THE CIVILIZATION OF THE AMERICAN INDIAN SERIES

(*Complete list on page 293*)

INDIANS OF THE WOODLANDS

FROM PREHISTORIC TIMES TO 1725

INDIANS OF
THE WOODLANDS

From Prehistoric Times to 1725

BY GEORGE E. HYDE

UNIVERSITY OF OKLAHOMA PRESS : *Norman*

102419

BY GEORGE E. HYDE

Corn Among the Indians of the Upper Missouri
(with George A. Will) (Cedar Rapids, 1917)
Red Cloud's Folk (Norman, 1937. New Edition,
Norman, 1957)
The Pawnee Indians (Denver, 1951)
A Sioux Chronicle (Norman, 1956)
Indians of the High Plains (Norman, 1959)
Spotted Tail's Folk: A History of the Brulé Sioux,
(Norman, 1961)
*Indians of the Woodlands: From Prehistoric Times
to 1725* (Norman, 1962)

Library of Congress Catalog Card Number: 62–16480

For Dr. John M. Christlieb
and his wife Elizabeth R. Christlieb

Preface

THE PRESENT BOOK is a companion volume for my *Indians of
the High Plains,* which was so well received that it appeared useful
to prepare a second volume, on the Indian tribes between the Ohio
and the Great Lakes, from the Hudson to the Mississippi, embracing
the prehistoric and early historic periods. Both books were written
along the same lines, utilizing historical, archaeological, ethnological,
and traditional materials. This method is termed ethnohistory and
is supposed to be something new; but it implies the use of all available material, and that was a method known to Greek historians
before the time of Christ.

In the nineteenth century our scholars were employing ethnology
in an effort to trace the historic Indian tribes back and link them
with their prehistoric ancestors, and linguistics was regarded as the
master key that would unlock the secrets of America's past. This
single-line method of research produced much interesting material,
but it did not solve the problem. During that period, from about
1825 to 1925, American archaeology was in the main a guessing game;
but in the 1930's it was completely reorganized along scientific lines,
and plans were made for very extensive operations, which it was believed would bring quick results. The organizers of the new archaeology realized that the one-line method was not a good one and they

pledged themselves to the full utilization of historical, ethnological, and traditional materials, as well as archaeological ones. This pledge seems to have been forgotten by many archaeologists. They do refer to historical and ethnological materials now and again; but most of them seem to regard Indian tradition as childish nonsense. If it were not for Indian tradition, they would be today formulating archaeological theories about what tribe had lived in the earth-lodge village on the Sheyenne Fork of the Red River of the North, and making theories concerning the date of the village ruins. As it is, they have in Indian tradition the fact that this village was that of the Cheyenne tribe and that it dates to the middle of the eighteenth century.

When I wrote my book *The Pawnee Indians,* the new archaeology was just getting started, and I had very little definite information concerning the Iroquoian tribes of the East. I did not realize that these tribes belonged to the same stock as the Caddo and Pawnee tribes west of the Mississippi; but it now is obvious that the Iroquoians left the Caddoans in the south, probably in the lands west of the Mississippi, in prehistoric times and migrated toward the north and east. Even in the nineteenth century, historians and ethnologists had decided that in late prehistoric times there was a mass of Indians of the Siouan stock in the Ohio Valley and that these tribes had migrated northward, into Iowa, Minnesota and Wisconsin, and to the south and east, into Carolina and Virginia. The new archaeology confirms this and adds very interesting evidence, which shows that the oldest center of the Siouans was in Kentucky, that they were there in archaic times, and that in early Woodland times they migrated northward into Ohio, Indiana, and Illinois, and south into Tennessee, northern Alabama, and Carolina. Then the Iroquoians came from the southwest and intruded on the territory of the Siouans and their northern Algonquian neighbors, and an Iroquoian people, termed the Adena folk, settled among the natives of the Ohio Valley, introducing among them a new religion and the practice of building mounds and other earthworks. Thus the Ohio Mound Builder or Hopewell culture originated; and not in very ancient times, but at a period so near to the historic that both the Delaware tribe and the Iroquois of New York State had traditions concerning these Ohio Mound Builders and their empire, and its destruction.

These, seemingly, are the main facts of prehistory in the north-central woodlands: the archaic and early times with the primitive Siouan and Algonquian natives living by hunting and fishing; the coming of southern Indians, mainly Iroquoians, bringing a new religion that had to do with gods and goddesses in the heavens: sun and moon and star deities, an elaborate cult of the dead, mound building, the establishment of villages, and the beginning of agriculture.

In this book I have made use of every form of material available to me. The earlier chapters naturally depend mainly on archaeology, and here I have attempted to show my appreciation of the great service the new archaeology has performed in uncovering the facts concerning our early Woodland Indians and their way of life. In the later chapters I have depended more on historical and traditional material, supporting this when possible with archaeological material. The book as it stands is an experiment, and how much use it may be remains to be seen.

I wish here to express my appreciation for the aid I have received from many friends at the universities and museums who have supplied me with information. To Thorne Deuel of the Illinois State Museum, I am indebted for the use of drawings showing the types of Mound Builder or Hopewell people, their costumes, hair arrangement, and equipment. I wish to thank Miss Doris Quick for the fine maps she made for the book, and for the drawing of the winged catlinite pipes of the Siouan Indians. To Miss Catherine Beal and the other staff members of the Omaha Public Library, I wish to express my thanks for their aid in obtaining scarce books that were needed.

George E. Hyde

OMAHA, NEBRASKA
SEPTEMBER 10, 1962

Contents

Illustrations

INDIANS OF THE WOODLANDS

FROM PREHISTORIC TIMES TO 1725

And the Great Spirit made the Earth
in the form of a flat oval,
and he made four beasts
and four serpents and placed them
in the water under the Earth
to hold it firm;
but the Four Winds blew
and the Earth shook.

CHAPTER ONE

North Wind

IN ARCHAIC TIMES the northern woodlands and forests, between the Hudson and the Mississippi, were thinly occupied by groups of wandering hunters and fishermen who almost certainly belonged to the great Algonquian linguistic stock. They are supposed to have migrated from northeastern Asia, coming into Alaska and thence moving on toward the southeast. Lewis H. Morgan, when he wrote on Indian migrations a century ago, gave his opinion that the shores of Lake Superior and the country to the west of that lake were the center from which the Algonquians migrated toward the south and east; but modern archaeology has made it fairly clear that this Indian stock occupied the lands from Labrador down into New England at a very early period, and some Algonquian groups had even found their way into Virginia and the Carolinas. This stock also held the lands north of the Great Lakes, as far as Hudson Bay; they extended along the St. Lawrence and apparently held both shores of the Great Lakes.

Anthropologists have described the Algonquians as rather tall people, with dolichocephalic skulls: longheaded, with long and rather narrow faces. They have been termed the Sylvids, the Woodland people, and in the archaic period they were divided up into small groups, widely separated, wandering in the forest, hunting game, fishing, and gathering nuts, acorns, roots, and berries. They had no fixed abodes, but lived in movable camps; there are only scanty traces of their occupation of the land; and as time has destroyed all indications of their life, except for stone, bone, shell, and a little copper found in their campsites and graves, we have little direct evidence of their condition and the details of their daily life. However, they were clearly in a very primitive state. They had not yet learned to make pottery, and the practice of growing food crops was unknown to them. Archaeologists believe that they did not know the use of the bow. Their stone projectile points seem too large to be arrowheads and indicate the use of a spearlike weapon possibly hurled with a throwing stick that enabled a man to cast his spear with greater force and to a greater distance.

By traditional accounts, these very early times were marked by peace; and as the northern woodlands seem to have been held by people of the same blood and language, and as the search for food was a never ending task, it is probable that wars were few and of a rather mild character. A clash between two small groups of warriors, a man or two wounded, was probably thought to be a great affair, worthy of their making up boasting songs to commemorate it.

The French, who knew these northern Woodland Indians from as far back as the year 1500, described them as stern-faced, rather gloomy people. They had their short and wild periods of feasting, dancing, and pleasure; but on the whole life was a very serious affair to them. Almost every winter they starved; and this did not mean going without food for a day, but actual starvation. The little group of Indians moved through the snow-blanketed forest, seeking game and finding nothing to kill. They boiled and made soup of their leather moccasins and beaver-skin robes; they dug in the steel-hard ground for frozen roots, ate lichens and bark; and day by day the march was slowed as the people weakened. Children and old people fell, unable to go on, and were left for the ravens, the eagles, and the wolves to devour. The killing of moose or deer was like a reprieve from death to the people; and with hope reviving, they moved on through the forest toward some favorite fishing station on the shore of a lake or bank of a river, where they knew the never failing spring run of fish would come to save them.

In early spring, group after group came to the fishing stations until quite a large number of people had assembled. They fished

4

with nets, and they must have had birchbark canoes at quite an early date. Lewis H. Morgan wrote that fish and rabbits were the principal food of these northern Indians; but his information came mainly from nineteenth-century Indians who simply did not know what conditions were in early times. The early Algonquians called the St. Lawrence River the Fish Country; but they had fine fishing stations along the Great Lakes, usually at places where there were rapids in streams and the spring fish-run was dependable and very heavy. Mid-March was the Fish Running Moon of the Huron Indians of Lake Huron; mid-April was the Earth Drying Moon. When the last snows were melted and the ground dry, the Indians left the fishing stations and went into the forest to build deer-runs and take deer. Groups of Indians went to small lakes and to marshes at the season when fledgling waterfowl were still too young to fly, and they caught great numbers of ducks, geese, and swans in the same nets they used for fishing. They sometimes pursued the young waterfowl in canoes and killed them with sticks. This we know from the *Jesuit Relations* volumes for the period 1620–70 and from Cheyenne and other Indian traditions. Beaver and other fur-bearing animals were killed or trapped at certain seasons, and most of the tribes made warm beaver robes for winter use by sewing several tanned beaver skins together. As winter came on, the groups of Indians hid their canoes on the shores of lakes or banks of rivers and went into the forest on their winter hunt.

These early hunters of the north, ignorant of the cause of things, were in fear of their environment. They believed in the power of evil rather than the strength of goodness. Their world was full of spirits, most of which were inimical to man. When the ice in the rivers and lakes broke up in the spring with mighty crashes, roars, and moans, they said that it was the evil spirits, confined under the ice, breaking their way out to freedom. The Ice God was a terrible being who destroyed men. The Water God ruled the Great Lakes, holding storms in his hands to hurl at men in canoes and drown them. When some Indians camped on an island in Lake Superior, they found chunks of pure copper and loaded their canoes with them; but they had hardly set forth on their journey when a mighty voice came rolling over the waters, shouting, "Who are these thieves that have stolen my children's playthings?" Then the angry god loosed a great storm and sent it hurtling after the fleeing canoes.

It is supposed to have been in archaic times that the Indians of the north discovered copper. It was the only metal known to them. Float copper and copper in a matrix of rock, buried under a few feet of soil, was to be found in the lands along the south side of the Great Lakes, all the way from northern Minnesota east into Ontario. It was apparently on Isle Royale that, by tradition, the Indians found and stole the copper nuggets that were the treasure of the god of the lakes. Once they were acquainted with copper, they found it in nuggets here and there on the surface of the ground, and they also dug shallow pits, to get at the copper with rock matrix, knocking the copper out of the rock. They did not know the art of melting metal, but worked the copper while cold, beating it into shape and then often grinding and polishing it.

The Old Copper period in the North is a puzzling development. These Indians were in the Stone Age, and the only hard materials they were used to working with were stone, bone, shell, horn, and wood. When they obtained copper, they used it to make copies of the older stone and bone weapons and tools; thus the peculiar crescent-shaped knives of Eskimo type were apparently made of stone at first and were then reproduced in copper. This Old Copper culture extended from the region north of the Great Lakes south into northern Illinois and eastern Iowa. In the east it went into New York State. Intertribal trade brought copper to the Ohio Valley, and even farther south.

The primitive Indians of the north apparently had a rude form of religion, based mainly on fear. They feared the waters, the forest, and rocks; they were in dread of animals, reptiles, and even birds. They believed that winds and storms were produced by hostile forces. Every living creature had an Elder Brother, made in the same form, but of huge size and with great supernatural powers. An Indian never killed an animal without making an offering to propitiate the Elder Brother of his victim.

These northern Indians had great faith in the power of dreams and visions, and any being that appeared in a dream (a bear, an eagle, or even a rock or tree) became a personal protector and guardian spirit. The dreamer then obtained some small token to symbolize his protector, and carried it in his medicine bag, guarding it as his most precious possession, praying to it, asking its advice, and making offerings to it. With such supernatural protection, the In-

6

dian lost much of his fear of the evil forces that surrounded him. They might alarm him at times; but he had faith that, as long as he did nothing to offend his guardian spirit, he was safe.

To the south and west of the Algonquian area the woodland country was occupied in archaic times by a different Indian stock. These people were formerly called Sylvids, like the Algonquians; but more recently G. K. Neumann has termed them the Iswanids, which means River People in the language of the Catawba Indians, a Siouan tribe of North Carolina. There can be little doubt that the Iswanids were all, or most of them, Siouans. Unlike the tall Algonquian tribesmen of the north, they were of medium stature, with rather high, vaulted heads, short faces, and medium-broad noses. Their skull type was brachycephalic.[1]

These Siouans must have originally lived in very much the same manner as the Algonquian tribes toward the north—wandering about, hunting and fishing, with no fixed abodes—but the land that they occupied, centering in northern Kentucky, had a milder climate than the Algonquian country, and certain conditions favored the forming of permanent villages on river banks. One of the great attractions lay in the abundance of shellfish—mussels or clams. Camping on the river banks at favorable points, the Indians lived largely on shellfish and threw the shells and other camp refuse on the ground; thus in time they built large shell mounds, on top of which they established villages. For this reason their type of culture has been termed Indian Knoll. It was first found on the bank of the Green River in northern Kentucky, but there are other early village remains in southern Indiana and Ohio. The shell mounds on which these Indians built their huts covered from three to seventeen acres, and in times of flood they formed islands, for they were from four to twelve feet in height. The Indians buried their dead in pits dug in the tops of these shell mounds.

Judging by the imperishable implements, made of stone, shell, and similarly hard materials, found in the shell mounds, these Siouans of the Archaic period had a culture as rude as that of the Algonquians of the north; but the Indians in Kentucky not only occupied the shell mounds but lived in rock shelters and caves where nitrates in the soil have preserved wooden implements, fabrics, and other

[1] James B. Griffin, *Archeology of the Eastern United States*, 19, 177.

materials that display a culture adequate to the needs of primitive hunters and fishermen. Here was found proof of the use of the atlatl or spear thrower. These implements consisted of a wooden shaft, fifteen to twenty-two inches in length, with a socketed antler hook glued to one end with asphaltum; neatly made weights of stone, shell, or antler, increased the force of the throw. The spear and spear thrower were the principal weapons of these Indians. The people possessed woven fabric breechclouts, robes, perhaps shirts of dressed skins and cloth, woven bags, and baskets; they ornamented their garments with small shell beads, wore necklaces of shell, bone, and stone beads, and of perforated animal teeth. Pendants were made of conch shell or perforated canine teeth of such large animals as the bear. These Indian Knoll people buried their dead in pits with the bodies usually flexed but sometimes placed in a sitting position. A peculiar custom was the burying of a dog with his master. Such burials were often those of children, and sometimes a turtle rather than a dog was buried with the child.

The Omaha Indians had in their tribal sacred bundles an ancient bear canine tooth and a large clam or mussel shell, which fact, taken with the tribal tradition of former residence in the Ohio Valley, suggests that the Omahas were of the old Indian Knoll shell-heap group.

What makes these Kentucky Indian Knoll folk peculiarly interesting is the fact that they are the earliest Indian group whose movements can be followed with any degree of certainty. They migrated slowly toward the south, southwest, north, northeast, northwest, and, perhaps, the west, taking their type of crude culture with them. To the historians this situation strongly suggests that these Indians were a homogeneous stock, speaking one language, and that as their population increased, they spread in every direction from their old central area.

Their most interesting movement, perhaps, was to the south. In their earlier stage, before they had pottery, they spread down into Tennessee and northern Alabama. Then some of them went east of the Blue Ridge Mountains into the Piedmont district of northern North Carolina. Here they brought a culture similar to that in Kentucky. This North Carolina culture is termed Radin by the archaeologists. It developed into a later culture called Yadkin, and that in turn developed into Uwharrie, which was late enough in time to verge on the historic period. Toward the end of the Uwharrie period these

Siouan Indian Knoll Culture and Its Migrations

Indians formed tribal groups, and they then emerged on the page of history as Siouan tribes: the Tutelo, the Saponi, and others.[2]

When the Indian Knoll folk from Kentucky arrived in the North Carolina Piedmont district, the lands there were occupied by southern Indians, who hunted and camped in small family groups. They had vessels of steatite or soapstone, and later they made clay vessels,

[2] *Ibid.*, 305–308; William Snyder Webb and William Delbert Funkhouser, *Ancient Life in Kentucky*, 127–28.

tempering the clay with crushed soapstone. There was an abundance of shellfish in the North Carolina streams; but these Indians do not appear to have eaten shellfish. They preferred to hunt big game. When the Siouan Indians invaded the Piedmont they drove a wedge into the population of southern Indians, split them apart, and forced them to retire. These early Siouans are described as fierce warriors and great hunters. They later developed pottery, lived in tribal groups in villages, and built circular huts with central fireplaces lined with stone slabs. They buried their dead in cemeteries outside the villages, in circular pits, the bodies closely flexed and accompanied by ornaments and stone pipes.

The Siouans of the Radin group seem to have invaded the North Carolina Piedmont region from East Tennessee at a relatively late period, after the use of pottery and pipes had developed. It seems to be a fair inference that the Radin people left Green River in Kentucky and drifted slowly southward; that in East Tennessee they and other Siouans developed the use of crude grit-tempered pottery and learned to smoke tobacco, using tubular stone pipes. The Siouans who remained in the upper Tennessee River Valley had a culture resembling the Radin culture of North Carolina quite closely in some important features. Both groups lived in villages of circular huts, buried the dead flexed in round pit graves, used straight tubular stone pipes, and made crude grit-tempered pottery with fabric and cord marks on its surface.[3]

The evidence contained in J. B. Griffin's *Archaeology of the Eastern United States* indicates that the Indian Knoll folk in archaic times developed this shell mound culture and spread it probably through most of northern Kentucky. Their shell mounds are found on the Mississippi in western Kentucky; they are found on the Tennessee River in Henry and adjacent counties in western Tennessee; and north of the Ohio River they occur in southern Illinois, Indiana, and Ohio. Extending up the Tennessee River, these Indians established themselves in the Pickwick Basin in northern Alabama. They apparently also occupied East Tennessee and from there went across the Blue Ridge Mountains into the North Carolina and Virginia

---

3 Griffin, *Archaeology of the Eastern United States*, 33, 199, 306. Some archaeologists suggest that the Upper Valley folk of East Tennessee were Cherokees. I have drawn my own conclusion that they were probably Indian Knoll folk.

Piedmont. But that, as already stated, seems to have been a later migration, after the people had learned to make pottery and about the time of the beginning of the Adena period, when a southern Indian group moved northward and replaced the older Indian Knoll culture of Kentucky with their own. The rock shelter and cave remains in Kentucky seem to be of the Indian Knoll type, but of a later period, after the practice of growing crops had been established.[4]

North of the Ohio River the Indian Knoll people formed shell mound settlements in southern Indiana, in Dubois County, north of the Green River Indian Knoll settlements in Kentucky, and near Clarkesville, opposite Louisville, Kentucky, where the Falls of the Ohio are located. Farther up the Ohio the Indian Knoll folk crossed near the mouth of Kentucky River and went northward into Dearborn, Franklin, and Randolph counties, Indiana. The Falls of the Ohio at Louisville seem to have been a favored spot for Indian occupation in these early times. It was probably a good fishing station, and Indian Knoll sites have been found there.[5] As in Indiana, in southern Ohio the prepottery Indian Knoll settlements are found widely scattered, and there seems to be no break between these early occupations and the later ones that include pottery. This indicates that the same Indians continued to live in these areas; but some archaeologists view the shifting cultural traits as an indication of a new occupation. Thus the stone-slab mound burials have been regarded as a possible indication of a change in the Indian population; but these stone-slab mounds occur in southern Indiana and in other areas which, at an earlier period, had been held by Indian Knoll folk, and there is little reason for doubting that in Ohio, Indiana, northern Kentucky, and southern Illinois the Indian Knoll people were the main part of the population from archaic times on into the Mound Builder period. In Adams County, Ohio, near the great Serpent Mound, the village ruins show a lower and earlier occupation by a people of the Indian Knoll type. The culture is of the Kentucky rock-shelter pattern, and if there is any difference between pre-

---

[4] *Ibid.*, 304; H. C. Shetrone, *The Mound Builders*, 420. Some archaeologists doubt that the rock shelter and cave deposits belong to Indian Knoll people. The broad occupation of a very large area by the same Indians is apparent; but some men, when they find a small new trait in a culture, wish to bring the Indians into court, compel them to produce identity cards, and prove their good intentions.

[5] "Notes and News," *American Antiquity*, Vol. V, No. 4 (April, 1940), 341.

pottery Indian Knoll and the rock-shelter culture, it seems to lie mainly in the later date of the rock-shelter occupation. The stone-slab burial mounds are another feature of the later Indian Knoll culture. Along the Ohio River, from near Cincinnati to the Serpent Mound, a distance of about seventy-five miles, stone-slab graves are found on both sides of the Ohio, and some of them contain material of the Hopewell or Mound Builder culture. This at least hints at a continuance of Indian Knoll people on into the Mound Builder period in southwestern Ohio and across the river in Kentucky.[6]

The Indian Knoll penetration of Illinois is of prime interest. These Siouan Indians from the Green River in Kentucky came into Illinois in archaic times and scattered out, evidently in hunting camps; but in the Carbondale district in Jackson County, in the southwestern part of the state, they established a village which the archaeologists term Crab Orchard, and here the same physical type of Indians lived from archaic times to near the close of the prehistoric period. Other Indian Knoll folk went to the north, to Fulton County, north of the Illinois River, and established what is called the Black Sand center. Near them were Indians, perhaps of a different stock, whose remains have been given the name of the Red Ocher or Roskamp focus. The Black Sand folk are said to have been of the Kentucky Indian Knoll physical type; but Neumann has cast doubt on this, stating that these Indians had long heads and long, narrow faces of what he terms the Otamid type.[7] However, the Black Sand folk had cultural traits that came from Indian Knoll—not from Green River in Kentucky, but from the Tennessee River Indian Knoll centers at Eva in West Tennessee and at Lauderdale in northern Alabama. At a later period the Faulkner folk, another Indian Knoll people who had migrated from the Tennessee River into southern Illinois, moved north and joined the Black Sand people, imposing their culture on the Black Sand folk. These Indians on Illinois River in Fulton County now had pottery and had emerged from the Archaic into the early Woodland stage.

The Red Ocher folk of western Illinois were believed by G. K. Neumann to be early Iroquoians. They used quantities of red ocher in burials, a trait that was widespread in early times but that, on

---

[6] Griffin, *Archeology of the Eastern United States*, 84, has a discussion on these points. See the same author's *Fort Ancient*, 60.

[7] Neumann, in Griffin, *Archeology of the Eastern United States*, 24.

the whole, seems to have been of southwestern origin. It was a burial trait of the early Pueblo tribes of New Mexico and of the Marksville center in Louisiana, which was probably Caddoan. Thus the use of red ocher in graves, introduced among the Caddoans, may have been passed on to the Iroquoians, who were of the Caddoan stock. Red ocher was a feature of the Glacial Kame culture in northern Ohio and on eastward into the Iroquoian area of northern New York. If the Red Ocher folk in west-central Illinois were really Iroquoian, the vexing problem of the route by which the Iroquoians reached their later homeland in New York and Ontario might be solved. These Red Ocher folk seem to have entered Illinois from the west in the area now occupied by the city of St. Louis. From this point their scattered camp or village sites extend northeastward into Fulton County.

It is a curious fact that, although the first groups of Indian Knoll folk to enter Illinois seem to have come from the Green River center in Kentucky, the later groups appear to have come from Tennessee River. The Fulton folk, who left southern Illinois and moved north to take over the Black Sand area, were succeeded in Massac and Pope counties in the south by the Baumer folk, who appear to have come from Tennessee River and who brought a culture that was markedly affected by contacts with southern Indians. They had adopted the southern type of rectangular hut and the southern practice of tempering pottery clay with crushed limestone. But these people were of the Indian Knoll physical type, not southern roundheads, and Baumer implements were generally of the old archaic Indian Knoll type. Baumer had many traits in common with the Indians of Candy Creek in East Tennessee, and the Candy Creek culture seems to be a development of the Indian Knoll folk, who came into East Tennessee in archaic times and developed through Upper Valley and Watts Bar into the Candy Creek culture.

As is shown in J. B. Griffin's *Archaeology of the Eastern United States,* archaeologists in general agree that the Indians in Illinois were probably of the same stock from very early times on through the Hopewell or Mound Builder period.[8] These Illinois Indians were mainly or wholly of the Indian Knoll stock; the Radin people came from Indian Knoll, ending their migration in the Piedmont district in North Carolina and Virginia, where they presently emerged in

[8] *Ibid.,* 180, 189.

historic times as Siouan tribes. Since the Indian Knoll folk had also migrated into southern Indiana and Ohio, into Tennessee and northern Alabama, the inference is that the Siouans occupied Kentucky in archaic times and spread from there to the north and south. This is a situation that historians and anthropologists have long suspected; but they were without solid evidence. This evidence has been produced by modern archaeology, and, with the aid of Indian tradition, historical material, and linguistics, we can now assert that the Siouans were the earliest inhabitants of Kentucky of whom we have a record; that they were a homogeneous group, so much so that their physical type and general culture were very similar, from northern Illinois down into North Carolina, and their language, even after centuries of migration, was still close enough for many of the groups to understand each other's dialects. Indeed, Lewis H. Morgan stated that the Tutelos of the southern Piedmont spoke a dialect close to that of the Winnebagos in faraway Wisconsin. Many archaeologists will probably reject this view of the early Siouans, although their own evidence strongly supports it.

To complete this brief sketch of the Woodland Indian in the lands from the Ohio Valley northward in archaic and early Woodland times, one more stock must be referred to: the Iroquoians, those tribes in Ontario, New York, and western Pennsylvania who spoke dialects of the Iroquois language and were blood kinsmen of that nation. As is well known, the Iroquoians were related by blood and language to the Caddoan tribes and Pawnees, who occupied lands west of the Mississippi. The period of separation of the Iroquoians from the Caddoans is unknown. Some linguists have stated that the event occurred thousands of years ago, and they adduce as a comparable case the thousands of years it has taken the English language to get as far as it is from Russian. These scholars evidently never heard of the case of the Skidi Pawnees, who have a tradition that they formerly dwelled in the Allegheny country near the head of the Ohio and, being attacked by enemies in later prehistoric times, fled west and joined their Pawnee kinsmen in Nebraska. It did not take them thousands of years to close the gap between their dialect and that of the Pawnees. More probably the two dialects became fused within a century.[9]

[9] When I wrote my book *The Pawnee Indians,* I knew the Skidi tradition that they had migrated westward from an older home in the Allegheny region; but,

There has been a long controversy, with both archaeologists and anthropologists taking part over the date and circumstances of the Iroquoian migration into their historic locations. Some authorities have thought that these Indians followed the Appalachian Mountains and thus reached Pennsylvania; others have depicted a migration eastward, up the Ohio; while a third group believed that these Indians crossed the Mississippi somewhere near the mouth of the Missouri and moved eastward to the Detroit district, going on from there into New York and Ontario. No one could produce any solid evidence to support his opinion; but in recent years the new archaeology has produced evidence which, although it does not prove a case, throws some light on the question.

G. K. Neumann stated that the Red Ocher folk who were in Illinois in archaic times were Iroquoian. These Indians apparently came from the west, crossing the Mississippi in the St. Louis area and moving up to Illinois River, in Fulton County. They were a crude people, without pottery. They had obtained copper from the Great Lakes, and one of their characteristics was the use of red ocher in burial rites. They seem to have left Illinois; then, farther eastward, in southern Michigan, northeastern Indiana, and northwestern Ohio a similar type of Indians who used red ocher in graves appeared. These were the Glacial Kame folk. The kames were knolls of gravel and sand, formed in glacial times, and these Indians buried their dead in pits in the kames. Here they had copper from the Great Lakes and also conch and other marine shells, evidently obtained in trade from the Indians of the Ohio Valley as some articles from the Glacial Kame district have been found in Kentucky. The Glacial Kame culture is evidently later than the Red Ocher culture of Illinois, as the Indians now had tobacco pipes. They also had harpoons, which are characteristic of early Iroquoian culture. This Glacial Kame culture began in early Woodland times and went on apparently into the era of the Mound Builders, the Hopewell period.

Neumann states that at the time of early Glacial Kame a similar folk, with brachycephalic skulls, came into the Lake Ontario district

as I knew of no supporting evidence, I discounted the story. Now I have learned that the Skidis brought into Nebraska pottery typical of the Iroquoian district in the western New York and Allegheny country; also that the Omahas had a tradition that the Skidis accompanied them on their migration from the Ohio Valley westward.

of New York. Point Pennsylvania, an early Iroquoian culture on the shore of Lake Ontario, also used red ocher in graves and had harpoons.

Here we have a suggestion in modern archaeology of the route followed by at least part of the Iroquoians during their migration eastward. Probably other Iroquoian groups migrated along other routes: through the Ohio Valley, or along the Appalachian Mountains. We know that (perhaps at the same period) there was a Caddoan migration northward, into Kansas and Nebraska; and here we have a tree-ring dating which indicates that the Caddoans were in Nebraska as early as the year 1300.

The later history of the Iroquoians supports the view that they came into their historic locations by different routes, and in separate groups, for the Iroquois Proper regarded the Huron-Neutral-Erie group to the north and west of them and the Iroquoians of Pennsylvania to the south as distinct tribes.

Taking a general view of the Indians in the woodland country between the Hudson and the Mississippi, in archaic and early Woodland times, we note the development of village life, the introduction of pottery and tobacco pipes among the Indian Knoll folk, who were Siouans, and the coming of the Iroquoians, who also seem to have had villages and to have used pottery and pipes. We can even trace the migration of these two Indian stocks with some certainty, and the fact that they migrated suggests that their population was increasing. The Algonquians of the north and northeast were certainly also active at this early period; but there seem to be few indications of migration. Some of the Algonquians did develop village life and learn to make pottery, but in general the Indians of this stock continued to be wandering hunters and fishers.[10]

---

[10] The main sources for this chapter are Griffin's *Archeology of the Eastern United States,* and *Indians Before Columbus* by Paul S. Martin, George I. Quimby, and Donald Collier. As this book, it is hoped, will appeal to the intelligent general reader, I have not pinned down every little bit by inserting a footnote reference to the source of each statement made.

CHAPTER TWO

South Wind

AT THE CLOSE of the Archaic period and in the early Woodland times that followed, the Indians of the woodland country east of the Mississippi and north of Tennessee began to develop an incipient civilization. Many of the Indians were no longer content to worship earth-bound animal gods alone, and they turned their eyes to the heavens, seeking new gods. The growing of crops came like a miracle —a new discovery that added to the food supply and made it possible to cease wandering in camps and to establish permanent villages. Earthenware pottery came into use, taking the place of the old roasting pits and other primitive methods for cooking food, and pipes and tobacco came, as a feature of a new religious faith, perhaps, but also as a solace to men's hearts. The bow and arrow had taken the place of the older spear and throwing stick. There were conservative groups even in those far-off times, and part of the tribes clung to old ways, shunned the new gods, and regarded with abhorrence the wicked new custom of wounding Mother Earth's skin with hoes made of flint or shell, thrusting alien seeds into her flesh to force her to produce hitherto unheard-of crops.

In archaic times there had been a drift southward, some of the northern Sylvid Indians finding their way in little groups as far down as the mouth of the Mississippi. Now, in early Woodland days, a tribe of southern Indians migrated northward. They were small folk with round heads and rather broad faces, unlike the northern Sylvid people, with their greater stature and longer and narrower faces. The archaeologists call these Indians from the south the Adena folk, the name coming from the Adena estate near Chillicothe in Ohio, where the first of the big Adena mounds was excavated.

It was mainly these Adena Indians who brought a new faith, and the practice of burying the dead in large mounds, into the Ohio Valley. Where they came from is not clearly known. Some archaeologists have surmised that the Adena folk came from Mexico or Central America, or that they obtained their exotic cultural features from one of those regions; others believe that the Adenas came from northeastern Asia by way of Alaska. What is definitely known is that they were a southern people with what G. K. Neumann terms rugged brachycephalic skulls, and that they seem to have come north into the Pickwick Basin on the Tennessee River in northern Alabama, where they made contact with the older inhabitants (Indians of the Kentucky shell mound group, who were evidently Siouans). The archaeologists found no indication of war or conquest; the older shell mound Indians continued to occupy the lands in Tennessee, Kentucky, southern Ohio, and southern Indiana; yet the Adena folk found their way to the upper Ohio River and took possession of that region. If there was no war, we might assume that the Adenas made friendly arrangements with the Siouans in the Pickwick Basin and, with the assistance of those people, made their way in peace through the Siouan country to the Ohio, where they settled with the approval of the Siouans.[1] What appears to be the best evidence that these Adena folk were typical southern Indians lies in the fact that they practiced head-flattening, occipital deformation being present in nearly all skulls, and bifrontal flattening common. This was the result of binding the heads of infants tightly to their cradleboards.[2]

1 Martin, Quimby, and Collier, *Indians Before Columbus*, 263–67, 371; Griffin, *Archeology of the Eastern United States*, 23, 178–80, 358. The assumption that the Indian Knoll people were Siouans is mine.

The Siouans seem to have mingled with the Adena folk on the Tennessee River in northern Alabama to initiate a new culture termed Copena, which is of somewhat later date than Adena.

2 Griffin, *Archeology of the Eastern United States*, 86. Head-flattening was a practice of the southern tribes from very early times. Harrington found skulls

The Adena Indians were clearly a wandering group, as crude as any of their neighbors. It is doubtful that they previously had pottery or had learned to plant crops; but they had acquired what was apparently a new religious concept, mainly concerned with elaborate funeral ceremonies, and it was this feature of Adena life that made their people conspicuous. There was something in the new faith the Adenas brought northward that struck deeply into the minds and hearts of neighboring Indian groups; and the Adena cult of the dead, if we may term it that, spread into West Virginia, southern Ohio, northern Kentucky, Tennessee, and, perhaps, down into Alabama and Georgia. Since this happened about the time the making of pottery, the planting of crops, and the use of tobacco were introduced, a kind of social revolution seems to have begun in early Adena times. Curiously enough, even while they were leading in the spreading of a new faith, the Adena Indians were borrowing the methods and tools necessary for everyday life from their Woodland neighbors, and presently the character of their simple culture became, in its main features, a woodland culture.

Burial mounds were the heart of Adena cultural life, an expression of faith that was at its roots a cult of the dead. The mounds were carefully constructed, very symmetrical, and their contents indicated that the people were steeped in funeral ceremonial practices. Some of the smaller mounds seem to indicate that the Adena burial cult started, as some other southern burial complexes did, in simply placing a man's body in his own hut and then burning it. On the other hand, the great Adena mounds indicate an elaborately developed ceremonial for group burial, with a mausoleum in the center of the mound in which the chief or king and other important personages were entombed. There were carefully made clay cremation basins in the mounds, and it is conjectured that most of the commoners were cremated.[3]

Archaeologists are of the opinion that the majority of burial mounds in Ohio (and the number is very great) are of Adena ori-

thus deformed in graves on Red River in Louisiana that seem to date to Early Woodland times. In the Ohio Valley head-flattening continued to be an Indian custom in some districts on into late prehistoric times.

[3] Griffin, *Archeology of the Eastern United States*, 357; Martin, Quimby, and Collier, *Indians Before Columbus*, 266.

gin, and this is certainly true of burial mounds in northern Kentucky. As time passed and the size of the mounds and complexity of their internal arrangement grew, the Adena folk seem to have developed ceremonial centers at which the people gathered seasonally, to hold great ceremonies in honor of the dead. The heart of the Adena world seems to have been in the neighborhood of Chillicothe on the Scioto. Another center was at Miamisburg, north of Cincinnati, a third at the site of Cincinnati, and a fourth in southeastern Indiana. They had a great center on the Kanawha River in western West Virginia, and another on Grave Creek, farther to the northeast in the same state, in Marshall County.

The earthworks in the vicinity of Charleston, West Virginia, called Adena remains by Shetrone, consist of large burial mounds, great earth-walled circles, rectangles, and ovals, supposed to have been used for tribal ceremonial gatherings; and village ruins. These works are on the west bank of the Kanawha River, where the bottomlands are wide and suitable for growing crops. Along a stretch of river some six miles in length there are fifty burial mounds and ten or twelve great earth-walled enclosures, some of which embrace as much as thirty acres inside their walls. There are here also many stone-slab graves or cairns. One of the big mounds here had at the center near the base an area enclosed with posts, evidently some kind of building. In the middle of this enclosure lay a skeleton with the remains of a copper headdress still resting on the skull. In preparing this burial, a circular space some sixteen feet across had been covered with elm bark, then a layer of white ashes had been placed over the bark, and the body of the chief or king had been laid on the white ashes. A second layer of bark had been laid over the body. Around the dead chief or king, a number of men had been buried in a circle, their feet toward the spot where their chief lay. These bodies were wrapped in elm bark. The men on the east side of the circle each had a fine stone lance-head at his side; the skeletons at the north side of the circle had a stone dart-head and some mussel shells; the five skeletons on the west side of the circle had nothing buried with them. The largest and finest lance-head in the burial lay beside the dead chief in the center of the circle. In another mound there was a log structure at the center of the base, and inside this structure lay the skeleton of a chief who had been seven feet, six inches tall and nineteen inches across the shoulders. This man had six heavy copper bracelets on each wrist, a hammered copper gorget lay on the breast, and a thick sheet of mica lay on one shoulder. There were beads on the skull, and beside each hand lay three handsome stone lance-heads. Like all the lance-heads found in these mounds, these were especially fine work and seemed to be new and unused.[4]

The Adena people, occupying southern Ohio, southwestern Indiana, western West Virginia and northern Kentucky, must have had a large population, even though tribal centers were widely separated. They are the earliest people in the Ohio Valley whose villages can be clearly visualized. Their villages were of two to five huts, and groups of such small villages formed large settled areas. The huts probably housed more than one family each. They were circular, about thirty-five to fifty-five feet across. They had wall posts in pairs, the posts slanted slightly outward, so that the hut was wider at the eaves than at floor level. The wall posts had withes woven across them, forming wickerwork walls which must have been covered with some material. The peaked roofs were covered with sheets of bark. Some huts from sixty-five to ninety feet in diameter are supposed to have been community houses or, perhaps, the homes of chiefs.

It is difficult to credit the view of some archaeologists that the Adena folk did not have agriculture. These same men tell us that the Adenas had developed a highly organized social order that enabled them to build by their united efforts the great burial mounds and the vast walled circular, rectangular, and oval enclosures that formed a part of their community centers. Indians who lived by hunting, fishing, and gathering wild vegetable products had to move about to find game and other food; and they could not remain at one place in large gatherings or have the organization and discipline necessary for the planning and construction of great community works. Primitive man has no love for manual labor. There are just two motives that will make him work hard: stark danger that forces him to build defensive structures, and a burning faith that unites communities and even entire nations and submerges the individual in mass religious activity.

The latter incentive seems clearly to have been the moving spirit among the Adena folk. These Indians had brought into the Ohio

---

[4] Shetrone, *The Mound Builders*, 239, 243; Cyrus Thomas, *Report on Mound Exploration, Twelfth Annual Report*, B.A.E., 414–17.

Valley a new faith, a faith that had a strong appeal to the northern Indians and that spread in one form or another west to the Mississippi and possibly up the great valley to the Sioux in Minnesota. It spread eastward into New York and Pennsylvania, and some of its features went southward into Alabama and Georgia.

An older generation of archaeologists had quite a lot to say about sun worship among our early Indian tribes. The modern archaeologists generally ignore this subject. Nevertheless, some of the elaborate Adena burials seem to be those either of great leaders or of the type of Sun Kings that later appeared among such tribes as the Natchez along the lower Mississippi. When the Sun King of the Natchez died, his principal servants or officials were expected to submit to being strangled, so that they might accompany the Sun King on his journey into the spirit land. Some Adena burials suggest such a practice. It is difficult to explain in any other manner the burial of a great man in the center of a log structure under a mound, with ten or fifteen other men placed around him in a circle. These were not burials of bare bones but of bodies; and how are we to explain the death of ten or more leading men at the same time and at the moment of the passing of the great chief or king unless we assume a custom similar to the Natchez practice of strangling the king's servants at the time of his death?

The northern Indians, up to the coming of the Adenas, evidently had a faith that was connected with earth-bound animal gods. The Adena practices look very much like the worship of gods in the sky. Cremation had a very strong hold among the Adenas, but chiefs or kings and their servants were usually not cremated. Many years ago Daniel G. Brinton suggested that in some manner the Indians of our southern states had picked up the practice of cremation from the Indians of Nicaragua, who believed that no person could achieve immortality except through cremation. The smoke from cremation fires was supposed to carry the souls of the dead to their home in the heavens.

Smoking was at first, it would seem, a religious rite, the sending of prayers in a smoke cloud to the gods of the sky.[5] The great calumet pipes had birds' heads and wings attached to the stems, for birds flew high in the air and might, perhaps, be regarded as messengers, to bear man's prayers to the gods.

[5] Brinton, quoted by Reuben Gold Thwaites in *Jesuit Relations*, XX, 310.

The Adena folk had many small stone tablets on which were engraved rude formalized representations of birds of prey: eagles, hawks, and owls. These bird tablets have the look of being crude imitations of Mexican work. Some archaeologists point to the effigy mounds of stone, representing the eagle, in central Georgia as possibly connected with the Adena bird symbolism.

There seems to be no background for the great earth-walled circular, rectangular, and oval enclosures that were a part of the Ohio Mound Builder (Adena and later Hopewell) ceremonial life. These enclosures usually had mounds inside the walls, regarded as evidence that the enclosures were ceremonial centers. There are usually no indications of huts, and that seems to deny the theory that the enclosures were walled villages. The other theory, that the enclosures were walled gardens in which maize and vegetables were grown, is merely absurd. There is one clue that may be mentioned. At a somewhat later period than Adena times some of the Indians of Georgia, who were of the same physical type as the Adena folk, had ceremonial enclosures, not surrounded by earth walls as in Adena, but enclosed within log-picket palisades, interwoven with reeds and then plastered with clay. Inside such an enclosure there was a large council house, and outside the wall was a conical mound. Near this mound was a smaller burial mound. Some distance from the big enclosure was a death house or mortuary, rectangular with rounded corners and built partly underground. The mortuary was probably used for storing the bones of chiefs and prominent men. When it was full, it was burned and the ground around it was enclosed inside a circular clay-plastered wall. This circular enclosure then became the common burial field for the villagers. There is here a bare hint of the purpose for which the Adena enclosures were built. These Georgia coast Indians, termed Irene culture by the archaeologists, but apparently the Guale or Cusabo Indians of early historic times, used the big pentagonal enclosure for councils and tribal meetings and the big circular enclosure as a cemetery, which was first sanctified by having the chiefs and the headmen buried there and then was used for the common people. Farther north in Georgia the Indians of the Macon Plateau sometimes employed the Adena type of burial, in a log structure beneath a large mound.[6]

[6] Martin, Quimby, and Collier, *Indians Before Columbus*, 380–83.

M. S. Maxwell, in Griffin's *Archaeology of the Eastern United States,* expresses the view that the Adena people brought nothing into the Ohio Valley beyond a burial complex.[7] But behind that burial complex was a new faith that apparently turned the attention of the northern Indians from their earth-bound animal gods and disclosed to them gods in the sky and, perhaps, gave them their first real hold on a belief in life after death. This was not a mere burial complex; it was a religious revolution. Coming at the time of the introduction of crop-growing and the making of pottery, the impact on the native tribes must have been very great. Yet there was no apparent displacement of the older native groups. They remained where they had been; but six of the seven Indian knoll population centers took up agriculture, and as nearly as one may judge, they also adopted the Adena faith and its cult of the dead; they then developed in Ohio and Indiana a mound-builder complex, based on Adena beliefs but almost wholly a northern woodland culture. Part of Kentucky was now apparently in the hands of the Adena Indians; but they seem to have given up the practice of constructing large mounds and ceremonial centers. Farther south, in northern Alabama, the old Indian Knoll population of the Lauderdale center seems to have been replaced by an intrusion of southern Indians with an Adena-like culture, which is called Copena. Perhaps part of the old native stock remained, becoming fused with the intruding southern folk.[8]

The Adena people had wide connections, exchanging materials with tribes near the Great Lakes and southward to the sea. They had copper, probably obtained from the Glacial Kame Indians of northern Ohio and Indiana, who were contemporary with Adena. They had conch and other marine shells, and they obtained mica from the North Carolina Indians. Adena traits are found to the eastward into western New York; westward they reach into southern Illinois, but there is some reason for suspecting that it was the old Indian Knoll

---

[7] Maxwell, quoted in Griffin in *Archeology of the Eastern United States,* 179.

[8] The Indians on the Tennessee River, at Eva in West Tennessee, and at Lauderdale in the Pickwick Basin, northern Alabama, were clearly of the Kentucky Indian Knoll race. So, also, perhaps, were the Indians in East Tennessee. In Adena times these districts were invaded by southern Indians who either pushed out or assimilated the older population, producing the Copena and, evidently, the Hamilton culture. Some archaeologists conjecture that the Hamilton folk of the upper Tennessee River were early Cherokees.

population of Kentucky that spread the Adena traits to New York and Illinois. Radin, the Indian Knoll Siouan group in North Carolina, was contemporary with Adena. In the late Radin period, or early in the Yadkin times that followed, these Siouans of the North Carolina Piedmont began to fortify their villages with log stockades. They also developed agriculture.

The Adena period was a time that might be termed revolutionary. A new faith was introduced into the Ohio Valley; agriculture came in, the population increased, and villages became more numerous and larger in size. The groups began to take the shadowy outline of tribal entities, and even the cautious archaeologists begin to mention tribal names, as, for example, when they surmise that the Hamilton culture of East Tennessee may have been developed by the early Cherokees. They begin to theorize about the Iroquoian tribes.

As was stated in the first chapter of this book, there is some reason to believe that the Red Ocher folk of Illinois and, farther east, the Glacial Kame Indians of northern Indiana and Ohio may have been Iroquoian. Glacial Kame was contemporary with Adena, and some exchange of copper and other products took place between the Glacial Kame folk and the Indians of the Ohio Valley.

The situation in the lands to the north and northeast of the Ohio Valley in Adena times is difficult to determine; but one thing stands out, and that is the fact that the two main features of Adena culture, mound-building and cremation, did not spread among the Indians to the north and northeast. The Iroquoian tribes, for example, never took up mound-building or cremation. Like the Adenas, the Iroquoians seem to have come from the south; but they retained their own religious beliefs and their own burial customs, and all through the mound-building period of the Ohio-country the Iroquoians seem to have regarded the Mound Builders as aliens and enemies.

W. A. Ritchie, an authority on early New York archaeology, stated that about the time of Adena a wave of Indians intruded into western New York, coming from the upper Great Lakes. This movement may mark the coming of the Iroquoians into New York and Ontario; but W. N. Fenton, an authority on the early Iroquois, said that they came from the southeast, driving a wedge through the native Algonquian population to reach their later home in western New York.[9] The

9 William A. Ritchie, "Cultural Influences from Ohio in New York Archae-

Iroquoians were certainly southern Indians. They had a religion in some ways similar to that of the Adenas; they had villages and soon were planting crops. From Iroquois tradition it is obvious that the Iroquois hated and feared the Mound Builders of the Ohio Valley because the Mound Builders were apparently very numerous and well organized for both peace and war.

At the present time we have not sufficient evidence to form useful conclusions about what happened in Adena times. It would appear that Adena was not a highly material culture, but had a faith mainly concerned with a cult of the dead, which strongly appealed to the older native population of the Ohio Valley, who were evidently Siouans. These natives took up the Adena faith, adding their own woodland material culture to it and developing it in Hopewell times that succeeded Adena into the high culture of the Mound Builder period. That such a view is broadly correct is shown by the fact that the mound-building complex in the north spread strongly only into areas known to have been held by the Siouans at the dawn of historic times. Even in the closing years of the seventeenth century and on into the early part of the next century, the Siouans continued to build mounds, in western Iowa and northward into Manitoba.

ology," *American Antiquity*, Vol. II, No. 3, 182–83; W. W. Fenton, in *Smithsonian Misc., Colls.*, C (1940); Griffin, *Archeology of the Eastern United States*, 48–49. The Point Peninsula culture at the east end of Lake Ontario seems to be the first definite trace of Iroquoian culture. It is said to have come from the west or north in Adena times.

CHAPTER THREE

North Wind II

THE ADENA CULTURE did not fade and die. The religious beliefs and the cult of the dead with its impressive ceremonials, introduced into the Ohio Valley by the southern Adena folk, seem to have
caused a great spiritual awakening among the northern Indians, and
presently the northerners, outnumbering the Adena folk by about
three to one, took over the new culture in that part of Ohio where
the Adena people had established their main centers. The Adena Indians were not driven out. The northern people seem to have simply
taken the leadership and to have brought Adena faith and culture
into full power. This is what our fathers termed the Mound Builder
period. The modern archaeologists have labeled it Hopewell, the
name coming from the Hopewell estate near Chillicothe on the Scioto
River, where the first Mound Builder site was systematically excavated.[1]

We know a great deal more about the Mound Builders today

---

[1] The Hopewell culture is named for Captain M. C. Hopewell, on whose farm
near Chillicothe in Ross County, Ohio, these mounds and other works were located. The group of works was surveyed and mapped by Caleb Atwater in 1820
and partly excavated by Squier and Davis in 1846. W. K. Moorehead did some
excavation here in 1891–92, and the Ohio State Museum has been in charge of
the work since 1922.

(thanks to the new archaeology) than we did fifty years ago; but we still know too little concerning this great period of awakening and striving for a better life, which was to produce the highest culture the Indians within the limits of the United States ever achieved. The finding of both Adena and Hopewell remains in the same burial mounds suggests that the two peoples continued to live side by side in some districts. There is other evidence to support such a view; but the two physical types, the southern roundheaded folk with most of the skulls flattened from binding on a cradleboard and the taller and longheaded northern type, remained distinct, the northern Indians outnumbering the southern overwhelmingly. This was in Ohio, north of the Ohio River. South of the river, in Kentucky, the Adena southerners seem to have now predominated; and, curiously, here they ceased to build the great ceremonial centers that were a feature of their old districts in Ohio and West Virginia.

The district near Chillicothe on the Scioto had been the heart of the Adena culture, and it continued to hold that position in Mound Builder or Hopewell times. The Hopewell ceremonial centers were here on the Scioto, to the east at Marietta on the Muskingum, and to the west on the Great and Little Miami rivers. The great Mound Builder centers were a considerable distance north of the Ohio River. These Indians were not big river valley folk; they preferred locations on smaller streams, such as the northern tributaries of the Ohio.

There is a watershed extending across northern Ohio from east to west. The district to the north of the watershed in Mound Builder times was apparently unoccupied by Indians except close to the shore of Lake Erie, where the lands were held by tribes that seem to have been mainly Iroquian with, perhaps, some Algonquians. Ohio south of the watershed was woodland, except for some small areas of open prairie. The principal trees were the white oak, walnut, maple, hickory, beech, chestnut, ash, and elm. The red cedar was the only evergreen, and it was a sacred tree of those Siouan tribes who had traditions of being in the Ohio Valley in prehistoric times.

In the 1880's it was estimated that there were ten thousand mounds and one thousand earth-walled enclosures in southern Ohio, the great majority of them relics of the Mound Builders. In Ross County (a great Mound Builder center) there were five hundred mounds and one hundred large walled enclosures. The enclosures within earth walls are in the forms of circles, squares or rectangles, octagons, and other shapes. The big ones enclose up to one hundred acres of ground, and the archaeologists conjecture that great religious and social gatherings were held in them.

As the archaeologists visualize it, the Mound Builders first chose the site for a village and then nearby the site for a ceremonial center: for a temple and a big earth-walled enclosure. For the building of their sacred structure or temple, they first removed the surface soil, to obtain a level and firm surface; they then set the posts, usually in a circle or oval. They set the wall-posts close together, and sometimes they set interior posts, to divide the structure into chambers. There is some evidence that these sacred buildings had walls of wattle and daub, interwoven twigs plastered with clay, and it is conjectured that the structures were roofed. Sometimes they built a different type of sacred structure: a large enclosure with a wall of stone and earth and sometimes a palisade of posts on top of the wall. In some instances the area inside had one or more small circular enclosures walled with palisade posts. In these sacred structures the dead were buried with elaborate ceremony. When the sacred enclosure was judged to be filled to its capacity, the people assembled to hold religious rites, and the timbers of the sacred enclosure were set on fire. The people rushed forward and threw baskets of earth on the flames. Here we have a community mass-cremation ceremony, and the casting of earth on the burning sacred structure was the initial stage in the building of a great burial mound.[2]

It is stated by the archaeologists that cremation was the custom followed in the great majority of Mound Builder or Hopewell burials —not the cremation of bodies, but of disarticulated bones. This seems to indicate that most of the Mound Builders had the custom of the later historic tribes who exposed the dead on scaffolds raised on posts or in a mortuary hut, then cleaned the bones and often kept them for community rites held at stated times, when all the bones were buried with great ceremony. Here we seem to have evidence that the Mound Builder burial practices were the basis for the feast of the dead, a custom followed by historic tribes all the way from New

[2] Shetrone, *The Mound Builders*, 191. Shetrone wrote before the modern scientific archaeology was born, and some recent archaeologists are inclined to ignore his work. He made mistakes; but on the whole he was a careful observer, capable of drawing conclusions, which so many scientific archaeologists, preoccupied with the study of minutiae, seem to be unable to do.

York to Minnesota. Shetrone remarks that the Mound Builder burials indicate a belief in a future life, with more concern for the dead than thought for the living. The finest articles were placed in the burial mounds and were usually broken or "killed," so that they would be dead and could go with their dead owner to the spirit world. The burials inside the sacred structures seem to have been of prominent persons, as a rule. They were usually buried in the flesh, laid out in their finest articles of dress, on a burial platform carefully made of puddled clay. A conch shell was set at each corner of the burial platform; the body lay inside a log crib; bark was often used beneath the body or as a covering; weapons, tools, and ornaments were placed with the body, and the body and the grave offerings were sprinkled with red ocher. There were sometimes indications that the body was left on the burial platform until the flesh decayed, for the bones had been rubbed or painted with red ocher. There were indications that the Mound Builders in different localities had their special preferences in burial customs: in some districts they preferred to bury the dead extended at full length on the back; others flexed the bodies; and still others preferred cremation. Some made the burial crypts of logs, others of stone slabs. Cremation basins were in the burial mounds, carefully made of puddled clay. They were rectangular, some of them as much as three feet in width and ten in length. Some seemed to have been used only once and others over a long period.[3] One of the peculiar features of some of these burials was the multiple interment of several men in a circle. Sometimes the men lay on their backs with their heads toward the center of the circle and their bodies forming the spokes of a wheel; in other burials the skeletons were seated in a circle. In one mound on the lower Kanawha the men were in a circle around a very tall man whose equipment and ornaments suggest that he was a great chief or king. In a mound in eastern Wisconsin the skeletons sat in a circle facing a sacred conch-shell vessel that stood in the center. The Santees, a Siouan tribe of South Carolina, had kings who possessed the power of life and death over all members of the tribe. When the king died, he was buried in a mound, with great ceremony. Like their kinsmen the Mandans of faraway North Dakota, the Santees practiced scaffold burial, later cleaning the bones and making them into bundles.

Many of the Ohio mounds contained material that to these In-

3 Griffin, *Archeology of the Eastern United States*, 91.

dians must have seemed rich treasure. Some burials included thousands of freshwater pearls, beads made from marine shells, copper ornaments, and finely made weapons and tools of various kinds of stone. With the burials of prominent persons there were even finer objects, including textiles and copper headdresses and breastplates. W. K. Moorehead discovered the burial of a prominent man, whom he termed the Antlered King. The skull of this individual had a fine headdress still resting on it, with two branches of deer antlers, made of wood covered with sheet copper. Similar antler headdresses have been found in other burials. These burial mounds contained fairly clear indications of a noble class and even kings and queens. In the Hopewell mound near Chillicothe, where the Mound Builder culture was first carefully excavated, a burial was found of a young man and woman laid extended on their backs side by side. The woman had strings of pearls about the neck, wrists, knees, and hips; she had copper-covered buttons near her neck, copper bracelets, and other ornaments. She and the man at her side both had copper ear spools, large circular wooden ear ornaments covered with sheet copper. Both had long copper rods near the sides of their heads, necklaces of rare grizzly-bear teeth from the distant west, copper breastplates, and— of all things—both of them had copper nose-covers. This man and woman lay at the heart of the great central mound of the Hopewell group, and the mound was filled with other burials and cremations.[4]

Comparing these burials with the simple deposition of remains in pits in early times, we must admit that the Mound Builder culture was a rich and splendid one. And it must have been the kind of culture that produces kings, a priestly class, and a religion expressed in public pomp and ceremony, all apparently closely connected with a cult of the dead. In the burials mounds, but unconnected with burials, there were deposits of fine objects, and these have been termed sacrificial offerings. In the mound in which the young man and girl described above were lying side by side but apart from the actual burial, there was found a great spade-shaped weapon with rounded point. It was fashioned with great skill from a lump of black obsidian, a volcanic material found only at one place: in the cliffs near the head of the Yellowstone River in Wyoming, over two thousand miles from the mound in which this find was made. This was a feature of the Hopewell or Mound Builder culture, the bringing of rare

4 Shetrone, *The Mound Builders*, 211–12.

materials from distant places. In this same mound was found a huge, well-made quartz spearhead and two long narrow copper axheads, one sixteen inches in length and four to five inches in width, weighing over thirty pounds. These huge weapons of stone and copper were obviously for ceremonial use, and similar ones were found in many mounds.[5] In one mound a huge deposit of flint disks was found. These were evidently the offerings brought by a throng of Indians who attended a ceremony. The flint had come from several quarries far away; the disks numbered eight thousand and were finely made. In the mounds children were buried, sometimes with their mothers. The children had the same kind of tools, weapons, and ornaments as the adults, but in miniature. One small boy had a set of stone marbles buried with him. A toothless old chief was buried with a trophy head at his side. The head had a copper plate shaped like a helmet, which was lined with a fabric cap or bonnet. Extra skulls, evidently war trophies or the collected skulls of ancestors, and cut human jawbones with the teeth still in them were often in the graves.[6]

Some authors, particularly during the first half of the last century, were enthusiastic in their accounts of the civilization of the Mound Builders. Perhaps it was a civilization, compared with the very simple life of the earlier Indians; but the contents of the mounds strongly suggest that the Mound Builders were in their everyday life barbarous, and that it was only in their all-absorbing interest in religion and ceremonials that they had any interest in a higher life. Archaeological finds now and again suggest the barbarism of these Indians. The extra skulls found with some burials are not proved to have been war trophies, but the cut human jaws in the graves must be trophies; and from accounts of southern tribes, who had cultures similar to that of the Mound Builders and who were observed by Europeans after the year 1540, we know that enemy skulls and other grisly trophies were treasured by individuals and even kept in temples. The Iroquois seem to have had a faith similar to what we would suppose the Adena and Hopewell Mound Builders had developed; and the Iroquois were certainly barbarians, who made personal ornaments from enemy skulls and tortured captives to death. The Skidi

[5] *Ibid.*, 148–49.
[6] *Ibid.*, 101–104.

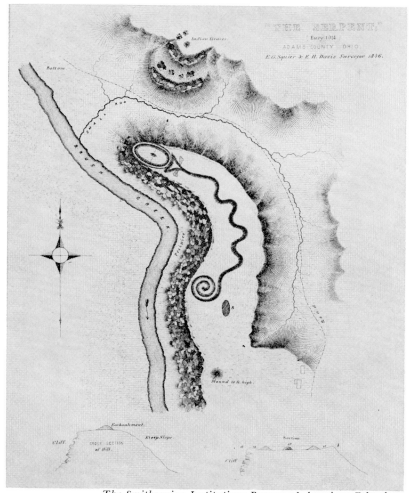

The Smithsonian Institution; Bureau of American Ethnology

The "Great Serpent" in Adams County, Ohio, is among the most cele-
brated of the effigy mounds constructed by the Mound Builders. It
measured 500 feet in length, or 1,330 feet following the convolutions.

The Smithsonian Institution; Bureau of American Ethnology;
Photographed by D. I. Bushnell, Jr.

The Cahokia Mound in Madison County, Illinois, is all that remains
of a strong center of Mississippian culture established by southern
Indians at Cahokia, opposite the present city of St. Louis.

Pawnees had a religion concerned with the sun, moon, and stars, which they may have brought to Nebraska from the old Mound Builder area. They made human sacrifices to their goddess, Morning Star. Again, the burials in Adena and Hopewell mounds, in which the body of a chief or king is surrounded by a circle of men's bodies, can only be accounted for by assuming that the servants of the chief or king were killed, to accompany him in death. All these clues and hints point to a barbarous social condition, and there is nothing to support the view that the Mound Builders had reached a stage that might be termed civilized.

Perhaps the most striking feature of Mound Builder culture was the ceremonial center, with its great earth-walled enclosures. The enclosures were geometric in form: circles, squares, rectangles, ovals, octagons, crescents, and combinations of such shapes. Although the Indians who laid out these vast enclosures had no knowledge of mathematics and no instruments, their great circles, squares, and other forms, made by rule of thumb, were sometimes close to being geometrically perfect.

The Mound Builder center at Newark in Licking County, Ohio, is a typical example of these great ceremonial centers. There is an earth-walled circle enclosing thirty acres, another of twenty acres, an octagon of twenty acres, and a rather irregular square enclosing fifty acres. These great enclosures are connected by avenues bordered on each side by earth embankments, and these avenues are almost as well laid out as modern engineers' work. The largest circle, enclosing thirty acres, is now the county fair ground. After centuries of weathering and other damage, the encircling wall is still five to fourteen feet high, thirty-five to fifty-five feet wide at its base. Inside the wall is a ditch, twenty-eight to forty-one feet wide and eight to thirteen feet deep. To realize the vastness of these Newark works, it may be stated that in historic times most of the walled and stockaded Indian villages in the northern states embraced less than five acres and many included only two or three acres.

Great centers, such as the Newark center just described, stand within a few miles of each other. There are at least five great groups in Ohio, embracing at least a dozen centers almost as impressive as the Newark works. General William Henry Harrison, ninth president of the United States, campaigned against the Ohio Indians and saw the Mound Builder earthworks before they were diminished or obliterated by a growing white population. He was greatly impressed by these Indian works and expressed the view that a very large population had worked over a long period to construct them. Strangely enough, modern archaeologists have failed to find any clear indications of Indian villages of the Mound Builder period, and as late as 1950 they were not able to specify the type of hut constructed by the Mound Builders and were still speculating on the possible locations of villages. With nearly all of the archaeologists agreeing that the great circles, squares, and other enclosures were purely for ceremonial use and denying that the walled enclosures could be villages, the extent of the population and the location and type of their villages are left to conjecture. It may be remarked, however, that at the period following Mound Builder times, walled enclosures, circular and rectangular, were nearly always fortified villages. In some instances, as among the Guale Indians of the Georgia coast, the arrangement was somewhat similar to the archaeologists' theories concerning the Mound Builders; that is, the villages were outside the walled enclosures, and the enclosures were used for tribal councils and ceremonial gatherings. The walled enclosures for such purposes were pentagonal; in a separate area these Indians had a mortuary house, square and partly underground. When this mortuary was filled, they set it on fire and then turned the surrounding land into a common cemetery, encircled by a wall.

We also obtain clues to the purpose of the Hopewell earth-walled enclosures from the practices of the Yuchis, a Siouan tribe living on Tennessee River in early historic times that may very well have been a portion of the old Mound Builder population. One of the Yuchi names for their people was Offspring of the Sun. The villages of this tribe had an open square in the center, which was regarded as sacred ground. It had a temple or sacred hut at each of its four corners, and it was in the square that the religious and social gatherings of the people took place. This square was said to symbolize the Rainbow in the Sky World, where the Sun, from whom the tribe was descended, had undergone certain ritualistic ordeals. These ordeals had been taught by the Sun to the Yuchis, and they evidently formed a main feature of Yuchi religious ceremonial. Indeed, the Yuchis believed that the Sun was their father and had originated all their sacred rites and social customs. This tribe not only had common huts covered with bark and mats; they also had huts with wattled walls, plastered with clay, which may have been the type of some Mound Builder huts.[7]

Everyone who has written of the Mound Builders has dealt more or less at length with the wonders of the mounds and the vast walled enclosures. Few have referred to a matter that is a great wonder, the amazing industry of the people who built these mighty works. In historic times the Indian of the woodlands between the Mississippi and the Hudson had no desire to labor with his hands. That was women's work, and the women were too busy with housework and crop-growing to accomplish anything further. The Mound Builders seem to have had a burning faith that led them to construct great mounds and enclosures. They had a faith in themselves and in their race and its future that the historic Indians had lost. Left undisturbed, the Mound Builders and similar groups would have gone eagerly on, treading the great highway that led upward into civilization, a highway along which they would have met despotic Sun Kings, priestly clans with their blood-stained rites, human slavery and oppression; but through it all they would have kept their energy and their faith in themselves and their race's future.

The material culture of the Ohio Mound Builders was magnificent, but it is to be doubted that the common people had much share in it. Leading men had handsome headdresses made of copper or of dressed leather or fabric, ornamented with fresh-water pearls or beads cut from marine shells. Their garments were similarly ornamented. Besides quantities of copper ornaments, they had some of silver, and rare ornaments might even be covered with a very thin sheet of real gold. They had some iron, probably meteoric iron. They had not learned the art of heating or melting metal; their copper was hammered, the few bits of iron were probably sharpened by rubbing them on gritstone. They had learned to make fabrics, some of which have woven colored designs. They probably had cloaks made of fur and cloaks woven from the brightly colored feathers of birds. They wore

[7] Gaule Indians, Martin, Quimby, and Collier, *Indians Before Columbus*, 380–82; Yuchi Indians in F. W. Hodge (ed.). *Handbook of American Indians North of Mexico*, II, 1006. Griffin, *Archeology of the Eastern United States*, 359, has statements that seem to show that Mound Builder hut remains were inside some Ohio enclosures and even under the earth walls surrounding the enclosures.

leather moccasins and woven sandals, and they had large stone pipes —red, green, and other colors—many of them beautifully carved into the forms of birds and animals.

These Indians had ransacked half a continent in search of materials which they regarded as rare. They had vessels, probably for drinking, made of big conch shells from the coast. Mica, in thick silvery sheets, used for mirrors and ornaments, came from the Piedmont of Carolina and Virginia. Copper from the Great Lakes, galena or lead ore from the Mississippi perhaps, black obsidian and huge grizzly-bear fangs for necklaces from the Far West, shark teeth from the Gulf, and brown chalcedony from the Missouri River in North Dakota. Some archaeologists have pictured a primitive traveling salesman, setting out from Ohio and going to the Gulf or the Great Lakes to exchange their wares for rare materials. This trade most probably was from tribe to tribe, the commodities passing through many hands before they reached Ohio. Primitive Indians regarded everyone outside their own local group as potential enemies, and any traveling salesman from Ohio in all likelihood would have ended up with his head displayed on a pike over some alien village gateway.

From figurines made by the Mound Builder potters we obtain much information about the dress and appearance of these people. They wore copper-covered ear spools, and the men had breechclouts of leather or fabric, the women short skirts. One outstanding feature is the hair arrangement of the men. One man had a round tuft of hair at the center and front of his head, the rest of his hair being cut short or shaved. Other men had two round tufts, one on the front of the head and one at the back; others left only a long narrow ridge of hair from the forehead to the nape of the neck. Archaeologists have asserted that there is no archaeological evidence that any Siouan Indians ever lived in the Ohio Valley. These hair styles of the Mound Builders seem to deny that assertion, for the five Siouan tribes—the Osages, Quapaws, Kansas, Omahas, and Poncas—who had traditions of a former residence on the Ohio all had clan haircuts resembling these Mound Builder styles. Each clan had its special style of haircut; and when the boys reached a certain age, their hair was cut in the clan fashion with ancient ritual, for the haircutting was regarded as a sacred matter.

The Mound Builders constructed hilltop forts, some with earth, others with stone walls. These forts seem to have been built to guard against enemies coming from the north.[8] One fort, in Ross County, embraces an area of 150 acres; Fort Ancient on the Little Miami River, north of Cincinnati, has an interior area of 100 acres. Inside some of these forts there are clear indications of village sites, with mounds and village refuse; yet some archaeologists maintain that the forts were for ceremonial gatherings and not for defense. They base their opinion largely on the fact that the Mound Builder forts usually have the moat or ditch inside the wall, a custom which military men state would render the forts useless. But primitive Indians did not fight with firearms, and George Catlin, after 1830, saw the Mandans defending a fortified village with the ditch inside the wall, in Mound Builder fashion, against an enemy assault. The Mandan warriors stood on the inside slope of the wall, shooting arrows through the openings between the pickets of the stockade on top of the wall, and they beat off the enemy with little difficulty. The Mandans told David Thompson, after 1790, that although the warlike Sioux often attacked their villages with the moats inside the walls, the Sioux had never succeeded in breaking into a village.

In reviewing the Hopewell or Mound Builder period in Ohio, one cannot avoid the strong impression that the Indians of this time had created a new era of barbaric pomp and splendor. We need not fall into the error of assuming that the Indians of the Ohio Valley were only half-naked savages before Hopewell times, for we know from the finds in Kentucky caves and rock shelters that this was not the case. The pre-Hopewell Siouans of the Indian Knoll groups were well and even handsomely equipped; they had cloth fabrics and probably woven fur and feather cloaks; they were skilled wood carvers, and had handsome ornaments. But they had nothing comparable to the fine material culture of the later Mound Builder period. And this was not all pomp and show. There are strong indications of the well-being of the common people in Mound Builder times, of a population increase, and of villages becoming larger and more numerous; pottery, which was a needed convenience, became more abundant and better in quality.

At this period one may for the first time pierce the dark curtain of prehistory and begin to glimpse Indian groupings into stocks and

[8] Thomas, *Report on Mound Exploration, Twelfth Annual Report,* B.A.E., 704. It is not likely that there was a military plan of defense. Each Mound Builder center probably had its own hilltop fort as a place of refuge in time of danger.

tribes. Even the cautious archaeologists have stated that the Hopewell centers in Ohio are so homogeneous that the occupation of most of Ohio by people of a common stock may be assumed. To the anthropologist and historian this seems obvious, and much more may be assumed. For this culture was now spreading in many directions, and apparently moving rapidly and with some force. The new religious beliefs must have accelerated this spread. The Mound Builder faith was like fire driven by a wind, like a great light penetrating into dark places. The spread seems to have been strongest into Kentucky, Tennessee, Indiana, Illinois, and Wisconsin, with weaker penetrations into Missouri, Iowa, and Minnesota. Michigan seems to have been uninhabited or very thinly occupied by Indians in early Woodland times; but in middle Woodland times it was held, probably by Algonquians and some Iroquoian groups, and these were influenced to some degree by Ohio Mound Builder culture.

Assuming—and it is a fair assumption—that the Indians in Kentucky, Tennessee, and Illinois in early Woodland times were Siouans, we might make the further assumption that, when the Adena folk brought a new faith and culture into Ohio, some Siouans were attracted to the new development and moved north of the Ohio River. The more conservative groups remained in Kentucky and Tennessee. Southern Illinois seems to have been conservative also. It took its cultural features from Kentucky and Tennessee.

Thus, when the Mound Builder faith and culture spread westward, it went into southeastern Indiana quite strongly. It then jumped to Fulton County, Illinois, north of Illinois River, and from here it spread in every direction: into eastern Wisconsin, across the Mississippi into Missouri and Iowa, up the Mississippi into western Wisconsin and eastern Minnesota. It also spread southward, into southern Illinois. Modern archaeologists are averse to making conjectures, particularly about Indian stocks and tribes; but the spread of Ohio Hopewell or Mound Builder culture has led them to suggest that there was a tribal grouping of Indians of the same language in Ohio, and a similar situation in Illinois.[9] We do not need archaeology to tell us this. Primitive men always lived in tribes. The important point is that archaeology has produced new evidence that indicates quite clearly that part of the Ohio Mound Builders belonged to the Siouan

[9] Griffin, *Archeology of the Eastern United States*, 360.

stock and were in friendly contact with other Indians, evidently of the same stock, in Tennessee, Indiana, and Illinois, and particularly with Indians on the Illinois River, in present Fulton County. We can even state that the Mound Builders living at the Turner villages, at or near the present Cincinnati, traded painted pottery human figurines to the Indians on Illinois River.[10]

Indiana archaeology was rather neglected up to 1950, which is a pity, for it is in the southern portion of that state that we might most probably find traces of the Siouan groups that included the Osages, Quapaws, Kansas, Omahas, and Poncas. These tribes had traditions of former residence on the Ohio or Wabash, and it is very probable that they were there in Mound Builder times, taking part in that cultural development. In Indiana large Hopewell or Mound Builder centers are rare; but the Indians in southern Indiana built mounds containing burials of Mound Builder type. They also built small mounds on high ground in lines, a feature of the Effigy Mound culture, which was unquestionably a Siouan development.

In Illinois the Indians in archaic times had been mainly of the Kentucky Indian Knoll type, and therefore in all probability Siouans. They remained there through the slow development of early Woodland and on into middle Woodland times, with few changes. They were probably hunters and fishermen, spending most of the year wandering in small camps; but they had developed some villages, were making pottery, and possibly were learning to grow little crops of maize and vegetables. Then the Mound Builder faith and ceremonial practices came among them and startled them into wakefulness. It was like a revolution.

In Fulton County, on the north side of the Illinois River, the crude and poky little villages in the stream valleys sprang to life, as from a dream. They took up the new Ohio religion. They did not attempt to build the huge earth-walled enclosures that were the spectacular feature of the great Ohio centers, but they began to bury their dead with all the pomp and ceremony of the new faith. They imported from Ohio, or made among themselves, the necessary ceremonial equipment. As in Ohio, on the Illinois River nothing was too good for the dead. Copper breastplates and ornaments, garments decorated with pearls, and fine objects made of rare obsidian and

10 *Ibid.*, 159.

39

other scarce stone were placed with the dead. Sometimes they covered the dead with a tent of woven cloth, pinning down the edges neatly with long skewers of bone. Handsome stone platform pipes of Mound Builder type, big drinking vessels made of marine shells, and necklaces of grizzly-bear teeth were included in the grave offerings. Instead of sprinkling red ocher in the graves, as was done in early times, they broke up sheet mica and sprinkled the silvery bits in the graves. Here in Illinois, along with the religious upsurge, came agriculture, to become a definite feature of daily life; and villages increased in number and size.[11]

In southern Illinois the Indians were apparently of a somewhat different type from those along Illinois River. They were originally of the same stock; but they were conservative, and their relations were not with the Ohio Indians, but more often with the people in Kentucky and Tennessee. Those men who imagine that Indians in early times used the great rivers as highways are sadly at fault. The Indian route down the Ohio River from Ohio to southern Illinois seems to be imaginary. The trails were not by water, but across Indiana to Illinois River. The Indians in southern Illinois did take up the Mound Builder faith, but they apparently obtained their knowledge of it from Illinois River folk, and they still clung to many of their old ways.

The Mound Builder faith and type of burial spread from Illinois River to the district near Lake Michigan, in southeastern Wisconsin and northwestern Indiana; it spread across the Mississippi into eastern Iowa and northeastern Missouri, up the Mississippi into western Wisconsin and eastern Minnesota, and here it faded out. In all these areas the new religion and customs spread among Indians who were in all probability Siouans. There are only two other Indian stocks we need to mention: the Algonquians and the Iroquoians, and there is no evidence that the spread of Hopewell or Mound Builder culture from Illinois River reached any sizable groups belonging to these two stocks. Moreover, none of the Indians here in the west and north developed the Mound Builder culture as it was known in Ohio. They took up the religious and burial customs, but they did not construct the vast earth enclosures of the Ohio Mound Builder centers. One

---

11 *Ibid.*, 118, 153–54; Martin, Quimby, and Collier, *Indians Before Columbus,* 293–94.

feature of the development in Wisconsin is curious. In Ohio the Mound Builders built a few effigy mounds: the Great Serpent Mound in Adams County, some lizard mounds, and, reportedly, some bird and bear mounds. In Wisconsin the Indians took this practice up and built literally hundreds of effigy mounds: birds, bears, serpents, lizards, and turtles; mounds representing other creatures and a few supposed to represent men. The building of these effigy mounds was certainly the work of Siouans of the Winnebago, Iowa, Oto, Mandan, Hidatsa, and Crow groups. They spread their effigy mounds all over southern Wisconsin, down into Illinois, across the Mississippi into Iowa and Minnesota; and they took the effigy custom with them on their migration, across Minnesota to the Red River of the North, on to the Missouri, and even to the Souris River in North Dakota and Manitoba.[12]

Men who are inclined to smile when a reference is made to the Siouan Indian part in the Hopewell or Mound Builder cultural spread should study this effigy mound development. It seems to come from Ohio and from the eastern centers of the Mound Builders. It evidently had its roots in the Adena and Hopewell absorption in bird and animal symbolism. The Adena folk are connected in some manner with the bird effigies in Georgia, and both the Adena and Hopewell Indians regarded the serpent with veneration. They made serpent heads of copper, and coiled serpents were carved from stone and covered with copper or silvery mica; the Great Serpent Mound is supposed to have been constructed in Adena times. The Hopewell people may have continued the effigy mound construction; for there is a birdlike mound at Newark, and at the mouth of the Scioto the central mound in the Tremper site seemed to be a bear effigy. Across the Ohio River, in Greenup County, Kentucky, Rafinesque reported a bear mound, which modern archaeology has failed to locate. It is well known that many of the fine carved stone pipes of the Mound Builders are in the form of birds and animals. These people also made small turtles of copper, which have been found both in Ohio and in Illinois. The point that is difficult to understand is why, with all this absorption in bird, animal, and serpent symbolism, the Ohio Indians built so few effigy mounds, and why the Siouans of Wis-

[12] J. T. Short. *North American Antiquity*, 37; *Iowa Archaeological Society Journal*, Vol. V, 13–16.

consin made effigy mounds the outstanding feature of their Mound Builder type of culture.

Mound Builder culture seems to have come into eastern Iowa from the Fulton County, Illinois, villages. There was an important center of this culture on the Maquoketa River in Jackson County and another near Amana, farther south and some fifty miles west of the Mississippi, in Iowa County. Along the Mississippi the mounds of Hopewell or Mound Builder culture are found from near Dubuque to Keokuk, at the mouth of the Des Moines. These Mound Builders of eastern Iowa displayed the Ohio lavishness in handsome objects made of copper and fine stone. They had fresh-water pearls with which to adorn their persons, handsome stone pipes carved in the form of animals, mica for mirrors and ornaments, and woven fabrics. They also had agriculture, a sure indication of a rather high culture. In northeastern Iowa the Effigy Mound folk have left their strange remains: big earth mounds in the form of birds and bears, birds on the wing, bears marching in procession across the land. These remains are of the Mound Builder culture and of the same period as the burial mounds farther to the south in Iowa.

In Missouri there were Indians in early Woodland times who used the Siouan type of burial in stone vaults under mounds. The remains of this folk are called Boone culture by the archaeologists. The people seem to have remained on through the Mound Builder period, and at that time the Ohio religious faith and burial customs came into Missouri from Illinois, with the usual result that the crude native culture was lifted to a higher and rather splendid level. But this was only in certain areas: along the Mississippi (the land that St. Louis now sprawls across was once covered with Indian mounds and other works, partly of this middle Woodland period), but some of the bearers of the Ohio faith and culture went as far west as the present site of Kansas City, where they established a large center and extended their occupation into northeastern Kansas and northeastern Oklahoma. The type of culture in this Kansas City Mound Builder area has a close resemblance to that in Fulton County, Illinois, and may have come from there.[13]

13 Griffin, *Archeology of the Eastern United States,* 140; A. C. Spaulding, in *Fifth Plains Conference Notebook,* I, 106–107.

The Mound Builder faith and burial customs went up the Mississippi, evidently from Fulton County, Illinois, into western Wisconsin and eastern Minnesota. There can be no doubt that the Sioux already occupied Minnesota at this early time. They were evidently a crude and conservative group, wandering in small hunting camps, with few and very small fixed villages. They seem to have been affected by the new faith, but they did not have the means or leisure for developing the Mound Builder type of culture. In their burials there are none of the copper breastplates, gorgets, and ear spools usual in the Mound Builder burials in Illinois, no fine stone pipes, pearls, or other rich offerings to the dead. The sparse Sioux settlements or little villages of this period are near the present cities of St. Paul and Minneapolis, in a country of lakes and, in early times, great marshes. The Sioux gathered wild rice in the marshes, and even when the growing of crops became a matter well known to them, they did not plant corn or vegetables but continued to gather wild rice. Thus they failed to establish large fixed villages, and their way of life continued to be simple and crude. They did adopt the Mound Builder burial customs, but they evidently cut these practices to fit their own way of life. Wandering about in small camps the greater part of the year, they exposed the dead, probably on scaffolds raised on tall poles. When the flesh decayed, they cleaned the bones and made neat bundles of them, which they carried about from camp to camp.

In the early spring all the little camps met at a common gathering place, decided on the year before. This spring gathering was termed by the French traders the *rendezvous,* and its big feature was a Feast of the Dead. This was obviously the Sioux version of the Mound Builder burial ceremonies. Every family that had had a death brought out the handsomely wrapped bundle of bones; a feast was held, and the bones were buried, the best offerings obtainable being given to the dead or to their living relatives. The Brulé Sioux winter count or pictograph record kept by Brown Hat, alias Baptiste Good, records these Feasts of the Dead under the designation of Commemoration of the Dead, down to the middle of the nineteenth century, and there is some reason for supposing that the ancient rites were practiced at Rosebud reservation, South Dakota, as late as 1890. The Brulés did not keep up the old practice of carrying about bundled bones. Instead, each family made a small buckskin doll, representing its dead relative; and when the ceremony took place, all the families brought the buckskin dolls to be mourned over and to be given handsome offerings.

There must have been a Siouan group along the eastern side of the Mississippi in northern Illinois and southern Wisconsin that was different from the Sioux. There are no clear indications that the Wisconsin Indians had agriculture in Mound Builder times, and this probably meant that the people were in moving camps, engaged in hunting, fishing, and gathering wild vegetables and fruits. But they were strongly affected by the Ohio faith and burial customs, and each group of Indians built both conical burial mounds and large effigy mounds. Here in northern Illinois and in Wisconsin the people had most of the fine things produced by the Ohio Mound Builder folk. They had copper breastplates, ear spools, and other ornaments; fine polished-stone gorgets and carved stone platform pipes, animal-tooth ornaments (made of copper and silver), and fine stone weapons, including knives made of brown Dakota chalcedony, brought apparently all the way from Knife River on the Missouri in North Dakota—which is an indication that, like the Ohio Mound Builders, the Indians on the Mississippi in Illinois and Wisconsin were obtaining rare materials from distant places. Like the Sioux of Minnesota, the Indians in Wisconsin in Mound Builder times seem to have exposed their dead on platforms, and later they held group burial ceremonies and placed the bundled bones in mounds with lavish grave offerings. This suggests again that these Indians did not have big fixed villages, but wandered about in camps. These were the probable conditions at the beginning of the Mound Builder period. As the culture was introduced into Wisconsin, at least a part of the population seems to have taken up agriculture and established villages.

The effigy mounds are the striking feature of this period in southern Wisconsin, extending down into northwestern Illinois and across the Mississippi into eastern Minnesota and Iowa. They may indicate the migration of the Iowa and Oto tribes, but a lengthy and minute study would be necessary to demonstrate that fact.[14]

In southeastern Wisconsin the Hopewell culture seems to have come up from Fulton County, on Illinois River. Here there are

[14] Martin, Quimby, and Collier, *Indians Before Columbus*, 300–307; Shetrone, *The Mound Builders*, 193, 306–307; Griffin, *Archeology of the Eastern United States*, 115.

groups of effigy mounds, mainly to the south and west of Lake Winnebago, extending west to Wisconsin River and down that stream to the great effigy mound center near its mouth. In Waukesha County, close to Lake Michigan and south of Lake Winnebago, the remains seem to indicate the beginning of the mingling of Mound Builder culture with that of the natives. Here the strange effigy mounds were developed: bird, turtle, and perhaps panther mounds. The bird and turtle mounds spread westward into Dane County; lizard mounds appear here; some are farther north, near the south end of Lake Winnebago. The serpent mounds seem to start at the south end of this lake and extend off toward the northwest into Minnesota and on into Dakota. There do not seem to be many serpent mounds. Turtle and bird mounds went west with the serpents; bear mounds (some may be buffalo) are on lower Wisconsin River and extend across the Mississippi into northeastern Iowa. They are usually accompanied by bird mounds. There seems to be a chance in all this that someday we may be able to trace the migrations of several groups of Siouan Indians through a study of these effigy mound groups.

Mound Builder culture may have been brought into southern Michigan by actual Indian colonists from Ohio, for the Michigan type of this culture includes the earth-walled enclosures of the great Ohio centers. This is curious. It might mean that here Ohio Indians came among people of an alien stock, perhaps Iroquoians, and that they therefore built a community on the Ohio plan, either to impress the natives or to serve them for defense against attack.[15] What are termed the Goodall sites in southwestern Michigan are of Hopewell times and affected by that culture; but the population seems to have been Iroquoian; and this is true also of the other two centers, in southeastern Michigan, called Gibraltar and Younge. Shetrone speaks of a big Hopewell center on Grand River, near Grand Rapids: eight groups of mounds, a total of forty-six mounds, containing Hopewell type of material; but here again, the natives who built the mounds may have been Iroquoians. Unlike Illinois and Wisconsin (Siouan territories), Michigan had many circular earth-walled enclosures which were undoubtedly villages once defended by wall and log stockade. Whether these villages belong to the Mound Builder era or a later time is not clear. In southwestern Michigan there were many

15 Shetrone, *The Mound Builders,* 280–82.

tracts of cultivated land termed garden beds, the exact purpose of which has always been a puzzle. These tracts have very even straight or slightly curved rows, and in a photograph they look like sheets of corrugated iron. The Indians planted maize and vegetables in hills, widely spaced, and not in regular rows. One suspects that the garden beds are old Indian tobacco gardens. The Iroquoians were famous tobacco growers, and the presence of these garden beds may be additional evidence that this district in southern Michigan was held by Iroquoian tribes in Mound Builder times. Indeed, there is much reason for believing that at this period groups of Iroquoians held lands in northwestern Indiana, northern Ohio, and southern Michigan, which seems to strengthen the theory that these Iroquoian Indians did migrate eastward from the Mississippi in Illinois, and that in Mound Builder times they held lands from eastern Illinois to the eastern end of Lake Ontario.

The Mound Builder religion and culture did not spread strongly toward the east or northeast. The country in those directions was held by Iroquoian and Algonquian tribes that did not take kindly to the idea of mound-building; and east of the Allegheny Mountains, mounds were either absent or rare. The Indians in New York and Pennsylvania in archaic times were apparently Algonquians; but about the time southern Indians brought the Adena culture into Kentucky, West Virginia, and Ohio, there was what W. A. Ritchie terms an influx of new people from the upper Great Lakes into western New York. These folk had the custom of putting red ocher in graves, and other traits that suggest their identity as Iroquoians. They established a center at Point Peninsula, at the eastern end of Lake Ontario. Meantime, other groups with Iroquoian-like culture appeared in West Virginia and Pennsylvania, and their culture, which resembled that of Adena, began to influence the earlier Algonquian population. Some of this influence seems to have come from Adena in the Ohio Valley; and when the Hopewell Mound Builder culture succeeded Adena, the influence of the Ohio culture on the Indians in New York, West Virginia, and Pennsylvania continued to be felt— but not very strongly. A few mounds of the Ohio type appeared in the extreme west of New York, but there are only a few Indian centers in which the Ohio cultural influence is marked. Meantime the opposing culture of the Point Peninsula Indians continued to spread. This Point Peninsula culture is divided into three phases. In the

46

second phase it picked up some Mound Builder traits from Ohio. The third phase was contemporary with the fading of Mound Builder culture, and Point Peninsula III is rather clearly an Iroquoian culture that had won out in a protracted competition with Ohio Mound Builder culture.[16]

The Ohio Hopewell or Mound Builder culture sent some of its traits through West Virginia, Pennsylvania, and even into Virginia; indeed, the culture found by the first Europeans along the Middle Atlantic coast had some features of the Ohio Mound Builder type, but without mounds. In these early times the Indians in West Virginia seem to have been Siouans, or at least part of them were; in western Pennsylvania there were Iroquoian groups, but perhaps of a different origin from the New York Iroquois, and the same or similar type of Iroquoian folk who lived in Pennsylvania apparently extended down from eastern West Virginia into Allegheny, Bath, Page, Rockingham, and Shenandoah counties in northwestern Virginia.[17] Near Pittsburgh, in Washington County, Pennsylvania, were mounds of Ohio Hopewell culture showing Iroquoian traits, and in both West Virginia and Virginia the sites with Ohio Hopewell culture have similar Iroquoian traits. Moreover, after the Ohio Mound Builder culture had faded away, the Indians of the new Ohio culture, termed Fort Ancient[18] by the archaeologists, continued to trade with and influence the Iroquoians in West Virginia, Pennsylvania, and Virginia. This is an interesting situation. It hints that the two Iroquoian groups were distinct; that the group in Pennsylvania, West Virginia, and Virginia had friendly relations with the Ohio Valley tribes in Mound Builder times and on into early historic times, and that the Iroquoians in western New York, northern Ohio, and Ontario were not friendly either with the Iroquoians of the southern group or with the Ohio Indians. In early historic times the Iroquois or Five Na-

16 Ritchie, "Cultural Influences from Ohio in New York Archaeology," *American Antiquity*, Vol. II, No. 3, 183; Griffin, *Archeology of the Eastern United States*, 48–50, 59; Martin, Quimby, and Collier, *Indians Before Columbus*, 250–51.

17 Griffin, *Archeology of the Eastern United States*, 60–62.

18 Fort Ancient culture was misnamed. The older archaeologists found a Mound Builder fort in western Ohio and named it Fort Ancient. They found village ruins near the fort and mistakenly thought that the people of these villages had built the fort, so they termed the village culture Fort Ancient culture. It later turned out to be a culture that came after the Mound Builders, the latest prehistoric culture of Ohio, which seems to have lasted down to 1650 or even later.

tions were the bitter enemies of these southern Iroquoian groups and waged vindictive war on them until they were destroyed.

The culture of the Ohio Mound Builder does not appear to have affected to any marked degree the tribes dwelling to the south of the Ohio Valley. Those in Kentucky and Tennessee seem to have been conservative, clinging to old ways, and farther south the southern tribes had their own peculiar culture, which in some areas was on a level with that in the Ohio Valley. At Marksville on the Red River of Louisiana there was a culture almost identical with that in Ohio, and there was trade between Ohio and Louisiana, northern copper and other rare materials being traded for southern products.

When one attempts to weigh the results of the development of the Mound Builder culture in the Ohio Valley, he finds the task an almost impossible one, because of the lack of definite information. We have few confirmed facts beyond those provided by archaeology; and here in the United States, where the ancient peoples had no system of writing, archaeology has little to exhibit beyond the dry bones of peoples and cultures. The comparison of pottery traits and types of tools and weapons made of stone, bone, shell, and other materials is interesting; but it tells us little about the beliefs and social conditions of the Indians involved, and one can learn little about a people of the past by studying the bare skeleton of their material culture.

It was not with new types of pottery, stone knives, and projectile points that the Mound Builders made their deep impression on the minds of the northern Indians, but with imponderable things of the spirit. They seem to have introduced a new system of sky deities and new and definite ideas of a future life among tribes that worshiped in the main only earth-bound animal deities, and this new faith was such a powerful force that it shook primitive people out of their sloth and set them to doing arduous work with their hands. There was no such spirit among the Indians of later periods, who detested and avoided manual labor. They were warriors who would not demean themselves by working. Their ancestors in Mound Builder times worked, and with a spirit and purpose that is most impressive.

If the Cult of the Dead and the Feast of the Dead among northern tribes came out of the Mound Builder faith—and there is excellent reason for thinking that they did—we will have to admit that the new faith, brought into the Ohio Valley in those far-off times, spread

48

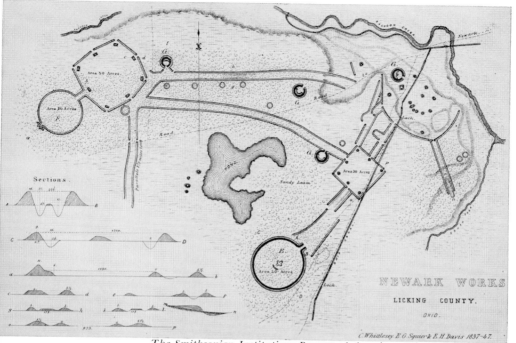

The Smithsonian Institution; Bureau of American Ethnology

The prehistoric Newark Works are located on a plain thirty to fifty feet above the bottom land at the junction of two branches of Licking River, near Newark, Licking County, Ohio. Divided into two sections connected by two walled avenues, the works consist of a series of square, circular, and octagonal enclosures with mounds and ditches and spread over nearly four square miles.

James B. Griffin, Archeology of the Eastern United States;
Courtesy University of Chicago Press

At left is a Hopewell woman from Log Tomb of Dickison Mound 478. The necklace of ground shell beads with the wolf-mandible and hawk-skull pendants was found with the skeleton as were the beads at the feet. At right is a Hopewell warrior found with the necklace of disk-shell beads and human-mandible pendants, a spearhead, and small shell rings and hawk claws which are shown above as decorations on the breechcloth.

north into the cold lands beyond the Great Lakes and from the Hudson west beyond the Mississippi, and it kept a hold on some tribes that was still strong in the eighteenth century. This Cult of the Dead was not a thing that the old beliefs in animal gods could produce. It had to do with sky deities and a clear belief in a future life.

One hundred years ago, and even sixty years ago, there was much talk among scholars of sun worship and sun priests and kings among our Indians in early times. The modern archaeologist has little to say on this subject, although some of the discoveries in the Mound Builder area strongly suggest that there were kings and a priestly cast among these Ohio Valley Indians. When ten or fifteen adult males are found in a single burial and are known to have been buried in the flesh apparently at the same time, one man in the center with the trappings of royalty, the others seemingly his lieutenants or servants, it is difficult to avoid comparing the burial with the known customs of such southern tribes as the Natchez Indians, who when the Sun King died, strangled his principal officials and servants so that they might accompany him to the spirit land. The Mound Builder culture spread as far as Virginia; and when the first whites came, the Virginia Indians had kings and priestly groups.

The Jesuits in the seventeenth century termed the Illinois Indians and the Hurons of Ontario sun worshipers, and there were indications of sun worship among other northern tribes. Together with the sun worship often went a belief that all people were the children of the Sun, who had created them in the Sky World and then sent them down to live on earth. In this faith the feminine Moon was a goddess and the stars were deities.

The Skidi Pawnees are a tribe with a clear record of sun, moon, and star worship, and they made human sacrifices to Morning Star to insure good crops and successful hunting. The probability that the Skidis dwelled near the head of the Ohio before migrating westward after the year 1650 renders it possible that their form of religion was close to that of the Ohio Mound Builders.

The Dhegiha Siouans (Osages, Omahas, Poncas, Kansas, and Quapaws) had a tradition of an origin in the Sky World, which seems to be quite similar to that of the Yuchis. These Dhegihan tribes still had fragments of customs and traditions that apparently had to do with sun, moon, and star worship in the nineteenth century. Lewis H. Morgan, in his journals, speaks of a similar sun, moon, and star cult among the Crows of Montana. The Iroquois of New York also had myths of a Sky World and of the doings of the sun, moon, and stars. These myths were the basis of Iroquois religion. Thus it may be that, in Adena and Hopewell times, a new sky faith was brought into the north-central woodlands by southern Indians, producing a religious and social revolution that, if the Indians had been left to themselves, might have produced an Indian civilization comparable to that of Mexico. But war and the coming of Europeans brought chaos, and the incipient civilization in the Ohio Valley withered and died.

CHAPTER FOUR

West Wind

THE MOUND BUILDER INDIANS in the Ohio Valley brought their culture to a height that may well be termed spectacular, and then it began to fade and presently vanished. Archaeology cannot explain this. The archaeologists admit that, after more than a century of excavation and study in the centers of Mound Builder or Hopewell culture, the disappearance of this culture is an even greater mystery than the puzzle of its origin.[1]

Let us leave archaeology and turn to the livelier field of Indian tradition. Nicolas Perrot was a fur trader and interpreter in Canada from before 1650 until after 1689, and in his memoirs he set down traditions that he had picked up from the Algonquian and Iroquoian tribes. Men who are familiar with Indian traditions know that it was quite possible for our Indians, relying solely on memory, to recall events as far back as two centuries, but that these stories have an occasional taint of fiction. Perrot's traditions may therefore have referred to the period 1400–50, and that probably means to the time when the Mound Builders of the Ohio Valley were in their prime. He does not refer to them; he probably did not know of their existence, for the stories he set down were those of the tribes in Ontario, New York, and along Lake Erie in northern Ohio.

[1] Griffin, *Fort Ancient*, 307.

According to these traditions the Indian population was not large in early times, and the people lived by hunting and fishing. They wandered in the forest and along the lake shores in small groups, living mostly in moving camps. Then some of the Indians—all Iroquoians, apparently—obtained maize and the seeds of vegetables; and they formed fixed villages and lived by growing crops. They did not know how to hunt, but the wandering Algonquians visited the villages at harvest time and traded meat and skins for maize and dried vegetables. Here there is a touch of fiction. We know from similar village Indians on the Missouri and Arkansas Rivers in the eighteenth century that the villagers did know how to hunt but were prevented from going freely on hunts by hostile wandering hunter tribes, and that some of the villagers preferred the safe and rather lazy life of their towns to the hazards of the hunt. For both reasons, these Indians stayed at home, obtaining meat and skins from visiting groups of hunting Indians.

This early period, as Nicolas Perrot suggests, was a time of peace. The Iroquoian villagers and the Algonquian rovers and hunters got along well for a time. Then a group of young Iroquoians went on a hunt with a camp of friendly Algonquians, intending to spend the winter with them in the forest. Some of the Algonquians grew jealous and alarmed. They feared that if these young Iroquoians went home, they would teach their own people the secrets of successful hunting. Then the Iroquois would kill their own game, and there would be no market in the villages for the meat and skins brought in by the Algonquian hunting tribes. So the Algonquians murdered the Iroquois youths, buried their bodies in the snow, and reported to their relatives that the boys had accidentally fallen into a river and been drowned. But when the snow melted in the spring, some Iroquois found the bodies of the youths and knew that they had been murdered.

A war followed the discovery. It was probably started by the vengeance-seeking Iroquois, but the Algonquians were hardier than the village Indians and more active. They proved themselves to be better warriors, and the Iroquois faced a hard struggle. At first the Algonquians defeated the Iroquois, but then the Iroquois began to fortify their villages by surrounding them with high log palisades, to train their youth for fighting, and to attack the Algonquians with very large war parties. As the war continued, the Iroquois had to do their own hunting. They went into the forest in large communal groups and probably spent the winters in search of game. The Algonquians made life miserable for them by setting ambuscades for their hunters, driving off the game they sought, and sending war parties to their camps, where the old people, children, and a few warriors who had remained at home were unable to defend the stockaded villages.[2]

Now, this was probably in the Mound Builder period, and we cannot doubt that some similar condition existed in the Ohio Valley, with wild hunting tribesmen plaguing the Mound Builder villagers. The archaeological evidence is that the Mound Builders established their great ceremonial centers in a time of peace, when the wilder tribes were strongly inclined to accept the new religion and to be the loyal friends of the southern Indians who had brought this new faith and the impressive cult of the dead into the Ohio Valley. We can easily understand how different the situation would have been if war had started. Like the Iroquoians, the Mound Builders were concentrating on village life, growing crops, and holding great religious gatherings. Like the Iroquoians, they probably depended on the hunting tribes for part of the meat and skins they required. War would put an end to such an arrangement; the Mound Builders would have to do their own hunting, and when they went on extended hunts in large communal groups, they would be harassed by the wild tribes, who would also send war parties to attack the villages, held weakly while most of the people were with the hunting camps. In time war did come, and archaeology shows that the Mound Builders constructed forts near their population centers as places of refuge in the event of enemy raids.

It must be obvious that a time of peril and harassment would have a very serious effect on the life of the Mound Builders. If they adhered to the custom of flocking to the great centers to take part in religious ceremonies, the wild hunting tribes would plunder their villages in their absence. Little groups of people on their way to the ceremonial centers would be massacred, and in time the people would cease to believe that their gods really protected them. They would turn against the priests of the religion; and if they had kings, their faith that these kings were divine beings who could protect them

---

[2] Perrot, in Emma H. Blair's *Indian Tribes of the Upper Mississippi*, I, 42–46.

would be destroyed. The unity of the Mound Builder groups would have been shattered, and each group would have stayed in its own district taking measures to protect itself. The faith and the high culture with its splendor would be gone.[3]

When we turn to Illinois, where the Mound Builder faith and cult of the dead had taken strong root, we find evidence of peace and an increase in both population and the number of villages. Then the Hopewell or Ohio Mound Builder culture in Illinois began to fade away; the people abandoned their undefended villages in the stream valleys and built new ones on the bluffs, where they could defend themselves better. Indians whose culture is termed Maple Mills by the archaeologists came into Illinois from the north, bringing a seemingly Siouan culture down from Wisconsin.[4] About the same time the southern Indians who had built a strong center at Cahokia, opposite the present city of St. Louis, extended their influence to Illinois River in the north. The Mound Builder culture on Illinois River vanished, the native population evidently mingling with the northern invaders and the Cahokia Indians from the south. About this time two groups of invaders came into extreme southern Illinois and put an end to the Mound Builder culture there. Then these invading Indians formed a settlement in Massac and Pope counties in southern Illinois, and from tree-ring dating we learn that they established their settlement about 1450. Here we seem to have a date for the fading of the Mound Builder culture in Illinois.[5]

[3] Here we may turn to what is one of few references made by Indians to the Mound Builders. The reference occurs in the quaint, mythology-like history of the Iroquois written by a partly educated Iroquois, David Cusic, and is contained in Henry R. Schoolcraft's *Historical and Statistical Information Respecting the History, Condition and Prospect of the Indian Tribes*, Vol. V. On page 635, Cusic records that at an early date the Iroquois were much troubled by snakes, which one suspects may mean the Ohio Indians. The Iroquois sent a prince or chief to visit the Emperor in the Golden City, the capital of the empire, and after a time the Emperor built many forts "almost penetrating the Lake Erie," which caused much fear among the Iroquois, who held the lands along the south shore of the lake, so they determined to defend their lands. This makes the Mound Builders the aggressors; but there are no Mound Builder forts in the north; they are all close to the Mound Builder centers and clearly for defense.

[4] Probably Siouan because they came from the Siouan area in Wisconsin and brought with them pottery of the "Lake Michigan" type, which is now termed Effigy Mound pottery and is certainly Siouan.

[5] Griffin, *Archeology of the Eastern United States*, 155–58.

We have yet another way to check on what happened to the Ohio Mound Builders, and that lies in the Delaware tribe's "Walam Olum" or Red Score. This tribe had an ancient song, recording the tribal migrations and early wars, and to keep the events in memory, they made a painted tally on either birchbark or wood. This was in the form of pictographs, each representing an episode in tribal history. Probably the Delawares adopted this method for recording their migrations after they came in contact with Europeans around 1600. The Walam Olum therefore may show a blurred memory of events back to the year 1400.

The tale opens with a group of Algonquian tribes in the land of snow and ice, which some authorities suppose was Labrador. The tribes in the group are set down as the Delawares or Leni-Lenápe, the Shawnees, Conoys, Nanticokes, and Mohicans. All these tribes, except the Shawnees, ended their migrations near the Atlantic coast and were found by the first Europeans in Delaware, Maryland, eastern Pennsylvania, New Jersey, and southern New York.

The Walam Olum states that these tribes migrated from the land of snow and ice, moving toward the southwest. They came at last to a great island, the beautiful land of the Snakes. They drove the Snakes out and occupied the island. This island was perhaps the southern peninsula of Michigan, and from archaeology we learn that the Ohio Mound Builders had a colony here and that the early natives were evidently of Iroquoian stock. Further, archaeology seems to show that Algonquian tribes later came into the peninsula and built villages, defended by log palisades.

The Walam Olum next records that the Delaware group of tribes spread southward into the beautiful land of Akolaki, the Shore Land, the Big Fir Land, which seems to be the land of the Akowini, the first "Snakes" whom they fought. The Delawares drove them eastward. The land was apparently located on the south shore of Lake Erie. Here the Delaware people learned to plant crops and settled down for a long time; then a drought came, and they went on to Shillilaken, the Buffalo Land, beyond the Mississippi. This part of the story is very improbable. These Indians had plenty of game and fish in the Lake Erie district; if crops failed and they had to hunt to obtain food, they could have hunted and fished where they were. Even if they desired buffalo meat, there were great herds of buffalo on the Illinois prairies and probably to the east, in Indiana. There is no indication in Illinois archaeology of an invasion of Algonquian people at this period. Moreover, the Walam Olum states that on the Mississippi they met the Mengwi or Iroquois, who crossed the river to the north of the Delawares and were moving eastward. This again is evidently myth. The probability is that the Delaware group drifted southward from the Lake Erie country into Ohio.

The Delaware group now sought to enter a rich land in the Ohio Valley, a land of towns and forts held by a powerful people they called the Tellegwi or Taligewi. They sent a messenger asking permission to settle in the Tellegwi land, but this request was refused. They were offered safe passage through the land, but soon after this a party of their warriors was slain by the Tellegwi. War followed. The Walam Olum states that the Delaware group advanced from the west and after a long war defeated the Tellegwi and drove them south. The victorious Delawares settled in an old Tellegwi center on the lower Wabash, where they dwelled for a long time. Then the Shawnees and Nanticokes left the Delaware group and moved southward; the rest of the group started to migrate, evidently eastward, and had a bitter war with the Towakon or Father Snakes. In this struggle the Hurons, called the Talamatuns in the Walam Olum, aided the Delaware group. The Father Snakes may have been Iroquoian or Siouan.[6] The Delawares now went on eastward to their historic location in Delaware, New Jersey, and New York.[7]

In reviewing the Walam Olum narrative, one is struck by the probability—indeed, the certainty—that the Delaware group of tribes came into the Ohio Valley in Mound Builder times, fought the Mound Builders, tarried in the land for a long time, and then moved eastward, leaving the Shawnees behind. The narrative lacks detail concerning the Ohio country. It was a rich land of towns and forts; but the only people mentioned are the Tallegwi and Towakon, and the only other information is that the Ohio River was called

[6] Hodge's *Handbook of Indians North of Mexico* conjectures that the Towakons were Senecas. My own suggestion is that they may have been Mound Builders of Siouan stock. *Wakon* in the Winnebago dialect meant snake. In other dialects it meant spirit or perhaps god. There was a Siouan tribe in South Carolina called "Woccon," which seems to be another spelling of Wakon.

[7] I am using the version of the Walam Olum found in W. W. Beach's *Indian Miscellany*, 1877. I have not seen the new edition of the Walam Olum.

Telegahonah and that the lands along the Ohio from its head west to the Wabash were called Alligewi-neng, the Land of the Alligewi or Telligewi. In the Walam Olum the Delawares assert that their group settled on the Wabash, the western border of the Telligewi country. This casts doubt on their claim that they drove the Telligewi out and occupied their country. One might even extend this doubt and assert that the whole story of the migration is greatly exaggerated, that the Delaware group was never in the west, and that the great island of the Snakes was not the southern peninsula of Michigan, but the island of Montreal in the St. Lawrence, which is known to have been held by the Iroquois, termed Snakes by the Algonquians, at an early period. But such a view is not tenable. The Delawares and Shawnees were very closely related in dialect to the Miamis, Sacs, and Foxes; and these tribes are known to have occupied the southern peninsula of Michigan, perhaps at a date a little later than the Walam Olum times. The Miamis—they are the Wemiamik or Beaver Children of the Walam Olum—may even be surmised to have penetrated into Ohio at a time when the Mound Builders still continued their old pomp; for when the French came among them in the country near the southern end of Lake Michigan, the Miamis had a head chief who was treated like a king of divine birth. He was followed wherever he went by a drove of officials and servants who attended him with reverence and instantly provided anything he desired. This concept of a divine king was utterly strange in the north, and the Miamis must have picked up their ideas of divine royalty from Indians who had rulers of the Sun King type.[8]

Little as the Walam Olum tells us concerning the Indians of the Ohio Valley, it does suggest that they were Mound Builders, and it gives them a name, Tellegwi or Allegwi, from which comes the name Allegheny. For a century it has been surmised that the Tellegwi were the Cherokees, an Iroquoian tribe with a vague tradition that they formerly dwelled in the Ohio Valley, perhaps in eastern Kentucky. But no one has ever succeeded in connecting the Cherokees with the Mound Builders convincingly. When first definitely known to the Europeans, the Cherokees were south of the mountains in North Carolina. They may have retreated there from the Ohio Val-

---

[8] Miami king as quoted by Perrot in his memoirs, in Blair's *Indian Tribes of the Upper Mississippi*, I, 223.

ley, but we have no proof of that. It may be noted that Cherokee would be Tellegwi if we altered the pronunciation, turning *Ch* into *T*, *r* into *l*, and *k* into *gw*. The Walam Olum does not call the Cherokees Tellegwi but terms them Otaliwako, explaining that this name means Snakes, or Enemies. No one seems to have observed that this name is a variant of Tellegwi and apparently also of To-wakon, the name of the other tribe the Delawares fought in the Ohio Valley. Here are implications that, in the view of the early Algonquians, the Indians in the Ohio country were Snakes, and as for the tribe called Towakon, it is stated that in later times the Delawares called the Osages Wakon, meaning Snakes. In early historic times the Algonquians had extended the name Snake to include many tribes of both Iroquoian and Siouan stock. They called the Sioux Nadowe, Snake or Adders; the Iroquois they called Real Adders, and even the Iroquoian Hurons, who were the friends of the Algonquian tribes, were called Adders.

It would be interesting to learn in what manner the Delaware group in their early migrations picked up the name Wakon. In the dialect of the Winnebago group, Wakon meant Snake, while among the Dhegihan Siouan tribes it usually meant Spirit or God. The Osages had a subdivision named Wakon, which was translated as meaning Serpent; and the name of the Osage tribe is a French spelling of Wasase or Wazhazhe, which meant Serpent. The Osage tradition was that their tribe lived on the Ohio in a district which the Shawnees later inhabited, and the Walam Olum asserts that the Shawnees were evidently on the Wabash with the Delawares in Mound Builder times. This seems to suggest that the Osages were part of the Mound Builder population.

The Walam Olum states that after the Tellegwi were defeated, the Shawnees left the Delawares and moved southward. This has been accepted by some scholars as meaning that the Shawnees at this early time moved south to Savannah River on the eastern borders of the present Georgia; but that is obviously not correct, for the Shawnees are referred to in Iroquois tradition as dwelling near the south shore of Lake Erie at the time of the Iroquois war with the Adirondack group of Algonquians in 1535–60. The Adirondacks despised the Iroquois as peaceful farmers. They began a war with them, defeated them, and finally forced them to remove southward into the lake district of New York. The Iroquois began to train their men for war, and first they attacked the unwarlike Shawnees, defeating them and carrying off youths whom they forced to serve in the Iroquois ranks. They defeated the Adirondacks and drove them from the shores of the lower Great Lakes, where they dwelled. Then the Iroquois attacked the Shawnees and drove them southward.[9] Cadwallader Colden adds that the Iroquois later attacked the Shawnees again and drove them south,[10] apparently to the Ohio, where part of the Shawnees were still living in 1669. The Shawnee movement to Savannah River seems to date after 1650; and the Delawares, when they explained the meaning of the Walam Olum in later times, used their knowledge of the Savannah River move and wrongly assumed that the Shawnees went south after the first Tellegwi war. Actually, the driving of the Shawnees south after this war seems to mean that they had lived near the southern shore of Lake Erie and were driven down into Ohio, probably before 1570. A later migration took them to Savannah River.

One is wise to be on guard against Indian traditions of great conquests. The Walam Olum claim that the Delaware group drove out the Tellegwi in the first war is probably greatly exaggerated. The second war, with the Father Snakes, looks like a Delaware retreat. Their group split up, the Shawnees and Nanticokes going their own way, the Delawares heading east, across the Allegheny Mountains. As to the destruction of the Mound Builder centers in Ohio State, archaeology indicates that the attack came from the northeast and was apparently an Iroquoian movement. Archaeology also indicates that at least part of the old native population remained, mingling with the invaders. This period of invasion is termed the Intrusive Mound period by archaeologists. The invaders buried their dead intrusively in the old Mound Builder earthworks. During this period the great Mound Builder centers seem to have fallen into the hands

[9] Perrot, in Blair, *Indian Tribes of the Upper Mississippi*, I, 227; Cadwallader Colden, *History of the Five Indian Nations of Canada*, I, 5–7.

[10] Colden, *History of the Five Indian Nations of Canada*, I, 2–3, 7. Perrot states that the Shawnees made war on the Iroquois (more probably the Neutrals) and forced them to remove toward the east and settle along the shores of Lake Ontario. The Michigamea group of the Illinois confederacy had a tradition that the Shawnees were created and given a home in the lands to the southeast of Lake Michigan. This may be a faint memory of a time when the Shawnees really occupied those lands.

of crude people who cared little for the Mound Builder pomp and ceremony. Under such conditions the rapid decay of Mound Builder culture was assured.

One final word concerning the Delaware invasion of the Ohio Valley: In 1955 archaeologists made an announcement which, stripped of its professional jargon, meant that they had found Delaware village ruins and burials of a later time in the country east of the Alleghenies and that the cultural remains exhibited clear connections with the culture in central Ohio on the late middle Woodland time level which is the period of the Hopewell Mound Builder culture. This appears to confirm the statements in the Walam Olum that the Delaware group of tribes was in Ohio at the time of the Mound Builders and that they remained there long enough to pick up some Mound Builder cultural traits, which they took with them to their new lands east of the mountains and close to the Atlantic shores.[11]

There were two racial groups responsible for the development of the Mound Builder culture in the Ohio Valley: the southern Indians, termed Adena by the archaeologists, and a northern element, probably Siouan by race, coming from the old Indian Knoll centers in Kentucky. Archaeologists seem unwilling to admit that any Siouans took part in the Hopewell or Mound Builder phase; they prefer the Algonquians, although there is no evidence that any large group of Algonquians were in the Ohio Valley until the Delaware group arrived. And this group did not come to construct the great Mound Builder centers, but to destroy them. Some archaeologists now seem inclined to accept the southern Adena folk as the Tellegwi of the Walam Olum and to make a conjecture that they were Cherokees.

In any attempt to identify the northern Indians who joined the Adena folk in creating the Ohio Mound Builder centers, the tribes of the Siouan stock seem to have a much stronger claim than the Algonquians. The claim for the Siouans has been damaged in the past because of the faulty, piecemeal presentation of their case. The newer archaeology has strengthened their case by showing that Indian Knoll culture was Siouan and that the people of this culture were in the Ohio Valley from archaic times into the Hopewell or Mound Builder period.

11 "Reviews," *American Antiquity*, Vol. XXI, No. 2, 192.

From historical and traditional evidence, we obtain additional proof that the Ohio Valley was occupied by Siouan tribes. At the opening of historic times, the great valley had been emptied; all the tribes had been driven out by Iroquois wolf packs armed with guns; but there was an almost complete circle of Siouan tribes surrounding the Ohio Valley, to the north, northwest, west, southwest, south, and southeast. The Iroquois closed in the circle to the northeast. Even without further evidence, this situation would suggest that the Iroquois had driven Siouan tribes out of the Ohio Valley toward the west. To support this view, we have the definite statement of the five Dhegiha Siouan tribes—the Osages, Quapaws, Kansas, Omahas, and Poncas—that they formerly dwelled on the Ohio River and migrated westward, evidently after the year 1650. There is some evidence that other Siouan tribes were driven out toward the southeast and found refuge in northern Virginia.[12]

The French explorers and missionaries provide considerable evidence to support the view that the Iroquoian tribes had driven large Siouan groups out of the Ohio Valley before the year 1673. Unfortunately, the French were somewhat careless in making their statements, and this has made it a simple matter for doubters to point out inconsistencies and to assume the attitude that the French accounts are worthless. The evidence is as solid as any reasonable man could expect to obtain from casual French reference and from Indian traditions that were not written down until after the year 1800.

In the first place, we find that the tribes of the Illinois confederacy, who spoke Algonquian, gave the general appellation of Akansa or Akansea to the Siouans they alleged had lived in the Ohio Valley. This name was later applied by the French to the Quapaws alone; but it is obviously a form of the name Kansa, and the Kansas were a tribal group of the Dhegiha Siouans, who had a tradition of former residence on the Ohio River. When these Siouans were driven from the valley, they evidently fled in confusion. Their groups were broken up; part of the Kansas fled down the Mississippi with the Quapaws, but the main body went up the Mississippi and up the Missouri. One group joined the Osages; another apparently moved

12 The Monetons and Monahoac are two Siouan tribes that may have migrated from the Ohio Valley to Virginia. The first of these tribes evidently left the Ohio as late as 1670.

northward through Iowa with the Omahas and Poncas. All this is proved by the fact that each of the tribes listed above had a subdivision named Kansa.

It was the Illinois Indians who told the French, between 1673 and 1686, that the Akansea group had formerly lived on the Ohio. The French set the Akansea down on maps, some of which were so crude that it is difficult to judge just where the Indians were really located.

The Dhegiha tradition may be told briefly. These Siouans claimed that their five tribes lived together as one people on the Ohio, and sometimes they asserted that the location was the lower Wabash, or a district later occupied by the Shawnees.[13] Savannah was another name for the Shawnees, and some French maps set down the old Savannah settlements between the Cumberland and Tennessee rivers, at their mouths, and on the Ohio River. This traditional information implies that at least part of the Siouan tribes dwelled on the north side of the Ohio, perhaps on the lower Wabash; and that when they were attacked from the northeast, they fled across the Ohio and settled on the southern bank. A century ago, Lewis H. Morgan wrote that the Osages—perhaps the leading tribe of the Akansea group—had a tradition that they dwelled on the south bank of the Ohio before the Shawnees came there.[14] The Omahas and Poncas told J. Owen Dorsey that their ancestors lived with the five Siouan tribes on the Ohio. The tribes migrated down the Ohio to the Mississippi. There the Quapaws left and went south, while the other tribes crossed the Mississippi and moved up to the Missouri River. The Kansas told Morgan that their tribe lived on the Ohio and moved with the Osage and Omaha groups across the Mississippi and to the Missouri, where they built a village. They even gave him the village name and its meaning. The Osages also remembered this village; but these Indians seem to have located the village too far down the Missouri River. After two centuries, they remembered the village, its name, and some landmarks; but they had the location wrong.

These traditions, because they lack detail and are often inconsistent have been termed vague and unreliable by some anthropologists.

13 Two good sources for the Dhegiha migration traditions are J. Owen Dorsey's "Migrations of the Siouan Indians" in *American Antiquity*, XX, and Dorsey, *Siouan Sociology, Fifteenth Annual Report*, B.A.E., 191.

14 Morgan, "Indian Migrations," in Beach's *Indian Miscellany*.

Supported by French evidence of the period 1673–1700, however, they are reliable in a general way, and they supply some most important information.

For the period when these five Siouan tribes dwelled in the Ohio Valley, the French use the name Akansea and do not normally refer to the other tribal names. Father Gravier visited the Akanseas or Quapaws in 1700 and stated definitely that they had formerly lived on the Ohio, but had been driven westward before 1673. A Dutch map of 1720[15] shows the Akansea in their former location on the Ohio. This map also seems to show the group again, as Axansa, west of the Mississippi, in the present state of Missouri.

The early French writers confused the situation by making occasional loose or inaccurate statements. Thus Father Cosmé, in 1690, wrote that the Osages and Akansea lived on a branch of the Missouri at a time probably anterior to 1670, and that the Osages left the Akansea here and moved westward. There can be little doubt that this French writer said the Missouri when he meant the Mississippi, and that the branch stream was the Ohio. In 1682, Father Douay confused this same information by stating that the Osages and Akansea dwelled on a tributary of the Missouri, that the Iroquois made cruel war on them, and that the Akanseas fled down the Mississippi with part of the seventeen Osage villages accompanying them. Here again the Missouri is pretty obviously the Mississippi, and the tributary stream is the Ohio.

In the tables of Indian population for the year 1829, in Schoolcraft's *Indian Tribes*[16] it is set down that the Osages assert that the Akanseas or Quapaws were formerly a part of the Osage tribe, but left them while they were dwelling on the Ohio River.

Exactly where on the Ohio these Siouan tribes lived is still in doubt, and archaeology has failed to supply any definite information. The reference to the Wabash in the traditions is not very helpful; for it is pretty obvious that these Indians regarded the Wabash as the main river, and they called the river below the mouth of the Wabash by the same name. The Ohio was a minor stream, ending in its juncture with the Wabash. The Osage statement that they lived on the river in a district later occupied by the Shawnees might mean some-

15 Justin Winsor, *The Mississippi Basin.*
16 III, 594.

where near the mouths of the Cumberland and Tennessee rivers, or it might refer to the older Shawnee occupation along the Ohio from near Cincinnati down to near the Louisville Falls. In this connection we may note that the Popple map, dated 1733 and found in Justin Winsor's *The Mississippi Basin,* names the Cumberland or Tennessee (it shows them as a single river) the Hogahegee, Callamaco, or Acenseapi. These are clearly the names of tribes that formerly lived on this stream, and the last named is the Akansea with the Algonquian ending *sipi,* meaning river. This confirms the Siouan tradition that they lived on the south bank of the Ohio near the Cumberland-Tennessee.

Of the five Dhegiha Siouan tribes in the Ohio Valley, the Omahas were given prominence by nineteenth-century anthropologists, who used Omaha tradition largely and accepted the Omaha statements that their tribe was the leading group. Old information on such matters is the best. In 1758, Louis de Kerlérec, a French official in Louisiana, stated, on the information of traders who had spent years among the Indians, that the Grand Osages were the oldest or leading group and that the Little Osages, Kansas, and Quapaws were merely offshoots from the Grand Osages. He did not even mention the Omahas, who presumably were only another offshoot from the same Osage group.[17]

Some anthropologists used to state that Osage meant Wazhazhe; and when they were asked what Wazhazhe meant, they said it meant Osage. We might clear that up. Osage is the French form of Wazhazhe, the real name of the Osage tribe which means Serpent or Snake. About the time Kerlérec set down his report on the Osages, Jean-Bernard Bossu, a French naval officer in Illinois, met a party of Osages who were reverently carrying in procession the dried carcass of a monster snake which they called their *manitou,* their god.[18]

We must here refer to the Honga, the apparent ancestral name of the Ohio Valley Siouans. The name meant Fish, and probably resulted from the practice among primitive folk of deifying their principal source of food and regarding themselves as the children of that food source. The Winnebago Siouan group of Wisconsin had a similar native name, Hochangara, meaning Great Fish. The Popple map

---

17 A. P. Nasatir, *Before Lewis and Clark,* I, 51.

18 *Ibid.,* I, 50, n.134.

referred to above shows the Cumberland or Tennessee branch of the Ohio as the Hogahegee, Callamaco, or Acanseapi and, as we have noted, the last of these names is Algonquian and means Akansea River. To this we may add that the first name, Hogahegee, might refer to the Honga, the old group in which the Omahas were the leaders. This is pure surmise; but these old names for the Tennessee and Cumberland clearly refer to tribes formerly dwelling on or near the rivers, and we are justified in seeking to identify these tribes. The name Akanseapi clearly shows that the Quapaws lived on or near these streams, and this makes it probable that other Siouan groups were in the same district.

This account of the Siouans in the Ohio Valley would not be complete without some reference to the Mosopeleas. La Salle probably learned about this tribe in the winter of 1666, when a Seneca family visited him at his place on Montreal Island and gave him much information concerning the Ohio country. He later obtained additional information, and he included the Mosopeleas in a list of tribes on the Ohio that had been destroyed by the Iroquois in 1681 or 1682.[19] He also gave information to mapmakers, and they placed the Mosopeleas on their maps, as Franquelin did on his 1684 map. This map has a group of villages north of the Ohio River marked "Masapelia, 8 villages destroyed," and the Ohio is termed "Ohio or Masapeleacipi or Alighin," the last name being Allegheny, a name applied to an upper branch of the Ohio.[20]

Some scholars were very much pleased when they came across these traces of a big Indian group named Mosopelea in the Ohio Valley. They wrote extensively about this tribe; they suggested that the In-

[19] La Salle's list of tribes destroyed in the Ohio Valley, in Pierre Margry's *Découvertes et établissements des Français*, I, 27–28. Among the destroyed tribes, La Salle lists the Ouabache. This seems to cast doubt on the accepted belief that Wabash is an Algonquian word meaning White Water. It looks very much like a Siouan word, perhaps Wabasha. That was the name of a famous line of chiefs among the Sioux, and it meant Red Leaf. The river may have taken its name from Kaintuckie, the tribe to which La Salle refers. He also lists the Kentaientonga as a destroyed tribe. *Tonga* may be the Siouan tonga meaning great or big, and this tribal name seems to be the same one that David Cusic refers to in his Iroquois history as the Kaintuckie Nation, which he states first lived on the east (north) side of the Ohio, but the tribe was attacked by the Iroquois and driven to the west (south) side of the river and, as La Salle records, was destroyed.

[20] Franquelin's map, 1684, in Griffin's *Fort Ancient,* 20.

dian village ruins of Madisonville (at Cincinnati), which are seventeenth century in their final date, were the remains of the eight Mosopelea villages of La Salle. Then John R. Swanton connected the Mosopelea with the Ofo tribe and declared that they were Siouans. Some archaeologists, who were maintaining that there was no archaeological evidence of Siouans in the Ohio Valley, now turned their guns on the Mosopelea tribe and finally concluded that no such tribe ever existed.[21] But Marquette and Joliet reportedly met the Mospeleas in 1673 on the east bank of the Mississippi below the Ohio, and they set the tribe down on their maps near the other Siouan fugitives, the Akansea group. In 1682, La Salle encountered a few Mosopeleas among the tribes of the lower Mississippi, and he was given a Mosopelean boy by the Akansea chief. This evidence refutes the contention of the archaeologists that the Mosopeleas were a myth.

In the closing years of the seventeenth century an English mariner, Daniel Coxe, sailed into the lower Mississippi, where he obtained information concerning Indian tribes from the French. He made a map on which he placed the Ouesperie tribe on the north bank of the Ohio. John R. Swanton pointed this out, and stated that the Ouesperie and the Mosopelea were the same. Swanton should have added that the French had difficulty with the sound of the letter *w* and often substituted *m*, as in "Misconsin" for Wisconsin. At times they used *ou* for *w*, and they often used *b* and *p* interchangeably. This is most important, for it suggests that the Mosopeleas were not only Siouan but probably that group of Siouans who had the name Wasabe, meaning Black Bear. These Wasabes were still important groups among the five Dhegiha tribes in the nineteenth century, and they were particularly important among the Osages.

The French were obviously exaggerating, or misinformed, when they asserted that the Iroquois had destroyed the Mosopeleas. Like the other Dhegiha groups, the Mosopeleas probably split up when they were driven out of the Ohio Valley. We know from the French that part of the Osages split off and went south with the Quapaws, and with them went a group of Poncas. There were in the nineteenth century Ponca groups among the Osages, Kansas, and Quapaws; and the old Wasabe or Black Bear group was as badly split up as the Poncas, but their main body was with the Osages.

21 Griffin, *Fort Ancient,* 27–28.

This information establishes several large Siouan groups along the Ohio in the seventeenth century, but were they there in Mound Builder times? It seems pretty obvious that they were; for archaeology shows that the Indian Knoll folk of Kentucky moved into Ohio and Indiana in archaic times, and archaeology failed to find evidence of a violent dislocation of the native population when the Adena folk came into Kentucky and Ohio and started the building of mounds and great earth-walled enclosures. Archaeology shows that there was a village of the Indian Knoll folk (Siouans) at the site of the Great Serpent Mound in Adams County, Ohio. This was evidently a Siouan district before the Serpent Mound was built, and with our knowledge that the Siouans of Wisconsin were the principal builders of animal and serpent mounds we are justified in conjecturing that the effigy mound impulse in Wisconsin may have been started by the Siouans of Ohio in Mound Builder times. Archaeologists, however, prefer to ignore the Siouans and to suggest that the Algonquians were the northern Indians who joined with the Adenas to create the Hopewell mound centers. But there is no archaeological evidence to suggest an early Algonquian occupation of the Ohio Valley; and the arrival of the Delaware group, long after the mound culture had been developed, seems to be the first solid evidence of Algonquian groups on the Ohio River.

It has been remarked many times by scholars that the Mound Builders must have had a large and fairly settled population, well organized and controlled, to enable them to construct the great earthworks in the Ohio Valley. This is obviously true, and it is one reason for believing that the Algonquians were not Mound Builders. They were a fiercely independent people who would not brook attempts to discipline or control them. It is true that Father Marquette, in 1673, described the Shawnees of the Ohio Valley as a docile people who permitted the Iroquois to lead them away into captivity like sheep; but these Algonquian Shawnees were people armed only with flint weapons, and completely helpless in the face of Iroquoian attacks made with firearms. These same Shawnees, in later years and when properly armed, were famous fighting men.

The Siouans of the Dhegiha group had indications in their social organization, even late in the nineteenth century, that they had formerly been very much under the control of hereditary leadership. They were organized in tribes, half-tribes, and gentes or clans; and each tribe was divided into a war side and a peace side, like the more advanced southern tribes, which had red villages that led the tribe and controlled it, and white villages that grew crops, worked and, theoretically at least, were supposed to leave war-making to the red villages.

As far as organization and discipline were concerned, the Dhegiha Siouans would have fitted neatly into the Mound Builder way of life, which was pretty obviously controlled by ceremonial ritual. Even after 1800 these Dhegiha tribes had the remains of highly developed ceremonial life. They had more of it than was good for them, for it must have killed individual initiative. The smallest acts of daily life were ruled by ancient ritual. One group kept the sacred corn and the corn rites and told the people when they might plant their seed. Each family had to obtain a few kernels of the sacred corn first and perform endless ceremonies before the actual planting. Even going to war was ceremonial, and the required rituals seem to have been far more important than striking the enemy a swift blow.

These Dhegihas had a form of religion that, from what we know, would have fitted conditions in the Mound Builder way of life. Their religion featured both sky spirits and earth-bound animal gods or patron protectors. Tribes like the Omahas honestly believed that the Sun was their father and the Moon their mother; that their people were originally in the sky; that the Moon told them they must descend and live on earth; that a female redbird gave them human bodies, and that they flew down from heaven and alighted on a huge red oak tree, apparently in the Ohio Valley. There the animal gods took control, provided them with maize seed and game to kill, and supplied their other needs.[22]

Even in the 1880's after their tribes had been decimated by epi-

[22] Dorsey, *Siouan Sociology, Fifteenth Annual Report,* B.A.E.; Alice Fletcher and Francis La Flesche, *The Omaha, Twenty-Seventh Annual Report,* B.A.E. One suspects that different Dhegiha gentes or clans had different origin myths, some claiming an origin in the sky and others on earth or in the water. Part of the Omahas and Osages (possibly their Honga division) believed that a shell was their ancestor and god. The most sacred object the Omaha tribe possessed was its ancient clam shell (*unio alatus*), and as the Omahas were Honga folk, this shell may hark back to the time in archaic days when their ancestors lived on the clam-shell mounds along Green River in Kentucky. This ancient clam shell had inside it a little parcel wrapped in native fabric, the warp of which was twisted vegetable fiber and the woof made of rushes.

demic diseases and enemy attacks, these Dhegiha Siouans had among them groups of Thunder people, usually a war-leader group, Sky people, Earth people, and Water and Wind people. They had Sun people called Carry-the-Sun-on-Their-Backs and Turtle people called Carry-the-Turtle-on-Their-Backs; they had Star people and Rain people, and they had a group among the Osages who kept ancient fire rituals which seem to hark back to times when sacred fire was kept in a temple.[23] The Elk people were often termed homosexuals and, like other primitive folk, the Dhegihas seem to have regarded them as a mysterious and sacred group. They were leaders in some religious rites and probably were like the homosexuals the French colonists noted among the Florida tribes in the sixteenth century: males who dressed like women and did women's work, but went to war to serve as rescuers and nurses for the wounded. Among the Dhegihas the Elk people were connected with the Moon and were perhaps her servants. The women of one Omaha group had many Moon names, mostly New Moon names, and the girls of the group held Moon rituals at the time of the rising of the new moon.

All of this has the sound of a people who had achieved a rather high cultural status; but it is obvious from the seventeenth-century French accounts that the Dhegiha tribes were savages. The men wore strings of beads dangling from pierced ears and noses. They were hunters and warriors, and disdained doing any work around the villages. To the casual French observers all their religious beliefs had to do with animal gods, and the only thing that set them apart from the wild Algonquian hunters of the north was their good order and good nature. The Quapaws were well disciplined and obeyed their chiefs; but they were also lively, talkative, and often laughing— quite different from the grim and usually silent northern Indians. This is not a denial that the Dhegihas were Mound Builders, for there is enough archaeological evidence to suggest that, with the exception of their ceremonial and religious life, the Ohio Mound Builders may have been little better than savages. There are many examples in history of peoples who developed rather high cultures and were then cast down into a condition of savagery or barbarism when attacked by cruder and hardier folk. This was presumably what happened to the Mound Builders, and it is not strange to find that surviving groups

[23] Dorsey, *Siouan Sociology, Fifteenth Annual Report,* B.A.E. His fourteenth Osage group, Fire people and South Wind people.

should have lost most indications of their higher culture very quickly. Mound building was a main trait of that culture, and we know that the Omahas and Osages continued to build mounds into the eighteenth century. The Omaha mass burial of their slain people in mounds on the Big Sioux and in northeastern Nebraska are examples of the persistence of basic Mound Builder traits into the eighteenth century.

CHAPTER FIVE

South Wind II

T H E F A I L U R E of the Mound Builders to maintain their high state
of cultural development in the Ohio Valley and in the Illinois country cannot be explained from archaeological evidence alone. There
were human forces at work that cannot be perceived by a study of
characteristic pottery designs and types of implements and ornaments
made of stone, bone, shell, and copper. There was a religious element
at the very roots of the Mound Builder rise to power that archaeology
cannot visualize, and the indications of the presence of Sun Kings
and sun worship among the Hopewell Indians are generally ignored
by archaeologists.

Turning to the south, we find that when the Adena Indians came
into the Ohio Valley and laid the foundations of the Mound Builder
state, an almost identical mound-building culture was developed on
Red River in Louisiana, in the Marksville district. Curiously, the
makers of the Marksville mounds are said to have been Sylvids, northern, longheaded people; and there are many hints that the Indian
population in the southern states was becoming mixed at this time—
as it was in the Ohio Valley—and consisted partly of longheaded
northern Indians and partly of southern roundheads. There is even
a suggestion that some Siouans and Algonquians had drifted into

the far south; but most of the Indians on and near the lower Mississippi seem to have belonged to the Tunican, Natchezan, and similar stocks, and these were sun worshipers, ruled by Sun Kings. Their culture extended eastward into the Florida Gulf Coast area and into southern Georgia.[1]

It was the coming of the Muskhogean people, a fighting race from the lands west of the Mississippi, that seems to have heralded the coming of a new day in the south. A new cultural pattern, the Temple Mound or Mississippi pattern, came in, with features that appear to have been brought from Mexico or Middle America. Some of the Muskhogeans fought their way eastward into central Georgia, driving out or subordinating the older population to their rule. Another Muskhogean advance is supposed to have started from the Mississippi near the mouth of the Ohio, later to join up with a northward Muskhogean push from Tennessee into the Ohio Valley; while yet another advance of the people bearing the new culture crossed the Mississippi in the district where the city of St. Louis now stands and formed a great center at Cahokia in Illinois. The earlier type of Mississippi culture had intruded into Ohio during the period in which the Ohio Hopewell or Mound Builder culture was strong. There were temple and pyramid mounds in the Marietta district and also on the Scioto,

---

1 F. R. Eggan, in Griffin, *Archeology of the Eastern United States,* 44. To put it simply, this earlier mound period in the south developed among the Natchez, Taensas, and other tribes along the lower Mississippi an agriculture and a religion of Sun worship which featured the keeping of sacred fire in a temple and the sacrificing of captives to the Sun by placing their severed heads on wooden pikes on the wall that surrounded the Sun Temple. The ruler was believed to be the younger brother of the Sun. There was a royal clan of Suns, male and female, a class of nobles and court officials. When the Sun King died, his courtiers and servants submitted to being strangled by public executioners so that they might accompany their master to the spirit world. The Sun King and his officials had absolute control over the people, pretending that any order they issued had been given by the Sun in the heavens to his younger brother, the ruling Sun.

Taking into account the known intercourse of the Indians of the Ohio Valley with these southern mound builders and noting the finds in Ohio mounds that hint at kings—the burial of servants in the same grave with their master and similar clues—it seems very probable that the secret of the faith and political organization of the Ohio Mound Builders was simply that the Adena folk, coming up from the south, introduced a Natchez-like religion complete with Sun King, temples, sacred fire, and the despotism of a ruling class.

but little seems to be known concerning this introduction of the Temple Mound culture into eastern Ohio.[2]

The archaeological evidence suggests that the intrusion of these southern Indians into the Ohio Valley and the lands along the east side of the Mississippi in Illinois was a peaceful penetration. There was no apparent dislocation of the older native occupants of the country although these southern intruders were certainly Muskhogeans, and they were a pugnacious people—a conquering race. They followed one practice that exhibits tolerance and even kindliness toward alien folk: they often gave peace to a conquered tribe, took them into an alliance, and finally adopted them.

In Illinois and southern Indiana these invaders seem to have come among Indians who were Siouans. There is no escaping the fact that the Dhegiha Siouans, a very numerous group, were on the Ohio—almost certainly in Indiana and perhaps in other districts farther up the river. As for Illinois, archaeology tells us that the early inhabitants were of the Kentucky Indian Knoll type, which means that they were Siouans. The archaeologists state that there is no indication of a change in the Indian population of Illinois from Archaic and early Woodland times almost to the end of the prehistoric period, which indicates that the original Siouan occupants of the state were still there when the Mississippian Indians brought in their Temple Mound culture.

When we review the situation in Illinois and in Wisconsin and eastern Minnesota, we find that the Illinois Indians adopted with enthusiasm the faith and culture of the Ohio Hopewell or Mound Builder folk. This new culture was first strongly developed on the Illinois River, mainly in Fulton County, and from here it spread toward the north and south, and across the Mississippi into eastern Iowa. In southern Wisconsin, particularly in the Lake Winnebago district, the Mound Builder culture took on a particularly Siouan character, turning to the building of effigy mounds, linear mounds, and conical burial mounds, usually arranged in lines. When Hopewell mound culture faded in the Ohio Valley and in Illinois, a Hopewell offshoot, the Effigy Mound culture of Wisconsin, continued to

[2] Griffin, Fort Ancient, 257, 259; Eggan, in Griffin, Archeology of the Eastern United States, 44–45; Shetrone, The Mound Builders, 409–10.

grow. It spread westward to the mouth of Wisconsin River and then across the Mississippi into northeastern Iowa and southeastern Minnesota. In Illinois it extended in a diluted form as far south as the thirty-ninth parallel, almost down to the mouth of Illinois River; and it made its appearance, also in diluted form, in southern Indiana.[3] This Effigy Mound culture was undoubtedly Siouan in origin. It had its beginnings in a Siouan area in Wisconsin, in the district later oc-

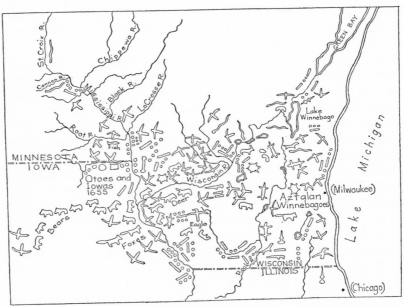

The Flowering of Siouan Culture in the North—The Effigy Mounds of Wisconsin, Iowa, and Minnesota

cupied by the Winnebago, the Iowa, and the Oto tribes. The Missouri tribe also belonged to this group; and we must suppose that the Mandans and the Hidatsa-Crow tribe, all closely connected lin-

---

3 Shetrone, *The Mound Builders,* 317–18; Thomas, "Catalogue of Prehistoric Works East of the Rocky Mountains," *Bulletin* 12, B.A.E., archaeological maps of Illinois and Indiana. I have termed the extension of Effigy Mound culture down into Illinois and southern Indiana diluted because there are few or no effigy mounds found there, but the culture is characterized by linear mounds and lines of small conical burial mounds.

guistically with the Winnebagoes, were in Wisconsin or northern Illinois and took part in the making of Effigy Mound culture.

As they took this peculiar culture farther toward the west and south, the Indians ceased to build effigy mounds; but they continued to construct the small circular burial mounds in lines on high ground and the strange elongated linear mounds which were shaped like the letter I or L. In the west, along Red River of the North in Dakota and Manitoba, these Siouan Indians—evidently the Mandans, Hidatsas, and Crows—developed the practice of using large stones to make effigies. Instead of building mounds, they outlined the forms of turtles, serpents, birds, and other animals by setting small boulders in the ground. They took the peculiar linear mounds as far as the Souris River in North Dakota and Manitoba. The linear mounds and the strings of small circular burial mounds also extended down the Mississippi into northern Missouri.

This astonishing spread of the Effigy Mound culture from Lake Michigan to beyond the Missouri, from Manitoba down the Mississippi into Missouri State, and to the Ohio in Indiana, was undoubtedly the work of Siouan Indians, mainly or wholly of the Winnebago stock. The spread indicates a close-knit and vigorous Indian stock. extending its influence far toward the west and south. The purpose of the effigy mounds is a mystery. Some of these mounds had a burial place in them, usually at the point where the heart of the animal represented by the mound would be; but they were not intended primarily for burial purposes. The effigies and the strange linear mounds had some place in the religious practices and ceremonial life of the Siouan Indians. In the Ohio Valley the Mound Builders had constructed two large serpent mounds, one or two bear mounds, a bird mound, and some lizard or alligator mounds. This makes it a possibility that the Siouans of Wisconsin adopted the effigy mound custom from the Ohio Indians. An attempt to show that the effigy mounds of the Wisconsin area were built to represent the animals for whom the Siouan clans or gentes were named proves unsuccessful. There was no group among these Indians that bore the name of Lizard, Turtle, Swallow, or Goose, and apparently none called Serpent; yet there are effigy mounds representing all of these creatures.

The great clusters of effigy mounds and linear and circular burial mounds in such areas as Lake Winnebago and the district at the mouth of Wisconsin River suggest population centers; but the Effigy Mound period seems to have been before crop-growing was introduced into Wisconsin, and there was no possibility of village life without crops. These Siouans were roving hunters and fishermen, but they had the custom of gathering at the end of winter. Each tribal group had its favored spot for this annual rendezvous. When the people came out of the forest where they had hunted in small groups during the winter, they met together at a chosen place for a period of social and ceremonial activity. It must have been at such gatherings that the religious ceremonies were held, and the Feast of the Dead was probably the most important event. Persons who died during the winter were wrapped in bark or furs and placed on high scaffolds or in trees. The families later gathered the bones, cleaned them, and placed them in a neat bark container. At times they covered the parcel of bones with furs ornamented with strings of shell beads. At the rendezvous all the families brought out the bundled bones of their dead, and the Feast of the Dead was held. The bundles of bones were placed together, sometimes accompanied by gifts to the dead, and a mound was raised over the common grave. In some small burial mounds there were as many as forty-five burials of bundled bones. Some burials of bodies occur—probably persons who died while the people were gathered for the annual ceremonies. Cremation was also practiced to some extent.[4]

Thus, before the coming of the southern Temple Mound Indians into the Ohio Valley and into Illinois, the Siouans of Wisconsin and northern Illinois kept up the Ohio Mound Builder culture in their own peculiar Effigy Mound practices; and they not only maintained it, they spread it far to the west and south. There is no clear archaeological evidence that the Algonquians or any other alien stock intruded into the Siouan area—Wisconsin and Illinois—until the coming of the Mississippian Indians from the south. In the Ohio Valley there seems to have been some intrusion by Iroquoian tribes, who pushed in among the surviving Mound Builders, taking advantage of their loss of vigor and unity. Some Algonquian intrusion into the

---

[4] For the Effigy Mound period, see J. W. Bennett, in Griffin, *Archeology of the Eastern United States,* 111–16; Thomas, *Report on Mound Exploration, Twelfth Annual Report,* B.A.E. The Feast of the Dead among the Sioux and Crees is described by Pierre E. Radisson in his narrative, *Voyages of Peter Esprit Radisson.* The Feast of the Dead among the Algonquians and Iroquoians is described in detail in several volumes of *Jesuit Relations,* edited by Thwaites.

Ohio lands from the north also seems to have taken place. In Wisconsin the Siouans were probably strong and kept the Algonquians out until early in the seventeenth century.

There are two theories concerning the advance of the Mississippian Indians into the Ohio and Illinois districts. Some scholars believe that these Muskhogean tribes came from west of the Mississippi and formed great centers of Temple Mound culture in Georgia and adjacent states from which they spread out in every direction. The second theory is that they crossed the Mississippi in groups at points widely separated, extending from the St. Louis district in Missouri down into Louisiana. The archaeological evidence is inconclusive. Some of these Mississippian folk appeared in East Tennessee and established a strong center on the upper Tennessee River. These folk seem to have been Muskhogeans of the group termed Creeks, and they apparently confined their activities in the north to making raids into eastern Ohio.

The main Mississippian intrusion in the north was into Illinois and along the Ohio eastward to beyond the Wabash in Indiana. They established two main centers: one called Cahokia on the vast, rich alluvial plain which stretches along the east side of the Mississippi directly opposite the present city of St. Louis and is called the American Bottom, and a second in Pope and Massac counties on the north bank of the Ohio in southern Illinois. This second center is called Kincaid by the archaeologists, and here tree-ring dates were obtained which seem to show that the Mississippian Indians formed their settlement in this district about 1450 and were solidly established by 1520. The thriving middle period lasted from about 1520 to 1580, which means that the Mississippian occupation of Illinois and the lower Ohio Valley dates to the time when the Europeans made their appearance all along the eastern North American coast from Mexico to the St. Lawrence.

The Kincaid Mississippian settlement included sixteen mounds which had temples and chiefs' or kings' houses built on their tops. There were several villages. The earlier villages were not large. The huts were of the southern open-cornered, rectangular, wattle-and-daub type. The people lived by farming and by hunting and fishing, and they had trade relations with Indians in the Memphis district in West Tennessee and those in southeastern Missouri. In the middle period Kincaid increased in size and impressiveness. The mounds were larger, and the villages were also large and were carefully arranged with the huts built in orderly rows around the central plaza. Some of the huts had closed corners and were better suited to the northern climate than the older open-cornered ones. In this period Kincaid sent out colonies. One was established in Kentucky at the mouth of the Ohio. A second, called Angel by the archaeologists, was located on the north side of the Ohio, east of the mouth of the Wabash and west of the present town of Evansville, Indiana. A third colony seems to have been established up the Wabash. It was a strongly fortified town. In this period Kincaid extended its trade relations, obtaining articles from as far south as Alabama and trading with Indians of the Upper Mississippi region for native articles. The closest relations were with the Tennessee-Cumberland Indians of Tennessee and the tribes in southeastern Missouri.[5]

Cahokia was a much greater center than Kincaid, perhaps the mightiest of all the centers of Temple Mound culture. It was contemporary with Kincaid and had trade relations with that center. There were about eighty big mounds in the Cahokia group. The great temple mound is the largest ever built within the limits of the United States, its earth content being larger than that of the great pyramid of Cheops in the Nile Valley. The extensive villages of Cahokia have been almost completely obliterated by the plow and the grading machine, and even the type of huts is left in doubt. But Cahokia sent colonists northward to the Illinois River valley and farther north into Jefferson County in southeastern Wisconsin; and from the remains in these areas, it is obvious that the Cahokia villages were very similar to those of Kincaid. The huts were mainly rectangular wattle and daub, and in Wisconsin they seem to have had bark roofs instead of the thatch preferred in southern regions. Both on the Illinois River and in Wisconsin, the main Cahokia villages were fortified with earth walls and stockades of tall log pickets. This refutes the archaeological claim that the Mississippi culture tribes made a peaceful penetration into the north. In Illinois and Wisconsin and in the Kincaid area on the Ohio, the main villages were fortified. Moreover, in Wisconsin there were Woodland Indian graves—probably Siouan—containing bones that had imbedded in them the

---

5 This brief description of Kincaid is mainly taken from M. S. Maxwell's account, in Griffin, *Archeology of the Eastern United States*, 188–89.

typical Mississippian small, triangular, notched arrowheads.[6] This is firm proof that the Mississippians were fighting at least some of the native tribes. Archaeological evidence indicates that the Cahokian colonists lived in friendship and mingled peacefully with part of the native stock in Wisconsin and on the Illinois River. In Wisconsin it seems certain that the Winnebagoes and perhaps the Iowas and Otoes were friends and allies of the Cahokians and probably aided them in raiding other native tribes. At the big Cahokian town in Wisconsin —called Aztalan by archaeologists—there were clear indications of cannibalism on an extended scale. This meant raids on native tribes to obtain victims for cannibal feasts.[7]

The Mississippian Indians of Cahokia had a colony on the Missouri near the present Kansas City. Archaeologists term it the Steed-Kisker aspect of Cahokian culture; and here we may have a faint ray of historical light penetrating the twilight of archaeology, for Auguste Chouteau stated in his historical notes written in 1816 that the Illinois tribe—heirs to the old Cahokian territory—claimed lands west of the Mississippi in the present state of Missouri. Their claim was bounded by a line from the mouth of the Des Moines River to the divide that separates the waters of the Mississippi from those of the Missouri, along this separating ridge from near the head of Buffalo Creek southeast to a point north of the mouth of the Gasconade River, then south to the mouth of the Gasconade, along the dividing ridge between the Gasconade and Missouri rivers and southeast to "the negro fork of the Maramec (or fish) River," and then eastward to the mouth of the Ohio. Here we have the definite land claims that the Illinois tribes inherited from the Cahokians; and, what is more, Chouteau states that the lands in southern Iowa and Missouri formerly belonged to the Moinguena tribe of the Illini, then to the Michigameas. Finally, after the Indians were too weak to occupy

[6] Bennett, in Griffin, *Archeology of the Eastern United States*, 120.

[7] *Ibid.*, 120. Archaeologists found clear evidence of cannibalism during Mississippi times in southern Illinois and also across the Mississippi in Missouri. The Cahokians of Aztalan, in Jefferson County, Wisconsin, were clearly cannibals. As the Winnebagoes were evidently living in friendly contact with Aztalan and after 1600 were accused by the neighboring tribes and the French of being notorious cannibals, we may assume that they acquired the habit of eating human flesh from their Mississippian allies. They also acquired the other Mississippian vice, male homosexuality. The authorities for the latter statement will be found farther on in this volume, where the Winnebago-Illini war is chronicled.

these lands, the French of Illinois used the district as a hunting ground where they could go to obtain meat for their families.

Archaeologists term the Temple Mound culture of these Mississippian tribes a splendid manifestation, the highest culture ever brought into the lower Ohio and upper Mississippi areas. It was also the last of the prehistoric cultures. It was characterized by fine shell-tempered pottery made in many forms. These tribes probably were skilled workers in wood, and they had fine garments and ornaments. From the *Jesuit Relations* we obtain hints that the big towns held trading fairs to which people flocked from nearby villages, some even coming from distant tribes. In the south some of these Mississippian Indians had advanced to the point where they lived solely by growing crops; hunting had been given up by the common people, who seldom tasted meat; but the Mississippians of the Ohio and upper Mississippi valleys had not reached this stage of development. Sun Kings probably ruled. Archaeology produced evidence of one interesting difference between the Mississippian Indians of the Ohio and those of the upper Mississippi. The former had tobacco pipes in large numbers; but the Cahokians appear to have had no pipes at all. Another feature of this Mississippian culture was the lack of gifts to the dead in graves. The Hopewell Mound Builders had lavished gifts on the dead, but the Mississippians usually put only some food and drink with their dead.

It seems incredible, but neither history, Indian tradition, nor archaeology gives us any information about the identity of these Mississippian tribes in the north, although they lived at the close of the prehistoric period and even on into early historic times. The Indians of Cahokia had built about eighty big mounds; and Shetrone described one of their villages as extending along Cahokia Creek for a distance of seven miles, the village being about one mile in width for all that distance. These Indians still inhabited this district after the year 1650; yet we have no evidence as to the tribal identity of these people. The French were interested only in trade and in the conversion of the Indians to Christianity. As traders and priests, they dwelled among the Indians for a century, within sight of the mighty Cahokia mound, and never once referred to its builders or even recorded the names of the tribes that had formerly lived in the district. Still, we have a few clues outside the inconclusive evidence of archaeology. Thus, the Chickasaws claimed the Tennessee lands and are said to have had villages near the mouths of the Tennessee and Cumberland rivers prior to the year 1700. This suggests a Muskhogean occupation as far north at least as the Ohio; and as the Indians of Kincaid culture are said to have had connections with the Cumberland and Tennessee river tribes, particularly with the Indians in the Memphis district, this suggests that the Mississippi culture tribes in the north were Muskhogean and part of them Chickasaws.

After 1700, when there was a plan for a Chickasaw alliance with the French, the chiefs of that tribe suggested that their people should be aided by the French in colonizing the lands on or near the Wabash. Here is a faint hint that the tribe had formerly held lands on the Wabash and wished to return with French support. The Chickasaws were a vigorous fighting race. In 1541, De Soto apparently found them, or part of the tribe, in northern Mississippi State, a fact which casts a doubt on their being in the Ohio Valley before the year 1500, which is the period indicated by the tree-ring datings at Kincaid in southern Illinois. But archaeology suggests that the Chickasaws were in West Tennessee in Kincaid times, and the tribe in early historic times had a landing for its boats at the Chickasaw Bluffs at Memphis, and two other landings higher up the Mississippi. They were raiding the Quapaws near the mouth of Arkansas River in 1673–90; and in 1699, they were vigorously raiding the Algonquians of the Illini group in Illinois. It was the French alliance with the Illini that turned the Chickasaws against the French and caused them to ally themselves with the English.[8]

We now come to the story of Aztalan. This is the name the archae-

[8] John R. Swanton, "The Indian Tribes of North American," *Bulletin 145,* B.A.E., 177–80; Hodge, *Handbook of Indians North of Mexico,* I, 261; Benjamin Franklin French, *Historical Collections of Louisiana,* III, 124. The Algonquian Illini are supposed to have destroyed or driven out the Mississippian Indians, perhaps adopting some of them. John D. G. Shea stated that the Michigamea tribe was adopted by the Illini, and Marquette recorded that the Michigameas did not understand the Algonquian tongue. The Chapousa tribe, allies and neighbors of the Michigameas, were perhaps of the same stock, and not Algonquians. Groups, long extinct, that were part of the Illini confederacy but perhaps not Algonquians were the Michigamea, Chapousa, Chinko, Coiracoentanon, Albivi, and to these we might add the Cahokias themselves, the Tamaroa, and Moinguena, who lived on the Des Moines in Iowa. Some of these tribal names sound more Muskogean than Algonquian. The statement that the Chickasaws asked for French aid to enable them to colonize the Wabash lands is from Father Douay's memoir, in French's *Historical Collections of Louisiana.*

ologists have long applied to the ruins of a fortified Indian town in southeastern Wisconsin. The Mississippian Indians of Cahokia, having established themselves among the native tribes on Illinois River, went up into Jefferson County, Wisconsin, and there built a great frontier fortress. They seem to have also pushed up the Mississippi, perhaps into southwestern Wisconsin; but there they had no great town like Aztalan. This town was on a tributary of Rock River. It had a frontage on the stream of about five city blocks in length, and it extended back from the water a distance of about two city blocks. The town was an irregular rectangle in shape and was surrounded by an earth wall which was looped every eighty feet or so. Apparently a watch tower was set inside each loop. There was a tall stockade of log pickets atop the wall. The wall construction seems very similar to the Mississippian village wall at Angel and to that of another Mississippian fortified town near Nashville, Tennessee.

The earth wall at Aztalan had a length of approximately 1,750 feet and enclosed an area of about 17 acres. This indicates a very large town with a big population. The town was open and without fortification on the side facing the stream; inside the walls were two big pyramid or temple mounds and a plaza for holding religious and other ceremonies. The huts of the inhabitants were grouped facing this plaza. These huts were evidently the typical Mississippian wattle-and-daub dwellings. There is some indication that on the death of a householder, his body was placed in his hut, and the dwelling was then burned down. The gateway into the town was defended by wing walls on either side. Outside the gate there was a long row of small mounds in the tops of which tall poles had apparently been placed. This has been termed an avenue of banners. There appear to have been several small villages surrounding the main town.[9]

At Aztalan there was abundant evidence of two peoples living together, the Mississippi Indians and the native stock, who were undoubtedly the Siouans of the Winnebago group. The pottery found at Aztalan tells its own tale. It is partly fine-quality Mississippian pottery of Cahokia Old Village date, partly Siouan pottery of the Effigy Mound period, and partly a mingling in which the Siouan Indians adopted the features of the finer Cahokia pottery. From this

9 For Aztalan, see Shetrone, *The Mound Builders*, 302; Griffin, *Archeology of the Eastern United States*, 119–21; Martin, Quimby, and Collier, *Indians Before Columbus*, 313–15.

mingling at Aztalan—and apparently at other Cahokian centers on the Mississippi near the mouth of Wisconsin River—developed the next phase of Siouan culture in the upper Mississippi Valley, which is termed Oneota.[10]

At Aztalan and also in village ruins of the same culture and period near the mouth of Wisconsin River, there are clear indications of cannibalism. Archaeology has recorded this fact and let it go at that; but to the historian the cannibalism of the Aztalan and Cahokian Indians is another matter that connects these southern Indians with the Winnebago Siouans of Wisconsin, who, from about the year 1640 on, were described by the French as notorious cannibals. The district on the Mississippi in southwestern Wisconsin and across the river in northeastern Iowa and southeastern Minnesota is believed to have been held by the Iowas and Otoes, two tribes originally belonging to the Winnebago group; and since cannibalistic evidence was found in this area, it seems a fair inference that the Siouans of the Winnebago group were infected with the habit of eating human flesh by the Aztalan Indians, with whom they were living and whom they admired because of their higher culture.

Aztalan, a Cahokian outpost, was probably established as a trading center to obtain certain northern products, including Lake Superior copper. There are clear indications that the native population flocked to Aztalan and that part of the natives, presumably the Winnebagoes, established themselves in permanent villages near Aztalan. The southern Indians were agriculturists. There is little or no evidence of the growing of crops in Wisconsin at the earlier period; but now the practice must have started, and with it came the custom of living in permanent villages instead of moving about in hunting camps. And here, from historical evidence, we can indicate a date which is more

[10] Lake Michigan pottery, now termed Effigy Mound pottery, and therefore Siouan, was mingled with Cahokian pottery at Aztalan. Sites of later date in eastern Wisconsin and on the Mississippi in Wisconsin, Minnesota, and Iowa exhibit a culture developed from Effigy Mound and Aztalan into a new phase called Oneota. By archaeological dating, Aztalan was occupied in Cahokia Old Village times but seems to have lasted on into the later Cahokian period. By tree-ring dating, Aztalan might have been inhabited until 1580 or 1600, but one suspects that the town was still in use at a later date. Indications of cannibalism were clearly evident in the Orr Oneota area on the Mississippi, where the states of Wisconsin, Iowa, and Minnesota touch each other. This Oneota area is generally supposed to have been occupied by the Iowa tribe, but the Otoes may have been there also.

than an archaeological conjecture. Aztalan and the rise of the Winnebagoes to power dates to the beginning of the seventeenth century,
as will be demonstrated presently in this narrative.

Aztalan must have been a thriving center for a considerable time,
long enough to influence strongly the way of life of the Siouan natives. The southern Indians were obviously on friendly terms with
part of the natives, and equally obviously warring with other native
groups, who must have been Siouan since there is no evidence of
the presence of any Algonquian tribes in Wisconsin at this time. Native graves have been found with the peculiar Aztalan type of stone
arrowheads imbedded in the bones, proof that the southern Indians
were raiding part of the native population. As the Aztalan people
were bringing in captives for their cannibal feasts, we have here a
second proof of war. But presently something happened; Aztalan
was abandoned, and the southern Indians left Wisconsin. Archaeology cannot explain this, but we may find a reason for the flight
of the Aztalan population if we turn toward the northeast, where
the historic period had already opened.

In the north and northeast the Indians were all Algonquian and
Iroquoian. The Algonquians were the old native stock, wandering
groups of hunters and fishermen. The Iroquoians had intruded into
the area, coming from the southwest; and about the time of the rise
of the Mound Builders in the Ohio Valley, some of the Iroquoians
had started to grow maize and other crops and had established themselves in fixed villages. An archaeological conjecture as to time fixes
the coming of the Iroquoians about 1440.[11] The Iroquoian tribes
have been divided by anthropologists into two divisions. The Eastern Division was made up of the Mohawks, Onondagas, and Oneidas,
all Iroquois Proper; the Western Division included the Senecas and
Cayugas (Iroquois Proper), with the Hurons, Tionotatis or Tobacco
Hurons, Eries, Neutral Nation, and the Andastes of Pennsylvania.
By Iroquoian tradition the Neutrals were the parent group from
which all the Iroquoian tribes had separated.[12]

The Point Peninsula culture, found in lower Ontario and in central and northwestern New York, is said to be early Iroquoian. It in-

11 Fenton, *Smithsonian Misc. Colls.*, C, 164–84.

12 Ritchie, "A Perspective of Northeastern Archaeology," *American Antiquity*,
IV, 97.

cludes ceremonial burials in the manner of the Mound Builders of the Ohio Valley and is partly contemporary with the Ohio culture; but the Iroquoians never adopted the custom of mound-building. In time the Iroquoian population increased; their villages were larger and were placed in rugged country in defensible locations, many of the villages being protected by an earth wall or a stockade of tall posts set firmly in the ground. A moat was usually outside the stockade or wall.[13]

Here we are obviously on the edge of the historic period. This is the time the Iroquois Proper were driven from their lands along the St. Lawrence and went south to establish themselves in their historic locations in the lake country of central and northwestern New York. This is apparently the period referred to in the legends collected by Nicolas Perrot in 1650–89 and by Cadwallader Colden in the eighteenth century. It is probably also the period referred to by David Cusic in his Iroquoian legends, which depict the tribe as living in fortified villages and the Indians of the Ohio country as having great towns and forts and being the enemies of the Iroquois. The Perrot and Colden tales do not refer to the Ohio tribes, but concern the Iroquois and Algonquians. Perrot described the Iroquois of these early times as farmers living in villages. His Algonquians were wild rovers and hunters, who came to the Iroquois villages to barter meat and skins for maize and other village products. The Iroquoian tribes also grew great quantities of tobacco and had a large trade in this product with the Algonquians. In the *Jesuit Relations* we are informed of another article of barter; for it states that the Algonquians were much better at making charms than the Iroquoians and that the wild hunters invented charms to bring health and success in life and to protect the owner from evil. They sold these charms and incantations to the Iroquoians at very high prices. Perrot depicted the Algonquians as more intelligent than the Iroquoian villagers, more vigorous, and bolder and better warriors. He stated that, in these very early times, the Iroquoians did not even know how to hunt game, which is one of those exaggerations that creep into Indian tradition to make the narrative more interesting to primitive folk. Colden confirmed much of what Perrot had said. He stated that the Iroquois

---

[13] Griffin, *Archeology of the Eastern United States*, 50; Thomas, *Report on Mound Exploration, Twelfth Annual Report*, B.A.E., 542.

dwelled along the St. Lawrence, near Montreal; and the Algonquians, called the Adirondacks, occupied the river some three hundred miles above the place called Three Rivers on the St. Lawrence.

It was apparently in the sixteenth century that the split between the Hurons and the Iroquois occurred. The Hurons were more numerous than the Iroquois. They seem to have sided with the Algonquians; and when Cartier came up the St. Lawrence in the summer of 1545, he found the Hurons in possession of the lands that Colden states were formerly held by the Iroquois. The year 1570 is usually given for the founding of the great Iroquois confederacy of the Five Nations.

If the Iroquois had been peaceful folk in early times, by 1570 they had taken up war in real earnest and made themselves masters of this new profession. They are said to have put eight thousand warriors in the field when they went to drive the Hurons from their picket stockades along the St. Lawrence; and they did such a thorough piece of work that the Hurons fled westward to the shores of the lake that now bears their name, leaving the St. Lawrence Valley from the site of Quebec to above the site of Montreal uninhabited and desolate. By 1600, the Iroquois were spreading terror among the Algonquians of southern New York and New England and were even sending war parties into Virginia. The Mohawks were the fiercest of the Iroquois. Their name means "Cannibals." They were the Iroquois tribe farthest to the east. To the west of them was the big Onondaga Iroquois tribe, wise in council and usually inclined to peace. West of these was the small and fierce tribe of the Oneidas, over half of their force adopted Huron and Algonquian captives who had been taught by their masters to be as fierce and pitiless as any born Iroquois. The Oneidas raided toward the southwest, as far as Tennessee and Georgia. West of the Oneidas were the Senecas, the most westerly Iroquois group and the most numerous. In the seventeenth century they were reported to have thirty villages and to be harrying the tribes in the Ohio Valley. They were termed the most warlike and most ambitious for power of any of the Iroquois. In between the Mohawks and the Onondagas dwelled the Cayugas, the smallest of the Iroquois tribes.

John R. Swanton was of the opinion that, as late as the year of Cartier's visit to the St. Lawrence in 1545, the five Iroquois tribes were independent and sometimes made war on each other. J. N. B. Hewitt believed that it was about the year 1570 that the two wise men, Dankanawida and Hiawatha, started their crusade and induced the Iroquois to cease their quarreling and form a league.[14] Many scholars have admired the Iroquois and praised them for developing the highest form of organization and Indian government north of Mexico, and that is understandable if we wish to close our eyes to the cold-blooded Iroquois policy of aggression that devoured one neighboring tribe after another, to the Iroquois' delight in torturing captives to death, and to their indulgence in cannibal feasts. It is little excuse that the tribes who were enemies of the Iroquois were often equally cruel, equally fond of torturing unfortunate captives, and also given to eating human flesh. If the Iroquois were a superior race, they should have cultivated some feelings of humanity. To term them the Greeks of America is absurd. Francis Parkman came nearer to the truth when he called them kinsmen of the wolves. Hitler's fanatical Nazis would have hailed them as brothers.

Judging by the Walam Olum and some other Indian traditions, it was the Hurons who aided the Delawares in their attacks on the Ohio Mound Builders, and it was also the Hurons who first attacked the Shawnees. The Hurons were a more numerous group than the Iroquois Proper. They were evidently on more friendly terms with the Algonquians; and when the war between the Iroquois and the Algonquians started, the Hurons sided with the latter against the Iroquois, who were of their own blood. After 1545, the Iroquois sent an army northward, took the Huron villages on the St. Lawrence by surprise, slaughtered part of the enemy, took many captives, and forced the survivors to flee westward. By 1600, the Iroquois were in central and northwestern New York, the Hurons were east of Lake Huron. South of the Hurons, and between them and the Iroquois, was the big Neutral Nation, occupying lands along the north shore of Lake Erie and the south shore of Lake Ontario. This tribe was striving to be neutral in the wars between the Iroquois and the allied Hurons and Algonquians. The Erie tribe or Nation du Chat extended along the south shore of Lake Erie. To the northeast, north,

---

[14] Swanton, "Indian Tribes of North America," *Bulletin 145*, B.A.E., 39; J. N. B. Hewitt, *Iroquoian Cosmology, Twenty-first Annual Report*, B.A.E., and *Forty-third Annual Report*, B.A.E.

and west of these Iroquoian groups were numerous Algonquian tribes of wandering hunters. All the Iroquoian groups lived by growing crops, including tobacco. They had many towns fortified by earth walls and tall stockades of logs set upright in the ground. There was good reason for these fortifications. The land was seething with war; the old village and agricultural population had been driven from the St. Lawrence, and the fine country along the Richelieu River, between the St. Lawrence and Lake Champlain, which had formerly been heavily populated, was now deserted and desolate. Without pity the Iroquois had set about the systematic devouring of all neighboring tribes.

By this time all the tribes knew of the coming of a strange race of write-skinned men to the shores of the land. They came in great canoes with white wings spread to the winds. Columbus came first, and after him came many other adventurous navigators. By 1510, the Spaniards had found the coast of Florida; in 1521, Ponce de León and his Spaniards invaded Florida; in 1523, Cortez landed in Mexico. In the north John Cabot had planted the flag of England on the east coast of Canada in 1498; and Verrazano, in the service of France, had coasted northward from Carolina or Virginia in 1524, entering New York Harbor and then proceeding on north along the coast. French fishing vessels were frequenting the east coast of Canada by the beginning of the sixteenth century. In 1539, De Soto landed in Florida with an army of six hundred men, many of them mounted and in armor; and for the next three years the army marched through the south, plundering, killing, or enslaving the Indians as far north as Arkansas and northern Georgia and west into Texas.

The news of the white man's coming must have spread quickly as far inland as the Ohio Valley and the Upper Mississippi. At first the strange beings were regarded as gods; but the cruelties of the Spaniards altered the Indian view, and some tribes soon changed the designation from gods to demons. In the far northeast the situation was different. The French met the Indians in friendly wise and soon opened a trade with them, giving worthless French articles for furs, which the Indians at first regarded as of little value. It was with the Algonquians that the French made their first contacts; and presently the rivers were filled with birchbark canoes as the Indians came down to the coast to trade furs for trinkets, for cloth, and for precious iron hatchets and knives. The tribesmen learned very quickly that their old weapons made of flint, bone, wood, and antler were very poor things when compared with French iron implements; and the Algonquians lost no time in using their new weapons to terrorize neighboring tribes.

Jacques Cartier sailed to the Canadian coast in 1534 and examined the mouth of the St. Lawrence. He believed that this river led to a seaway through which he could reach the Spice Islands of Asia. In 1535, he returned to the coast and sailed up the St. Lawrence. In September he reached the site of Quebec, where the Indians had a large town called Stadacona on the hill. In the lowlands, crops of maize and vegetables were ripening. Cartier found the great valley on both sides of the river occupied by Indian towns and covered by their fields of growing crops. On Montreal Island he found the town of Hochelaga on a high hill or mount. This town was defended with a triple line of log stockades, one line within the other. Galleries or platforms lined the stockades, and stones were piled on them ready to hurl down on the heads of attackers. The land about the town was covered with growing crops. The Indians he saw here between Quebec and Montreal Island were evidently Hurons, and perhaps they were the two clans called the Rock and Deer People, found among the Hurons after 1600. They were evidently among those inhabitants of the St. Lawrence whose towns were taken by surprise and destroyed by the Iroquois army at an uncertain date between 1545 and 1595.[15]

Cartier made his last voyage up the St. Lawrence in 1543. In 1603, Champlain came up the river and found the Indians Cartier had visited gone, their towns destroyed, their maize fields desolate. He found a few camps of Algonquians, who were constantly on the watch for the dreaded Iroquois raiding parties. In the meantime the French had sent a colony consisting mainly of prisoners to establish a settlement at Quebec. The unfortunate Frenchmen held out for one bitter winter and then abandoned the place. In 1606, Champlain with the Canada Company partners, De Monts and Pontgravé, established a colony in Arcadia; and Champlain, having been appointed governor, went up the St. Lawrence and on July 3, 1608, landed at Quebec with twenty-eight men and built a fort.[16]

[15] Hodge, *Handbook of Indians North of Mexico*, I, 555, 616; II, 632; Samuel de Champlain, *Voyages of Samuel de Champlain, 1604–1618*, II, 183.
[16] J. H. Schlarman, *From Quebec to New Orleans*, 22–23.

The French at Quebec began trading with the Indians, who were mostly Algonquians. From the first these Indians urged Champlain to come with some of his men, armed with guns, to aid them against the Iroquois; and in 1609 the French leader with two of his followers accompanied a large war party of Algonquians and Hurons on an incursion into the enemy country. They marched south from the St. Lawrence along the valley of the Richelieu River through lands that had been dotted by Indian towns not many years back, but had been desolated by the inroads of the savage Iroquois. On the shore of the lake that now bears the name of Champlain, the war party of Indians and French encountered a force of two hundred Iroquois warriors, who advanced boldly to the attack. Champlain and his two men fired their arquebuses, and three Iroquois chiefs fell. The Iroquois, who had evidently never seen a gun before, fell into a panic and retreated.

At this time, 1609, the Iroquois had a few French knives which they had captured from Indians who traded with the white men; but most of the Iroquois warriors were still armed with flint knives and similar primitive weapons. The Indians who traded with the French had a temporary advantage; but they frittered it away by making small nuisance raids on the Iroquois, coming home in triumph with a few scalps and captives. These Algonquians and Hurons evidently had no unity, no real leadership, and no plan. The Iroquois had all these; and when they struck, they followed up their blow and left the enemy shattered.

Champlain attempted to teach his Indian allies the rudiments of effective warfare. In 1615, he went with a few Frenchmen to the Huron country, north of Lake Ontario, between the small Lake Simcoe and Lake Huron. The Hurons had many towns, some of them protected by log stockades; and they had a larger population than the Iroquois. Their hatred for that tribe was intense, for two of the Huron tribes had been driven from their towns on the St. Lawrence by the Iroquois and forced to flee to the other Hurons for protection. The Hurons were planning an expedition to destroy a fortified Iroquois town. Encouraged by the presence of Champlain with a few Frenchmen, armed with guns, and by the news that their allies, the Andaste tribe of the Susquehanna River in Pennsylvania, would join them with five hundred men, they gathered their forces and set out for the Iroquois country. Meantime, the Andastes were engaged in harvest festivities and forgot to gather their five hundred men and carry out their part of the united plan. In the Oneida country the Hurons and French attacked a strongly fortified Iroquois town but failed completely in their efforts to break into it. The great expedition then split up. They made a few small attacks, lost a few warriors, lost courage, and returned home. During this expedition, Champlain noted that the Iroquois fortifications were much better planned and constructed than those of the Hurons. He also observed that the Hurons caught the Iroquois men at work harvesting their maize crop. The warriors were working with their arms piled on the ground near them. When the Hurons took them by surprise, they were not armed; but seizing their weapons, they drove the Hurons off in a fierce onset.[17] At this time, the Dutch were on the Hudson, had made friends with the Iroquois, and were trading arms to them. The Algonquians and Hurons had lost the opportunity that their early acquisition of French weapons had placed in their hands. Armed by the Dutch, the Iroquois went grimly to work, systematically destroying their enemies.

The French had barely established themselves on the St. Lawrence when they began to record instances of Indians indulging in feasts of human flesh. This very distasteful subject has been avoided by American scholars with the result that there is a widespread belief that the American Indians, unlike any other savages in the world's history, were rather nice people, inclined to be friendly and peaceable before the whites came and brutalized them. In justice to the whites it should be observed that every one of the Iroquoian tribes, who were the most advanced groups in the northeast, had the custom of torturing captives to death and then feasting on the flesh of their victims. By the time the French came, this custom had been adopted by some of the Algonquian tribes; and there is archaeological evidence that the Siouans of the Winnebago group in Wisconsin had picked up the habit, evidently from the southern Indians of the town of Aztalan. The origin of the custom of eating human flesh is obscure; but the Iroquoian tribes were from the southwest, and their kinsmen, the Caddoans of the country west of the Mississippi, also were eaters of human flesh. We might conjecture that the custom was introduced into the north by southern Indians.

The primitive hunters in the northern forest suffered frequently

[17] Francis Parkman, *Pioneers of France in the New World*, 410–16.

from outright starvation. Caught in the forest in winter with no food, they wandered about in desperation seeking game, some of their people falling and dying in the snow of stark starvation. On such occasions a few individuals saved themselves by eating the flesh of their dead tribesmen; but that was not habitual cannibalism, and most of the people shunned the men who had been guilty of eating human flesh. Among the Iroquoian tribes it was a different matter. They habitually, and with every indication of pleasure, tortured their victims, men and women and sometimes children, to death, and then feasted on the flesh. They did it with their village full of food. It was out-and-out cannibalism, and they were proud of it. The French attempted to shame them out of the habit, and occasionally they made a convert; but as a rule these tribes only ceased to hold cannibal feasts when the whites put a stop to intertribal warfare, and there were no longer any enemy captives to be eaten.

The main purpose of this brief account of the tribes in the northeast is to link them up with the tribes in Illinois and Wisconsin, tribes that were still in the prehistoric period from the archaeological angle. Champlain began to hear vague accounts of these western tribes as soon as he came among the Hurons. The Jesuits started a mission among the Hurons in 1633, and also picked up vague or poorly understood statements concerning these tribes in the west. The tribes were Algonquian, mostly in Michigan, and beyond them the Puants or Stinkards, the Winnebagoes.

It is obvious from the French accounts that these western tribes were being warred on by both the Hurons and Neutrals before the French came among the Hurons. It was a situation we might expect. While part of the tribes were at war, some groups were paying friendly visits to the western tribes and trading with them. Even before the French came, this intertribal trade was probably in existence, and as soon as the first French ships appeared on the lower St. Lawrence, some of the Algonquians took up the business of trading French articles to the Hurons and even to tribes beyond Lake Huron. Ottawa, meaning "traders," was the name for these trading Indians. By the time that Champlain and the Jesuits penetrated to the Hurons, some Huron families had adopted the practice of making annual canoe voyages down the St. Lawrence to exchange their furs for French goods, and—like the Ottawas—these families gave up trapping to obtain furs and went into trade. They spent their winters visiting western tribes and exchanging cheap French trinkets and a few metal knives and hatchets for furs that were worth far more. It is obvious from the French accounts that even before French goods were available, this intertribal trade was of considerable importance. In autumn the roving camps of Algonquian hunters came and camped at settled villages, large groups of Algonquians spending entire winters at the Huron and other villages, where they traded their furs and other forest products for maize, dried vegetables, tobacco, and other village products. The Algonquians were famous makers of charms to bring luck or to ward off evil, and they traded these charms to the Hurons at high prices. One of the most famous of these Algonquian charms was supposed to insure good fishing. Some pretty girls were selected and formally married to the fishing nets of the tribe. This was intended to delight the fish spirit as the brides were to be his, and in appreciation he was supposed to cause the nets to be always full of fish when they were drawn from the water. The Algonquian camp that taught this charm to the Hurons probably spent an entire winter at the Huron village, being feasted and loaded with gifts while they taught the Hurons the proper rites and songs to be used in marrying their girls to their fishing nets.[18]

When we examine the Algonquian traditions and the early French statements, we find that at this period, which by archaeological dating was late prehistoric, the Algonquians held the Michigan lands. Earlier, in middle Woodland times, at least the southern peninsula of Michigan was apparently held by Iroquoian groups. By the late Woodland period the Algonquians had pushed down into the peninsula. Roving hunters at first, these Algonquians had picked up from Iroquoian neighbors the practice of growing crops; and they had formed villages, some of which were fortified by log palisades. In these times, around 1600 to 1625, Mackinac Island, off the north shore of the southern Michigan peninsula, was populous. It had thirty villages and was a famous Algonquian fishing center. On the mainland of the southern peninsula, the Nation of the Fire or Mascoutens had several "castles" or stockaded villages; near them were the Potawatomis; over to the east, near Saginaw Bay, the Sacs, who gave their name to the bay, had their settlements, and the Foxes and perhaps the Kickapoos were near them. To the south, near the southern shore

18 This is a *Jesuit Relations* story.

of Lake Michigan, were the Miamis and Illini. The Ojibwas were in northern Michigan, at and around Sault Ste Marie.

This southern peninsula of Michigan was a fine land for Indians in these far-off times. It may have been the Great Island which the Walam Olum states that the Delaware group of Algonquians invaded, driving out the native inhabitants, whom they termed Snakes, perhaps Iroquoian folk. The district at the straits near the present Detroit seems, from archaeological evidence, to have been held first by Iroquoians, then by Algonquians. This district was called Tiosahrondion—the Place of Beaver Dams. On both sides of the straits beaver were particularly abundant. Elk hunting was also excellent here, and there was more rich beaver country toward the south and west, between the Maumie River and the upper Wabash. This area was clearly held by the Algonquians around the period 1600–40; but the Iroquois claimed the Detroit lands by right of conquest, asserting that they destroyed the native tribes in 1654.

Apparently these Algonquian tribes, intruding into the southern peninsula of Michigan, had made war on and driven out certain Iroquoian tribes before the year 1600; but after that date the tide turned. The Iroquoians obtained French weapons, and, aided by the Algonquian Ottawas, they attacked the Michigan Algonquians vigorously. Champlain heard of these Iroquoian attacks on the western Algonquians as early as 1615. The Neutrals, aided by the Ottawas, were raiding the Michigan tribes in 1626. By about 1630, Champlain obtained an account of the Puants or Stinkards—the Winnebagoes of Wisconsin—and he set them down on his map of 1632; but his knowledge of the west was from Indian information, and he put the Winnebagoes in Michigan, north of the Sault Ste Marie.

Here we have fairly accurate historical information on a period which archaeology terms prehistoric. Tribes as far to the west as Lake Huron were being armed by the French. The Iroquois were being armed by the Dutch. The Algonquians of Michigan were under heavy attack by the Iroquoians and Ottawas, and in Wisconsin the powerful Winnebago group of Siouans was evidently in alliance with the southern Indians of Cahokia, having a strong colony of these southerners living among them at Aztalan. The Illini were apparently not yet in the present state of Illinois, to which they gave their name, but were close to the southern shore of Lake Michigan, which was called Lake of the Illinois. The Ottawas were trading Indians. Every

94

spring they went down the St. Lawrence in fleets of birchbark canoes to trade furs to the French; and on returning to their homeland, they sent out parties to spend the winter trading for furs among the western tribes. They had formerly trapped their own furs; but now it was more profitable to trade French trinkets, knives, and hatchets at very high prices to the simple western natives for their furs. Like the traders they were, the Ottawas had few scruples. They joined their Iroquoian customers in making war on their own Algonquian kinsmen. It was often cheaper and simpler to attack and plunder a tribe of kinsmen than to spend an entire winter in bartering for their furs.

Here we have a situation that seems clear enough. War and trade were disrupting the tribes in Michigan. In Wisconsin the strong and haughty Winnebagoes, allied with the southern Indians in Illinois, were face to face with an Algonquian intrusion into their sphere of influence; and they apparently met the threat boldly by taking the offensive. Nicolas Perrot, the French trader, heard the account of this battle from Indians who had taken part in the events. The story was that in prehistoric times, when the western Indians had only flint weapons, the Winnebagoes attacked and ruined the Illini. That tribe, aided by Algonquian kinsmen, then attacked and ruined the Winnebagoes. From the French sources we can add many details to this simple statement. Champlain had heard of the Winnebagoes about 1630. The tribal name was Algonquian, and some said that it meant Stinkards, while others asserted that the name referred to the salt- or evil-smelling water. This tribe was sometimes called the People of the Sea, from a tale that they had formerly dwelled by a sea in the west, supposed by the French to be near China.[19] From Indian information Champlain set the Winnebagoes down on his map in northern Michigan; but the map clearly shows Lake Winne-

[19] Our anthropologists have accepted the salt- or evil-smelling water explanation of the name Winnebago; but the French sources refer to the Winnebagoes as sodomites and cannibals, and in the *Jesuit Relations* for 1638, XV, 155, this tribe is termed the stinking people, *des gentes puants*. Thwaites here inserted a footnote to the effect that it was the Winnebagoes and not the water of the lake that stank. We also have the seventeenth-century name for Lake Michigan, "The Great Lake of the Algonquians or of the Stinkards," which was applied before the lake was termed the Lake of the Illinois. Father Brebeuf wrote in 1636 that *Aweatsiwaenrhonon* was the Iroquoian name and that it meant Stinkards. His text shows that the Indians thus named were the Winnebagoes.

bago and the Fox River flowing from the lake. It has these turned around, with the river flowing south, whereas the fact is that the lake is in Wisconsin and the river flows northward. This map shows the Winnebago town on Fox River, not far north of the lake, with the caption *"La Nation des Puants."* It shows another village, unnamed, on the opposite bank of the river, and a third village, also unnamed, on the west shore of Lake Winnebago. It does not show any other tribes near the Winnebagoes, but it sets down the Mascoutens, on the southern peninsula of Michigan, south of Sault Ste Marie and of Mackinac Island.[20]

It is interesting to note that, when the French came among the Hurons, east of Lake Huron, they began to hear vague reports of the Siouans of Wisconsin and Minnesota, of the Winnebago group and the Sioux. As the years passed, reports came in that the Siouans were making war on their Algonquian neighbors, who were still mostly without metal weapons. In 1636, the Jesuits reported that the Winnebagoes were attacking the Amikwa or Beaver tribe in the lands of northern Michigan and were even warring with the Hurons. A peace was made; but members of the Beaver tribe fortified their village for protection against the Winnebagoes, and then the Winnebagoes killed two Beaver men and made a feast of their flesh. The war was resumed. In 1638, groups of Huron trading Indians were going to the tribes near Sault Ste Marie to trade with the Algonquians there. In 1641, French traders met Potawatomis fleeing from the Sioux. The Potawatomis were evidently in northern Michigan, but presently they crossed the water into the peninsula of southern Michigan. In the autumn of 1642, two Jesuits, Father Charles Raymbault and Father Isaac Jogues, voyaged to the Sault Ste Marie, where they met two thousand Algonquians of different tribes and heard of the Sioux, who dwelled in about thirty villages at a distance of eighteen days toward the west, nine days by canoe along Lake Superior, and nine days up a river that evidently entered the lake from the south-

20 Copy of part of the Champlain map of 1632, in *Collection of the State Historical Society of Wisconsin*, XI, 24. Boisseau map in *Jesuit Relations* for 1643, XXIII, 233. This map shows the Winnebagoes on the southwest shore of Lake Winnebago as *"Nation des Puants"* or Nation of Stinkards. The Fox River flowing from the lake is marked *"Rivière des Puants."* The map shows the *Nation du Feu* to the southeast of the Winnebagoes, evidently near the southern end of Lake Michigan.

west. The Sioux were reported to be at war constantly, mainly with the Crees to the north and with the "Irinions" (Illinis?).

Champlain and other French leaders at Quebec were greatly interested in the Indian tales concerning the Winnebagoes, particularly as there were vague reports of a sea in the west, not far from the Winnebago country. They still believed that China was not far to the west, and they had a theory that some of the tribes near the Winnebagoes were Tartars. The Quebec men now chose Jean Nicolet, who had lived for many years among the Indians and spoke their languages, to go to the Winnebagoes; and they were so sure that he would meet Tartars in that region that they supplied him with a superb mandarin robe of crimson brocade embroidered with birds and flowers in brilliant colors so that the Tartars he might meet would regard him as a high official and treat him with respect.

Nicolet is said to have left Quebec in early July[21] and to have gone to the Hurons, where he induced some Huron men, probably traders familiar with the western Indians, to accompany him. The Winnebagoes, according to the Jesuit account, were at war with the Hurons at this time; but still Nicolet induced seven Huron men to accompany him. They went by canoe from Lake Huron, through the Straits of Mackinaw, then south into Green Bay. Nicolet may have picked up a force of Algonquian warriors in the Mackinac district, for the *Jesuit Relations* of 1643 states that he had four hundred

---

[21] I am very uncertain as to the year of Nicolet's visit to the Winnebagoes. Hodge, in *Handbook of Indians North of Mexico,* states on several pages that the date of Nicolet's visit was 1634 and that Nicolet found several Algonquian tribes at Green Bay. These tribes certainly were not there until after 1640, and Nicolet did not refer to them, as far as I can learn. Parkman was in doubt, stating that Nicolet visited the Winnebagoes "in 1635 or 1638." W. J. McGee, in *The Siouan Indians: A Preliminary Sketch, Fifteenth Annual Report,* B.A.E., 196, says 1639. This may be the correct date. Nicolet came to Canada in 1618 as a boy and spent two years among the Island Algonquians, then eight or nine years with a second Algonquian group, all before he was selected as the most experienced man available for the Winnebago expedition. One authority says he went to the Winnebagoes in 1643; but that is the year of his death, as recorded in the *Jesuit Relations* for that year, and he did not die until several years after his return from the Winnebagoes. I have studied what Justin Winsor and the learned contributors to his *Narrative and Critical History of America* have said about Jean Nicolet, and I do not believe that they knew all the facts or that their opinion concerning the date of Nicolet's visit to the Winnebagoes is final.

Algonquians with him when he visited the Winnebagoes to make peace.

The Hodge *Handbook of Indians North of Mexico* asserts that Nicolet found the Winnebagoes near Green Bay, "wedged in by Central Algonquian tribes, particularly the Sauk and Foxes and the Menominee";[22] but in the Nicolet narrative in *Wisconsin Historical Collections,*[23] there is no mention of any tribe near the Winnebagoes, and that tribe was far up Fox River, away from Green Bay. Moreover, the *Jesuit Relations* asserts that in 1634 the Winnebagoes were warring on both the Hurons and Algonquians; and it is evident that the Algonquians did not come into the Green Bay and Lake Winnebago country until after 1634, most of them probably after 1650.

On nearing the Winnebago town, Nicolet sent some of his Hurons to inform the natives of his approach. He then put on his mandarin robe and advanced boldly toward town with a loaded pistol in each hand. He must have fired his pistols, for we are told that the Winnebago women and children fled in terror and called him a spirit who held thunder in both hands. He was received with marked respect by the Winnebago leaders, and the chiefs gave a feast in his honor. But he found no Tartars, and he learned that the Tartars who supposedly came in ships to visit the Winnebagoes were Sioux who came in dugout canoes.[24]

It is unfortunate that we have only meager accounts of Nicolet's visit to Wisconsin. His story and the accounts of the Winnebago war with the Algonquians form a most important link between history and archaeology. Nicolet evidently found the Winnebagoes in what archaeology terms the Lake Koshkonong phase of Oneota culture, with the southern Indians from Cahokia perhaps still inhabiting their great fortified town of Aztalan. Yet, none of the French accounts speak of any Indians except the Winnebagoes. Both the Cham-

---

22 Hodge, *Handbook of Indians North of Mexico,* II, 958. We may note that La Potherie says that toward the end of the Winnebago war with the Algonquians, and probably after 1640, the Winnebagoes sent a great force to attack the Foxes in southern Michigan, and this and other facts prove that the Algonquians were in Michigan, and not at Green Bay in 1634–40.

23 XI.

24 Henry Juan, *Jean Nicolet, Collection of the State Historical Society of Wisconsin,* XI.

plain map of 1632 and the Boisseau map of 1643, show the main Winnebago town on Fox River, close to Lake Winnebago. This seems to prove that up to 1640, the Winnebagoes were in the middle period of the Lake Koshkonong development, which starts south of Lake Winnebago and then extends north to Fox River and down that stream to near Green Bay. There is not a word in the French accounts about the Winnebago tribal make-up or the identity of their allies; yet we must suspect that in 1630–40 the Iowas and Otoes were in close alliance with their Winnebago kinsmen and that the southern Indians may still have held their great fortified town of Aztalan, to the south of Lake Winnebago. Whether the Iowas and Otoes were near Lake Winnebago at this period is unknown; but even in the nineteenth century the Winnebagoes, Iowas, and Otoes had an ancient song, which the Iowa missionary stated was in the old Winnebago dialect, which recounted how the three tribes had lived together in a great fort of earth and timber on Rock River—where the earth-and-timber fortress of Aztalan was located.[25]

The French accounts do not state what Nicolet did among the Winnebagoes beyond attending feasts. He is said to have left the tribe and gone on toward the south and west where he visited the Illini, perhaps on Illinois River. There is no reference in the contemporary reports of a Winnebago war on the Illini, but such a war may have been in progress in a district so remote that rumors of it did not reach the French.

As has been said, the assertion of the French implied that the powerful Winnebagoes attacked and ruined the Illinis before these Indians had any metal weapons and that then the Illinis struck back and ruined the Winnebagoes. This second and last phase of the war ended about 1630. This does not fit in with the Nicolet information, and it does not agree with the more detailed French account.

La Potherie evidently had some of the manuscript writings of Nicolas Perrot that are now lost, and his account of the war was based mainly on the Perrot material. He begins by stating that the Winnebagoes, at the time when they were armed only with flint weapons,

[25] Schoolcraft, *Indian Tribes,* III, 267. Beyond this ancient song, these Indians had no memory of the time when their people lived in the earth-and-timber fort. See also *ibid.,* IV, 231.

were very powerful, were making war in every direction, and were feared by all neighbor tribes except the Menominees. The Menominees were the only tribe that was at all friendly with the Winnebagoes, and even this friendship was based on fear, the Menominees living in dread of their powerful neighbors. The Winnebagoes were ruthless and wicked, and they were cannibals. At this time the Ottawas, living near Lake Huron, were trying to extend their trade in French goods westward. They sent a party of their traders to the Winnebagoes. That tribe scorned French goods and did not even desire French iron knives and hatchets. The Winnebagoes, however, received the trading Indians with every mark of friendship, lulled them into a feeling of security, and then made a treacherous attack, killed all the Ottawas, cooked them, and ate them.

When the Ottawas heard of the fate of their trading party, they were infuriated; but it was impossible for them to strike back at once. They apparently adhered to the ancient Algonquian custom—practiced by the Cheyenne tribe down to the middle of the nineteenth century in plains wars—of waiting one winter to strike a real blow at an enemy. The Ottawas sent parties to all related and allied tribes urging them to join in a crusade against the hated Winnebagoes. They waited through the winter and spring, and then in summer they gathered their forces and went in fleets of birchbark canoes to invade the Winnebago lands. They probably had a number of men armed with French guns, most of the rest having French knives and hatchets. The Ottawas were the leaders. They seem to have taken the Winnebagoes by surprise, for La Potherie states that they fell into confusion, part of the people blaming the group that had killed and eaten the Ottawa traders. There was quarreling and division, almost civil war. Part of the Winnebagoes (perhaps this means the Iowa and Oto tribes and other allied groups) held aloof. Nicolet had stated that the Winnebagoes (and allies?) had about four thousand warriors; but now when the Algonquians struck and most of the people either fled or kept out of the fighting, the Winnebagoes are said to have gathered four to six thousand "men" in a single village, where they apparently held out. Such a force in an Indian village seems incredible, and in all probability the number given represents the total population of the village, including women and children, and probably less than one thousand fighting men. We might conjecture that the Winnebagoes took refuge in the fortified town of Aztalan. At any rate, La Potherie states that pestilence broke out in the crowded town, killing all but fifteen hundred "men," by which we may assume he meant people.

The Indian could not keep up a siege for any long period. Each warrior had only a pack of parched corn and dried meat, and when that was consumed, the fighting force broke up, going home or setting out to hunt game in small groups. This was probably how the siege of the Winnebago town ended, and what happened next was typical of the Indian. The Winnebagoes, instead of seeking peace, made up a war party, which La Potherie asserts numbered five hundred men, and set off in a fleet of canoes to cross Lake Michigan and attack the Fox tribe in the southern Michigan peninsula. The fleet of canoes was caught in a storm on the lake, and the Winnebago warriors were drowned.

The Algonquians now made a peace or truce with the Winnebagoes. That tribe was in a dreadful situation. They had lost a great many people, game had left their lands, and they were starving. La Potherie states that the Illini took pity on the stricken tribe and sent five hundred men, including fifty chiefs, to bring a store of food to the Winnebagoes. This has a strange sound. Indians were not much given to being charitable to defeated enemies; but the Illinis had a reputation for being different from the other Algonquians, who looked down on them as poor, spineless folk. The Illinis were now evidently living in northern Illinois, where they must have been near the southern Indians of Cahokia, who were old friends and allies of the Winnebagoes. Thus it may have been Cahokian influence that induced the Illinis to go in friendly wise, to aid the Winnebagoes. That tribe welcomed the visitors. There was feasting and dancing; and while the Illini warriors were dancing, the treacherous Winnebagoes cut their bowstrings and then made a sudden attack, killing all the Illinis, cooking them, and having a great cannibal feast. La Potherie says that the great enclosure (ruins of the stockaded village?) where this affair took place was still marked with the piled-up bones of the slaughtered Illinis late in the seventeenth century. The *Jesuit Relations*[26] reports that the massacre of the Illini visitors

---

[26] LIV, 237.

by the Winnebagoes occurred about the year 1639, and that in re-
venge for the murder and eating of their people, the Illinis struck a
heavy blow against the Winnebagoes.

War was resumed, and the Winnebagoes, in fear of the vengeance
of the Algonquians, left their village and fled to an island in Lake
Michigan. This island was near the west shore of the lake. The Illinis
came in force, but they had evidently marched by land from northern
Illinois. They had no canoes and could not cross to the island. Other
Algonquian tribes, with canoes, offered to come to the aid of the
Illinis, but that tribe wished to deal with the Winnebagoes unaided.
They went home. In winter they returned, crossing to the island on
the ice; but the Winnebagoes had left and gone on their winter hunt.
The Illinis followed their trail for six days, then came upon them
and attacked, killing nearly all the men and, evidently, carrying off
the women and children. A few Winnebago warriors escaped and
found refuge among the Menominees. This ended the wars, but later
another almost incredible event occurred. The Illinis are said to
have released the Winnebago captives and permitted them to return to their old lands between Lake Winnebago and Green Bay to
form the nucleus of a revived Winnebago tribe. The pride of the
Winnebagoes had survived all disasters. They had always had an
hereditary head chief. Now all their chiefs were dead, the children of
the chiefs had been slaves among the Algonquians, and the proud
tribe refused to be ruled by a chief who had been a slave. There was
a warrior, a commoner, who had fought bravely in the war and had
escaped, badly wounded. He had remained free, and now he was made
head chief of the new Winnebago tribe. Reduced to a mere remnant
of their former strength, the Winnebagoes kept their pride and haugh-
tiness, with the result that they had no friends. All the Algonquian
tribes, now their neighbors in Wisconsin, detested them.[27]

When we attempt to fit in the historical account of the Winnebago war with the Algonquians and join it to the archaeological
evidence, it would appear that this war occurred at the time when
Aztalan was held by the southern Indians of Cahokia or at a slightly

27 This narrative of the Winnebago wars is mainly from de la Potherie, in Blair,
Indian Tribes of the Upper Mississippi, II, 293–96. The narrative states that the
Winnebago village at which the bones of the murdered Illini were piled up was
within sight of the island in Lake Michigan to which the Winnebagoes fled. The
village was therefore close to the shore of Lake Michigan.

later date. There is no hint in any of the French accounts that alien southern Indians were in Wisconsin or Illinois at the time of this war; but the French, little interested in such details, may have omitted them. With the mighty Cahokia mounds within sight of their mission and trading post over a long period of years, the French were not enough interested to mention the mounds or to refer to the tribes that had built them.

In the nineteenth century the Winnebago tradition was that when the cognate tribes left them in Wisconsin, the Iowas left first and the Otoes last. All three of these tribes had a tradition that their ancestors had lived in a great wood-and-earth fort on the head of Rock River, which may have been Aztalan. Archaeology informs us that Aztalan was burned and abandoned toward the close of the Old Village period at Cahokia; and that period, by Kincaid tree-ring dating, seems to mean after the year 1600. This appears to make it at least probable that Aztalan was still occupied when the Winnebago war began. Moreover, there are Aztalan cultural remains on the Mississippi near the mouth of Wisconsin River, close to a big Siouan occupation of the Oneota period, which are certainly either Iowa or Oto culture of the period after 1600. The evidence suggests intimate relations between the southern Indians of Aztalan and the Winnebagoes, Iowas, and Otoes around 1600–50. Evidence of cannibalism, practiced at Aztalan and a feature of the Winnebago history in this period, is found in the archaeological remains, apparently Iowa or Oto, near the Mississippi; and there the trail of cannibalism ends.

There can be little doubt that the migration westward which is featured in the traditions of the Iowas and Otoes took place at the time of the defeat of the Winnebagoes by the Algonquians. Archaeological evidence indicates that part of the Winnebago group had a great center of population near the mouth of the Wisconsin, and across the Mississippi in northeastern Iowa, in the Effigy Mound period, which is earlier than the Aztalan period; but we must keep in mind that the old Winnebago group not only included the Iowas and Otoes, but the Missouri tribe and probably also the Mandans, Hidatsas, and Crows. Some of these tribes had evidently migrated to and beyond the Mississippi in Effigy Mound times. Of these movements we have no traditional accounts, and the evidence of archaeology is scanty. It may be observed, however, that the Hidatsas and Crows seem to have taken Effigy Mound culture with them on their westward and northward migration, and they kept this type of culture even after they reached North Dakota and Manitoba. What little archaeological evidence we possess suggests that the Mandans remained on or near the Mississippi long enough to pick up the rectangular hut of the Cahokia southern Indians and also their early custom of setting the huts in regular rows in the village.

It has been generally accepted that the Illinis were in Illinois at a very early period and that they probably took the lands there by conquest, but both modern archaeology and the historical evidence seem to cast doubt on this view. The Illinis were probably with the closely related Miamis in the lands near the southern end of Lake Michigan; and when the French first heard of the Illinis, soon after the year 1600, they called Lake Michigan "Lake of the Illinis," because the tribe lived near the lake. Living near the lake and hunting westward, the Illinis would have had to go into the Illinois lands, for the lands in Wisconsin were strongly held by the Winnebago group. When the Winnebago strength was broken, the Illinis had a choice of lands they might occupy, and they preferred the valley of Illinois River. Archaeology shows that in late prehistoric times the Illinois Valley was invaded by northern Indians. The old native population, perhaps Siouan with some admixture of southern Cahokian people, lived in unfortified villages in the valley lands; but now the people built new villages on the bluffs, where they could defend themselves. This was evidently a time of invasion and confusion. Archaeology suggests that the natives were Siouan Indians bearing Oneota culture, later in time than Aztalan, mingling with Cahokian southern Indians and perhaps other groups.[28] The Illini occupation of Illinois River seems to date this period, right on the edge of historic times.

The view that the Illinis invaded Illinois State and swept away the powerful Cahokian tribes is not reasonable. It is based on the belief that all the tribes of the Illini confederacy were Algonquians, but that is little more than conjecture, and modern archaeology seems to refute it. The Illinis were either near Lake Michigan or on the upper Illinois River at the time of the Winnebago war. That was apparently in late Old Village Cahokia times; and, instead of being conquered or destroyed, the Cahokian Indians continued to hold the lands along the Mississippi, from near Illinois River down to the

28 Griffin, *Archeology of the Eastern United States,* 156–58.

Ohio; and they not only held on, they developed a new and finer Cahokian culture, which continued to exist perhaps into historic times.[29] Archaeology gives no clear evidence that the Cahokian Indians were ever conquered. With no French evidence to aid us, we can only conjecture that the Illinis attacked some of the Cahokian groups, those on Illinois River for example, and incorporated the survivors into their tribe. They then may have formed an alliance with the other Cahokians. The French had nothing to say about this. They did state that, unlike the other Algonquians, the Illinis were Sun worshipers like the Cahokia folk, that the Illinis did not believe in dreams as the other Algonquians did, and that the Illinis had a peculiar way of cutting their hair, with locks left above the ears, which was not an Algonquian style but resembled the haircuts of some of the Siouan Indians and of the Hopewell or Ohio Mound Builder folk.

Whether the Cahokian tribes of Illinois were conquered or not, their attempt to colonize northern lands had failed. They had to retreat from Wisconsin and then from northern Illinois. The southern Indians who had intruded into the Ohio Valley also retired southward, under attack of the Iroquoian tribes. And thus was ended, at the close of the prehistoric period, the last effort of the southern tribes to colonize lands on the Ohio and the upper Mississippi.

[29] *Ibid.*, 150, 160–61. A study of the early Illini leaves one with a strong impression that the Peorias and part of the Kaskaskias were true Algonquians, but that most of the other so-called Illini, particularly the Cahokias, Tamaroas, Michagameas, and Moinguenas may have been southern Indians and not Algonquians. The name Cahokia stuck so persistently to the district in which the great mound and population center had been, that it seems probably that Cahokia was the name of the principal tribe of southern Indians here in Illinois.

CHAPTER SIX

East Wind

IN LATER PREHISTORIC TIMES the main Indian group in
the northeast was composed of a number of Iroquoian tribes who
were obviously immigrants from the south or west. They were similar
in some ways to the southern Indians who had come into the Ohio
Valley and developed the splendors of the Mound Builder culture.
The Iroquoians, however, were not Mound Builders, but judging
by Iroquois legends and some archaeological evidence, were the
enemies of the Ohio Mound Builders and took a leading part in the
destruction of Mound Builder civilization.[1] Mound-building and the
construction of great earth-walled enclosures were features of the
religious and ceremonial life of the Ohio Indians; but among the
Iroquoians, although religion and popular beliefs were probably very
similar to those held by the Ohio Indians—a combination of belief
in sky gods and earth-bound animal and nature gods—the Iroquoian
tribes contented themselves with believing, and what manual labor
they performed was expended on the practical work of growing crops

1 This is indicated in the Iroquois legends of the giants in the Ohio Valley, who
made war on them, and in the archaeological evidence of Iroquoian intrusion into
the Mound Builder area in the late period termed the Mound Intrusion time. The
Intrusive Mound culture is clearly Iroquoian. It comes from the Iroquoian lands
in the northeast, and also from a small area in the southern Michigan peninsula.

and constructing villages. They thus built up a material culture much higher than that of the roving camps of Algonquian hunters and fishermen, who made up the second great group of Indians in the northeastern woodlands.

Taking root in their new lands, evidently in a period of relative peace, the Iroquoians grew in population and physical well-being. Their villages usually had a large surplus of crops, and the Algonquians came on visits, bartering furs, copper, and other forest and lake products for maize, vegetables, tobacco, and other village commodities. Thus the Iroquoian tribes developed a material culture based on village life and the growing of tobacco and other crops; they lived under the rule of hereditary chiefs, counting descent in the female line, and they were well organized for social and religious life. Contrary to their own legends, they did not live entirely on their crops and were not ignorant of hunting and fishing methods. Every group went into the forests seasonally on large communal hunts, and they were skilled in building fish weirs in the streams near villages and in making fishing nets.

The one thing they had not achieved was unity. They were not only fighting their Algonquian neighbors, they were raiding each other. Even the Iroquois Proper were fighting among themselves before they learned a great lesson and formed a league and brotherhood of their five nations about the year 1570. Putting power into the hands of the federal chiefs, the Iroquois grew strong. The Hurons attempted to form a league of their own; but they lacked the wisdom and discipline of the Iroquois, and their league was little more than a pretension of friendliness and mutual aid among their tribes. Personal renown in war and little honors were more important to most of these Indians than peace could ever be, and they fell to fighting neighbor tribes or even their own close kinsmen when any slight excuse could be found for resorting to violence.

The difference between the Iroquois themselves and such Iroquoian tribes as the Hurons was marked and evidently had its roots far back in prehistoric times. It was a matter of mind and spirit. Defeated in early wars with the Algonquians, the Iroquois went grimly to work, to train themselves for survival and for conquest. They disciplined their people and trained their youth for war, teaching them the shame of weakness and the folly of showing pity for defeated foes. The Iroquois have been termed the ancient Greeks of

America. It would be more correct to style them the Prussian Junkers or, better still, the Hitler Nazis of the Indian world. They had the same haughty faith in their being a master race as the German fanatics, the same cold-blooded pitilessness in dealing with weaker peoples.

The rise of the Iroquois power does not appear to date farther back than the forming of their league. They had suffered defeat and had been driven from their lands along the St. Lawrence and forced to retire southward in New York before Jacques Cartier sailed up the river in 1535. The coming of the French favored the enemies of the Iroquois. At first the French came in fishing vessels to the coast and the mouth of the St. Lawrence, where they met and traded with Algonquian Indians; but the Indians at once recognized the great superiority of the French iron knives and hatchets as weapons over the flint ones they were accustomed to use, and the French trade grew rapidly as the Indians bartered furs for French articles. The French weapons aided the Algonquians and their Huron allies; but by the year 1600, the Iroquois had some iron knives and hatchets. Still, their enemies were better armed.

The Iroquois, haughty and aloof, usually scorned to have any friendly dealings with the Algonquians. The Hurons, on the other hand, although they at times fought with the Algonquians, usually were friendly; and as winter came on each year, large fleets of Algonquian bark canoes came to the Huron country, between Lake Huron and Lake Ontario, where the Algonquians spent the cold months trading furs, copper, and Algonquian magic charms for maize and other village products. Thus, probably even before the French arrived, the Hurons had made alliances with several Algonquian tribes.

The Algonquians were rated by the French as braver and better warriors than the Iroquois; but they were roving hunters, fiercely guarding their freedom, and they would not submit to discipline. They could not act together for any length of time; but, after making one combined attack, they broke up into little groups and went off on separate hunting and fishing expeditions, forgetting their war enterprises for the rest of the year. The Hurons, being village Indians and closely related by blood and language to the Iroquois, would have done better to ally themselves with that group; but ancient quarrels with the Iroquois had left a bitter hatred in Huron hearts for that tribe and all its ways; and, instead of imitating the Iroquois sub-

mission to leadership and discipline, the Hurons copied the Algonquians in some ways. The result was that there was no real unity
among the Hurons towns, no sound leadership in war, and feuds and
jealousy prevented any effective common action even in times of
crisis.

The Hurons imitated the example of the Algonquians and began
trading with the French. Before long a very large number of the Huron men were spending nearly all their time in trading journeys.
They went down the St. Lawrence in the spring in fleets of canoes,
loaded with furs and with their native tobacco, which they traded
for French goods. Coming home in late summer, they set out in small
trading parties and spent the winter among western tribes, trading
goods for furs.[2] Thus some Huron families enriched themselves, and
the number of Huron traders increased rapidly. They thought only
of profit, even while their tribe was at war with the Iroquois and
every man needed to be at home, ready to fight at any moment. Most
of the Huron men who stayed at home were idle. They neglected the
defenses of their villages. The stockades were in bad repair; some
of the villages had no stockades, and when the chiefs urged the men
to come and work on the village defenses, they were disregarded.

There was no peace. The Hurons and Algonquians were sending
war parties to raid in the Iroquois country, and the Iroquois were
responding by sending large war parties against the Hurons and Algonquians. About 1610, the Iroquois were still poorly armed. They
had obtained some iron knives and hatchets from tribes that traded
with the French, but their arrows were still tipped with flint. They
used war clubs and probably thrusting-lances. The Algonquians and
the Iroquoian tribes had armor made of hardwood slats bound
strongly together; they carried small wooden or leather shields, and
they had obtained sword blades from the French, which they used
as points for their lances. The Iroquois had wooden clubs with
sharp iron blades set into the wood. There was no peace, and peace

2 For the early trade of the French relations between the Hurons and Algonquians, the authorities are Samuel de Champlain's *Voyages,* II; Perrot, in Blair,
Indian Tribes of the Upper Mississippi, I, 196–98; Thwaites, *Jesuit Relations,*
XXIII, 191; *ibid.,* LIV, 127. The Algonquians were trading with the French before
1530, going down the St. Lawrence with fleets of bark canoes laden with furs. The
Hurons did not take up the trade until Champlain established Quebec, but by
1610 they were sending annual fleets of canoes down the river to trade.

for any length of time was impossible. Every Indian man had just one ambition, to distinguish himself in war, and he never missed an opportunity to start a fight. Even in winter they went on long war journeys, traveling on snowshoes.

The Neutral Nation, dwelling between the Hurons and the Iroquois, in the district along Niagara River, was neutral in the war between the Huron-Algonquian allies and the Iroquois. They were said to have been the ancestral group from which the Hurons and other Iroquoian tribes had broken off, and they were rude folk who scorned trading and did not wish to have the French among them. Though called Neutrals, they were engaged in raiding Algonquian tribes in the Michigan country, and the Ottawas were aiding them in these attacks. It was perhaps the attacks of the Neutrals and Ottawas, around 1600, that compelled the Illinis to leave Michigan and move westward to their historic location in Illinois. After 1625, the Neutrals and Ottawas were still making war on the Algonquians of southern Michigan, but now it was mainly the Nation du Feu that they were attacking. This nation was either the Mascoutens or the Potawatomis, Algonquians who had imitated the Iroquoian tribes and were cultivating the soil and living in fortified villages.[3]

Most of this fighting in the first quarter of the seventeenth century seems rather aimless and futile to us today. The Iroquois were the only tribe that had anything like real policy, purpose, and discipline; but it is difficult to find much to admire here. The Iroquois deliberately planned their treachery, pretending friendship, going through imposing peace negotiations, lulling their intended victims into a feeling of security, and then attacking them by surprise and slaughtering them without mercy. The Iroquois leaders had a master plan; they were going to eat the other nations, as they grimly put it, and they worked steadily toward that end.[4]

Luck was on their side. Their enemies had the advantage of trade with the French; but soon after the year 1600, the Dutch came to the Hudson, and the Iroquois not only obtained all the iron knives and hatchets required, but also firearms. The European governments

[3] Schoolcraft, *Indian Tribes*, IV, 205.

[4] References to arms and warfare are in various volumes of *Jesuit Relations;* also discussed by Perrot, in Blair, *Indian Tribes of the Upper Mississippi*, and by La Potherie, in Blair.

concerned in the colonization of Canada, the Atlantic coast, and the Hudson Valley had no real Indian policy. The whites were interested mainly in the trade for furs, and they gave little aid to their Indian allies beyond trading weapons to them. The only seriously planned enterprise was that of the Jesuits, who came into the Huron country in 1632 with a plan to establish missions and build a theocratic state called Huronia, in which the Indians, turned into Christian pacifists, would attempt to survive among enemy tribes. It was a Jesuit dream that could never come true, and the efforts of the zealous missionaries only aided in weakening the Hurons and contributing to the final disaster that destroyed them as a nation.

The Dutch built a fortified trading post near the present Albany in 1614, and their trade with the Iroquois was now regular and heavy. In 1626, they bought the island of Manhattan from the Indians and established their principal center there. In 1629, an English fleet sailed up the St. Lawrence and captured the French town of Quebec, which they held until peace was made in Europe in 1632. This disaster practically killed French enterprise among the Indians of the St. Lawrence and lower Great Lakes until after 1632. Some French traders, like Jean Nicolet, were stranded among the Indians and remained among them, seeing no white man again until the English left Quebec. In addition to this disaster, the English captured the French fleet for Canada in 1628, and most of the Canadian traders and all their stocks of goods fell into enemy hands.

Deprived of French aid and most of their trade in European goods, the Ottawas, Hurons, and Neutrals seem to have spent the years when the English were at Quebec in making war on western tribes. Nicolas Perrot states that the Hurons made peace with the Iroquois, and we know from the Champlain and Jesuit records that the Hurons were at war with tribes as far west as the Winnebagoes of Wisconsin. It was to make peace between the tribes, and probably to renew trade, that Nicolet made his venturesome canoe journey to the Winnebagoes. At this time, 1634-40, a fleet of Huron canoes went down the St. Lawrence every spring, laden with furs and native tobacco. The Hurons traded with the French and went back up the river, reaching home about August. They then formed trading parties and went to trade their French goods to the Tobacco Hurons or Petun, who dwelled three days' journey west of the Hurons on the shore of Lake Huron, to the Neutrals in the Niagara district, to some Algonquian tribes, and even to the distant Winnebagoes.[5]

In all the early French accounts there are few references to the Eries or Nation du Chat, who were close relatives of the Hurons, living along the southern shores of Lake Erie. The *Jesuit Relations* for 1653 states that the Eries were moving eastward about 1635, which suggests that they were being attacked by tribes dwelling to the west of them. There are almost no references to the tribes in the Ohio Valley in the French records prior to 1665. These Ohio tribes were apparently Siouans and some Algonquians, particularly Shawnees. That tribe had a story that the Hurons were raiding them, evidently prior to 1640, and that at least part of the Shawnees were forced to remove south of the Ohio River. It is to be suspected that the Eries were making war on the tribes along the Ohio. The Eries were a warlike people, reportedly using poisoned arrows; and the Dutch of New York called them the Satanas or Devils. It is to be observed again that the invaders of Ohio at this period brought an Iroquoian type of culture with them, the Mound Intrusion culture. They seem to have come mainly into eastern Ohio, into the Scioto country, the heart of the old Hopewell or Mound Builder lands. From these few and scanty references to the Ohio country, it is obvious that the Mound Builder power had been destroyed before the French came among the Hurons, soon after 1600.

In 1633, a handful of brave Jesuits made the dangerous voyage from Quebec to the Huron country. They accompanied the canoe fleet of the Hurons, returning home from trading with the French. Filled with zeal and high hopes, the Jesuits soon began to glimpse the almost insurmountable obstacles that barred the way to a general conversion of the Hurons. The chiefs and leading men among the Indians at once began to stir up hatred against the white priests, and even the few Hurons who were inclined to listen to the Jesuit teachings seem to have regarded the priests as a new type of medicine-men, who, they hoped, might cure their bodily ills and teach them charms that would give them success in crop-growing, hunting, fishing, and war. Few of the Hurons were interested in a white man's paradise.

The Hurons were termed the most populous of the Iroquoian tribes. In 1639, the Jesuits stated that the tribe had 32 villages, large

5 Thwaites, *Jesuit Relations*, XV, 155.

and small, 700 bark longhouses, 4,000 families, 12,000 adults, and perhaps a total population of around 20,000.[6] Some of their long-houses were as much as 240 feet in length and housed many families. These Indians had several big villages with triple log stockades; but the Jesuits soon noted that the village defenses were built on a poor system and were in bad repair. They advised the Huron chiefs to re-build the stockades, to give up the bad practice of making the stock-ades circular, to make them rectangular, with a tower at each corner. They assured the chiefs that a handful of men, armed with arque-buses, could fight off any Iroquois attack, but the Hurons ignored the advice and left their defenses in a state of neglect.

The French made a terrible error in not sending armed men among the Hurons to build a fort and live permanently with the Indians. The Hurons looked up to and respected armed Frenchmen. The Jesuits came solely to propagate the faith, and the Hurons, observing the meekness of the priests, insulted, abused and robbed them, often threatening to kill them. Desiring martyrdom, the Jesuits offered no resistance, and their passivity simply encouraged the brutality of the Indians. The priests had only one defense: to resort to magic trickery, and that they refused to use. The Hurons believed that the Jesuits were magicians and feared their supernatural powers. Slowly the mis-sionaries won over a few of the Indians, but the partial acceptance of the white man's religion only added to the confusion among the Hurons. It further split the Indians by adding a Christian *versus* pagan feud to all the other quarrels that divided the tribe into hostile factions, and the pagans—vastly in the majority—began savagely to persecute the Indian Christians.

In 1636, three years after the Jesuits came among the Hurons, a plague broke out in the Indian villages and killed a great many peo-ple. The Jesuits were so completely immersed in their efforts to spread Christianity that they hardly referred to the pestilence and did not describe it. It may have been bubonic plague. In the following year the plague spread into every Huron village, and half the popu-lation is said to have perished. The Indians blamed the Jesuits, ac-cusing them of bringing this terrible disaster on them and of plotting to destroy the entire tribe by magic. The chiefs held a council and planned to massacre the missionaries; but when the Huron canoe

[6] This careful estimate of the Huron population was made after the pestilence or plague of 1637–38 had carried off about half of the Hurons.

fleet came home in early autumn from trading with the French at
Three Rivers, the trading Indians, who were better acquainted with
the French than the stay-at-homes, used their influence to halt the
plan to kill the missionaries. Famine followed the pestilence, spreading among several tribes. The Neutral Nation was in such dreadful
condition that parents sold their children into slavery to obtain a
small supply of maize. By 1638, conditions were improved, and the
Hurons once again sent a war party against the Iroquois. Coming
home with many Iroquois captives, they tortured the prisoners to
death, then cooked them and had a great cannibal feast.[7]

The Ottawas, an Algonquian group, lived along Ottawa River,
about one hundred leagues above the Saguenay, in a land of rivers,
lakes, and mountains. They were among the first of the Indians to
open a trade with the French, and by 1600 they were supplying the
Hurons and certain western tribes with French goods, which they exchanged for furs. They went annually down the St. Lawrence with
their canoe fleets laden with furs to trade with the French. Knowing
the French well, they looked down on less sophisticated nations, particularly those that had no French knives, hatchets, or metal kettles
and still used flint weapons and earthenware pots which they made
themselves. The Ottawas apparently took advantage of these tribes,
cheating them in bartering for their furs, and at times simply attacking them by surprise and robbing them. The Ottawas presently
made an alliance with the Neutral Nation, whose villages were in
the Niagara River country between Lake Ontario and Lake Erie.
The Neutrals had to go only a short distance westward to get into
the southern peninsula of Michigan, and it was against the tribes
there that the Neutrals and Ottawas were warring vigorously from
about the year 1600 on. This war on the Michigan Algonquians was
at its height after the French resumed control on the St. Lawrence,
about the date 1632; and by 1640 the Neutral and Ottawa war parties
were violently attacking the Michigan tribes, particularly the Nation
du Feu and the Mascoutens. In the summer of 1643, the Neutrals sent
a great war party, said to have numbered two thousand men, and
assaulted and took the main castle of the Nation du Feu. The stockade surrounding the village was defended by nine hundred warriors;
but, after a siege of ten days, the attackers broke in, slaughtered part

[7] Thwaites, *Jesuit Relations* for 1636-38; Parkman, *The Jesuits in North America,* 137.

of the garrison, made captives of the rest, and burned seventy of the captured warriors at the stake. The Neutrals took about eight hundred women, children, and old men. They blinded all the old people by slashing them across the eyes with knives, and then turned them out in the forest to starve or be eaten by wild animals. Afterward they marched home in triumph with their hundreds of captured women and children.[8]

The Nation du Feu or Fire Nation has been identified by historians as the Potawatomi tribe and also as the Mascoutens. It may be remarked, however, that these early Algonquian inhabitants of the southern Michigan peninsula were so closely connected by blood and language that it is difficult to determine just which tribes were included under the term Nation du Feu. It is quite probable that the name referred to a confederacy of tribes, similar to the Seven Council Fires of the Sioux and the council fires of the grouped Iroquoian tribes. Unlike most of the other Algonquians, who were wandering hunters and fishermen, these Algonquians of the southern Michigan peninsula had imitated the Iroquoian way of life, settling down, growing crops and tobacco, and living in villages, some of which were strongly stockaded and termed "castles." The tribes involved were the Potawatomis, Mascoutens, Kickapoos, Sacs, and Foxes. The Miamis and Illinis appear to have belonged to a separate group.

A fog of mystery has surrounded the Mascoutens. Their name in one form meant Fire People, and they are therefore identified as the Nation du Feu; but the Potawatomis are also termed Nation du Feu, and by making a slight alteration in the name Mascouten, the meaning is changed to Small Prairie People. They have therefore been termed the Prairie Potawatomis, a group whose existence continues to this day. It is to be observed, however, that there were small prairies in the southwestern corner of Michigan, where the prehistoric garden beds, which may have been tobacco gardens, are found; and they may have been the home of the Mascoutens in the seventeenth century, and from these small prairies their name may have come. They were not living with the Potawatomis in the eighteenth century, but they continued a separate tribal existence as an independent tribe, more closely associated with the Illini than with the Potawatomis.

[8] Thwaites, *Jesuit Relations*, XXVII, 25. For the Ottawas, see *ibid.*, XXVII.

The war on the Nation du Feu recounted in the French records is undoubtedly the war on the Bone Indians, set down in the Ottawa and some other Algonquian traditions. These Bone Indians or Assegun are said to have dwelled in the Mackinac district in Michigan when the Ottawas and Ojibwas first entered that country. These tribes attacked the Asseguns and drove them southward, and the tradition asserts that the Bone Indians were the makers of the Michigan garden beds and had also made large deposits of human bones at certain places. Presumably this last assertion refers to the kind of communal burial of bones in ossuaries which was a feature of the burial customs of some Iroquoian tribes, and may have been adopted by the Algonquians of southern Michigan. The attempt of some authors to connect the Osage tribe with the Bone Indians is not convincing. At this period, and probably for centuries back, the Osages were in the Ohio Valley.

The accounts in *Jesuit Relations* indicate that this war of the Ottawas and related Algonquians, such as the Ojibwas, on the Nation du Feu and other Algonquians of southern Michigan, went on from about 1600 until the destruction of the Hurons and Neutrals by the Iroquois after 1648. This affords us historical evidence concerning the time of the removal of the Algonquian groups from the southern Michigan peninsula into Wisconsin. Those authors who assume that these tribes were in Wisconsin, near the Winnebagoes, when Jean Nicolet visited that tribe have no solid evidence to support their conclusions. The Winnebagoes were still an unbroken and powerful people when Nicolet came among them. The defeat of the Winnebagoes by the Ottawas and Illini dates after Nicolet's death. Moreover, part of the story implies that, after they had been defeated by the Algonquians, the Winnebagoes sent a force of warriors in canoes eastward across Lake Michigan, to attack the Fox tribe and other Algonquians in the southern Michigan peninsula. This fleet of canoes was destroyed in a storm and the Winnebago warriors perished.

The movement of the Illinis into Illinois is related to this problem. The evidence of the *Jesuit Relations* and other French narratives seems to indicate that the Illini movement westward was at a late date, perhaps after the year 1630. They were living near the southern end of Lake Michigan when the Jesuits first heard of them, and for this reason the lake was called the Lake of the Illinois. The story that they were in Illinois State when Nicolet came among the Winnebagoes does not have any solid basis. We do not know where the Illinis lived when the Winnebagoes defeated them, or later when the Algonquians defeated the Winnebagoes. The statements in *Jesuit Relations* that the Illinis and kindred groups came from a sea in the west and migrated eastward to Lake Michigan seem to be a part of the French illusion that China, Tartary, and a sea were to the west of the Winnebagoes. The fact seems to be that the Illinis and Miamis were near the southern end of Lake Michigan at the period when the Ottawas and Hurons attempted to open a trade with the Winnebagoes but only became embroiled in war with that tribe.[9]

The *Jesuit Relations,* even as late as 1653, show that the southern Michigan peninsula was occupied by Algonquian tribes. Groups of Ottawas and Tobacco Hurons, fleeing from the Iroquois, intruded into those lands; then, in the autumn of 1653, the Neutrals and Tobacco Nation—closely related to the Hurons and usually termed Hurons—assembled with the local Algonquian tribes at *A'otonatendi,* three days south of *Skia'e* (Sault Ste Marie) on the southern Michigan peninsula, and at this gathering the Neutrals and Tobacco Nation refugees had two thousand warriors—probably that number of people, not warriors alone. These refugees wintered at *Sken'ch'o'e* (Fox Place) in the direction of *Teo'chanontion,* which was probably the Detroit neighborhood. The name Fox Place probably indicates the location or former center of the Fox tribe, just as the name Panther Place indicated the center of the Panther or Erie nation.[10]

It was probably at this time of panic flight, after the Iroquois destroyed the Hurons and Neutrals, that the Algonquian tribes of the southern Michigan peninsula fled westward into Wisconsin. Indeed, the *Jesuit Relations* state that the Algonquians fled from Michigan

---

[9] Some writers state that when Nicolet visited the Winnebagoes, he left them and went toward the south and west to visit the Illini; but there seems to be no basis for this claim. It was after Nicolet's visit that Lake Michigan was given the name of Lake of the Illinois because that tribe lived near its shores, and in 1642 the Jesuits reported that the Illini dwelled near the southern shore of this lake and were constantly at war with the Sioux in the west.

[10] Thwaites, *Jesuit Relations* for 1653, quoted in Hodge, *Handbook of Indians North of Mexico,* II, 62. It is possible that the place where the Neutrals and Tobacco Nation wintered was the location of the Potawatomis. The place was *A'otonatendie,* and the Iroquoian name for the Potawatomis was *Atowateany* or *Ondatouatandy.* After 1750, the Wyandots, who were surviving Hurons, called the Potawatomis *Undatomatandi.*

in fear of the Iroquois. These Algonquians of Michigan are not known to have suffered from Iroquois raids prior to 1648. Their trouble was due to the persistent attacks of the strong Neutral and Ottawa tribes.

It was at this period, around 1640, that the French began to hear reports concerning the Sioux, a powerful and warlike tribe in the west, feared by neighboring tribes and termed, by the French, the Iroquois of the West. The Sioux, judging by archaeological evidence, must have been in Minnesota from middle Woodland times, the period of the Ohio Mound Builders. They were evidently a marginal people, crude folk, wandering hunters and fishermen, who took little share in the cultural development of the tribes east of the Mississippi. They had no big settlements, no notable earthworks; but they did learn to make crude pottery, and they adopted some of the Mound Builder religion and burial customs, placing their dead in small conical mounds.

It was evidently the Algonquian war with the Winnebagoes that brought the Sioux to the notice of the French. We do not know exactly what happened; but the Sioux were clearly engaged in these events, and the rather vague language of the Radisson narrative tells us that the Ojibwas, like the Ottawas, were engaged at the period (1600–30) in trading French goods to western tribes, that they became involved in a war with the Sioux, and, evidently, were driven east into the Sault Ste Marie lands. The other French reports, that the Sioux drove the Illinis eastward to Lake Michigan, probably refer to events after the Winnebago war, when the Illinis and some other Algonquians advanced westward to the Mississippi, became involved with the Sioux, and were driven back eastward. The Sioux evidently followed the Algonquians, for in 1670 the Jesuits reported that the lands around Lake Winnebago were uninhabited because of Sioux raids into the district.

The early French accounts gave the Sioux a high reputation. The Sioux, it was said, kept their promises better than the more sophisticated tribes to the east of them. They were fine warriors; but they did not attack neighboring tribes, except in retaliation for attacks on their own people, and they did not have the nasty eastern Indian custom of torturing prisoners at the stake and then cooking and eating them. In fact, they were simple folk, and the Algonquians seem to have despised them as bumpkins who had never seen a white man and were so ignorant that they did not even know that furs were valuable.

The *Jesuit Relations* for 1642, giving the first vague reports concerning the Sioux, stated that the tribe grew only a little maize and tobacco and that they had about thirty villages; but from later reports it seems that only one village was a permanent one and that the others were hardly more than camps, moving from place to place seasonally. The Sioux lived near the head of the Mississippi, in a land of lakes, marshes, and forest, and the marshes contained vast areas of wild rice. The Sioux, mostly wanderers and hunters, were not tempted to settle down and cultivate crops, for they could obtain wild rice by going into the marshes when the grain was ripe, pulling the tall plants over a canoe, and shaking the rice off. They put the rice into leather bags and trampled it to separate the grain from the chaff. Wherever they went in their moving camps, they had a supply of wild rice in sacks, and that was better food than maize. After 1650, some of the Sioux seem to have grown little patches of maize, and they are reported to have planted small tobacco gardens. Autumn was the time for wild-rice harvesting. In March, when the snow was usually still on the ground, the streams just beginning to thaw, and the wildfowl winging in from the south, the Sioux went to maple groves and made sugar. This was the season when food was often very scarce, and sometimes the Sioux families lived for weeks on maple sugar and little else. As late as 1800, certain Sioux families claimed particular maple groves as their property, asserting that they alone had the right to make sugar from the sap of the trees in these groves.[11]

It was no compliment to the Sioux that the Jesuits termed them the Iroquois of the West. Like the Iroquois, the Sioux made war on their neighbors, but Sioux war consisted of small raids with occasional heavy attacks and lacked entirely the grim purpose of the Iroquois, to exterminate their enemies. The Sioux seem not to have been guiltless of the two worst Iroquoian practices, torturing enemies to death and holding cannibalistic feasts, but there was little resemblance between the two tribes. The Iroquois were culturally advanced. They lived in well-organized communities, in strongly fortified villages, and were deeply interested in crop-growing. The Sioux were a crude people, who lived in wandering camps. These two tribes resembled each

[11] Blair, *Indian Tribes of the Upper Mississippi*, II, 32–33; Thwaites, *Jesuit Relations* for 1642, chap. 12.

other only in being feared by neighboring tribes and in the fact that they both had seen the wisdom of forming leagues or confederacies to maintain peace among themselves. By tradition, the Sioux had formed the Seven Council Fires, comparable to the Iroquois Five Fires; but the Sioux did not make use of their united strength, as the Iroquois did, to "eat" all the neighboring nations. There seems to be only one instance in these early times of the Sioux torturing a captive to death, and the victim evidently deserved his fate. An Ottawa chief, he invited a Sioux chief to bring his family on a visit to the Ottawa village, then treacherously killed them and made a cannibal feast of their flesh. This story will be set down in more detail farther on in our narrative.

The Iroquois were now obtaining a regular supply of firearms from the Dutch of New York. The tribes supplied by the French were almost without firearms, except for a few, like the Ottawas, who traded regularly and had become well acquainted with French weapons. Most of the tribes had a low opinion of these weapons. They said that a good man could loose eight or ten arrows while a man with a gun was firing one shot. But the Iroquois prized their guns and employed them with much effectiveness. By 1643 they had four hundred guns.

The Jesuits were very happy over their small successes among the Hurons, and they were planning to start missions among the Neutrals and the Tobacco Nation. The latter tribe, closely related to the Hurons, lived in nine villages to the west of the Hurons, in a mountainous district near the south shore of Georgian Bay, Ontario. The Hurons had been at war with them for many years, but had made peace, about 1640. Angry with the Jesuits, whom they accused of bringing pestilence into their country and killing over half of their people in a decade, the Hurons spread false reports about the priests to prevent their going among the Neutrals and the Tobacco Nation. Still, the Jesuits persisted in their plans for the new missions.

Then the Iroquois took a hand in the proceedings. The Huron, and also the Jesuit, line of communications with the French settlements at Quebec and Montreal was along the St. Lawrence waterway. The Iroquois blockaded that route by sending war parties, partly armed with guns, to ambush all canoes going down or up the river. The plan was carefully and shrewdly made. One war party would block the river for a certain period; then a second party would come and relieve the first, which would return home. It was almost impossible for any travelers to escape the Iroquois ambushes, and the French seemed powerless to do anything about it. Meanwhile, lurking groups of Iroquois infested the Huron country, and every day Huron women were being killed while at work in their cornfields. If the Hurons got on a trail and pursued the small group that had murdered some women, the pursuers fell into a clever Iroquois ambush and were destroyed.

The Jesuits reported little of this and continued to write of bright prospects for enlarging the mission field until 1643, when they had to report that the Iroquois had captured Father Isaac Jogues and two French mission servants on their way to Montreal. The Indians also captured the manuscript for the *Jesuit Relations* of that year, and the Jesuits among the Hurons became suddenly aware of the serious situation. They complained bitterly that no traveler was now safe on the St. Lawrence, and the Hurons and Algonquians, having had their trading fleets of canoes attacked and plundered, were giving up the practice of going down the river, to trade. With communications cut, both the missions and the Indian trade would be destroyed. Father Jogues escaped from the Iroquois, with the aid of friendly Dutchmen, and was sent home to Europe in a ship; but the situation of the Jesuits among the Hurons remained critical.[12]

It is easy for us today to realize that the French had moved into the distant wilderness too rapidly and with too few men, that they should have built forts and set small garrisons along the St. Lawrence and in the Huron country. But pioneers have to work with what resources are at hand; and, with no aid from the government in France, the French in Canada had done the best that they could. The unfortunate Hurons were to pay most of the penalty. They needed armed Frenchmen and a French fort in their country, and they had nothing beyond a few missionaries, living in Indian huts and splitting the people into embittered factions by preaching a faith which most of the Hurons had no intention of accepting.

In 1644 the French officials released an Iroquois warrior who had been captured by French Indian allies and turned over to the officials. This Iroquois went home, and later came back to the French settle-

[12] Thwaites, *Jesuit Relations*, XXIII, 267–69; *ibid.*, XXIV, 281; *ibid.*, XXV, 63, 287.

ments with two Iroquois chiefs. They brought with them one of the Frenchmen who had been captured with Father Jogues, and the chiefs offered to make peace, a proposal that the French eagerly adopted. Later, Father Jogues came back from Europe; and, with peace restored, the Jesuits among the Hurons took new heart and resumed their labors with fresh vigor.

The Iroquois peace of 1645 was with the French, and not with the Indian allies of the French. It was a peace that left the Iroquois free to carry out their avowed purpose of "eating" their neighbors. In 1647 the Senecas captured and destroyed a large, fortified town of the Neutral Nation, butchering most of the people and carrying off hundreds of captives. In the summer of 1648, large war parties of Iroquois entered the Huron country. They were discovered and the alarm was given. The Hurons were supposed to be ready. They had a few towns fairly well fortified with stockades; but most of their fortified villages were only death traps, and many of the groups in the villages had no intention of standing an attack. They had already chosen hiding places in the forest and on islands in the lakes, and they were ready to flee the moment the alarm was given. That was what they did when the Iroquois attacked in July, 1648; but probably the majority of the people remained in the fortified villages and attempted to beat off the enemy. The Iroquois burst into three of the fortified towns, slaughtering the panic-stricken people and rounding up hundreds of women and children to be enslaved.[13]

Late that same autumn, a force of one thousand Iroquois, mostly Senecas and Mohawks, set out to complete the destruction of the Huron Nation. They spent the winter in the Huron forests without being discovered; and in March, 1649, they took the Hurons by surprise, capturing three more big fortified towns and executing the usual Iroquois program of slaughter, torture, and burning. They broke into groups and set off in pursuit of the Huron fugitives.[14]

Many of the Hurons fled westward to the villages of the Tobacco Nation; but the Iroquois found them, and in December the alarm was given among the Tobacco Nation towns that the enemy was approaching. The warriors of the Tobacco Nation assembled in the fortified towns, armed and painted for battle. Eager to fight the Iroquois, they paraded in their finery, put on war dances, and feasted;

13 Hodge, *Handbook of Indians North of Mexico*, I, 588.
14 Parkman, *The Jesuits in North America*, 374–77.

but no Iroquois appeared. The war captains held councils and decided to march out and attack the Iroquois in the forest. And so the Tobacco Nation warriors marched off into the forest, and from their hidden ambush the Iroquois watched them go. They waited until the warriors were too far off to be recalled, and then they burst out of the forest and rushed the fortified town they intended to take. They threw firebrands over the stockade and set the bark longhouses afire. They stormed the town and began a general slaughter, striking down women and old people and throwing children into the burning houses. They plundered the town and rounded up captives from among the young women and children, then vanished into the forest. As they marched, they ruthlessly killed any of the women and children who could not keep up the swift pace they set.[15]

Between July, 1648, and December, 1649, the Iroquois wolf packs had destroyed the Hurons and the Tobacco Nation as organized entities. They had stormed the principal towns and slaughtered most of the people in them, they had carried off into slavery great droves of women and children, and they had left the Huron land a smoking wilderness. The war machine of the Iroquois was as horribly effective as that of the Nazis in 1940, and it was built on the same principle of ruthlessness and the application of explosive force against enemies who were unprepared. Firearms did not play a large part in these Iroquois attacks. They used very large war parties, trained to attack with speed and force and to cause panic in the enemy towns by their ferocious deeds of inhuman cruelty. The Iroquois also made full use of the Nazi technique of lulling the enemy into a feeling of security by the making of peace treaties, which were only made to be broken.

The Jesuits were stunned by the Huron disaster. All their bright hopes for founding a Christian state in Huronia had been swept away as by a whirlwind; most of their Indians lay dead in the ruins of their towns, and the greater portion of the Hurons to whom they had taught Christian meekness had meekly surrendered to the Iroquois. In 1650 the Jesuits abandoned the whole mission field and retreated to the French settlements on the St. Lawrence. At Isle Orleans near Quebec they gathered a few surviving Hurons, mainly Christian converts, and started a little mission among them. The Iroquois came and with honeyed words urged the Hurons to leave the French and

15 *Ibid.*, 405–408.

come to live happily among the Iroquois. Some of the Hurons migrated to the Iroquois towns; the Iroquois then sent war parties to Isle Orleans and murdered most of the remaining Hurons there.

The Neutral Nation was next on the Iroquois schedule for destruction. There were about ten thousand people in the Neutral towns; and, as their lands lay between the Iroquois country and the Huron land, they had striven to remain neutral for many years, hoping thus to avoid destruction. The Iroquois excuse for attacking them was that they had committed the hostile act of permitting fleeing Hurons to settle among them. In the winter of 1651, an army of six hundred Mohawks and Senecas invaded the Neutral country. The attack was made in winter because the Iroquois had found that to be the season for making their onsets most effective. Now the Neutrals proved to be easy victims, as the Hurons had been. Their towns were taken with all the customary acts of Iroquois cruelty, and most of the survivors were carried off as captives to the Iroquois land.

The Iroquois now paused in their work of exterminating their neighbors. They still had to deal with two groups that in earlier times had fought and beaten them and even threatened their existence as free tribes, the hardy and brave Algonquians and the fierce Eries. But, before attempting to deal with these tougher foes, the Iroquois needed time to recruit their military strength; and in 1653 they made use of another favorite weapon, diplomacy. They sent their most dignified and smooth-talking chiefs to the French and to the Algonquians. The Iroquois chiefs blandly told the French officials that their nation had always felt friendly toward the French and that there was no reason why the French and Iroquois should not continue to be the best of friends. This was a little quaint, considering that in the past five years the Iroquois had destroyed the tribes who were the particular allies of the French, had broken up the French missions, ruined the French fur trade, and turned most of Upper Canada into a wilderness dotted with ruined Indian towns and deserted cornfields. The Iroquois chiefs did not overlook the Jesuits. They held out the bait of possible conversion of the Iroquois people and invited the Jesuits to come to their towns and start missions. So the French made peace with the Iroquois, and the Jesuits entered the new mission field, only to find that there was nothing for them among the Iroquois beyond the strong probability that they would find martyrdom at the stake. Meanwhile, the Iroquois made a pretended peace with part of the Algonquians, broke the peace, made another, and broke that. They kept this up until they were ready to deal with the Erie Nation.[16]

The Eries were probably the most numerous of the Iroquoian tribes that the Iroquois had set out to destroy, and they had better organization and leadership than the Hurons or Neutrals. In earlier times they had badly frightened the Iroquois by their fierce attacks; and, even after they had witnessed the destruction of the Hurons and Neutrals, they were not afraid of the Iroquois. The Dutch of New York knew the Eries and called them Satanas, which indicated that the Dutch regarded the Eries as much more dangerous than the Iroquois. In 1653, the Eries still had few guns and were reported to prefer the bow as a fighting weapon.

Large numbers of Hurons had fled for refuge to the Eries, and the Iroquois made use of this fact to threaten the Eries. They said that the Hurons were stirring up the Eries against them; but while they spoke publicly in this manner, they were secretly preparing to attack the Eries. An Iroquois chief told the French at Montreal in May, 1653, that his nation intended to spend the summer making war on the Eries.

The Eries sent thirty ambassadors to the Senecas to renew the peace agreement already in force. One of the Eries accidentally killed a Seneca man, and the Senecas in a fury massacred all but five of the Erie ambassadors, holding the surviving five as captives. This was too much for the proud Eries to bear meekly. They sent a force of warriors and stormed a Seneca town; they ambushed a big Iroquois war party returning from the Great Lakes and killed eighty of the best Iroquois warriors; they sent war parties to lurk at the very gates of the Iroquois towns, and one of these war parties caught and carried off one of the most famous Iroquois chiefs. The Iroquois had intended for a long while to attack the Eries. They were seeking for an excuse to do so, and the Eries certainly gave them some handsome excuses.

The Iroquois marched with eighteen hundred men, including hundreds of warriors armed with guns. They had made every possible preparation for this expedition, and one of their war captains had even permitted the Jesuits to baptize him. He made a quaint use of his newly acquired Christianity; he dressed himself as a Frenchman

[16] Perrot, in Blair, *Indian Tribes of the Upper Mississippi*, I, 192–95; Parkman, *The Jesuits in North America*, 437.

and sent messages to the Eries threatening to induce the god of the Christians to destroy them if they did not submit. The Eries were not impressed. They are said to have gathered three to four thousand warriors in their principal town of Rique, into which was also crowded a mass of women, children, and old men.

The Iroquois found that conquering the Eries was not the easy matter that conquest of the Hurons and Neutrals had been. The Eries defended the town of Rique valiantly; the Iroquois had to use all their military skill, and their losses were very heavy; but in the end, hurling firebrands to set the town afire, they stormed the stockades and burst in. The Erie warriors were killed, and then "the Onondagas entered the fort and there wrought such carnage among the women and children that blood was knee deep in certain places."[17] In this siege the Iroquois suffered such losses that they had to remain at Rique for two months, caring for their dead and wounded. They took terrible vengeance on the helpless Eries within their reach for the losses they had suffered.

It took the Iroquois a few months to destroy the Hurons and Neutrals; it required nearly four years for them to finish their work among the Eries. Hewitt believed that the Eries had about fifteen thousand people at this time. Of this number, only six hundred surrendered to the Iroquois. The rest were killed, captured, or escaped. Some of the Eries apparently retreated southward to the Ohio Valley, where they formed new settlements. French maps and the assertions of La Salle indicate this. The Iroquois had taken a large number of Erie women and children as captives, but they had butchered the greater part of the Erie Nation.

During the wars with the Hurons, Neutrals, and Eries, the Iroquois had doubled or even tripled their population by incorporating droves of captives into their five tribes. They were now very strong and masters of a vast tract of territory. They were raiding the tribes in southern New York, in New England, in Pennsylvania, Virginia, Michigan, and Ohio; and generally they were successful. They now possessed fifty times the territory they could occupy; but their passion for killing was insatiable, and they were making long journeys to attack the distant tribes that they lumped together under the general name of Ontwagonha, the Far Indians. There was only one group of tribes anywhere near that the Iroquois regarded as a potential

17 Hodge, *Handbook of Indians North of Mexico*, I, 431.

danger, the Upper Algonquians of the Great Lakes, and particularly the tribes among whom the Ottawas were leaders. The Ottawas were primarily trading Indians, firm allies of the French, taking French goods to tribes as far west as Wisconsin and Illinois. The main Ottawa center was on Ottawa River at first, and about 1653 they held lands to the north of the Hurons. To the west of them were two related groups. Ojibwas and Missisaugas, two wandering tribes of hunters and fishers whose center was along the north shore of Lake Huron. The Iroquois first attacked these two tribes and drove them farther west and north. This caused the Ottawas great concern. They felt isolated and in danger, and at least part of their people fled to Manitoulin Island in Lake Huron. This was at about the time when the remnants of the Neutrals and the Tobacco Nation fled to the southern peninsula of Michigan, to seek refuge among the Algonquian tribes there, in 1652 or the following year. The Iroquois kept sending war parties against these tribes, and presently they sent (1654?) eight hundred warriors against the Ottawas; but that tribe was warned by scouts, and they fled in canoes from Manitoulin Island to an island in the entrance of Green Bay, Wisconsin, where "they fortified themselves at a place called Mechingan."[18]

Obviously, it was not before Jean Nicolet came to Wisconsin but years later, in 1653–54, that the Algonquians of the Michigan peninsula removed to Wisconsin; and they did not go there as conquerors, as some writers suggest, but as refugees, fleeing from the Iroquois. They did not go to hem in the conquered Winnebagoes, but to seek refuge near that tribe, now again growing in strength. The Potawatomis were evidently one of the first tribes to flee from Michigan. They went to an island in the entrance of Green Bay, which was later called Potawatomi Island. Then the fleeing Ottawas came to live on an island here, and the Tobacco Nation refugees from the Michigan peninsula came and settled on an island near the Potawatomis and Ottawas. Some French accounts state that these Indians were all on Potawatomi Island in the entrance to Green Bay, that the Potawatomis left the island and settled on the mainland at the head of the bay, and that the Ottawas and Tobacco Nation then held Potawatomi Island for a brief period.

[18] Perrot, in Blair, *Indian Tribes of the Upper Mississippi*, I, 153–56, 196–98; Hodge, *Handbook of Indians North of Mexico*, I, 588; Warren Upham, "Groseilliers and Radisson," *Minnesota Historical Society Collections*, Vol. X, part 2, 522–25.

This was the situation in eastern Wisconsin about 1652–53. These refugee Algonquians were waiting in fear to see what the Iroquois would do; and at this time the Illini started warring on the Miamis, their close kinsmen, who had evidently pushed westward from the southern end of Lake Michigan into northern Illinois, which was now occupied by the Illini. That tribe now attacked the Miamis and drove part of them northward to the lands west of Lake Winnebago, where they joined the Mascoutens.[19]

Radisson and his brother-in-law, Groseilliers, were in Wisconsin in 1654, the only Frenchmen recorded in the area since Nicolet had been there years before. Radisson's narrative is often vague and confused; but he mentions being among the Potawatomis, Ottawas, Hurons, and Mascoutens. He says that he and Groseilliers were among the Mascoutens in the late winter of 1654–55 and set off in search of a group of five hundred Tobacco Nation Hurons, who had fled to the Mississippi. The French accounts state that these Tobacco Hurons, fleeing from the Iroquois, went among the Illini. Perhaps that tribe was not particularly friendly toward the alien Hurons. At any rate, the fugitives now crossed the Mississippi and sought refuge among the Iowas in the buffalo prairies. This is supposed to have been when the Iowas had their village on Upper Iowa River, in northeastern Iowa. The Hurons (forest Indians) were very unhappy in the treeless prairies among the buffalo herds. They soon left the Iowas, went up the Mississippi, and built a temporary village on the island in the upper end of Lake Pepin, the wide stretch of the Mississippi near the present town of Red Wing, Minnesota. The Tobacco Hurons had evidently reached this island in 1654, as Radisson states that, in the spring of 1655, these Indians were newly arrived on the island and were without much corn because they had not had time to put in a crop.[20]

Afraid as they were of the Iroquois, these refugee Hurons, Tobacco Hurons, and Ottawas in the west continued to venture eastward to

19 W. C. Temple, "Indian Villages of the Illinois Country," *Illinois State Museum, Scientific Papers,* Vol. II, part 2, is the authority for the driving of the Miamis north into Wisconsin.

20 These Tobacco Hurons and their Ottawa friends apparently fled westward when the Iroquois destroyed the Hurons, before 1650. The *Jesuit Relations* for 1652–53 records that part of the Tobacco Hurons had fled to the Illinois country before that date.

trade with the French, and it was with one of their canoe fleets that Radisson and his brother-in-law set out from the French settlements for the upper country in 1654. The Iroquois now had the old route to the west blocked. The Indians the two Frenchmen were with left the St. Lawrence, went up Ottawa River, and on by Lake Nipissing into Lake Huron. They came to the Straits of Mackinac, and here heard of the Potawatomis and Mascoutens. In late winter, 1654–55, the Frenchmen went with Indians to the Mascouten village in Wisconsin.

Radisson's narrative was written in London, some years later. He had fled from Canada and joined the English. He evidently wrote his story to impress the officials and merchants in London, in the hope of obtaining employment in the English trade on Hudson Bay. His story is vague in many places, often confused, and one suspects that he at times resorted to pure fabrication. But the story can be checked with the brief account in the *Jesuit Relations,* which lacks detail but gives reliable dates and an honest account of the movements of Radisson and Groseilliers.[21]

When Radisson came into eastern Wisconsin, the refugee Hurons and Tobacco Hurons were in at least two groups, part near Green Bay and part on the Mississippi. The ones in eastern Wisconsin were those who had gone east to trade with the French and had returned home in the late summer of 1654. They and the two Frenchmen had stocks of French trade goods; and, late in the winter of 1654–55, a party was made up to go to the Hurons on the Mississippi, probably to trade with them. Radisson and Groseilliers went with this party of 150 Hurons or Tobacco Hurons. They had one Ottawa man with them. They went on snowshoes, men and women, "thwarting the land," to a river, where they camped for three weeks, hunting and making canoes. It is generally believed that this journey was from the Green Bay area to Wisconsin River, and that they now went up the Mississippi. Radisson states that they went up the river for eight days and then came to two sedentary tribes that grew crops. His spelling of tribal names is atrocious. He calls these tribes the "Pontonatenick" and "Mantonenock." They were certainly the Iowas and Otoes, and this is the first recorded meeting of white men with these

---

[21] Radisson, *Voyages of Peter Esprit Radisson.* An excellent study of Radisson's movement in Wisconsin and Minnesota, written by Upham, is in *Minnesota Historical Collections,* Vol. X, part 2.

tribes. The tribal name, as written by Radisson, had the Algonquian ending *uc*, which Radisson renders *nock* or *nick*. He used the M for W and his Mantonenock are surely the Matotenta or Watotenta, the old name for the Otoes. Pontonatenick evidently comes from Paoutet, the native name of the Iowas for their people. Radisson states that this nation was called the Scratchers. The Iowas were at times called the Dusty Ones, and one is reminded of the name Oglala among the Teton Sioux. It refers to scattering dust, to digging the ground and planting; and the Iowa nickname might have had the same origin. Tribes that were too primitive to cultivate crops usually jeered at those who did, saying that they were scratchers of Mother Earth's skin, dust-throwers. The fact that the Tobacco Hurons are said to have taken refuge among the Iowas seems to be a confirmation of Radisson's assertion that he found the Iowas and Otoes on the Mississippi, below the island on which the Hurons were located, in the spring of 1655.[22]

It was spring when the Radisson party came to the Iowas and Otoes. These Indians must have been in their permanent villages; for they had a big supply of maize, enough to trade to Radisson's party of over 150 persons all the maize needed for the rest of the journey up the river. Leaving these Indians, the party went on and presently came to the island on which the Tobacco Hurons had taken refuge. Radisson calls this the "first landing isle." Perrot says that it was Isle Pelee, Bald Island, the Prairie Island of today, in the upper end of Lake Pepin. The only known Indian village remains on this island are of what the archaeologists term Blue Earth culture. In all probability these are the remains of an Oto or Iowa village of late prehistoric times. The stay of the Hurons and Ottawas on the island was probably brief.

As soon as they reached the Hurons on the island, Radisson and his brother-in-law began to urge the chiefs to organize a strong party

---

22 It is often stated that at this period the Iowas were on Upper Iowa River in northeastern Iowa. Upham, evidently estimating eight days' travel up the Mississippi from the mouth of the Wisconsin, stated that Radisson found the two tribes, the Iowas and Otoes, in the vicinity of the present Winona, Minnesota, which is far above Upper Iowa River. However, the whole stretch of the Mississippi, from below the Wisconsin River to the Winona vicinity and even farther north, is clearly the old center of the Iowa and Oto group; and the whole district is dotted with village ruins, mounds, and other Siouan remains.

to go with the two white men to the French settlements on the St. Lawrence. The Hurons were badly in need of French goods, but the chiefs were almost horrified at this proposal. They said that the route to the French was blocked by the Iroquois, and their men and women, if they went, would all be killed. They said that Radisson and Grose-illiers must wait a year, then they would all go to the French.

These Tobacco Hurons were forest Indians. Their people had dwelt for a long time in the forests of the lower Great Lakes living in permanent villages, growing crops, and specializing in growing tobacco. They were said by the French to be poor hunters and poor canoemen, since they stayed at home most of the time. They obtained meat and skins from the Algonquians, who were wandering hunters, coming to the Huron towns seasonally to trade forest products for maize, vegetables, and tobacco. Having fled from the Iroquois to the upper Mississippi, these Hurons were in a strange environment, among tribes speaking alien tongues, who lived mostly in the prairies and hunted the buffalo. There were only about five hundred of the Hurons, a weak group, and they were having to beg for aid and seek protection from alien peoples. They had probably applied first to the Illinis and finding that tribe far from friendly had gone across the Mississippi, among the Iowas and Otoes. Now they were trying to plant crops on their island and attempting to obtain food by hunting.

Radisson states that he and Groseilliers spent the summer hunting with some Indians. They went for four months from river to river and met many tribes. It was probably from information he picked up among these Mississippi River Indians that he made the narrative of his pretended travels among the southern tribes.[23] That winter

[23] There is little that is incredible in what Radisson put into his account of the southern tribes, if he meant those down the Mississippi and on the lower Missouri and the lower Ohio. He said that the tribes were sedentary, living almost wholly on maize, pumpkins, and fish; using fishbone and other bone to tip their arrows; using wooden dishes and doing fine carving in wood, and having great red and green stone calumet pipes. His statement that these southern Indians were giants and that when they saw little people, men of ordinary size, they cried out and were afraid, is a form of tradition of the Iroquois and of tribes like the Arikaras who lived on the Missouri in the nineteenth century. Radisson probably picked up these tales at Green Bay or during the summer of 1655, when he was hunting with the tribes west of the Mississippi. His assertion that he met the southern tribes is probably false.

(1655–56), Groseilliers stayed in the Huron village on the island, trading for corn to be kept for the journey back to the St. Lawrence in the following spring. Radisson evidently went hunting, to obtain meat and furs. In the spring of 1656, about one thousand Indians assembled on the island, and the chiefs selected a large body of hardy men and women to make the long and dangerous canoe voyage to Montreal. After many adventures on the way, Radisson and Groseilliers reached the French settlement with thirty canoes, loaded with Hurons and furs, in August, 1656.

These Tobacco Hurons certainly returned home to the island on the Mississippi in safety. Meantime, the other group of their people, who had been living on an island in the entrance to Green Bay, decided to move to the mainland, to a point at the head of this bay near the Potawatomi village. Here, in 1657, they built a village surrounded by a strong stockade. They had been there only a few months when a party of six Iroquois appeared and boldly entered the village. The Hurons received them with assumed friendliness; but one Huron chief, Anahotaha, made a plot, and he and his followers took the six Iroquois by treachery and murdered them. The Hurons then became alarmed, fearing a larger party of Iroquois would come to the village, seeking vengeance. They deserted their handsome new village, the main body of people fleeing to join the Hurons on the island in the Mississippi. Chief Anahotaha and his followers fled eastward and sought protection among the French on the St. Lawrence. There, in 1659, he with forty of his warriors joined an expedition of seventeen Frenchmen and a few Algonquian warriors. At the Long Sault on Ottawa River, this force was ambushed by seven hundred Iroquois, and all were killed except five Frenchmen and four Hurons.[24]

Nicolas Perrot must have obtained his information from the Ottawas, and he featured that tribe's adventures on the upper Mississippi. He states that, fleeing from the Iroquois, they went to the river of the Iowas and up it to its head in the prairies, where they met friendly native tribes; but they hated the prairies and the buffalo herds and soon went to Isle Pelee on the Mississippi and built a village there. Then the Sioux came to visit them. Perrot brings in the Tobacco Hurons after all this had happened; but the *Jesuit Relations* and Radis-

24 Hodge, *Handbook of Indians North of Mexico*, I, 589.

son seem to indicate that the Hurons were the more important group and the Ottawas a minor one.

However, these Woodland Indians were now visited by the Sioux, who came to the village weeping. This was an ancient Siouan custom, to weep copiously as an indication of joy when meeting important strangers, but the Woodland Indians probably set the Sioux down as simpletons. The Tobacco Hurons and Ottawas were sophisticates; they were familiar with the French and were equipped with French articles, including guns. They cheated the simple Sioux in trading for their furs and other products, giving them trinkets and a few French knives, hatchets, and sewing awls. They fired their guns to frighten the Sioux, and probably succeeded. The Sioux had never seen a gun; they said the men who had them carried thunder in their hands, and thunder was a very terrible and deadly thing.

It is clear that the Hurons and Ottawas believed that they could have their will of the Sioux. They took every advantage short of violence, and then the Hurons took that final step. They caught a small group of Sioux alone on the prairie and murdered them. They cut the heads off the bodies and carried them away. Taking enemy heads as trophies was an Iroquois custom, and perhaps the Hurons hoped to persuade the Sioux that their kinsmen had been killed by the Iroquois. But the Sioux found the headless bodies of their kinsmen, and found signs on the ground pointing at the Hurons. They came on a small camp of Hurons in the prairie, captured them, and took them to the Sioux village. The Sioux kept the prisoners for a time, then the chief released them. Perrot stated that this was the usual Sioux custom, the Sioux being generous to captured enemies; but perhaps the Sioux were still in awe of the Huron and Ottawa guns and were unwilling to cause open war.

Being what they were, the Hurons and Ottawas regarded the release of the captives as a plain indication that the Sioux were afraid of them. These Woodland refugees had been treated with kindness by the tribes they found west of the Mississippi, but they probably felt no gratitude. In their view, people who were kind were weak. They might have taken the lands of the Iowa tribe, but they hated the prairie country. The Sioux country was much more to their liking, a fine land, similar to their old home near Lake Huron, a land of forest, lake, and marsh, teeming with game and fish. They now decided to conquer the Sioux, drive them out, and take their country.

They started by making a surprise attack on a small Sioux village. It was to be the usual Woodland affair—capture the village, slaughter the people, and produce panic among the Sioux; but the attack had hardly started when Sioux warriors came swarming out of nearby villages like angry bees and violently assaulted the attackers, defeating them and forcing them to retire. More and more Sioux came from other villages. They chased the Hurons and Ottawas back to their island village, where the frightened Woodland Indians worked frantically to fortify their village, to protect themselves from the Sioux. The Sioux did not assault the island. Instead, they kept sending small war parties to lurk near the island and to attack any group of Hurons or Ottawas who might venture out. They apparently made it impossible for the Woodland Indians to leave the island to go hunting or for any other purpose; and, after holding out for a time, the Hurons fled up Black River, an eastern tributary of the Mississippi, and built a village surrounded by a strong stockade near the head of this stream. The Ottawas from the island joined other members of their tribe, who had already built a village on the south shore of Lake Superior, at Chequamegon Bay.[25]

This was the situation about 1658. The dreaded Iroquois now took the field in Wisconsin and Illinois. Perrot says that the Ottawa and Huron bands that lived at Green Bay had defeated a small Iroquois force and had then fallen into a panic, fearing the Iroquois would come in great force against them. It was at this time that part of the Ottawas left Green Bay and removed farther west, establishing a village at Chequamegon Bay on the shore of Lake Superior. Father Jules Tailhan, the editor of Perrot, stated that the Iroquois war on the Illini and other western tribes dated from 1656 to 1667 and ended in the ruin of the Illinis, who fled west of the Mississippi. Hodge's *Handbook of Indians North of Mexico* used the date 1656 for the beginning of the Iroquois assaults on the Illinis, but the attacks before 1660 seem to have been made by small Iroquois parties. They alarmed the Indians of Illinois and Wisconsin, but did not do much harm.

25 This narrative of the Huron and Ottawa relations with the Sioux is mainly from Perrot, in Blair, *Indian Tribes of the Upper Mississippi*, I, 159–63. Tailhan, the editor of Perrot, noted that the *Jesuit Relations* for 1671 stated that the Tobacco Hurons and Ottawas fled to the Mississippi in 1652–53. This fits in with other French information.

It was about the year 1661 that the Iroquois sent a big force, eight hundred warriors, into Wisconsin. The French accounts of the expedition are not clear. Perrot states that the Iroquois force first went to a fortified Ottawa village and made peace with that tribe to keep them from interfering with their plan to attack other Algonquians. They then divided their force, sending part to attack the Ojibwas and Missisaugis, the other group to seek out the Foxes and Illinis. The latter force came into prairies where there were buffalo herds, clearly in Illinois. There were plenty of buffalo in Illinois at this date, and the Illini spent much of each year in the prairies, hunting buffalo. The Iroquois warriors, unused to prairie country and unfamiliar with the method of hunting buffalo, were bewildered, worn out, and hungry. But when they discovered a small camp of Illinis, they started a fierce attack on it. The Illini men fled; the Iroquois murdered the women and children. They then settled down in the captured camp to feast on the buffalo meat found in it and probably to eat the women and children they had killed, for it was the custom of these wolf packs to hold a cannibal feast in any camp they had taken. While they were feasting, parties of Illini warriors from a number of hunting camps came together, and took the Iroquois by surprise, and killed most of them. This, says Perrot, was the first contact of the Iroquois with the Illini.[26]

In the ensuing years, the Iroquois came back in force, again and again. They drove the Illini beyond the Mississippi, and evidently drove out at least part of the Miamis along with their Illini kinsmen. Perrot is not clear on all points; but he says that, when attacked by the Iroquois, the Wisconsin Indians and Illinis fled down the Wisconsin River and down the Mississippi, and he names the Kickapoos and Miamis as being among the fugitives. These Indians evidently went into eastern Iowa, into the lands south of those held by the Iowa and Oto tribes, perhaps down near the Cedar River, where Marquette noted part of the Illinis were living in 1673. We know from the reports of the Jesuits at La Pointe on Lake Superior that the Illini were still west of the Mississippi in 1670 and were making the long journey to the Ottawa Indian village near La Pointe to trade

[26] Perrot, in Blair, *Indian Tribes of the Upper Mississippi*, I, 165–67, 321; Temple, "Indian Villages of the Illinois Country," *Illinois State Museum Scientific Papers*, Vol. II, part 2, 14. The Illini flight beyond the Mississippi seems to date about 1665.

for guns and French goods. Perrot states that these Indians who had fled west of the Mississippi did not return to the east until he came to Green Bay with a large stock of trade goods, probably about the year 1670 or 1671.[27]

The Ottawas, by making peace with the Iroquois, had assured their own safety, remaining neutral while the Iroquois slaughtered their Algonquian kinsmen. Moreover, the peace made it possible for the Ottawas and their Huron allies to make annual journeys to the French towns on the St. Lawrence, to trade furs for French goods and guns. They then returned to their village on the shore of Lake Superior and spent the rest of the year trading French goods for furs with neighboring tribes. The Illinis came all the way from Iowa to trade with them, taking a trail that crossed the Mississippi south of the dangerous Sioux country. Thus, while Iroquois warred on the Illinis, that tribe obtained guns from the Ottawas.

Radisson and his brother-in-law, Groseilliers, took advantage of this situation; and, in the summer of 1659, they left Quebec with the Ottawa and Huron fleet of canoes and went with the Ottawas to their village on Chequamegon Bay. The two white traders spent the winter wandering among the Ottawas, Hurons, Sioux, and other tribes. Radisson wrote a long and rambling account of the Sioux, which is of little historical value. He found them warring with the Crees, who dwelt to the north. It was winter, and the Sioux and other tribes were wandering about, hunting. Radisson's journey to the Sioux of the Prairie is interesting primarily because it proves that this group was already in existence in 1659. The distance of this band from the Sioux of the other groups appears to have been grossly exaggerated by Radisson. His journeys were probably of only a few miles a day, and it is probable that the Sioux of the Prairie at that time were living in the prairies immediately west of the Mississippi, in the Sauk Rapids area.

Perrot informs us that at this period the Ottawas and Tobacco Hurons were still planning to destroy or drive out the Sioux and take their lands, but these ambitious conquerors were not Iroquois. They were few in number, and they lacked the Iroquois discipline, determination, and steadfast purpose. They were not even the equals of

[27] Father Allouez wrote in 1665 that the Illini, formerly very numerous occupants of ten large villages, were now west of the Mississippi and had been almost destroyed by the Iroquois. This seems to fix the date of the flight prior to 1665.

the Sioux in courage and skill at war. Their sole advantage lay in the firearms in their hands, and once the Sioux had gotten over the initial panic caused by the firing of these mysterious thunder-weapons, the Sioux, as Perrot tells us, offset the advantage the Hurons and Ottawas had in the use of guns by the employment of stratagems. They were better warriors than their attackers, braver and more skillful, and they probably had ten times the number of warriors their enemies had. Perrot gives details of these events, but without dates.

Part of the Sioux were living among the wild-rice marshes, between the Mississippi and the St. Croix River, to the north of the present city of St. Paul. Perrot speaks of the difficulty of attacking the Sioux effectively in this location, a land of lake and marsh, with only narrow strips of dry land here and there; and without canoes an attacking force could hardly operate at all. The Sioux were living in tiny villages of five or six families each, scattered through the marshes. They had canoes, usually described as dugouts, which was the type of boat used by southern tribes. The Hurons and Ottawas had canoes for use on their annual journeys to Quebec to trade, but they could not take their bark canoes overland for use against the Sioux.

The Huron and Ottawa plan for conquering the Sioux was to send small war parties to kill a few Sioux or carry off a few women and children. Even in this nuisance warfare, the invaders of the Sioux lands had little success. Perrot tells of one party of ten Huron warriors who set out to collect scalps and captives. They became involved in the maze of lakes and marshes, and while they were floundering about, the Sioux discovered them. The alarm swiftly spread to little Sioux villages, dotted all around the edges of the great marsh, and some three thousand Sioux, on foot and in canoes, set out to hunt for the unhappy Hurons. But the Hurons had vanished, each man of the ten going his own way, and most of them were lying hidden in the wild rice or reeds with only their noses showing above water. The Sioux leaders held a council and ordered their men to get the nets that were used in catching beavers. They had these nets strung across all the narrow paths through the marsh, with hawk bells obtained in trade from the Ottawas tied to the nets. That night the Sioux waited silently in their boats until they heard the bells attached to the nets tinkling; then they landed parties on each side of the spot where the bells had sounded and caught all the Hurons, who were creeping on hands and knees along the narrow ridges of dry land. Perrot and the Jesuits have much to say concerning the kind of treatment the Sioux showed to captive enemies; but on this occasion the Sioux took the Hurons to their villages, tied them to trees or posts, and left them to serve as targets for the small boys' archery practice. Nine Hurons were thus disposed of. The tenth, named Le Froid (Cold Man), escaped to tell the tale. Perrot's editor, Tailhan, says that this event occurred in 1662 or 1663. It seems to be a fair example of the Huron method of warring on the Sioux.[28]

One war party of Hurons captured a small number of Sioux and brought them to the Ottawa village at Chequamegon Bay. The Hurons were going to kill their captives and have a cannibal feast, but the Ottawas intervened, obtaining the release of the captives. This was in 1665 or 1666. The Ottawas and four Frenchmen now accompanied the captives to the Sioux country to open trade with that tribe. The Ottawas were keen traders. At this period, about 1665, they discovered tribes north of Lake Superior who had never seen a white man or any European goods. The Ottawas traded to these simple natives worn-out French knives, hatchets, and metal kettles for rich stocks of furs. But among the Sioux, the Ottawas had poor pickings. They found to their disgust that this barbarous tribe ate beavers without first skinning them and preserving the valuable fur. They had the same habit as the Siouan tribes of the Ohio Valley; they singed the fur off the beaver and then roasted the animal in its skin. The only beaver fur they usually had was what they wore as winter robes, and this fur often became ragged and very dirty before the Sioux were willing to trade their discarded winter garments to the Ottawas or Frenchmen.[29]

The Ottawas and Tobacco Hurons of Chequamegon Bay numbered about fifteen hundred, of which about five hundred were Hurons. The Jesuits had formed a mission among these Indians at La Pointe after 1660, Father Allouez laboring among them for some years, and Marquette then took over. Some of the Hurons had been baptized in their old country east of Lake Huron before the destruction of the Huron nation by the Iroquois; but most of the Hurons at Chequamegon were heathens, and practically all of the Ottawas scorned

28 Perrot, in Blair, *Indian Tribes of the Upper Mississippi*, I, 166–69.

29 *Ibid.*, 181. The statement that the tribes along the Ohio singed their beaver and roasted them in the skin was made by English traders around 1670.

the teachings of the priests and were thoroughgoing savages. They were very shrewd traders and good warriors in their fashion, but not fit to face the Iroquois in battle or, as it turned out, the Sioux either. The Ottawas at Chequamegon belonged to the Sinago or Black Squirrel clan and to the Kishkakon or Pike clan. These refugee Indians at Chequamegon had five small villages. Marquette had little success in spreading the gospel among them; but he was casting long-ing eyes at the great Sioux nation and at the Illini, who had been driven by the Iroquois beyond the Mississippi but were coming to Chequamegon to trade with the Ottawas and Hurons. Marquette hopefully presented some Sioux chiefs with colored holy pictures, telling them, among other things, that these pictures meant that they must keep peace with the Ottawas and Hurons. This the Sioux tried faithfully to do.

Little good came of that. The Sioux were willing to be friendly with the Woodland refugees, and one of their chiefs was very hos-pitable to a Sinago Ottawa chief, who was trading in the Sioux camp. The Sinago then invited the Sioux chief to visit his village at Che-quamegon. There would be feasting and gift-giving. The Sioux chief went there with a party of four of his relatives. The wily Sinago received the Sioux with every mark of friendship, then had them murdered and their flesh cooked. He then invited his friends to a cannibal feast.[30]

The Sioux now went to war. So did the Ottawas and Hurons. They had revived their old ambition, to destroy the Sioux and take the Sioux lands for their own home. Now, in 1669–70, they had a master plan. They were going to copy the methods of the Iroquois wolf packs, take the Sioux by surprise with a great force, slaughter them, and take their lands. Part of the Ottawas and Hurons went to Quebec to trade for arms and other supplies; part traded with Joliet, who was at the Sault Ste Marie at the entrance into Lake Superior with a big stock of guns and goods, in the fall of 1669 and on into the spring of 1670. Thus the two men who were to immortalize their names in 1673 by exploring the Mississippi were in the Lake Superior country in 1669–70, Marquette striving to promote Christianity, Joliet trading guns and abetting the Ottawas and Hurons in their plan to destroy the Sioux.

[30] The story of the Sinago chief's treachery and the cannibal feast is recorded by Perrot, in Blair, *Indian Tribes of the Upper Mississippi*, I, 188.

Being few in number, probably not able to put more than three hundred men under arms, the Ottawas and Hurons were seeking allies among the Algonquian tribes, among the Sacs, Foxes, and Potawatomis. They sent parties to these tribes, to bribe the chiefs with gifts of guns and French goods, and in this manner, as Perrot relates, they collected a force of one thousand men, mostly armed with guns, all with excellent French knives and tomahawks. The Sioux still used flint weapons, only a few of the men having iron knives and hatchets.

The invasion of the Sioux land came in late summer or early winter. The Ottawas and Hurons had been on the St. Lawrence in early summer with their fleet of canoes laden with furs. They had traded at Montreal and had then come home to harvest their crops. They had then taken all their people, including women and children, westward into Sioux land, and with them moved the Sac camp and other allies. At first their invasion went according to plan. They surprised and took some small Sioux villages, the Sioux men fleeing, the women and children being captured. But the Sioux men went to other villages and spread the alarm, and the Sioux warriors assembled with such speed that they caught the invaders while engaged in building a fort, in which they intended to shelter their women and children and their captives while continuing the conquest of the Sioux. The Sioux, attacking with reckless courage, threw them into a panic and sent them off into the forest in headlong flight. Perrot was probably exaggerating when he stated that nearly all the invaders perished, those who escaped the Sioux dying of hunger in the woods. They had been forced to drop everything, including food, equipment, and even arms, in their panicky rush to escape. The Potawatomis and Foxes were the first to flee, horrified by the numbers and fierceness of the Sioux; and most of the warriors of these two tribes escaped. Some fugitives, when they began to starve, killed companions and ate them.

The chief of the Sinago Ottawas, who had treacherously killed and made a cannibal feast of the Sioux chief and his four companions, was fleeing in company with his brother-in-law, a Sac chief, when they were overtaken in the forest and captured by the Sioux. The Sioux carefully kept these two captives, took them to a big Sioux village, and tied them to stakes. They then tortured them, which was by all reports an almost unheard-of act for the Sioux. While torturing the

Sinago cannibal, they cut slices of flesh off his thighs, roasted them, and forced him to eat his own flesh. The Sioux shot the other male captives to death with arrows.

These details of the invasion of the Sioux country are all from Perrot, but there are brief confirmatory statements in the *Jesuit Relations* for 1669–71. The volume for 1671 states that last winter the Ottawas and Hurons were at war with the Sioux; and in the spring these two tribes, fearing that the Sioux would overwhelm them, hastily abandoned their villages at Chequamegon Bay and fled eastward, the Hurons going to Mackinac Island, the Ottawas going farther east, to Manitoulin Island in Lake Huron. Marquette abandoned his mission near Chequamegon, at La Pointe, and followed the fleeing Hurons to Mackinac. Perrot was in the west at this time. He had been officially appointed to assemble the tribes and hold a great ceremony of taking possession of the Upper Lakes lands in the name of the King of France. He seems to have gone to Green Bay and to other Indian centers, coaxing the chiefs to attend the ceremonies; but he could not find the Ottawas and Hurons, who had fled and concealed their new locations, and they did not attend the gathering of the clans when France formally took possession of all the western country.

This chapter has been written mainly from historical source materials. When we attempt to support the historical evidence by making use of modern archaeology, we at once find ourselves groping in a twilight land where nothing stands out clearly; and we are confused by archaeological dating, which the archaeologists themselves admit is largely conjectural. There is so much important and interesting material that the archaeologists have gotten together that it seems a pity that we cannot fit this material into a historical narrative; but generally that is the situation. The period that archaeology terms Cahokia Old Village is the time when the great southern Cahokian fort and town of Aztalan was built in the Winnebago lands to the south of Lake Winnebago. From the association of the Winnebagoes with these Cahokian Indians came the new cultural aspect called Oneota, and in that time the Winnebagoes were at the height of their cultural development and their power. From the view of history, this is the period 1600–40, and the development of the great Oneota center in western Wisconsin, near the mouth of Wisconsin River and across the Mississippi in southeastern Minnesota and northeastern Iowa, we might presume was of this dating; but this western Oneota culture continued to develop, even after the year 1700, whereas the Winnebago Oneota culture seems to have been struck a shattering blow when the Ottawas, Illinis, and other Algonquian tribes defeated and, for a time, dispersed the Winnebago Nation. Meanwhile, the southern Indians of Cahokia developed out of the early or Old Village stage into a late cultural period, called by archaeology the Trappist period.

In southeastern Minnesota we have some apparently less advanced and less widely spread archaeological aspects, termed Blue Earth, Silvernale, and Cambria. They are all obviously the work of Siouans of the Winnebago groups. Some archaeologists term them Iowa tribal remains, while others prefer to conjecture that these remains are of the Oto tribe. The fact that these cultural remains seem cruder than Oneota has led some archaeologists to date them very early; but Cambria is certainly of late date, contemporary in part with Oneota. For all we know, these aspects in southeastern Minnesota may be the remains of less advanced Iowa or Oto groups, who for their own reasons did not take up the higher cultural features of Oneota. The Sioux, a bit farther north, were still in a crude state of cultural development in 1670.

Neither history nor archaeology provides an answer to the question about the fate of the great Cahokian centers along the Mississippi in Illinois, mainly south of Illinois River. These great southern Indian centers were still thriving in the Trappist period, which admittedly has a dating after the year 1640. Trappist is the time when the Illinis invaded northern Illinois and probably drove some of the southern Indians from Illinois River Valley. What occurred after that is a mystery. In time archaeology may be able to demonstrate what was the fate of the southern Indians of Cahokia, whether they were destroyed or driven southward or incorporated into the Illini confederacy. At present what slight evidence we possess seems to suggest that the Algonquian Illinis at first occupied only northern Illinois, particularly the valley of Illinois River, leaving the part of the state southward along the Mississippi to the southern Indians. Archaeology shows that these Cahokians still held the lands along the Mississippi in Illinois near the end of prehistoric times, by which is meant here a date around 1665 or even 1670. Therefore, if these Indians were driven out, it was almost certainly by the Iroquois. Some apparently fled across the Mississippi into Iowa; the Michigameas fled down the river into northern Arkansas.

The French statements, particularly those in the *Jesuit Relations,* suggest that the Illinis did not conquer or drive out the Cahokians, but mingled with them. The other Algonquian tribes detested the Illinis. This might have been because they had mingled with the alien Cahokia tribes and adopted some of their manners and beliefs. The *Jesuit Relations* assert that the Illinis were not like the other Algonquians; that they were docile where the others were fierce; that they were sun worshipers and did not have the dream religion of the Algonquians; and that they had a peculiar manner of cutting and arranging their hair that was not like that of the Algonquians. These French statements hint that the Illini had lived for a considerable period with or near the Cahokian Indians and had adopted many of their ways. It may be, however, that the French were describing the Cahokian tribes under the name of Illini, neglecting to note that part of the Illini tribes were Algonquian in type and customs.

CHAPTER SEVEN

East Wind II

AFTER THE IROQUOIS had destroyed the Hurons, the Tobacco Nation Hurons, the Neutrals, and the Eries (all nations of their own blood and language), they turned with unabated thirst for killing and conquest to the destruction of the Algonquian tribes of the upper Great Lakes and the tribes of the Ohio Valley.

In the last chapter a fairly detailed account of the Iroquois attacks on the Algonquian tribes was given. We now must turn to the Ohio country and attempt to follow the course of events there, from about the year 1600 to the end of the prehistoric period around 1680. It will be observed that, whereas, the historic period began in the Iroquois and Huron country before 1600 and started in the upper Great Lakes region before 1640, in the Ohio Valley prehistoric times continued until near the close of the seventeenth century. The reasons for this are that neither the French in Canada nor the English along the Atlantic coast obtained or recorded any definite information concerning the Indians in the Ohio country until about 1670, and that the archaeologists who have made most exhaustive studies of the Indian remains along the Ohio have failed to connect any known tribes with these village ruins, mounds, and cemeteries. They have made just one tentative attempt, by stating that probably the Shawnees had villages at Madisonville (Cincinnati), at the end of the prehistoric period, about 1665–70, and they base this view mainly on their having found a few handfuls of glass beads and small metal objects of European manufacture in graves at this location. After more than a century of labor, this is all that archaeology has achieved in the vital task of connecting known tribes with the Indian remains in the Ohio Valley.

In the earlier chapters of the present book it was maintained, on archaeological and other evidence, that in the early period, from Archaic on through early Woodland times, the native population of the Ohio country was wholly or mainly Siouan, and that the coming of a southern Indian group, termed the Adena folk by archaeologists, produced the Mound Builder or Hopewell culture, which was the work of the Adenas and of the native Siouan peoples. Then, late in the Mound Builder period, an invasion of Algonquians—Delawares, Shawnees, and others—combined with some Iroquoian groups, took control in the Ohio country, and Mound Builder culture was destroyed.

At the time when the Mound or Hopewell culture was beginning to disintegrate, archaeology records an intrusion into Ohio, apparently in the Scioto River area, of northern invaders, who took over some of the great Mound Builder centers and buried their dead intrusively in the old Hopewell mounds. The culture of this Intrusive Mound folk was mainly Iroquoian and has been traced to the lower Great Lakes region and also into the southern peninsula of Michigan. This intrusion may have been that recorded in the Delaware tradition, an invasion of the Ohio Valley by Algonquians in western Ohio, aided by Iroquoian allies, supposedly of the Huron or Erie group and not the Iroquois Proper. At the end of this intrusive period the Delaware group of tribes moved eastward across the Alleghenies. Some Iroquoians apparently remained, mostly in the Scioto country, and some Algonquians either remained in the Ohio country at that time or came down from the Great Lakes at a later period. A new cultural aspect developed in the Ohio Valley and has been termed Fort Ancient culture.

It is unfortunate that the archaeologists termed this latest cultural development Fort Ancient. This fort, a vast earthwork embracing one hundred acres of ground, is northeast of Cincinnati in Warren County, Ohio. It is a Mound Builder fortress. The nineteenth-century archaeologists gave the fortress the name of Fort Ancient; and, when village ruins were found near the fort, the culture in the villages was supposed to be of the same date as the fort, and thus the culture was called Fort Ancient. But it was later established that the Indian remains near the fort were not of the same period as the fort itself, but belonged to the most recent prehistoric period in the region.

Fort Ancient culture is of a lower type than the older Hopewell or Mound Builder culture. This culture is probably the work of a remnant of the old Mound Builder population and of the intrusive groups of Iroquoians and Algonquians, who had come into Ohio and mingled with remnants of the Mound Builder population. The intrusive burials in the old Hopewell mounds indicate this, and it is further suggested by the fact that the ruins of the Fort Ancient villages, which are in the old Mound Builder population centers, show that the Fort Ancient folk were exchanging pottery and other material with the Iroquoian Indians of the Whittlesey and Younge areas along the south shore of Lake Erie and in southern Michigan and northern Indiana. These Iroquoians, who were seemingly on good terms with the Intrusive Mound folk in Ohio, were almost certainly the Erie Nation.

At this period, when the Iroquoians of the north were intruding into the old Mound Builder area in Ohio, a second intrusion was coming from the south. This Mississippian intrusion was evidently very strong, and J. B. Griffin and other leading archaeologists have stated that without the help of Mississippian Indians the old population in the Ohio Valley could not have held out against the Iroquoian invasion from the north and Fort Ancient culture would never have developed. As it was, the Fort Ancient folk did hold out and developed a culture that was strongly Mississippian. This period of intrusion into the old Mound Builder country appears, from archaeological evidence, to have been one of breakdown and confusion. Part of the intruding Iroquoian Indians from the north seem to have penetrated to the Ohio River at the mouth of the Scioto, and another northern group, perhaps the Algonquian Shawnees, reached the river in the Cincinnati district.[1]

The Mississippian intrusion into the Ohio country appears to have

---

1 For Intrusive Mound culture, consult Griffin, *Fort Ancient,* 307–309; Martin, Quimby, and Collier, *Indians Before Columbus,* 278–87; Ritchie, "Cultural Influences from Ohio in New York Archaeology," *American Antiquity,* Vol. II, No. 2, 182–83.

come in two waves, in early Mississippi times and in the later middle Mississippi period. This Mississippian invasion of the Ohio lands seems to have come from East Tennessee, from the Tennessee and Cumberland rivers, and also up the Ohio from its mouth. The southern Indians brought their culture, including their truncated pyramid temple mounds, to the Scioto Valley; but their main settlements were along the Ohio River, in southern Illinois and southern Indiana. They had a real province along the north side of the Ohio River, extending upstream to near Louisville. Their intrusion was probably not a peaceable one, for they fortified some of their principal centers. These Mississippian folk of the lower Ohio Valley had their main connections with people of their own stock in southeastern Missouri and in the Memphis district. At Memphis there was a big Mississippian town; and to the east, between Memphis and the Tennessee River, near the modern town of Pinson, was a great Mississippian center of population. The early Mississippian intrusion into the Ohio lands was evidently not strong; it was the later middle Mississippian intrusion that had power and probably prevented the Iroquoians and other northern groups from taking over the Ohio lands.[2]

Archaeology, after over half a century of intensive study of the Fort Ancient villages and other remains, still depicts these Indians as mysterious groups whose tribal identity is unknown. This seems extraordinary, as these Indians were the last of the prehistoric inhabitants of the Ohio Valley, and some of their villages were still occupied when the French and English began to come into the Ohio country after the year 1670. Archaeology, Indian tradition, and the information of the French and English all depict the Ohio Valley as having a heavy Indian population at the period of Fort Ancient culture. These Fort Ancient Indians had taken over the great centers of the older Mound Builder folk, and they had, by archaeological count, over thirty villages. One tribe alone, the Shawnees, who are admitted by archaeologists to have been on the Ohio River in Fort Ancient times, were said by Father Marquette in 1673 to have had two main groups, twenty-three villages in one group, thirteen in the other. Some of these villages were probably small; but we know that at this period the Iroquoian tribes around Lake Ontario, Lake Hu-

[2] For Mississippian intrusion into the Ohio Valley, consult Griffin, *Archeology of the Eastern United States*, 190–91, 195; Griffin, *Fort Ancient*, 307; Griffin, *Late Prehistoric Cultures of the Ohio Valley*, 189.

ron, and Lake Erie and in New York had from ten thousand to over thirty thousand persons in each tribe, and the Fort Ancient folk were agricultural village-dwellers with communities similar to those of the Iroquoians.

As has been stated, these Indians were living in the old Mound Builder centers; but they were simpler folk than their predecessors of the mound period. The religious and ceremonial life of the Mound Builders, which had been their glory, had faded away, and these simple Fort Ancient Indians grew their crops and hunted and fished among the mounds and great circles, squares, and octagons of the Mound Builders.

Their population was clearly very mixed. They must have had part of the old Mound Builder folk among them. Some Fort Ancient centers show longheaded northern skulls in the burials, while others have mainly the roundheaded southern type and show evidence of artificial flattening, a practice of the southern tribes on into historic times.

In the archaeological studies of the Fort Ancient remains, there are many very interesting facts; but their meanings are obscure. The villages of the Fort Ancient people that center at Cincinnati had almost no contact with the villages to the east, on the Scioto, and the exchanges in pottery and other material that did take place between the two centers were made through Fort Ancient groups that lived south of the Ohio, in Kentucky. This situation might mean that the Scioto was held by Indians of a different group, hostile to the group at Cincinnati, the groups in Kentucky being perhaps neutral, friendly with both groups. The trade of the Fort Ancient Indians was, perhaps, mainly to the south; but they sent pottery and other materials eastward into Pennsylvania, a district occupied by both Iroquoian tribes and Algonquians, and into West Virginia and Virginia, where the inhabitants were Siouan, Algonquian, and Iroquoian. The Iroquoian tribes of Pennsylvania, West Virginia, and Virginia were evidently enemies of the Iroquois Proper; and the Fort Ancient folk seem to have had little contact with the last-named group. On the other hand, they had some trade with the Siouan Indians of Wisconsin and northern Illinois. They do not appear to have had any contact with the southern or Mississippi folk in Illinois, along the Mississippi River, at Cahokia, and other centers.

There is scanty information as to the village types of the Fort

148

Ancient Indians. On the Scioto the huts were evidently circular, with some of the Iroquois longhouse type; in other districts, farther west, the hut was usually of the rectangular Mississippian type. Except at the Feurt villages near the mouth of the Scioto River, the Fort Ancient Indians kept up the old Mound Builder custom of placing a food vessel and shell spoon in the grave so that the dead could eat. From this fact it would seem that, although the religious ceremonial life of the Mound Builders had degenerated, some fundamental beliefs were kept up in Fort Ancient times.

Another archaeological fact is that the Indians on the upper Scioto were forced out, evidently in late Fort Ancient times, probably by northern enemies, and retired southward to Feurt at the mouth of the Scioto, to Serpent Mound farther west, and to Fox Farm on the south side of the Ohio, southwest of Serpent Mound and southeast of the big Fort Ancient center at Cincinnati. This retirement hints at an Iroquoian attack from the north into the Scioto district. The Fox Farm Fort Ancient center, consisting of four village centers on both sides of Licking River, Kentucky, was of the same group as that at Cincinnati, showing that the Fort Ancient people here lived on both sides of the Ohio and made up, perhaps, the strongest population center of the Fort Ancient culture. This group also extended along the north bank of the Ohio westward into Indiana. By conjecture the Cincinnati and Licking River villages were Shawnee.

To the west of the Cincinnati Fort Ancient center on the Ohio in Indiana, near the mouth of the Wabash, there were villages in Fort Ancient times that do not show strong traces of Fort Ancient culture. This district is by tradition an area occupied by Siouan tribes in late prehistoric times, and it is to be observed that Siouan cultural features, coming down from Wisconsin and northern Illinois, went largely to the lower Wabash and to the Fort Ancient villages near Cincinnati. The southern or Mississippian Indians had a great center and fortress on the north side of the Ohio, near the present Evansville, east of the Wabash. The influence of this Mississippian center appears to have extended northward in eastern Indiana.

Another big Fort Ancient center was on the Little Miami River, to the north of Cincinnati. It is termed by archaeologists the Anderson focus, and it is here that the old Mound Builder fortress, called Fort Ancient, stands. This center shows a mixed population, round-head skulls of southern type, and a culture suggesting strong southern influence. As this district was apparently occupied by Adena folk from the south in Mound Builder times, and as these Anderson people of Fort Ancient times seem to have had frequent contact with the Indians on the Scioto, one is inclined to suppose that they were part of the old Mound Builder population which survived here on the Little Miami and to the east on the Scioto.[3]

Archaeology has had its opportunity to clear up this very confused situation in the Ohio Valley in post-Hopewell times and to identify at least part of the large Indian population with historic tribes. In this task archaeology seems to have failed, and the only remedy that most archaeologists have to offer is more and more intensive archaeological research in the Ohio country. To the non-archaeologist, another method for attacking this confused problem is apparent, and that is to try the experiment of adding Indian tradition and what historical evidence is at hand to the mass of archaeological material which, taken alone, seems to mean so little, from the point of view of Indian history.

David Cusic was an Iroquois Indian with some education, who, early in the nineteenth century, set down the traditions of the Iroquois in writing.[4] He had some knowledge of European history, and he employed this in an attempt to equate events among the Indians with European periods. His main landmark for dating was "the Columbus," meaning the coming of Columbus in 1492. In dating Iroquois events he is, like some archaeologists, inclined to attribute great antiquity to the matters with which he is dealing.

Cusic begins with the creation of the earth and goes on to a time when the Iroquois were being greatly troubled by giants, called Ronnongwetowanea. At this early period the Iroquois had the custom of going on tribal hunts in winter, leaving a few people at their permanent villages; and the giants came and attacked the villages, killing, plundering, and destroying. The Iroquois began to fortify their villages, and when they went away on winter hunts they left warriors in the villages to defend them. They also discovered that by going with very large war parties into the lands of the giants they could defeat these enemies. Speaking historically, the giants were probably the Algonquian tribes and, perhaps, the Ohio Mound Builders. The time was about A.D. 1400–1500.

3 For Fort Ancient culture, the main source is Griffin, *Fort Ancient*.
4 David Cusic, in Schoolcraft, *Indian Tribes*, V, 631–46.

About 2,200 years "before the Columbus," Cusic states that there was an empire to the south of Lake Ontario, and it was evident that this empire was the principal enemy of the tribes in the Iroquois region, for these Iroquoians now formed a confederacy and appointed a prince or ruler, who went at once to visit the emperor in his capital, the Golden City. This was evidently an effort to make peace; but the emperor built many forts, some near the Iroquois lands, and the Iroquois feared that they would lose their lands and freedom. This tale seems to refer to the Ohio Mound Builder power, to their emperor and to their capital, the Golden City, which in truth was the Copper City, copper being the precious metal of these northern tribes. Cusic seems to have been mistaken about the forts. Archaeology tells us that the Mound Builder forts were erected in the population centers, obviously as places of refuge that the people could flee to if their land was invaded. Cusic states that the war with the empire lasted probably one hundred years and was bloody. He adds that the northern tribes were hardier and more skilled with the bow than the people of the empire, and, in the end, they took all the forts and destroyed the empire.

Now Cusic tells us that after the fall of the empire there was great trouble. A monstrous horned serpent destroyed people; a great lake serpent caused terrible trouble, and the Iroquois tribes forgot their brotherhood and made war on each other. The Ottawas, who held the lands along the southern shores of the Great Lakes, attacked the Iroquois and invaded the Seneca country. Here the Ottawas are not the historic tribe of that name. It is a general term, synonymous with Algonquian. From other Iroquois traditions we know that the Shawnees were said to have occupied lands along the southern side of Lake Erie and to have been driven southward by Iroquoian attacks. Archaeology gives some support to such a situation, showing indications of an early Algonquian occupation of the lands south of Lake Erie, followed by a later Iroquoian occupation.

After the war with the Ottawas, Cusic asserts, the Iroquois sent an exploring party westward. They asked permission from the Ottawas to pass through their lands, south of Lake Erie. They went to Sandusky and then to the Mississippi, where the people of Duke Twakau-ah came out with drums and dancing to greet them. Beyond the Mississippi they came into a land of wonders, a district where there were flying fish and one in which the people had short tails. Coming back eastward, they returned home. The Iroquois chiefs now decided to make peace with the western tribes and sent an embassy to the Kentahkeh Nation, then living east (north) of the Ohio and now, Cusic states, living in Kentucky. This Kentahkeh Nation was intermarrying with the Ottawas, he asserts, which suggests that the Kentahkeh people were not Algonquians. Could they have been the Kentaientonga of La Salle, a nation on the Ohio who were destroyed by the Iroquois? They apparently are shown on some French maps as the Kenasintonton, high up the Ohio River. Could they have left their name on Kentucky River? Further on in his story, Cusic seems to speak of this Kentahkeh Nation again, as the Keattah-kiehroneah, the Iroquois form of their name; and he says that, at the time of the coming of "the Columbus" in 1492, the Iroquois attacked this tribe and drove it west (south) of the Ohio. At this point, he is speaking of the Iroquois war on the Erie Nation, not in 1492 but after 1650, and this suggests that the Kentahkeh Nation might have been Eries, or a tribe allied with that nation.[5]

The Delaware Indian tradition in the Walam Olum seems to give support to part of David Cusic's traditions. Both narratives depict a great power or empire in the Ohio country, Cusic claiming that the Iroquois destroyed this power, the Walam Olum claiming it was destroyed by the Algonquians with some aid from Iroquoian allies, not the real Iroquois but either the Hurons or some other group. The Delaware assertion is that they, the Shawnees and allied Algonquians, made the Wabash their center, and from there the Delawares advanced eastward to attack what Cusic terms the empire. The Shawnees took no part in the war, but moved southward. This does not agree with Iroquoian tradition which claims that the Algonquians, or Ottawas, including the Shawnees, were along the southern shores of Lake Erie and that the Shawnees were driven south into Ohio from there perhaps as late as 1600.

The traditions of the Siouan tribes of the Dhegiha group—the Osages, Quapaws, Kansas, Omahas, and Poncas—assert that their people were on the Ohio, in the Wabash area, in a district later occupied by the Shawnees. These Siouan traditions do not refer to any

5 Hodge, *Handbook of Indians North of Mexico*, II, 1072. Hodge states that Kentaienton was Gentaienton, an Erie Nation town of unknown location. But Cusic calls the Kentahkeh a nation, and La Salle terms the Kentaientonga a nation on the Ohio, destroyed by the Iroquois.

other tribes that dwelt in the Ohio country when they were there; with the exception of the Shawnees, they do not mention any tribes who came after them. Their traditions are empty of any references to early wars. The same things are true of the traditions of the second Siouan group, the Chiwere—Iowas, Otoes and Missouris. All these Siouan tribes were apparently driven from their old lands east of the Mississippi and forced to flee westward; and, being Indians, they had no long memory of defeats in old wars. All that we may adduce is that the Dhegiha group certainly were on the Ohio and were among the tribes there that the Iroquois attacked and either destroyed or drove out after the year 1650. The evidence to support this view will be set down presently.

These Indian traditions indicate that the inhabitants of the Ohio Valley, from Mound Builder times to about 1650 or 1670, were Siouans, Algonquians, and some Iroquoians. Archaeology seems to prove that even at a much earlier period than Mound Builder times the Siouans—the Kentucky Indian Knoll folk—were in Ohio, as far east as the Serpent Mound district, and also occupied a large area in southern Indiana. Their main center was in Kentucky. These Ohio Valley tribes, even in the time of high culture in the mound-building period, were probably only partly agricultural. They had permanent villages, ranging in size from small groupings of one hundred people to large settlements of several hundred; but they had to go on tribal hunts, just as the Iroquois did, probably spending several months of each year away from their villages. There were prairies with buffalo herds in Indiana, Illinois, and Kentucky, and the Siouan tribes of the Dhegiha group were probably buffalo hunters while dwelling in the Ohio Valley. The Quapaws of this group were going on buffalo hunts when first met by the French in 1673, and the rest of the tribes of the group were also buffalo Indians when first met, in Missouri and Iowa. J. B. Griffin has suggested that the Ohio tribes in Fort Ancient times were probably formed into confederacies, similar to the League of the Iroquois.[6] These Ohio tribes were primarily northern Indians with a basically northern Woodland culture, which had been affected by Iroquois, Mississippi, and Oneota culture. This last was that of the Wisconsin and northern Illinois Siouans and did not develop until about 1600, when contacts with the southern Indians of Cahokia produced the cultural development termed Oneota. Thus

[6] Griffin, *Late Prehistoric Cultures of the Ohio Valley.*

the Ohio Valley tribes, both in Ohio and Indiana, were in contact with the Siouans of the Winnebago group at the period when that group was very powerful.

Taking the Walam Olum Algonquian tradition with the Iroquois traditions, we may assume that the so-called empire of the Mound Builders in the Ohio lands was torn down by a combined attack of Algonquians and Iroquoians; but the Iroquois version does not mention an Algonquian occupation of the Mound Builder territory. It states that the Shawnees and "Ottawas" held the lands along the south shore of Lake Erie and that the Shawnees were later driven down into Ohio by Iroquoian attacks. Thus the first intrusion into the Ohio lands was that of the Intrusive Mound folk, who had an Iroquian type of culture and who apparently intruded into the Scioto Valley in eastern Ohio. This, we may assume, caused some of the Mound Builder population, particularly the Siouans, to abandon the Scioto. Some may have gone into West Virginia, Virginia, and North Carolina. Others perhaps went westward into the Cincinnati district and to the Wabash. This is conjecture, but it would explain why the Siouans were in the west in later times and why the intrusive burials in old mounds in western Ohio are of the Fort Ancient cultural type, while the intrusive burials in the Scioto district are of the Iroquoian type. It would mean that Fort Ancient culture had time to develop before the Cincinnati district intrusion. That probably does not indicate any great length of elapsed time; for the ordinary Mound Builder culture, the everyday culture, was not very different from the later Fort Ancient culture. It was the decay of the high religious and ceremonial culture of the Mound Builders that made the difference. Another difference was that the old settled conditions of Mound Builder times were gone. There was war. Groups shifted their locations, seeking safety, and many of them surrounded their new villages with stockade defenses.

Anthropologists have been inclined to picture a great Siouan occupation of the Ohio lands and the lands to the south, in Kentucky and western Tennessee. They include the Dhegiha group of five tribes, the Mosopeleas, Yuchis, Ofos, Biloxis, and some Siouan tribes that are supposed to have fled from Ohio into Virginia and North Carolina. Much of this anthropological material seems to be too conjectural. It may be correct, but it cannot be supported by solid evidence. Many archaeologists are inclined to discredit the whole Siouan tradition, but they cannot do this by simply rejecting all Indian traditions as unreliable, which is the attitude of some archaeologists. The presence of the Dhegiha Siouans in the Ohio Valley is solidly supported by French documentary evidence. The only real problem is the location of the Dhegihas and Mosopeleas and the date and circumstances of their flight from the Ohio lands.

Nearly all the leading archaeologists have denied that there are any remains in the Ohio Valley that can be attributed to the Siouan Indians, but it is to be observed that these archaeologists seem to be unaware of the type of culture the Siouans may have had while dwelling in the Ohio country. They are even in some doubt as to the type of Siouan culture established by the Dhegiha group after they went west of the Mississippi and came out into the clear light of historic times. They seem inclined to take the view that Dhegihan culture was Woodland, strongly affected by Mississippian culture of a late period. Uncertain of the exact type of this late Dhegian culture, archaeologists tell us that they have failed to find anything like it in the Ohio Valley, and they seem to think that this failure proves that the Dhegihas were never on the Ohio. To historians and ethnologists this is not acceptable.

The migration traditions of the five Dhegiha tribes contain practically nothing concerning their old home in the Ohio Valley. They speak of living on the Ohio, and some add on the Wabash. They give no explanation of why the tribes left the Ohio, but one Ponca tradition, quoted by James H. Howard in his college thesis on the Poncas, states vaguely that there was war, that the younger chiefs favored fighting, while the older and wiser chiefs were against it. This material is so vague that some archaeologists, who seem to resent any attempt to show that Siouan Indians were ever in the Ohio Valley, declare that the traditions are worthless. A fairer statement would be that these stories are an honest attempt by Indians to recall events of two centuries or more back, from memory alone. After all, the migration traditions of the Iowas and Otoes are every bit as vague as the Dhegihan traditions; yet archaeologists accept the Iowa and Oto stories as reliable, and make use of them to support archaeological opinions.

It is the supporting evidence that makes the vague Dhegihan traditions historically important. When the French came into the Mississippi Valley, the tribes there still had a clear memory of the time when the Dhegiha Siouans lived on the Ohio. The name Akansea, the old name of the Quapaw group, was still applied to the lower Ohio, and also to the lower Cumberland River. Marquette and Joliet placed the Akansea and other Dhegihas in their new locations, on and west of the Mississippi; but it was Father Douay, who was with La Salle in 1686–87, who first referred to the old location of the Osages and Quapaws. Douay was on the Mississippi but was speaking of the Osages on a branch of the Missouri. He asserted that in former years the Osages and Quapaws lived "on a branch of this river" but were driven out by the Iroquois. Some scholars have stated that Douay meant the Ohio, a branch of the Mississippi; others have maintained that he meant the tribes lived on a branch of the Missouri. His real meaning is exhibited by what Father Cosmé wrote a few years later, in 1699. Father Cosmé says that the Akansea or Quapaws and the Osages dwelt on the Ohio; the Osages left and moved westward; then the Iroquois made cruel war, driving the Akansea and part of the seventeen Osage villages southward, down the Mississippi, where they located on Arkansas River.[7]

In 1700, Father Gravier wrote that the Akansea tribe formerly lived on the Ohio. In 1829, the United States agent for the Osages wrote that this tribe claimed that the Quapaws were formerly a part of the Osages and that the Quapaws left them on the Ohio River. Lewis H. Morgan was told by the Osages, about the year 1847, that their tribe formerly lived on the Ohio, evidently on the south bank, in a district later occupied by the Shawnees. This seems to refer to the Shawnee occupation of the lands on the Ohio, near the mouths of the Wabash and Cumberland.[8]

A Dutch map dated 1720[9] shows the Akansea tribe on the south bank of the lower Ohio. It shows a second Akansea group (marked Axansa) west of the Mississippi, due west of the mouth of the Ohio.

7 Father Douay, in French, *Historical Collections of Louisiana*, IV, 222–23; Father Cosmé, in John Dawson Gilmary Shea, *Early Voyages Up and Down the Mississippi;* Father Gravier, in Thwaites, *Jesuit Relations.*

8 The Thevenot map (reproduced in Griffin, *Fort Ancient*) to accompany the Marquette narrative, made in 1681, shows the Shawnees along the north bank of the Ohio near a southern tributary, probably the Cumberland. Later maps show "Old Savannah settlement" (Shawnee village) on the south bank of the Ohio, between the mouths of the Cumberland and Tennessee rivers. The Indian agent's report of 1829 is in Schoolcraft, *Indian Tribes*, III, 594.

9 This map is in Winsor, *The Mississippi Basin*, 105.

The Popple map, 1733, gives the name Akanseapi (Arkansas River) to the Cumberland River. These maps confirm the statements of the French that the Akansea or Quapaws were on the Ohio or lower Cumberland at such a late date that the name of the tribe was still applied to these streams after the year 1700.

To these French references to the Dhegiha group of Siouans and their former residence on the Ohio, we may add the French material on the Mosopeleas. As was stated in Chapter Four of the present work, there is good reason for believing that the Mosopeleas were Siouans, and it is possible that they were the Wasabe or Black Bear group of the Dhegiha Indians. The information placing the Mosopeleas on the north side of the Ohio, high up the river, seems to have come mainly from La Salle. Minet was on board with La Salle during the voyage from France to Texas in 1686, and his map, showing the Mosopeleas on the Ohio, was made from La Salle's information. Franquelin must have had some of La Salle's notes when he placed the Mosopelea villages on his great map of 1684. These two maps show eight Mosopelea villages "destroyed," and La Salle includes the Mosopeleas in his list of tribes destroyed on the Ohio by the Iroquois. But the tribe was not destroyed; the eight villages were destroyed or abandoned and the surviving people fled, finding refuge in small groups, among the Taensa Indians on the lower Mississippi, among the Creeks, and probably among their Dhegihan kinsmen.

It is the view of some archaeologists that, like the Dhegiha claim to a former residence on the Ohio, the story of the Mosopeleas is a myth. These critics wish us to believe that Father Marquette, Joliet, and La Salle invented the Mosopelea tribe or that La Salle was so ignorant of the Indians in the Ohio Valley that he allowed some Indian informants to deceive him concerning the Mosopeleas. This is as astonishing a claim as the other contention, that the Dhegiha migration traditions are worthless myth. La Salle was a man of unusually keen intelligence. He was utterly absorbed in his plans for exploring the western country, the Ohio, and the Mississippi lands, and for years he never missed an opportunity to question Indians and French traders about the tribes in these distant countries. One winter a family of Iroquois stayed at La Salle's manor on Montreal Island for weeks, and La Salle probably questioned these Iroquois closely concerning the Ohio country. When he went westward in 1669, he was apparently determined to explore the Ohio; and he questioned the Senecas, those

Iroquois best acquainted with the Ohio Indians. Francis Parkman believed that La Salle did go down the Ohio to its mouth in this year, but the evidence is too slender to establish solidly that view. A great mass of La Salle's manuscript writing apparently has been lost. What papers did survive and were printed probably contain only a fraction of the information on the Indians which this very energetic explorer had put together between the years 1665 and 1685.

Our knowledge of the Mosopeleas is far too scanty, but we have some solid facts. They were a big Indian group, mainly on the north side of the Ohio River, far up the stream. They were evidently the Ohio Indians nearest to the Iroquois, and for this reason they suffered more and probably at an earlier date from Iroquois attacks than any of the other Ohio Valley tribes. They evidently fled in panic, splitting up into many groups and seeking safety among more distant tribes. They were supposed by anthropologists to have become extinct; but if they were the Wasabe or Black Bear group of Dhegiha Siouans, their descendants are living today among the Osages, Kansas, Omahas, and Poncas.

We have a number of clues that seem to support the conclusion that the Mosopeleas were Siouan and did belong to the Dhegiha group. The Coxe map (printed in Griffin, *Fort Ancient*) puts a tribe called "Ousperie" on the south side of the Ohio near the Mosopeleas, and the Hodge *Handbook of Indians North of Mexico* attempts to identify the Ousperie as a Quapaw group. Swanton considered them to be the Ofo, a Siouan tribe, driven south from the Ohio. But, are not Ousperie, Mosopelea, and Wasabe-rea the same name in varying spellings? John L. Buckner (quoted in Griffin, *Fort Ancient,* 179–83) believed that the Mosopeleas lived on the Scioto and also at Fullerton Field on the south side of the Ohio near the mouth of the Scioto. Near Fullerton Field, which was a Fort Ancient settlement, there was an effigy mound representing a bear. Across the Ohio, at the mouth of the Scioto, was another effigy mound of an animal. If the Mosopeleas were really the Wasabe or Black Bear group of Dhegiha Siouans, this bear mound might mark their old center, and the other animal effigy might mark another of their centers. The animal effigy mounds are so obviously of Siouan origin that one must suspect that this area in eastern Ohio and Kentucky was occupied by Indians of the Siouan stock in Mound Builder times.

The migration traditions of the Dhegiha group of tribes assert that their people moved down the Ohio, all in one group, and separated on reaching the Mississippi, the Quapaws moving down that river, the other tribes crossing the river and migrating on westward through Missouri State. The evidence set down on the preceding pages in this chapter seems to refute the traditional account. These Siouan Indians appear to have fled from the Ohio lands in separate groups. First the Mosopeleas and perhaps part of the Osages fled, part of them going south of the Ohio and then westward. They evidently found the Akansea or Quapaw group in the lower Wabash lands or across the river in Kentucky, left them there, and fled westward to the Mississippi; but, judging from the French evidence, the Akansea were soon also in flight from the Iroquois. In the Father Douay narrative, Marquette and Joliet are said to have met part of the Mosopeleas on the east side of the Mississippi, above the mouth of the Ohio and below the mouth of the Missouri, in 1673. The Marquette maps place the Akansea on the east side of the Mississippi above Arkansas River, and the Mosopeleas on the same side of the river, below the Arkansas. Obviously these Indians had recently fled to these locations to escape the dreaded Iroquois wolf packs; and the Osages had already reached Osage River, where the Iroquois apparently were still harassing them.

Those authors who attempt to depict the Dhegiha Siouans as dwelling west of the Mississippi as far back as the year 1000 or 1300 are only imagining things. These Dhegihans were recent arrivals west of the Mississippi when Marquette and Joliet came to the river in 1673, and some of them were still in flight from the Iroquois. The Omahas and Poncas—then one tribe—had fled the farthest, into northwestern Iowa; the Kansa tribe had fled to eastern Kansas; the Osages to Osage River. The Quapaws and Mosopeleas had fled down the Mississippi, along the east bank of the river. Part of the Shawnees were still on the Ohio; part had fled southward, and apparently the Piqua Shawnees had fled eastward into Pennsylvania.

If it is difficult to show in which parts of the Ohio Valley the Dhegiha Siouans had their villages before the Iroquois attacks displaced them, it is even more difficult to locate the older Shawnee settlements. About all that we have from archaeology is the statement that Shawnee culture was of Fort Ancient type, basically a Woodland culture with southeastern (Mississippian?) traits. To this is added the conjecture that the village ruins at Madisonville, in the Cincinnati vicinity, are probably Shawnee. The Delaware Indian tradition that the Shawnees were with them when they lived on the Wabash at a very early period and that the Shawnees moved south before the Delawares moved eastward is contradicted by the Iroquoian traditions that the Shawnees, sometimes apparently called Ottawas, dwelt along the southern shore of Lake Erie and were driven southward to the Ohio at a date probably later than 1550. Where the Shawnees went when they came down into Ohio we are not informed, but part of them were on the Ohio River, above the Louisville Falls, in 1669.

In 1673 Marquette stated that the Shawnees on the Ohio had twenty-three villages in one group and fifteen in another, the two groups being near to each other. He stated that the Shawnees were without metal weapons and that the Iroquois killed them with ease and rounded up great numbers of captives and carried them off. His assertion that the Shawnees were not warlike we may dismiss as nonsense. The Iroquois had firearms, and the situation on the Ohio was very similar to that on the Churchill River in the far north, where little groups of Crees, armed with Hudson Bay muskets, hunted the unfortunate natives, who were still armed only with stone weapons, like birds, and had them in such a panic that they fled in terror at the sight of distant smoke which might indicate the coming of a Cree war party. The Iroquois were forcing large number of Shawnee youths to serve in their wolf packs, and these Shawnees were good warriors.

The Ohio Valley Indians evidently had a very large population before the Iroquois began their work of destruction. As late as 1699, the Osages were given seventeen villages. They must have had many more before the Iroquois struck. The Mosopeleas had eight villages, and the Akansea group probably at least that number. The Shawnees had thirty-eight villages. Some of these villages were probably small; others formed large settlements, and many villages were evidently fortified by a surrounding earth wall and log stockade. To the Indians already listed we must add the southern or Mississippian Indians of the two big settlements called Kincaid and Angel by the archaeologists. They were on the north side of the Ohio in southern Illinois and Indiana. There were apparently other groups along the Ohio, including groups of Eries who fled there when the Iroquois destroyed their nation, and the Iroquoian group later known in Nebraska as the Skidi Pawnees.

About the year 1668, an Iroquois war party that had been raiding

160

on the Ohio came north and stopped at Mackinac Island with a number of Shawnee captives. The Ojibwas surprised these Iroquois, killing most of them and taking some of the Shawnees. One Shawnee came into the hands of the Potawatomis, who gave him gifts, including French articles, and sent him home. Another of the Shawnees, evidently from the same group of captives, came among the Nipissings, and Father Dollier obtained his release and took him to Montreal, where La Salle was staying at the time. It was from this Shawnee that the French obtained their first definite information concerning the Ohio Valley. The Shawnee said that on the Ohio a great number of tribes dwelt, but that no white man had ever been there. Other Indian reports said that single tribes on the Ohio had fifteen to twenty villages each.[10] In 1670, the English in Virginia obtained some information concerning the Ohio country. Two men, Batts and Fallam, visited the village of a Siouan tribe, the Monetons, on the Kenawha, and were informed that one day's journey below the Moneton village the river joined another, the Ohio, which flowed westward and had Indian settlements along it for a distance of twenty days' journey. At this time another Englishman, Gabriel Arthur, reached the upper Ohio and was captured by Indians, evidently near the mouth of the Scioto. Arthur reported that the Ohio Indians had no iron and no guns.[11]

In 1669, La Salle, who was planning to explore the Ohio, went westward with a party of French missionaries. Some Senecas, who were the Iroquois most familiar with the Ohio country, were with the party, and they informed La Salle and the missionaries that it was thirty days' journey from the Seneca towns to the Honniasontkeronons and Chaouanons (Shawnees) on the Ohio. Below these two tribes was a waterfall (at the present Louisville), and below the falls lived the Outagames and near them the Iskoussogos. Beyond, to the west, of the last tribes the woodlands ended and there were great meadows abounding with buffalo and elk and inhabited by unknown tribes.[12]

[10] John Witthoft and W. A. Hunter, "Seventeenth-Century Origins of the Shawnee," *Ethnohistory,* Vol. II, No. 1; Margry, *Découvertes et établissements des Français,* II, 111–71; Blair, *Indian Tribes of the Upper Mississippi,* I, 349.

[11] Griffin, *Fort Ancient,* 32.

[12] Witthoft and Hunter, "Seventeenth-Century Origins of the Shawnees," *Ethnohistory,* Vol. II, No. 1.

From these accounts it seems likely that the Dhegiha group of Siouans had removed westward before 1669. They are not named in the Seneca account of the Ohio in that year, and this Seneca statement places Shawnees above the Louisville falls, and the Iskoussogos, who may have been the Kispogogi division of Shawnees, below the falls. As to the Honnaisontkeronons, this is an Iroquois name, and the De l'Isle map of 1722 (reproduced in Griffin, *Fort Ancient*) puts them near a big lake north of the Ohio, perhaps Lake Erie. They may have been a group of fugitive Eries, living with the Shawnees. The main point is that these accounts of the Ohio after 1665 do not mention the Dhegiha Siouan group; but this fact supports the other evidence that the Dhegihas had fled from the Ohio by the date 1665.

The La Salle list of tribes destroyed on or near the Ohio by the Iroquois, which is in a letter he wrote in 1681 or 1682, throws additional light on the Indian inhabitants of the Ohio Valley before the Iroquois destroyed or drove them out.[13] La Salle is speaking here of tribes supposed to have been destroyed, and he does not appear to include the Dhegiha group, who were not destroyed. The list is as follows:

Illinois. (The Illinis), not destroyed, but driven beyond the Mississippi by the Iroquois.

Kentaientonga. This is the tribe David Cusic's Iroquois legends place north of the Ohio, stating that they were driven south of the Ohio and destroyed by the Iroquois. They are on the Minet map (reproduced in Griffin, *Fort Ancient*), made from La Salle information, 1685, which locates them on the south side of the Ohio, east of the Mosopeleas. The form of their name given by La Salle has the Siouan ending, tonga, meaning great or big.

Ganeiensaga. This name seems to have the Shawnee ending.

Chaouanons. Shawnees. Not all destroyed, but badly mauled by the Iroquois and driven out.

Ganeiensaga. The Hodge *Handbook of Indians North of Mexico* suggests that this was the name of an important Erie village of unknown location.

Ouabache. Here we have Wabash as the name of a tribe on the Ohio, destroyed by the Iroquois. This seems to discredit the usual belief that Wabash was an Algonquian name for the river and meant White Water.

13 La Salle, in Margry, *Découvertes et établissements des Français*, II, 236–37.

Tistontaraetonga. Another name with the Siouan ending, meaning great or big.

Gandostogega. The Hodge *Handbook of Indians North of Mexico* conjectures that this group were Conestogas, purely from a supposed resemblance of the name.

Mosopelea. Siouans; eight villages.

Sounikaaeronons. Iroquoian form of name.

Ochiatagonga. The Hodge *Handbook of Indians North of Mexico* conjectures that this tribe were Weas of the Illini group. *Tonga* is Siouan. Some Algonquin village names end in *ton.*

La Salle's list of tribes seems to include only Siouans, Shawnees, and some Iroquoians—probably fugitive Eries.

There seem to be no references in any of the French material to those southern or Mississippian tribes who had large settlements on the northern bank of the lower Ohio, what archaeologists term the Kincaid and Angel settlements. According to tree-ring dating from the Kincaid village ruins, this great settlement was still in use as late as 1613, and the probability is that these settlements were in existence for a generation after that date. These southern Indians probably did not leave the Ohio until the attacks of the Iroquois, after 1650. We still have no solid evidence regarding who these southern Indians on the Ohio were. When the French came to the Mississippi, after 1670, the Chickasaws were the only important group of southern Indians near the Ohio. There was a tradition that the Chickasaws formerly had a village near the mouth of the Cumberland River, which would be close to the old Kincaid settlement, below the mouth of the Wabash. It would also be in a district later occupied by the Shawnees and, by tradition, the old location of the Quapaw group of Siouans. In the 1680's, the Chickasaws wished to form an alliance with the French, and they urged that they be permitted to colonize the lower Wabash with French aid. This may support the view that they had formerly occupied lands on the Ohio in the Wabash district.

The Iroquois had been raiding into the Ohio Valley before the year 1600, but their early attacks were probably of a minor nature. After they obtained European weapons, particularly firearms, their first interest was to destroy the neighboring tribes of their own Iroquoian stock, whom they regarded as dangerous rivals. They destroyed the Hurons in 1648–49 and the Neutrals in 1650–51. In 1653–56, they destroyed the Eries; but groups of that tribe evidently escaped, part fleeing southward to the Ohio Valley. Meantime, the Iroquois turned on another group that they feared, the Upper Algonquians. They attacked the Algonquians in the Lake Huron district and in the southern peninsula of Michigan, driving them westward. The refugee Algonquians, with some Tobacco Hurons, had just established themselves in Wisconsin when the Iroquois discovered them and began to raid them again, about the year 1656. Next the Iroquois found the Illinis in northern Illinois and began making attacks on that group, driving them beyond the Mississippi, apparently in 1658. The Illinis were afraid to return to their old lands in Illinois until after 1670.

We have no date for the start of the heavy Iroquois assaults on the Ohio Indians; but by inference they began after the destruction of the Neutrals and Eries, perhaps about 1655, and it may have been the flight of the Eries to the Ohio River that attracted the strong Iroquois attacks to that area. When the Jesuit missions among the Hurons were destroyed, the missionaries shifted their attention to the Iroquois and went to their villages to seek converts or martyrdom. The Jesuits noted many instances of Iroquois war parties bringing in captives from the Ohio country, and the priests, at times, gave the name of the tribe being attacked as the Ontongannha, an Iroquois name reported to mean the Far Indians.[14] The Jesuits witnessed the torturing to death of many Ohio Indians and saw with horror the cannibal feasts that followed. The Iroquois feasted on the flesh of an Ohio Indian in one of their big longhouses; and after the feast the Iroquois, evidently including women and children, all began to shout and to beat on the inside walls of the house with sticks. They explained that they were driving the soul of the Ohio Indian out of the house, fearing that if the angry soul remained it would do them some great mischief.[15]

John Mitchell, the early Virginian geographer, states that in 1671

14 The Ontongannha are mentioned in the *Jesuit Relations* for 1661–62. They may have been the Outagames that the Senecas stated were on the Ohio below the Louisville Falls with another group called Iskoussogos in 1669. The Shawnees of Savannah River on the Georgia and South Carolina borders were called Outougannah (Thomas, *Twelfth Annual Report*, B.A.E., 694). This name, Outougannah, was Iroquois and meant, in their language, people who did not speak the Iroquois tongue. The Iroquois were raiding them as far back as 1661–62, as the *Jesuit Relations* of that period indicate.

15 Parkman, *La Salle and the Discovery of the Great West*, 15.

the Indians on the Ohio, mainly Shawnees, were engaged in a hot war with the Iroquois, and that in the following year, 1672, these Ohio Indians were partly exterminated, and partly captured and incorporated into the Iroquois nation.[16] Here we have a date for the last great campaign of the Iroquois against the Ohio Indians, but the Siouan tribes of the Ohio must have fled long before this final disaster.

From the Indian statements that have been quoted in this chapter and from the assertions of the English traders concerning the Ohio River, it is apparent that the valley of this stream was still heavily populated as late as 1670. This population was primarily Shawnee, with some assorted refugee groups, such as the Eries who had been driven down to the Ohio by the Iroquois, and perhaps some lingering Siouan groups. Nicholas Perrot stated that when he took possession of the upper Great Lakes country in the name of the King of France in 1671, the Iroquois attacks on the Algonquians of the upper lakes were thwarted; and the Iroquois then turned their attacks on the Indians of the Ohio country and on the Andastes of Pennsylvania, defeating that tribe and the Shawnees in many fights and carrying off Shawnee and Andaste captives to increase their own population.[17] It was about this period, 1670–75, that the Shawnees established strong settlements in the Nashville district in Tennessee, having retired from the Ohio Valley, and part of the Shawnees settled on Savannah River along the Georgia and South Carolina border in 1674. At this time, part of the Shawnees were making efforts to open trade with the French or to obtain French aid against the Iroquois. One party of Shawnees went north to the Miamis and from them to the Potawatomis to try to open a trade for French goods. About 1670, Marquette heard that the Shawnees had come to visit the Illinis. The Illinis reported that the Shawnees had quantities of glass beads but apparently no metal weapons. Finally, in 1675, the Iroquois overwhelmed the Conestogas of Pennsylvania, and the survivors of this tribe fled to the Potomac in Maryland.

Thus it would appear that when Marquette and Joliet reached the Mississippi in 1673, the Iroquois had already driven the Siouan tribes of the Dhegiha group to or beyond the Mississippi and had cleared most of the Shawnees out of the Ohio Valley, although Marquette

[16] Mitchell, in Griffin, *Fort Ancient*, 31–32.
[17] Blair, *Indian Tribes of the Upper Mississippi*, I, 226.

stated that this tribe was still on the Ohio. The Iroquois now claimed the Ohio Valley by right of conquest. The disaster to the old native tribes was probably much greater than is indicated here; for there was a mass of southern Mississippian Indians along the lower Ohio and along the Mississippi in western Illinois and eastern Missouri whose very names are unknown. Archaeology shows that large groups of southern Indians were in these locations until late prehistoric times; but, when the French came to the Mississippi in 1673, the southern Indians had vanished. We need not assume that the Iroquois were responsible for all this. The Illini and other Algonquians had probably displaced part of the southern tribes before the Iroquois arrived.

There has been considerable controversy about the extent of the Iroquois conquest in the Ohio Valley. When the French came to the Mississippi, they found the Iroquois raiding tribes to the west of the river; but Colonel George Croghan, who was Indian agent for the Iroquois from 1750 to 1781, stated that these Indians claimed the lands to the south of the Ohio as far as the Cherokee or Tennessee River, and on the north of the Ohio west to the Big Miami, only a short distance west of Cincinnati.[18] Despite their supposed superior mental abilities, the Iroquois seem to have had memories as bad as most other Indians. During the council at Lancaster, Pennsylvania, in 1755—less than seventy years after the Ohio tribes were driven out—the great chiefs of the Iroquois brought out a claim to the Ohio lands by right of conquest. Virginia claimed the Ohio Valley by right of royal charter, and the governor of Virginia denied the Iroquois claims, stating emphatically that the Iroquois had never conquered any tribe west of the Alleghenies. He was wrong, but the Iroquois chiefs had forgotten the Shawnees and other tribes they had driven out of the Ohio lands. They dropped their formal claim; but from 1670 on their war parties continued to rove in the Ohio Valley, through lands desolate and silent, stripped of all inhabitants by Iroquois attacks.

18 William Henry Harrison, *A Discourse on the Aborigines of the Ohio Valley*, 62.

CHAPTER EIGHT

East Wind III

THE MIGRATION TRADITIONS of the Dhegiha group of Siouans are, on the whole, poorly remembered accounts of the movement from the Ohio Valley westward, without much reliable detail. This has led some recent writers to mark off these traditions as worthless for the purposes of history, but this seems unjust. After all, these traditions state the main facts correctly, as can be demonstrated from historical and other evidence. They assert that the Osage and Omaha group crossed the Mississippi above the Ohio and below the Missouri and moved westward to a point near the mouth of Osage River, where they separated. The Quapaw or Akansea group left the Ohio and moved down the Mississippi to their historic location at the mouth of the Arkansas River. These statements are supported by French documentary evidence, by entries on old maps, and by anthropological evidence. It has been hoped that modern archaeology would give the final proof that these traditions are correct; but up to the present time archaeology has only confused the issue by insisting that there are no village ruins in the Ohio Valley of Siouan cultural type, to which they add various assertions that amount to an admission that they do not know what type of culture the Dhegiha Siouans had during the period 1600–1700. That being so, how would they recognize Dhegihan culture if they did happen to find it in the Ohio Valley?

There must have been a mass of southern Indians in southeastern Missouri until near the close of the prehistoric period. The remains of their culture are very impressive. There were strong towns surrounded by defensive walls, from a point opposite Union County, Illinois, down the Mississippi into the New Madrid district. Who these Indians were, we do not know; but it is probable that the Michigameas and their allies, the Chapousas, were living here and may have been here when the Dhegiha group of Siouans left the Ohio Valley. An English map of 1715 has the lower Missouri marked Anisissippi or Lennaw River. Lennaw seems to be a form of Illini, (Il)Lenaw, and that would indicate that tribes of the Illini confederacy held the lower Missouri to perhaps 1650.[1] We know that the Michigameas frequented the lands along the lower Missouri. Marquette found this tribe in northeastern Arkansas in 1673. They had fled there from enemies; but in later years they returned north, to what we may assume was their older habitat, and they then established a village in Illinois, not far from the mouth of the Missouri. These southern tribes along the Mississippi, from Arkansas and Mississippi State up to the mouth of the Missouri, were there when De Soto came in 1541–42. They were strong tribes, living in big towns, some fortified. They were ruled by kings and had fleets of big dugout canoes on the river. They were gone before Marquette and Joliet came down the river in 1673.

The Dhegihas of the Osage-Omaha group came from the Ohio into this stretch of the Mississippi Valley, above the Ohio, crossed the Mississippi and moved up to the vicinity of the present St. Louis, where they stayed for a time. The Kansa tribe and the Poncas had a dim memory of a village they occupied on the west side of the Mississippi above the Missouri. The Kansas even remembered the name of the village, Neblazhetame, Blue River Village. They called the Mississippi, above the point where the muddy Missouri waters join it, Blue River. This village, the tradition states, was on a peninsula with a mount or hill as an outstanding landmark. There is no known location of this character on the west side of the Mississippi, just

---

[1] English map of 1715, in Swanton, "Early History of the Creek Indians and Their Neighbors," *Bulletin 73*, B.A.E.

above the mouth of the Missouri, and there are no remains of a ruined village of any size. Gerald Fowke, the archaeologist, was of the opinion that the course of the Mississippi has changed here, that there was formerly a big bend, inside which there must have been a peninsula of land. On the south side of the Missouri, where St. Louis now stands, there were formerly the remains of big Indian settlements with many mounds; but these remains seem to have been of the southern Indian culture of Cahokia, which covered the east bank of the river, opposite St. Louis. Moreover, some of the traditions seem to mean that this peninsula and the mount were at a point some distance up the Missouri, not at the river mouth.[2] J. O. Dorsey believed, from his long study of the Dhegiha migration traditions, that these Indians ranged through the lands south of the Missouri, from near St. Louis west to the Osage River. The traditions state that at this period the Osage-Omaha group met the Iowas, but that the Otoes and Missouris were unknown to them. At the mouth of Osage River the Dhegiha group broke up; the Omahas, accompanied by the Poncas, went north into Iowa State and joined a village of Iowas on Des Moines River, a little to the southeast of the present city of Des Moines. The Kansa tribe went on up the south side of the Missouri to their historic location in eastern Kansas, while the Osages moved southward, along the Osage River.

Modern archaeology has failed to uncover any solid evidence either to support or to contradict the Dhegiha migration story, as far as the migration into Missouri State is concerned. The archaeological situation is absolutely baffling, up to the present time. To begin with, the building of the Bagnell Dam, which brought the extensive Lake of the Ozarks into existence, covered with water all the older Osage village ruins which would have displayed the type of culture this tribe had brought with it into Missouri State. Along the Missouri not one village ruin has been found that can be said with certainty to be Osage or to represent the older culture of any of the Dhegihan tribes. The Pinnacles—termed the Utz site by archaeologists—is four miles southwest of the town of Miami, in Saline County, Missouri. It is a location that might be conjectured to be the peninsula with the mount for a landmark mentioned in the Dhegiha traditions. The

---

[2] Dorsey, *Omaha Sociology, Third Annual Report*, B.A.E. Dorsey's earlier account of Dhegiha migration is in *American Naturalist*, Vol. XX (1887).

land here is very much cut up, with long ridges and isolated hills, standing 150 or more feet above the river bottoms below. On a high ridge is a fortified village with a type of earth wall defense said to be very similar to Fort Ancient fortified villages in Ohio and Indiana. On another ridge is an extensive village ruin. The culture shown is certainly Siouan and of late prehistoric date; but there are two types of culture, one characterized by grit-tempered pots and the other by shell-tempered ones. The latter smooth-surfaced ware is undoubtedly the product of Oneota culture developed by the Missouri tribe, a group of Indians known to have held this district from late in the seventeenth century into the nineteenth. The grit-tempered ware, the majority type, might be Osage; but there is no proof of this.

The archaeologists have had a great deal to say concerning the Top Layer in the Ozarks in southwestern Missouri and northwestern Arkansas. This Top Layer represents the late prehistoric occupation and, like the Pinnacles village ruins, it shows two types of pottery, a grit-tempered ware and a shell-tempered type that seems to be Oneota. One or both of these cultural types have been termed Osage by many archaeologists; but the older grit-tempered pottery may be Caddoan ware of the Brown Valley period, roughly contemporary with the Siouan Oneota culture. The shell-tempered pots in the Top Layer look like Oneota ware, but there is no proof that they are Osage pottery.[3]

Leaving the Osage-Omaha group in Missouri and returning to the Ohio Valley, we have some evidence that the Akansea or Quapaw group tarried on the Ohio for a time after their Osage-Omaha kindred had left. Indeed, the Akansea group, accompanied or preceded by the related Mosopeleas, seems to have been still migrating when the French came into the Mississippi Valley in 1673. They were still retreating from enemies who had driven them from the Ohio; and, unlike the Osage-Omaha group, they moved down the east bank of the Mississippi.

From the French accounts it is pretty obvious that the flight of the Quapaw group and of the related Mosopeleas was still in progress when Marquette and Joliet came down the Mississippi in 1673. The

3 Griffin, *Archeology of the Eastern United States*, 144, 149, 162, and figure 63. The Kansa tribe is said to have had grit-tempered pottery, and the Omaha (Mill Creek) pottery was grit tempered. The tempering of the Quapaw pottery is not definitely described.

Indians evidently were fleeing in confusion from the Iroquois, and this is shown by the mixed character of the Quapaw population. La Salle states that the Quapaws or Akanseas were an Illinois group, but that is impossible. They were Siouan Indians, and nothing could be clearer than their former residence on the lower Ohio; but it is quite possible that some groups of the Illinois confederacy, probably southern Indians of the Mississippi culture, joined the Quapaws at this time. Part of the seventeen Osage villages joined them, and in 1721, Father Charlevoix said that the Akanseas had five tribes, three occupying one village each and a fourth village occupied by two tribes.[4]

The Quapaw group is not likely to have fled all the way from their old location in the Ohio Valley to the Arkansas River in one panicky rush. The distance was great. They had to hunt and fish to obtain food, and they must have halted and formed villages where they could plant crops and gather the harvests. Coming from the Ohio, their easy course was to follow the east bank of the Mississippi southward, and it is here that we would expect to find remains of early Quapaw occupation.

James B. Griffin has stated that the Quapaw and Kansa culture was middle Mississippi; the Osage culture, middle Mississippi affected by Oneota culture; and Omaha (Mill Creek) culture, middle Mississippi with some Plains traits.[5] To the lay mind such culture among the Dhegiha Siouans is not unlike the predominant Fort Ancient culture that persisted in the Ohio Valley down to the year 1670.

We have spoken of the flight of the Dhegiha tribes from the Ohio, when attacked by the Iroquois, and this might be taken to mean the panicky rush of a confused mass of Indians who never halted until they had gone beyond the reach of the enemy. The traditions have no reference to enemy attacks and indicate an apparently leisurely migration westward and southward. The truth probably was that, when attacked, the Siouans deserted their villages and removed to new locations some distance away, where they thought that they would be safe from the Iroquois. When attacked again, they left their new location and moved on. At each move, we may imagine, there were differences of opinion, and part of the people either re-

---

[4] Charlevoix, in French, *Historical Collections of Louisiana*, III, 126.
[5] Letter from James B. Griffin to the author.

mained where they were or set off in a chosen direction, leaving the main group behind. The Iroquois probably did not maintain a steady pressure. They probably attacked once a year, or once in two or three years. The Dhegihan fugitives had to live, and that meant that they had to halt here and there to hunt and perhaps to build a village and plant crops. If this was the situation, it is curious that archaeology has failed to find likely sites for villages of the Dhegiha Siouans, except for a possible Osage village in Saline County, Missouri. It seems incredible that these Indians should have moved to these distant points without building some villages along the way. In 1852 the government agent for the Quapaws reported that the tribe had formerly lived in a village at or near New Madrid, on the west bank of the Mississippi, below the Ohio. There were ruins of Indian towns in the New Madrid district, and across the Mississippi in Kentucky and Tennessee; but, without a definite knowledge of what type of culture the Quapaws had, we cannot connect the tribe with any of these village remains.

It is a little farther down the Mississippi that we come to village ruins that might be attributed to the Quapaws or their relatives, the Mosopeleas. These are the Pecan Point and Walls sites, exhibiting a culture of late prehistoric date so recent that the villages contain much material of the so-called Southern Death Cult, which seems to date around the year 1650 in this district. The culture here is late middle Mississippi, the type of culture some archaeologists assume the Quapaws had. These Pecan Point and Walls villages may be divided roughly into two groups. In the north, on both sides of the Mississippi, between the north line of Tennessee and the city of Memphis, there are some six village sites, four on the west bank and two or more on the east. Just below Memphis, on the east bank, there are three more. These villages are very late prehistoric, but do not contain glass beads or other indications of trade with Europeans. The modern town of Walls is on the east side of the river, in northwestern Mississippi state. The village ruins near Walls start on the west bank, where there are four between Walls and the mouth of the St. Francis River on the Arkansas shore; then, below the St. Francis, there are three village ruins on the east bank of the Mississippi. These village ruins below Walls contain blue glass beads and some other trinkets of European origin.

Up to the present time archaeology has not made definite suggestions as to what tribe or tribes may have lived in these most interesting Pecan Point and Walls villages. The villages are in the very district in which the French locate the Akanseas and Mosopeleas in 1673. French maps place a group of Mosopeleas on the east side of the Mississippi south of the Ohio and north of the Arkansas River. Another Mosopelea location was on the east bank of the Mississippi, below the Arkansas River. The Marquette map and the Thevenot copy, made from the Marquette map, put the Akanseas on the east side of the Mississippi in 1673, not far from the mouth of Arkansas River; but later-day French information indicated that the Akansea village of 1673 was some thirty leagues north of the mouth of the Arkansas River, which seems to be the location of the Walls village ruins, near the mouth of St. Francis River. Marquette states that in 1673 the Akanseas had glass beads and a few metal knives and hatchets. That fact also is in agreement with the artifacts found in the village ruins south of Walls.[6]

With no help from archaeology, we might describe the culture of the Quapaw group, as recorded by the French between 1673 and 1700 —a fixed village life, some villages fortified, huts in the form of long rectangles, covered with cedar bark, and quickly falling in decay when abandoned. The Indians of this group went on tribal buffalo hunts and grew crops of maize, squash, and beans near their villages. As compared with that of the tribes below them on the Mississippi, their culture was rude, and the only gods among the Quapaws seemed

[6] Although the French locate the Akansea or Quapaw tribe in a general way between 1673 and 1690, the various statements do not agree exactly, and the old maps add to the confusion. Some of the maps show Old Kappa, the old village of the Quapaws, on the east bank of the river, nearly opposite the mouth of the Arkansas River, with Kappa, a later Quapaw village, on the west bank, higher up and near the mouth of the St. Francis. The French statement of 1758 (in Nasatir, *Before Lewis and Clark*, I, 53) puts the Quapaw village La Salle visited in 1682 here, at Kappa of the maps, on the west side of the river, thirty leagues above Arkansas River. This suggests that Old Kappa was the village Marquette visited in 1673; but Father Gravier, 1700, definitely locates the Marquette village just below the mouth of the St. Francis and states that he saw the defending wall but that the cabins inside the wall had disappeared. The Mitchell map of 1755 adds more confusion by placing Old Kappa on the east side of the river near the mouth of the St. Francis and "Ouyape" (Quapaw) on the east bank, opposite the mouth of Arkansas River. This confusion is annoying; but it is not historically important. The Quapaws were in this general district from before 1673 until after 1700, and it is for archaeology to determine in which village the tribe dwelt.

to be earth-bound animals. But they had the calumet ceremony, which indicates a kind of sun worship as well. The French were struck by the fact that the Quapaws were different from the silent and rather grim northern tribes, such as the Algonquians. They were good-natured folk, talkative and often laughing and joking.

If it is found that the Pecan Point and Walls culture is really that of the Quapaws, we may state that these Indians had a very late middle Mississippi culture, including the Death cult. This culture exhibited some traits (such as strap handles on pots and long stone chisels) which we may connect with Fort Ancient culture and others (such as flint hoes) which can be connected with the Illinois Cahokian culture. We may assert that they had trade relations with the Indians at Moundville in Alabama.[7]

The Mosopeleas, regarded by some archaeologists as a myth, undoubtedly migrated down the east side of the Mississippi at the same time as the Quapaws. It is all very well to assert that the Mosopeleas never existed or that La Salle stated that the tribe was destroyed on the Ohio by the Iroquois. Such a view ignores the fact that it was La Salle who started the tale that the Mosopeleas stopped Marquette and Joliet on the Mississippi and turned them back.[8] La Salle in 1682 was given a Mosopelea boy while among the Quapaws, and met a Mosopelea chief with a few of his people among the Taensas, farther down the Mississippi. Henri de Tonty, in his memoir of 1697, mentions meeting the Mosopeleas on the lower Mississippi, and, in 1701, Father Gravier met the "Ounspik" among the Tunicas, ten to

---

[7] I know that some archaeologists like to believe that the Pecan Point–Walls Indians obtained strap handles on pots from Moundville Indians; but strap handles were a characteristic feature of pots in Cahokia, Illinois, in the Cincinnati center in Fort Ancient times, in protohistoric Pawnee villages on Loup Fork in Nebraska, and among the Kansas of Kansas. Since there is pretty good reason for supposing that the Skidi Pawnees of the Loup migrated out of the Ohio Valley at about the time the Quapaws left, it seems more reasonable, taking the other evidence into account, to state that the Pecan Point–Walls strap handles may have come from Ohio.

[8] Griffin, *Fort Ancient*, 17, 20; Tonty, in Margry, *Découvertes et établissements des Français*, I, 568, 610. The reference to the map, on page 17 of Griffin's *Fort Ancient*, seems to show that Thevenot, who made the map, believed that the long-haired Indians with guns met by Marquette and Joliet below the Ohio and probably near Memphis were Mosopeleas. All the other evidence we have concerning that tribe refutes such an idea. This same Joliet map shows the Mosopeleas far

twelve large cabins of them, and these Indians were probably the ones Coxe termed the Ouspie. Coxe stated that they were close neighbors of the Mosopeleas on the Ohio and were driven south by enemies.[9] Tunica Old Fields are on the east bank of the Mississippi, close to the mouth of Arkansas River, and this spot probably marks an earlier location of the Tunica tribe. It is at least probable that the Ouspie, driven from the Ohio, came down the Mississippi, and a remnant of the group joined the Tunicas and were still numerous in 1701.

In attempting to discover what tribe or tribes made the Pecan Point and Walls villages, we must take into account the very late date of these villages (the southern ones contain a few European trinkets such as glass beads). The dating suggests that the makers of these villages were still there when Marquette and Joliet came down the river, and the only tribes mentioned by these explorers at this point on the Mississippi were the Quapaws and Michigameas. The latter tribe belonged to the Illinois confederacy but appears to have been composed of southern Indians of the Cahokian group. The culture of these Indians would be middle Mississippi and might fit into the Pecan Point and Walls type; but they do not appear to have had more than one village, and that was on the west bank of the Mississippi, above the Quapaws. These Pecan Point and Walls villages hint at a movement southward, the northern villages being earlier, the later ones showing the beginning of European trade. The villages are on both banks of the Mississippi, while the Michigameas were apparently always on the west bank, and the tribe seems to have moved back and forth, first south, then north again, to get

below the Arkanseas, just where the Marquette map shows them. The Marquette map does not show a second Mosopelean group, north of the Arkanseas. Marquette gave a letter to the longhaired Indians with guns, and this letter is supposed to be the one found among Colonel Byrd's papers in Virginia, which hints that the longhaired Indians were either Cherokee or Chickasaws, who were trading with the English. One suspects that it was La Salle and his followers who got the notion that these longhaired Indians were Mosopeleas, and that this led to the story that the Mosopeleas were in western Illinois and stopped Marquette and Joliet there and that the Marquette and Joliet narrative of their journey down the Mississippi was fraudulent. That I will never credit. Douay states that Tonty told him that when he went down the Mississippi to seek for La Salle (1687?), he met the Mosopeleas on the lower river.

9 Gravier, in *Jesuit Relations*, LXV, 129; Griffin, *Fort Ancient*, 24.

back into contact with their allies in Illinois. Their particular allies seem to have been the Tamaroas and the Chapousas.

One more remark concerning the Mosopeleas may be made. The Marquette and Joliet narratives of their voyage down the Mississippi are brief and without detail. They later placed on their maps many tribes, like the Mosopeleas, that are not mentioned in the narratives. On these maps they located with general correctness the positions of the Quapaws, Osages, Kansas, Omahas, and Iowas. The fact that they had these tribes correctly named and located is the strongest evidence that they were right in setting down the Mosopeleas as a tribe then in existence, and their location of this tribe is probably correct, although large numbers of Mosopeleas may have joined the Osage-Omaha group before 1673.

It must be admitted that we do not have satisfactory information concerning the Quapaw and Mosopelea groups or the Osage and Omaha groups at the period when they came out of the Ohio Valley. Their general movements are clear enough, but there are few details. When we turn to the tribes higher up the Mississippi at this same period, 1650–1700, we come out into the clear light of history. We can give a fuller account of the northern tribes, and in doing so, we obtain some additional clues about what had happened to the south, in the Ohio Valley and along the Mississippi from the mouth of the Missouri southward.

In the north the motivation back of all the tribal movements of this period is clear. The Iroquois had no sooner worked the destruction of their near-at-hand rivals, the Hurons, Neutrals, and Eries, than they turned on more distant tribes, the Upper Algonquians of the Great Lakes and the tribes in the Ohio Valley, with the object of subduing or destroying them. They began their destruction campaign in 1652 with the Algonquians, making the Ottawas a main target but also driving the Ojibwas from their older location along the north shores of Lake Huron. Then they drove the Algonquians and the Tobacco Hurons from the southern peninsula of Michigan westward into Wisconsin. The Algonquians and the Tobacco Hurons had the friendship and trade of the French, and if they could have united their forces, they might have held off the Iroquois or defeated them; but they were absorbed in old feuds and petty hatreds nearer home. If they had any policy, it was to injure each other to the extent of their ability. Their one attempt to unite their forces was aimed at defeating and driving from their lands the Sioux, who seem to have wished for peace with their Algonquian neighbors.

We do not know how or when the Sioux first came into conflict with the Algonquians; but perhaps it was during the war between the Winnebagoes and the Illinis at the period around 1630–45. During that war part of the Winnebago group—perhaps the Otoes and Missouris—seems to have fled beyond the Mississippi when the Winnebagoes were defeated and almost destroyed by the Algonquians; and this flight of their Siouan kinsmen may have brought the Sioux into the conflict. There are vague statements in the *Jesuit Relations* that the Sioux drove the Illinis and the Miamis from the Mississippi eastward toward Lake Michigan and raided them so persistently that the lands around Lake Winnebago were depopulated. Then more Algonquians fled from the Iroquois to Wisconsin. The Ottawas and Tobacco Hurons fled beyond the Mississippi and became involved in war with the Sioux, whom they were planning to drive from their country. The Iroquois wolf packs invaded Wisconsin and Illinois, and the fighting grew more disordered and deadly.

The northern Siouan tribes, the Winnebagoes in eastern Wisconsin, the Iowas, Otoes, and Missouris west of the Mississippi, seem to have taken no prominent part in these wars. The Winnebagoes had been shattered in their war with the Algonquians, about the date 1640. They were now a small group, living by sufferance among immigrant Algonquians in the lands between Green Bay and Lake Winnebago, where they had formerly been the most important tribe. Weak as they now were, they were haughty, looking down on the ruder Algonquians, and being detested for it by those tribes. The Iowas, Otoes, and Missouris were in the prairies west of the Mississippi, a land of buffalo herds. They lived in permanent villages, probably of bark or mat houses, cultivating crops and going on tribal buffalo hunts. In all the French accounts of the wars, these tribes in Iowa are hardly mentioned, and it is difficult to discover what part they played in events after 1650. By Sioux tradition, the Iowas and Otoes extended their territory up the Mississippi as far as Minnesota River, but the Sioux claimed that they attacked them and drove them farther south. Then the Iroquois drove the Illini west of the Mississippi, and the intrusion of the Illinis on their lands seems to have forced the Iowas, Otoes, and Missouris to move farther toward the west and south.

The Algonquian tribes that were in Wisconsin and northern Illinois after 1650 were the Illinis, the closely related Miamis, the Mascoutens, Kickapoos, Sacs, Foxes, Potawatomis and, in the north, the Menominees, and Ojibwas. The Menominees do not appear to have been warlike. The Ojibwas, coming along the southern shores of Lake Superior, made peace with the Sioux, and were permitted to occupy fine hunting lands claimed by that tribe in northwestern Wisconsin and northern Minnesota. Obtaining French goods in quantity, the Ojibwas traded with the Sioux; and thus, while the other Algonquian tribes were wasting their strength in futile intertribal wars, the Ojibwas increased in population and power.[10]

The Algonquians of Wisconsin included the tribe or tribes formerly known as the Nation du Feu, who had been a power in the southern peninsula of Michigan until driven out by enemies around the year 1650. This nation had lived in Michigan around Saginaw Bay and along the Maumee River. According to French information, they were located immediately south of the Mascoutens in Wisconsin; but the old name, Nation du Feu, now went out of use, leaving in doubt just what tribes were included under the name.[11] The Sacs and Foxes, in later times close neighbors and allies, were living apart in Wisconsin up to 1670 or later. The Foxes had taken over lands on what was now called Fox River (formerly River of the Winnebagoes). They were a strong tribe, warlike and haughty; and at an early date they began to hate the French with intense bitterness, never missing an opportunity to stir up trouble or to kill French traders.[12] The Sacs had lived at Saginaw Bay in Michigan and may have been a part of the Nation du Feu. They had an ancient grudge against the Illinis, and in 1766 one of their chiefs said that his people would go on hating the Illinis as long as the sun and the moon and the stars remained in the sky and that the bones of the dead Sac warriors would rise up and resume fighting the Illinis if they could do so.[13]

The Kickapoos were close in language to the Sac and Potawatomi tribes, and they were probably part of the old Nation du Feu. Like

---

[10] Blair, *Indian Tribes of the Upper Mississippi*, I, 276–79.

[11] Thwaites, *Jesuit Relations*, XX, 30; Franquelin map of 1684.

[12] Thwaites, *Jesuit Relations*, LIV, 225; *ibid.*, LV, 219.

[13] Temple, "Indian Villages of the Illinois Country," *Illinois State Museum Scientific Papers*, Vol. II, part 2, 94.

most of the Wisconsin and Illinois Algonquian tribes, the Kickapoos ate human flesh, and they seem to have kept the habit long after the other tribes had been shamed out of it by the French. This tribe had probably lost its strength before removing from southern Michigan to Wisconsin, and it did not play a prominent part in events after 1650.

Tailhan stated that the first big Iroquois incursion into Wisconsin was about 1661, when the Sioux drove the refugee Hurons and Ottawas from Prairie Island in the Mississippi, the Hurons building a fortified village near the head of Black River, the Ottawas establishing themselves north of the Hurons at Chequamegon, on the south shore of Lake Superior. It was to the Ottawa village that the Iroquois army came to make peace in an attempt to keep the Ottawas, who had many guns, quiet while the tribes closely related to them were attacked. Having made this peace, the Iroquois divided their force, sending the first division along the Great Lakes eastward to attack the Ojibwas and Missisaugis, and the second to deal with the Foxes on Fox River. The Iroquois seem to have bungled this first attack. They did not succeed in striking a heavy blow against the Foxes, and part of their army, wandering off southward into Illinois, got lost in the prairies, where there were herds of buffalo. A big party of Illini warriors took the field, surprised the Iroquois in the camp, and killed them all.

Tailhan states that this was the first encounter of the Iroquois with the Illinis and that the Iroquois soon came back in greater force and drove the Illinis, and evidently part of the Miamis and some other Algonquian groups, beyond the Mississippi. He says that this war ended about 1667, when the Iroquois made peace with the western tribes.[14]

From our scanty information concerning the Iowa, Oto, and Mis-

---

[14] Tailhan and Perrot, in Blair, *Indian Tribes of the Upper Mississippi*, I, 154–55, 165, 321. Edwin James, *Long's Expedition* (vol. XV of Thwaites' *Early Western Travels*) 132, gives the earliest version of the Iowa and Oto migration traditions. Here the Oto story is that the Missouris first left the Iowas, and moved to the mouth of the Missouri, where they built a village. The Otoes later left the Iowas and joined the Missouris. The Iowa tradition that their tribe moved to the lower Missouri seems to refer to the movement of one camp of Iowas only, and to a late period, perhaps as late as 1700. This band then moved up the Missouri and had a village on the east bank near the present Council Bluffs, Iowa, but that was after 1700.

souri tribes, it seems that they were along the Mississippi in eastern Iowa, probably extending northward into Minnesota, at this period. They do not appear to have been very warlike; and, with the mass of Illinis and other Algonquians driven across the Mississippi by the Iroquois and intruding on their hunting grounds, we may assume that these three Siouan tribes withdrew. From the Tailhan story we would suppose that the withdrawal was sometime between 1663 and 1667. The Dhegiha migration tradition states that, when the Osage-Omaha group migrated up the Missouri River, they did not find the Missouris or Otoes but made contact with the Iowas, who had a village on Des Moines River near the present city of Des Moines, and that these Iowas joined the Omahas and Poncas and with them moved up Des Moines River. The French maps put these Siouan tribes, including the Otoes, on or near the upper Des Moines at the period 1673–85, and the same maps, after 1680, put the Missouris on Missouri River, near its mouth, and mark a northern stream, either a tributary of the Missouri, or the lower Des Moines, "the River of the Otoes." The Iowa and Oto migration traditions are confused and do not seem to give the movements in the proper sequence. It was probably at this period, when the Algonquians were driven across the Mississippi by the Iroquois, that the Missouris moved down to the Missouri River and the Otoes, or part of them, moved down and joined the Missouris; but, judging by the French information, this was not until after 1665.

Even after 1665, French information concerning the tribes of the Illinois confederacy was faulty. The French at first listed this confederacy as having a very big population with scores of villages. The *Jesuit Relations* for 1658 gave the confederacy eight thousand warriors; but soon after 1660 the Jesuits established a mission among the Ottawas and Hurons at Chequamegon Bay and, in the *Jesuit Relations* for 1671, listed only eight Illini villages, with a total population of eight to nine thousand people. Father Marquette was at the mission among the Ottawas and Hurons, and he met Illini men, who were coming to the Ottawa village to trade for French arms and goods. He clearly places the Illinis west of the Mississippi; but they had to cross east of the river on their way north to trade, to avoid the Sioux. When the Illinis were refugees west of the Mississippi, they must have had a very hard time. They were being raided by the Iroquois from the east and were at the same time at war with the Sioux, who were coming down from the north to attack them. It may have been at this time that the Michigameas left the other Illinis and fled down the Mississippi into northern Arkansas. Other Illini groups may have occupied the land near the mouth of the Missouri; and if this is correct, we may assume that none of the migrating Siouan tribes—the Osage-Omaha or Missouri-Oto groups— could have occupied the lower Missouri Valley until the Illini tribes returned to their old lands east of the Mississippi. When driven west of the river by the Iroquois, the big Illini group of Peorias seem to have occupied the lower Cedar River, and with or near them was the little tribe of Moingwenas, for whom, perhaps, the Des Moines River was named by the French.[15] The big Kaskaskia group of Illinis occupied lands in eastern Iowa, north of the Des Moines, and some Illinis seem to have lived in Iowa, to the north of the Kaskaskias.[16] The Miamis, also driven west of the Mississippi, were probably in northeastern Iowa,

Although they had permanent villages and grew crops, the Illinis spent most of the year away from the villages, hunting. When they lived in Illinois, they hunted buffalo in the prairies, and when driven west of the Mississippi, they hunted buffalo in the Iowa prairies. They left their villages in September and went, either in dugout canoes or on foot, to their hunting grounds, where they broke up into small camps. The men of each camp went out on buffalo hunts, while the women, children, and old people stayed in the camps. They laid up large stocks of dried buffalo meat during the winter. In spring they hunted bear and deer, and in March they returned to their permanent villages, where the women prepared the ground and planted their corn and vegetables.

The Jesuits started a mission for the Ottawas and Tobacco Hurons at Chequamegon Bay on the south shore of Lake Superior about 1660. Father Allouez was in charge for a time; then Father Marquette took over. The priests had little success; some of the Tobacco Hurons

[15] The French had a habit of abbreviating some tribal names. They called the Akanseas *Les Arcs* and the Arkansas River *Des Arcs;* they called the Omahas *Les Mahas,* and so on. We might suppose that they called the Moinguenas *Les Moins* and the river they lived on *Des Moins.* The other explanations of the origin of the name Des Moines do not seem very satisfactory.

[16] When driven from Illinois River by the Iroquois in 1680, part of the fleeing Illinis turned up the Mississippi northward.

had been baptized in their old lands on Lake Huron, but most of the Ottawas had no interest in the white men's religion. The Ottawas were out-and-out heathen, jeering at the priests or abusing and threatening them. Marquette had hopes of converting the Sioux, who dwelled to the west, among the lakes and marshes. The Sioux seem to have made a good impression on all the Jesuits. They were upright people, inclined to be friendly and kind, and not at all like the treacherous and cruel Ottawas and Tobacco Hurons, who invited the Sioux to their villages and then killed and ate them.

All the attempts of the Algonquians to defeat the Sioux and take their lands failed. This tribe lived in moving camps among lakes and marshes, and in summer they traveled much in canoes, evidently dugouts. They had one permanent village which was regarded by the French as their main center, and it was reported to have some kind of fort. The Algonquians developed the practice of attacking the Sioux in winter, when the marshes and lakes were frozen and it was easier for war parties to travel through the Sioux lands; but in winter the Sioux were wandering about in small camps, and if the enemy did succeed in finding and surprising one camp, the Sioux from other camps swiftly assembled and drove off the attackers with heavy losses.

In 1666 the French officials, exasperated by Iroquois attacks, decided on a stiff policy for dealing with that tribe. Forts were built along the Richelieu River, which was a route the Iroquois wolf packs took in making raids along the St. Lawrence; and in September the largest force the French had assembled was gathered to invade the Iroquois country. Several hundred French regulars of the Royal Cardignon regiment, six hundred French settlers, and a force of Indian allies marched into the Iroquois country. The Iroquois fled to avoid a battle, and the French plundered and burned the Iroquois towns. Cowed for the moment by this disaster, the Iroquois made peace, which they kept more or less honestly for eighteen years. This peace was supposed to include the tribes allied to the French; but the Iroquois continued their attacks on the Algonquians of Wisconsin and Illinois and on the tribes in the Ohio Valley.[17]

The Sioux, aroused by the Ottawa and Algonquian attempt to destroy them in 1669, were vigorously raiding the Algonquians in Wisconsin, not forgetting the Illinis and some Miamis who were south

17 Schlarman, *From Quebec to New Orleans*, 40–41; Hodge, *Handbook of Indians North of Mexico*, I, 590.

of the Sioux and west of the Mississippi. The scales had shifted in favor of the Sioux. After their defeat in 1669, the Ottawas and Tobacco Hurons had abandoned their villages at Chequamegon Bay on Lake Superior and had fled east along the lakes to escape Sioux vengeance. Their villages had been the great western trading center for years, and the western Indians came to Chequamegon Bay in considerable numbers every year to trade for French weapons, kettles, and other goods. Now, with the Ottawas and Hurons gone, the Ojibwas occupied the Chequamegon Bay district, and the French traded regularly with them. The Ojibwas made an alliance with the Sioux and were permitted to hunt and trap on Sioux lands. Either because of this shift in the situation or because of a falling off in Iroquois raids, the Illinis and Miamis returned to their old homes, east of the Mississippi. The Sioux apparently followed them, and this was probably the time when Sioux raids greatly troubled the Algonquians in eastern Wisconsin and forced them to abandon the lands around Lake Winnebago.

Marquette, writing from the Chequamegon Bay district on Lake Superior in 1669, stated that to go to the Illinis, one went southward to the Kitchigami tribe, who dwelt inland in twenty big bark cabins. This tribe feared the French, wished to have trade with them, and were at war with the Illinis. The tribe was an Algonquian group, closely related to the Kickapoos and Mascoutens, and probably lived near those tribes on Wisconsin River. From this tribe one went on to the Miamis, and then crossed great empty lands and came to the Illinis, who were in two great villages and had from eight to nine thousand people. This probably refers to the Kaskaskia village of Illinis on upper Illinois River and to the big Peoria village farther down that river, at Lake Peoria. Thus, by 1669, the Illinis had evidently returned to their lands east of the Mississippi.[18]

In this report Marquette gives us a glimpse of conditions on the Ohio River and perhaps on the lower Missouri in 1668–69. He says that the Illinis who visited Chequamegon Bay to trade spoke of great nations who lived on a great river to the south of them in a warm country where two crops of maize were grown in a year. They said that the Shawnees came overland to visit the Illini villages in 1668.

[18] Marquette, in French, *Historical Collections of Louisiana,* IV, lvi; Hodge, *Handbook of Indians North of Mexico,* I, 705; Temple, "Indian Villages of the Illinois Country," *Illinois State Museum Scientific Papers,* Vol. II, part 2, 20.

This tribe dwelt three days' journey toward the east-southeast and had quantities of glass beads. Six or seven days below the Illini villages was another great river—probably the Missouri—on which lived tribes who traveled in dugout canoes. This may be a reference to the Michigameas and other tribes, and the Illinis seem to have regarded them as alien groups.

If one is inclined to pity the Illinis, first slaughtered and driven west of the Mississippi by the Iroquois, then attacked and driven east of the river by the Sioux, he should ponder Father Marquette's statement of 1669, that the Illinis were coming to trade with the Ottawas for French hatchets, knives, and some guns, and with these weapons they were raiding neighbor tribes who still had only flint weapons and were slaughtering them and carrying off great numbers of slaves. Almost invariably this was the practice of tribes that had been slaughtered by other tribes armed with French weapons. When they obtained such weapons, instead of using them to protect themselves from enemies armed with guns, they went off to slaughter neighboring groups who were still armed only with flint weapons. Father Allouez added a curious fact to the Marquette information. In 1677 he wrote that the Illinis had some guns, but were so slow and clumsy in using them that they did not employ them in real fighting, but kept them to terrorize tribes they were making raids on, tribes that still had only flint weapons and were thrown into a panic by firearms. For real fighting, he stated, the Illini warriors preferred the bow and club. They had long shields of buffalo hide, long enough to cover a man's entire body.

After the Ottawa and Algonquian war on the Sioux and the subsequent flight of the Ottawas and Tobacco Hurons, the Jesuits abandoned their missionary labors at Chequamegon and shifted to Green Bay in eastern Wisconsin, where they established a mission among the Winnebagoes, and in 1669 went up Fox River to visit the Algonquian tribes with the object of beginning missionary work among them. They found the Foxes on Fox River between Green Bay and Lake Winnebago, and the Mascoutens had a village a day's journey up Fox River from the Foxes. With the Mascoutens was a group of Miamis and Illinis. This group had a fortified village, and near or with them were the Kickapoos. Father Allouez described the Mascoutens and Kickapoos as rough and rude people; the Miamis he termed gentle, sedate, and friendly, with good manners. Yet, in the spring of 1670 a war party of Iroquois took six big bark cabins of Foxes by surprise when the men were away hunting, killing many people and carrying off thirty women; and it was the gentle Miamis who struck back at the Iroquois. They brought Iroquois scalps to the Foxes to dry their tears and a smoked Iroquois arm to make a feast.

Nicolas Perrot was in eastern Wisconsin at this time, 1669–70. He called Green Bay the Bay of the Foxes and Miamis. The Sac tribe and the Potawatomis were near Green Bay. The Potawatomis were then the most numerous group of the Wisconsin Algonquians, having seven hundred warriors. The Foxes had four hundred.

These Algonquians, caught between the Iroquois in the east and the Sioux in the west, were having a bad time. In 1668 the Sioux were heavily raiding the Illinis in the lands west of the Mississippi and were also attacking the Foxes and the other Algonquians in eastern Wisconsin. The Foxes had to remove to the neighborhood of the present Oshkosh. The other Algonquians moved nearer to Lake Michigan, to the Milwaukee and Chicago neighborhoods; but then the Iroquois struck at them, and the Miamis and Potawatomis moved southward, part of the Miamis spending their winters hunting in Ohio. The Fox tribe held to their old location; but the Kickapoos moved down Rock River into northern Illinois and the Mascoutens moved to a location north of the Kickapoos and south of Wisconsin River. The French accounts of the movements of these Wisconsin Algonquians are bewildering. Attacked alternately by the Iroquois and Sioux, each tribal group fled in a different direction, then returned to their old location, only to move again. The Miamis shifted back and forth and seem to have been as much at home on the Mississippi, in Wisconsin, or in Iowa as on the shores of Lake Michigan or in northern Indiana and Ohio.[19]

The French authorities had decided to explore new lands in the west and to take possession of those lands in the name of the French king. St. Lusson was sent west in the spring of 1671, accompanied by Nicolas Perrot as interpreter and by twenty Frenchmen. Perrot went among the Wisconsin Indians and urged them to attend the ceremony at Sault Ste Marie, at the entrance into Lake Superior, and there on June 14 the French solemnly took possession of the upper Great Lakes country in the name of Louis XIV and in the presence

[19] Marquette, in French, *Historical Collections of Louisiana*, IV, lvi; Hodge, *Handbook of Indians North of Mexico*, I, 705.

of a great gathering of Indians. This action of the French was an effort to prevent the spread of English trade among the tribes. The English were now in control in New York and had also established trading houses on Hudson Bay in the far north. The Crees in the north were already obtaining guns in quantity at Hudson Bay, and the Algonquians of the upper Great Lakes were showing signs of deserting the French and going to the English in New York to trade. To prevent this, in 1673 the French established Fort Cataroqui on Lake Ontario, at the site of the present town of Kingston.

The Jesuits were also giving much attention to extending their hold over the western tribes. They were pushing into new territory, in Wisconsin, and already had their eyes fixed on the Illinis, who were returning to their old lands in northern Illinois. Reports of a great river in the west had reached Marquette while he was doing mission work on Lake Superior and the plan for an expedition to explore the river was being evolved. A struggle for control of the Indians had developed. The Jesuits wished to keep traders out of the Indian country, accusing them of debauching the Indians with liquor and doing all they could to thwart missionary labors. The traders retorted that the Jesuits were secretly engaged in the fur trade themselves and were making great profits. The Indians were beginning to see the shadow of white control looming over them, and all of them, from the Iroquois in New York State to the tribes in Wisconsin, were beginning to suspect that the white men they had welcomed on their first coming were deadly enemies who would bring ruin on all the tribes. Thus the Jesuits, when they came into Wisconsin 1669–70, were derided and threatened, and the faith they were trying to spread was rejected with scorn. The mighty Iroquois, squeezed between the French in Canada and the English on the Atlantic coast, were seeking new power by conquering distant tribes in the west.

When Count Frontenac returned to Canada as governor in 1672, he had plans for exploration of new lands in the west. Intendant Talon informed him that the best man for such work was Louis Joliet, who had been educated by the Jesuits and had studied geographical astronomy. Joliet had been trading among the Indians of Lake Superior for some years, spoke the Algonquian language, and had heard Indian stories of a great river in the west, the Mississippi. The expedition to find the Mississippi was organized at once, and

Father Marquette, who had served at the mission on Lake Superior, was selected to accompany Joliet, probably to represent the Jesuits. Frontenac was no friend of the missionaries, but he had returned to Canada in an impoverished condition and was forced to accept Jesuit aid to pay the cost of the expedition to the Mississippi.

Joliet made his preparations at Quebec and Montreal and set out for the west late in 1672. At St. Ignace Mission at Sault Ste Marie, he picked up Father Marquette, and the two leaders spent the winter and spring completing their preparations and gathering information from the Indians concerning the Mississippi and the tribes near it. On May 17, 1673, seven men in two bark canoes left Mackinac Island. Joliet and Marquette were apparently accompanied by five French Canadians who had come with Joliet from the St. Lawrence in 1672. They went to the head of Green Bay and up Fox River, finding the Mascouten village high up this stream. The Marquette narrative states here that Mascouten means "the Fire Nation" in the Algonquian tongue, and that no Frenchmen had penetrated the country west of this village. This ignores the Radisson expedition to the Mississippi twenty years before.

The village was of three tribes, Mascoutens, Kickapoos, and Miamis. The first two were rough, rude, and evidently not very friendly. The explorers obtained two guides from the more friendly Miamis. On June 10, the party left the village and entered a maze of lakes and swamps near the head of Fox River. They then came to a short land portage into the Wisconsin River. Like most of the French they used the *M* and not the *W* in spelling Wisconsin, and they termed it Miskous or Meskousing. They saw no Indian villages on this river. On June 17 they reached the mouth of the Wisconsin and entered the Mississippi. For sixty leagues down the river they saw no Indians, but observed herds of buffalo and large numbers of deer. On June 25 they found a path on the west side of the Mississippi; and, leaving their men with the canoes, Joliet and Marquette went on foot along the path. At two leagues they came on a large village. Nearby were two more villages. The first village was on a river, the other two on a hill beyond. Joliet and Marquette shouted when they came near the first village, and two Indians came out, bearing calumets of peace, held toward the sun. They presented the pipes, which the white men smoked. Entering the village, the whites were met by an old man, stark naked, his arms extended toward the sun. He cried out that the sun was beautiful on this day when the white men came to his village. Joliet recorded that this first village—perhaps he meant all three—had 300 big cabins and 180 dugout canoes, most of them fifty feet in length. These Indians were Illinis; they were Algonquians; and, before coming to Illinois and to the Mississippi, they used the Algonquian bark canoes and must have learned to use dugouts from the southern Indians of the Cahokian group. The exact identity of the Indians in these three villages is not clear. They were all Illinis. Part were Peorias, and the head chief of the Illinis was with them. Their villages were in Iowa, and if the distance given, sixty leagues below the mouth of the Wisconsin River, is correct, they were either in the present Jackson County or in Clinton County, Iowa.

The party of explorers stayed with the Peoria group of Illinis until the end of June. On their departure they were given a sacred calumet of peace, which would protect them against attack by tribes farther down the Mississippi. The narrative of their journey[20] is barren of detail until they reach the mouth of the Missouri. The mouth of the Ohio is mentioned, and below here the party met a group of long-haired Indians armed with guns, who were friendly and gave the Frenchmen some buffalo meat. Next they came to the Michigameas, probably in northern Arkansas; and this tribe was hostile at first, but became more friendly when they saw the calumet of peace. Eight or ten leagues below the Michigameas they found the Akansea or Quapaw tribe. Here they decided to turn back, fearing the tribes farther down the Mississippi. On their homeward journey up the river, they took the route up Illinois River and found the village of the Kaskaskia group of Illinis on its upper course. These Indians were very friendly and guided the party eastward to the shores of Lake Michigan. The Frenchmen returned to their starting point on Green Bay and wintered there.[21]

The narrative of this most important exploration of the Mississippi is far from satisfactory. It was the target for criticism in later years by La Salle and his faction, who made it clear enough that they regarded the narrative as a falsification. They claimed that Joliet and

20 Thwaites, *Jesuit Relations*, LIX, 87–163.
21 Thwaites, *Jesuit Relations*, LIV, 167, 197, 205, 207, 219, 227; 231; *Ibid.*, LV, 20; Blair, *Indian Tribes of the Upper Mississippi*, I, 317; Temple, "Indian Villages of the Illinois Country," *Illinois State Museum Scientific Papers*, Vol. II, part 2, 58–59.

Marquette had not gone farther down than a short distance below the mouth of the Missouri and had manufactured their account of the lower river. The maps attributed to Joliet and Marquette, however, are more detailed than the narrative. They show many tribes not mentioned in the narrative, and most of these tribes are indicated as being in the districts in which later information locates them. These maps show a knowledge of the country and the tribes that is absent from the brief narrative.

It is difficult to credit the view of the La Salle party that Joliet and Marquette falsified the account of their explorations. These two men had high reputations among their contemporaries in Canada, and we have a simple explanation of the lack of detail in the published narrative. Joliet and his men left Green Bay in the spring of 1674 and made the journey back to the St. Lawrence. When they were within sight of Montreal, one of the canoes was upset in the Lachine Rapids, and two men were drowned, Joliet's strongbox holding the official narrative of the expedition, maps, and notes was lost. Joliet almost lost his life in this mishap. He went to Father Dablon, Marquette's superior among the Jesuits, and told him of the loss of the official report on the explorations. There was a second copy of this report in Marquette's hands, but Marquette fell ill of dysentery and died alone among the Indians on the shores of Lake Michigan. Before this news reached Montreal and Quebec, Father Dablon wrote, or had someone write, from Joliet's statements to him and from some notes, what he termed a brief abstract of the explorations, which was published in the *Jesuit Relations*. There was no pretense that it was a full narrative, as it was hoped to obtain the copy of the official report from Father Marquette and publish that later.[22]

The historical importance of the Joliet and Marquette material lies in the fact that it is the first reasonably clear account of the tribes along the Mississippi, from Wisconsin down into Arkansas, and that the maps solidly confirm the migration traditions of the Dhegiha group of Siouan tribes. Later French information proves that these tribes were driven out of the Ohio Valley by the Iroquois, probably after 1650, and the Marquette and Joliet maps prove that they had

[22] This matter of the loss of the official report and the making of the brief abstract is detailed in Schlarman, *From Quebec to New Orleans*, 56. Thwaites, the editor of *Jesuit Relations*, believed that Dablon wrote the brief account which was published as Marquette's.

reached their historic locations before 1673. The explorers found the Akansea or Quapaws on the Mississippi, near the mouth of Arkansas River. Marquette noted that the men of this tribe wore strings of glass beads in their noses and ears, and the finding of glass beads in the village ruins near the mouth of Arkansas in what the archaeologists term the Walls culture sites is a strong clue that these Walls villages were those of the Quapaws. Moreover, these maps prove that the Mosopelea tribe, termed a myth by some archaeologists, was real. The Marquette map puts this tribe on the east side of the Mississippi, about two-thirds of the distance up from Arkansas River to the mouth of the Ohio. That would be in the Memphis district, or a little south, in the Walls area, where the village ruins do not show glass beads or other European objects. Joliet's map was made immediately after his return to Quebec in 1674. In the location where Marquette placed the Mosopeleas, Joliet places a tribe called Aganatchi, not mentioned in other sources. He places the Mosopeleas on the east side of the Mississippi, south of the Akanseas. Thevenot, when he made a map from the original Marquette map in later years, seems to have noted the longhaired southern Indians, armed with guns, mentioned in the Marquette brief abstract as having been encountered below the Ohio on the east bank of the Mississippi; and he apparently conjectured that they were the Mosopeleas. At this point on his map he wrote, "*Aganahali; Monsoupleria; ils ont des fusils,*" and then followed the Marquette map, placing the Mosopeleas also on the east side of the Mississippi, south of the Akanseas. His Aganahali are probably the same as Joliet's Aganatchis, and both of these names seem to be from a southern Indian language, perhaps Chickasaw or Creek. One may assume that the Marquette and Joliet maps were right, that the Mosopeleas were on the east bank, south of the Akansea, and that Thevenot's conjecture that they were in the two groups, one in the Memphis district, was erroneous.

The Marquette map seems to disprove the conjectures of those scholars who assume that the Peoria group of Illinis, visited by Marquette and Joliet, were on the lower Des Moines. This map shows them on a river which is about due west of Peoria Lake in northern Illinois and far to the north of the Des Moines. The Marquette map places the Osages on the south side of the Missouri, with the Missouri tribe a little to the northwest of them. To the west of the Peorias, in northern Iowa, this map places the Illini group of

Moinguenas; to the west of them are the Otoes, west of these, the Omahas, and east of the Omahas, the Paoutets (Iowas). The Panas (a Pawnee group) are a little to the northwest of the Otoes and northeast of the Omahas. This is the location, obviously, as given in the Omaha migration tradition, which states that they left the Osages on the Missouri, migrated northward, met the Iowas near the present city of Des Moines, and went with them to a district near the upper Des Moines and the pipestone quarry in southwestern Minnesota. The Joliet map shows these tribes a little differently, placing the Panas on the Missouri, with the Paoutet or Iowas to the north of them. The map shows the Omahas east of the Paoutet, with the Otoes a little to the north of the Omahas. Joliet does not set down the Peorias or the Moinguenas.[23]

In speaking of the Illinis, Marquette observed that the Indians had some guns and other French weapons, and that they were employing these weapons to terrorize neighboring tribes who had only flint weapons. This was the beginning of the Illini slave-catching raids on the Siouans and Pani tribes west of the Mississippi, an operation which was interrupted in 1680 when the Iroquois drove the Illinis in panicky flight west of the Mississippi, and large groups of the fugitives had to seek refuge among the Osages, on whom they had been recently making slave raids.

These Algonquian tribes, driven west of the Mississippi, also tangled with the Sioux, and some time around 1672 the Sioux drove the Miamis back east of the Mississippi. Presumably the Miamis were in northeastern Iowa and were the first to be displaced by the Sioux; but, as Marquette found, the Kaskaskia Illinis also had to move back east of the river and were on upper Illinois River in the autumn of 1673.[24] These facts enable us to date the migration of the Osage-

[23] These maps, the Marquette, the Joliet, and the Thevenot, are reproduced in Griffin's *Fort Ancient*, on pages 14–16. The Marquette map, in French, *Historical Collections of Louisiana*, IV, 268, shows the Mosopeleas where Thevenot does, north of the Akanseas in the district where the longhaired Indians with guns were met. The Marquette narrative states that the Akansea men cut their hair short. As the Mosopeleas came from the Ohio River, they probably also had short hair. The Indians with guns met by Marquette had long hair and must have been southern Indians.

[24] It was probably after the year 1663 that the Miamis and Illinis were driven west of the Mississippi. Father Membré, in French, *Historical Collections of Louisiana*, IV, 154, stated that the Miamis had formerly dwelled beyond, presumably

Omaha group, for part of the Iowas had moved south to the Des Moines, near the present city of that name, and we may conjecture that this movement was caused by the intrusion of the Illinis and Miamis on the Iowa tribal lands in northeast Iowa. Here on the Des Moines this Iowa group was joined by the Omahas and Poncas, and the three tribes then moved up into northwestern Iowa.

The French information does not aid us much in attempting to follow the course of events in Iowa. Modern archaeology would be of great assistance, if we set aside the archaeological dating, which is conjectural and appears to be set for a much earlier time than the period with which we are dealing. It is difficult to escape the conviction that the many Mill Creek village ruins in Cherokee County, northwestern Iowa, are the Omaha and Ponca villages of the period 1650–80, and that the Oneota village ruins nearby are the remains of contemporary Iowa and Oto villages.

The French information does not make a clear picture. In 1680, Father Zénobe Membré mentioned the Ainoves, evidently an Iowa tribal group, as living near the Kickapoos, presumably in Wisconsin. It is possible that Iowas may have gone into Wisconsin to trade with the Kickapoos, and perhaps to live near them for a time. The French at this period added to the confusion by referring to the Nadouessie Mascoutens as a tribe in Iowa. Usually identified as Iowas, the name Nadouessie Mascouten was applied to both the Iowas and the Otoes.

The draft of the Franquelin map of 1684 shows the Oto and Missouri tribes on a northern tributary of the Missouri River, with the Omahas and Iowas to the north of them. It was apparently in the 1670's that the Otoes, or part of the tribe, went south, to live with or near the Missouris. J. O. Dorsey stated that the Otoes were on Osage River in 1687. All this confusion about the location of the Iowas and Otoes seems to have been the result of their erratic movements when the Algonquians intruded on lands in Iowa state, between the years 1665 and 1685.

Father Marquette described the Illinis as docile, friendly, and inclined to listen to the teachings of the Jesuits. He was burning with zeal to start a mission in the great Kaskaskia village on upper Illinois River. The missionary was still very ill, but he left Green Bay with

---

west of, the Illinis, but that by 1680 they were near Lake Michigan, east of the Illinis. Father Hennepin, writing in 1678 or 1679, said that the Miamis had formerly been in the west but had now crossed east of the Mississippi.

two Frenchmen and went in a bark canoe to the mouth of Chicago River, where his party wintered. In the spring they went to the Kaskaskia village, near the present town of Utica, Illinois. Marquette found that the Illinis of this village had increased their population very much since he had found seventy-four cabins in the village in the fall of 1673. They now had two thousand men and youths, not including women and children. The Indians were very friendly, and Marquette began his missionary work; but his illness increased and he had to give up his work and start for the Jesuit center on Mackinac Island. In mid-May he died on the shore of Lake Michigan.

The mission among the Kaskaskias was abandoned. In 1677, Father Allouez went to Kaskaskia and found a great town of 351 bark cabins, nearly five times the number Marquette had noted in 1673; but Allouez reported that the Kaskaskias had now been joined by seven other tribes of the Illini confederacy who had moved up Illinois River from the Mississippi. The great Indian town had its cabins arranged in a single row along the river bank, extending for several miles. The Indians were no longer the docile and friendly folk Marquette had described, and Allouez soon left the village.

La Salle was in France when Joliet and Marquette went down the Mississippi. He was seeking support at the French court for his plans of western exploration and for taking possession of the Mississippi Valley in the name of the French king. He obtained the backing he sought, and also the seigniory of Cataroqui (Fort Frontenac) on the north side of Lake Ontario, which he intended to employ as his base for operations in the west. He returned to Canada in September, 1675, with full powers from the French court to carry out Count Frontenac's western projects. By this time all the merchants and the Jesuits in Canada were bitterly opposing Frontenac and La Salle. Frontenac had returned to Canada as governor in an impoverished state, and he was employing high-handed methods to gain control of the fur trade and enrich himself. He had dismissed Nicolas Perrot, commandant or governor at Montreal, who was friendly with the Jesuit party; and the count was convinced that, with La Salle's aid, he could control the fur trade of the upper lakes, of the Mississippi and Ohio, and keep out the English of New York, who were trying to extend their trade to the lakes and the Mississippi. But, even after gaining the consent of the royal court, Frontenac had difficulty in starting his operations. Credit was required, and in November, 1677, La Salle returned to France. He came back to Canada in the autumn of 1678, accompanied by Father Zénobe Membré and Henri de Tonty, an adventurous Italian, who had lost a hand while serving with the French royal forces. Tonty's cousin, Daniel Greysolon Duluth, also came to Canada about this time, and was soon exploring the western shores of Lake Superior and penetrating the Sioux country near the head of the Mississippi.[25]

La Salle now went to Cataroqui (Fort Frontenac), north of Lake Ontario, and began building a fifty-ton vessel, which was to be the first ship to sail the waters of the Great Lakes. Up to this time the French had been greatly handicapped by having to transport their men and supplies through the lakes in fleets of birchbark canoes. La Salle's men built this ship, the *Griffin*, at the outlet of Niagara River; and in August, 1679, La Salle sailed with a large company of men and a big supply of trading goods and stores and reached Mackinac Island safely. He sailed on into Green Bay, where he loaded the *Griffin* with a rich cargo of furs—enough to pay most of the debts he and Frontenac owed. In France, La Salle had been forbidden to trade with tribes that the Ottawa Indians were supplying with French goods. This was to protect the Montreal traders, who supplied the Ottawas; but La Salle ignored the order and loaded his ship with furs obtained from tribes near Green Bay that had traded with the Ottawas up to this time. Warned by Indians of coming storms on the lakes, La Salle ignored their advice and sent his ship away. It was never heard of again.

Unaware of this dreadful loss, La Salle pressed on westward with a party of his men to lay the foundations for his exploration of the Mississippi Valley. He went to the upper Illinois River, and going down it he built Fort Crèvecoeur near the present city of Peoria as his base of operations. Here he was among the Illini, but most of the Indians were away hunting when the French arrived.

After driving the Illinis west of the Mississippi in the 1660's, the Iroquois had sent their own men into the Illinois country, east of

---

25 Schlarman, *From Quebec to New Orleans,* 85–87; Parkman, *La Salle and the Discovery of the Great West,* 85–91, 112–15, 126–28. The French had a ten-ton ship in Lake Ontario before the *Griffin* was built, but the *Griffin* was the first sailing ship to go through Detroit Straits into Lake Huron and Lake Michigan. La Salle had permission to trade only for buffalo robes, not for fine furs, but he disregarded this restriction.

the great river, to trap for furs. About 1672 some of the Illinis ven-
tured back into their old lands in Illinois, and here they found and
killed about forty Iroquois trappers. The Illinis were growing bold
again. Obtaining French knives, hatchets, and some guns from the
Ottawa traders, they were making slave-catching raids on tribes beyond the Mississippi; and now they had attacked the Iroquois. That
tribe had made dire threats of coming to eat the Illinis, but up to
the time of La Salle's arrival on Illinois River the Iroquois had not
struck a heavy blow.[26]

La Salle's purpose was to build a forty-ton vessel on the Illinois
River and later embark his men in it and explore the Mississippi to
its mouth, taking possession of the great valley in the name of the
King of France. He also wished to discover the sources of the great
river, and for this purpose he now sent Michael Accault, accompanied
by another *voyageur* and by Father Louis Hennepin, up the Mississippi in a canoe to explore; but the party fell into the hands of the
Sioux and were taken as prisoners to the principal Sioux village in
the marshes northeast of present St. Paul.

It was in February, 1680, that Hennepin and his companions set
out from Crèvecoeur. La Salle had only ten men left with him on
Illinois River. He was worried about his affairs in Canada, where his
enemies were scheming to induce his creditors to act against him and
seize his property and were even urging the Iroquois to attack the
Illinis, thus hoping to thwart his plans for an expedition down the
Mississippi. He now left Tonty in charge at Fort Crèvecoeur and set
out almost alone to find his way through the wilderness to Niagara
River. At or near Fort Frontenac he began to hear news that was
enough to destroy the courage of a lesser man. His ship, the *Griffin*,
had been lost with all its men and the cargo of valuable furs. A supply ship of his, coming from France, had been lost near the mouth
of the St. Lawrence with its cargo. The peddlers he had supplied
with trade goods, to exchange with Indians for furs on a commission
basis, had decamped into the woods and vanished; his creditors had
taken court action and seized all his property. Despite all these blows,
the indomitable La Salle got new credit, bought new stocks of goods,
recruited men, and set off to rejoin Tonty on Illinois River.[27]

[26] Temple, "Indian Villages of the Illinois Country," *Illinois State Museum Sci-
tific Papers*, Vol. II, part 2, 20.

[27] Membré, in French, *Historical Collections of Louisiana*, IV; Schlarman, *From
Quebec to New Orleans*, 89–90.

Meantime, Tonty was having plenty of trouble. He could not count on the handful of men left under his charge. They were discontented and mutinous. Father Membré was the only man he could depend on in a crisis. No work was being done on the boat, and the Illini tribe, on which he had to depend for protection and the very food he ate, was being alienated by rumors that La Salle was in league with their Iroquois enemies and had come to spy on them and that he had gone eastward to set the Iroquois wolf packs in motion against them. The Miamis, part of whom were now allied with the Iroquois, came to the Illinis near Fort Crèvecoeur and started intriguing against the French. These Miamis, recent enemies of the Illinis, had induced a Mascouten chief from Wisconsin to head their party on the pretence that it was a friendly Mascouten delegation. With a big stock of British kettles, hatchets, knives, and assorted trade goods to sweeten the minds of the Illinis, these men went to work undermining Tonty's weakened position. In a night council with the Illini chiefs, the Mascouten chief solemnly warned that La Salle and and his men were allied with the Iroquois and were only on Illinois River to prepare the ground and open the way for a fresh Iroquois invasion. This chief then presented the Illini chiefs with all the stock of trade goods as a proof of friendship and took his Miami young men out of the village, leaving the Illinis extremely suspicious of the French.

We here have another instance of the impossibility of uniting these Algonquian tribes against the Iroquois. The Miamis were so closely related to the Illinis that they had formerly been like one people, but they had quarreled and the Illinis had driven part of the Miamis from Illinois northward into Wisconsin before 1670. The Miamis in 1678–79 were angry with the Illinis and jealous of the French attention to that tribe. La Salle made a peace between the two tribes in 1679; but after that some Miamis went to the Iroquois country and suggested an attack on the Illinis to the Senecas. The Senecas gave them no encouragement, at least not in public, and practically ordered them to leave their villages. After this, part of the Miamis moved their village nearer to the Illinis; but that tribe was suspicious, fearing that this was a plot to get near enough to attack them by surprise.[28]

28 Membré, in French, *Historical Collections of Louisiana*, IV, 154; Parkman, *La Salle and the Discovery of the Great West*, 205, 265.

When he reached Mackinac Island on his way eastward, La Salle sent a messenger to Tonty, ordering him to go up Illinois River and examine a high rock near the old Illini village as a possible site for a permanent fort. This was Starved Rock, near the present town of Utica. The rock is a high, yellow sandstone cliff, just above the main Illini village, which was deserted by the Indians, who were away on the winter hunt when La Salle came to Illinois River. The legend was that a party of Illinis had taken refuge on this rock when attacked by the Potawatomis, long before 1680; and, besieged on the top of the rock, they had held out until they had died of starvation. Tonty, with a few followers, now went up the river to inspect the site for the new fort. On his return to Fort Crèvecoeur he was stunned to find that his men had plundered the stores and deserted, going off to hide themselves in distant Indian villages. This meant the end of La Salle's planning and labor in preparation for the exploration of the Mississippi to its mouth. The skeleton of the small vessel that was to carry his party stood on the bank of the Illinois River, abandoned by the skilled carpenters and shipwrights he had brought at such great expense from France. The supplies had been plundered, and Tonty was left with two priests and three greenhorns from France, who knew nothing about wilderness ways and were in terror of the Indians. The Illinis of the village near Fort Crèvecoeur were away hunting. When they came home, they moved their village up the river to the big summer village near Starved Rock; and Tonty, unable to feed even his remaining few men without assistance from friendly Indians, followed them up the river.

The great Illini village, usually called Kaskaskia, extended along the river bank from near Starved Rock to River Aramoni (the present Big Vermillion). The big bark houses were set along the riverside, with the dugout canoes drawn up on the shore. The village was over a French league (about two and one-half miles) in length, and it extended back from the river about one-fourth of a league. There were 460 bark houses, each sheltering several families. There were 2,400 families, and a total of about 6,000 people. Seventeen Illini tribes were present; but the population kept changing, as one group left to go hunting and another group arrived.[29]

29 Franquelin map of 1684; Parkman, *La Salle and the Discovery of the Great West,* 351; Temple, "Indian Villages of the Illinois Country," *Illinois State Museum Papers,* Vol. II, part 2, 21; Schlarman, *From Quebec to New Orleans,* 91.

197

This great village should have had twelve hundred warriors, the total for the group; but only four hundred were there. The rest were away, ignoring the danger of an Iroquois attack. Most of them were with a big war party in the Sioux country where they were carrying on what they called war, making minor attacks on Sioux groups, getting some scalps, and taking women and children captives, to be enslaved or to be tortured to death and then cooked and eaten. Like most of these tribes in Illinois and Wisconsin, the Illinis were notorious cannibals.[30]

Father Marquette, burning to establish a mission among the Illinis and blinded to the truth by faith, had described these Indians as kind, good, docile, and ripe for Christianity. Father Allouez, coming among them a few years later, was greeted with open hostility. His faith was jeered at, and threats were made against his life. He had left them in a very disillusioned state of mind. Father Membré, now with Tonty, gave the Illinis and the other tribes of the region a very bad reputation. He stated that they were incurable rovers, spending most of every year wandering about in hunting camps or on war excursions. The men were lazy, leaving the building of huts, the digging of the ground, the planting, and the harvesting for the women and girls to do. They were shockingly immoral, the village being full of boys dressed like girls and kept for immoral purposes. Most of the men, he declared, were cowards. They were too lazy to fortify the village, and when enemies appeared, they ran away, leaving the women and children to their fate. This was not the exact truth, for part of the Illini men were brave warriors, and they did not abandon their women and children when attacked. Like other tribes that were not fully equipped with firearms, they could not withstand the Iroquois and had no recourse but to flee when the wolf packs appeared. The chiefs in the village where Tonty and Membré were living had about four hundred warriors present. Of these about one hundred had guns of some sort, and they were no longer in the utter dread of the Iroquois that they had been a few years back when they had possessed nothing but flint weapons.

Except for excitement caused by rumors of an Iroquois attack, the summer passed fairly quietly. There was a Shawnee man from the

30 The statement that a large force of Illini warriors was in the Sioux country in the summer of 1680 will be found in French, *Historical Collections of Louisiana*, IV, 164.

Ohio Valley visiting in the Illini village. In early September he started on the return journey to his own land, and then came rushing back with a report that he had seen an army of six hundred Iroquois not far off and clearly intending to surprise the village. The Illini village was in an uproar. Scouts were hastily sent out to seek the truth concerning the presence of the Iroquois wolves. Some of the men accused Tonty and his companions, saying that they were spies for the Iroquois and had come among the Illinis to lull them into a feeling of false security and then betray them. They seized all the belongings of the French and furiously threw their goods and personal articles into the river. Some of the women began to load their children and property into the dugout canoes lying along the riverside, to be ready to flee if the enemy appeared. Scouts rushed into the village, shouting that the Iroquois were at hand.

The Illini men had dressed and painted for war. They crossed the river in dugouts and advanced toward the woods yelling, leaping, dancing, and singing. The Iroquois came out of the woods and advanced toward them, putting on the same sort of performance. Apparently, neither side was anxious to open battle. Tonty, with one or two of his Frenchmen, was in front of the Illinis. He now put down his gun on the ground and advanced toward the Iroquois, holding up a string or necklace of peace wampum. The Iroquois had a force of about six hundred men. They were mostly Onondagas with a few Senecas, and one hundred Miami warriors, blood relatives of the Illinis, now come to aid the Iroquois in destroying that tribe. Tonty and his party were instantly surrounded by a mob of wolfish savages. An Iroquois struck Tonty in the breast with a dagger; but the weapon glanced off a bone. Tonty, streaming with blood, boldly faced the scowling and yelling mob. One man got behind him and lifted his long hair, preparing to scalp him. An Onondaga chief stopped him. Tonty upbraided the chiefs. He told them that they were formally at peace with the French and their allies, who included the Illinis. He said that the Illinis had twelve hundred warriors and outnumbered the Iroquois, two to one, and that La Salle was near at hand with sixty armed Frenchmen. The chiefs were impressed; but now they got at the young Illini warrior who had come with Tonty, and he, badly frightened, told the truth—that his tribe had only four hundred men at the village and that there was no armed French force, only Tonty, three armed companions, and two unarmed priests.

An Iroquois warrior rushed up with news that the Frenchmen were firing at the Iroquois on the left end of the line. A chief ordered Tonty and his companions to stand out where they could be seen, so that it would be known that they were alive. The Illinis began to retire across the river to their village and the Iroquois advanced, some of them crossing the river. Neither side had done any real fighting, and as a picture of Iroquois prowess in war the performance is far from impressive.

In the village the Illinis had sent the women and children away, part into the woods, part down the river in dugouts to a bog or marsh in which there was an island of dry land as a place of safe refuge. The Illini warriors were in the village, attempting to hold the Iroquois off. The Iroquois kept on pretending that their only desire was peace. They released Tonty and his companions and sent them into the village with a peace belt of wampum and a friendly message. The two priests came from the village to meet them. Tonty was staggering, weak from loss of blood, but as full of fight as ever. He told the Illini chiefs not to trust the Iroquois, who were pretending that all they wanted was the furs in the Illini village to trade to the English in New York. Tonty said that some of them were openly declaring that they would not return home until they had devoured the Illini nation. More and more Iroquois were getting across the river and assembling outside the great village. The Illini men now set the village on fire, got into the dugouts, and fled down the river.

The Iroquois cautiously entered the village and began fortifying. There was no enemy in sight, but they were being very wary. They had killed a number of Illinis and had captured others, including women and old men. They set up stakes and tied victims to them to be tortured. They did not wish the French to witness their actions. Some packs of furs were brought and placed at Tonty's feet, and he was asked to go away with his Frenchmen. He angrily kicked the gift of furs aside; but there was nothing more that his weak party could do to aid the Illinis, and they now set off, to march to the shore of Lake Michigan.

With the French gone the Iroquois gave full rein to their savage inclinations. They tortured the captives to death, then cooked and ate their flesh. They plundered the village; they dug up every grave in the cemetery, tossing bodies and bones out on the ground. Part of the Illini dead had been buried on scaffolds, platforms of poles tied to long stakes set in the ground. The Iroquois threw all the bodies down. Some dead bodies were cooked and eaten. Before they left, the Iroquois finished the burning of the village. When La Salle came to this village some months later, it was still a scene of horror. Of all the hundreds of big cabins, all that remained were a few charred and blackened posts, standing in the ground. The village was swarming with wolves and buzzards, still feasting on the dead that the Iroquois wolves had left lying on the ground.

What followed now is a curious example of Iroquois warmaking. The main body of the Illinis had retired to the island in the bog, some distance down the Illinois River. The Iroquois, after remaining in the village for a day or more, moved down and encamped on the opposite side of the river, sending more peace messages to the Illinis. All they desired was to camp with their friends and be brothers. The Illini women and children fled again in the dugouts and the warriors sullenly faced the Iroquois for a time and then followed the fugitives down the river. They made another camp, and the Iroquois moved down and camped opposite to them and again sent messages. La Salle examined the ground some months later and reported that the Illinis made six camps in their flight down the river and in each instance the Iroquois formed a camp opposite to that of their intended victims. When the Illinis came close to the Mississippi, they split up, part moving up the Mississippi, part moving down, and part crossing into Iowa. Part of those who crossed the river fled all the way to seek refuge among the Osages in what is now Missouri State, south of the Missouri River, and part of the Iroquois pursued and attacked them while they were among the Osages. The Illini tribe of Tamaroas (one suspects that they were not Algonquians, but southern Indians of the old Cahokian group) remained encamped at the mouth of the Illinois River. Perhaps they trusted the Iroquois pretense of friendliness; more probably they lacked the necessary dugouts to continue their flight. When the Iroquois appeared in force, the Tamaroa warriors deserted their women, children, and old people and fled. The wolfish Iroquois then moved in on the defenseless Tamaroa families. Experts in judging human flesh, the Iroquois selected several hundred of the best young women and large children to be taken home to their villages, tortured to death, and eaten. They slaughtered the rest of the Tamaroas and settled down in their camp to hold a grand victory feast of human flesh. For years later the piles of Tamaroa women's and children's bones were a landmark on the river bank.[31]

31 This account of the Iroquois campaign on Illinois River in September, 1680, has been put together from the French eyewitness accounts of Tonty, Membré, and La Salle, printed in French, *Historical Collections of Louisiana*, vols. I and IV, and from the narratives in Parkman's *La Salle and the Discovery of the Great West.* See also Schlarman, *From Quebec to New Orleans*, 90–94, and Temple, "Indian Villages of the Illinois Country," *Illinois State Museum Scientific Papers*, vol. I, part 2, 32–34. This Iroquois army got home to their villages in 1681 with 700 Illini captives, most of whom they tortured at the stake and then cooked and ate. (*Jesuit Relations*, LXII, 71). In an Iroquois camp on the south bank of Illinois River, La Salle found trees stripped of bark, on which the Iroquois had recorded in signs the number of men under each chief, with the chief's totem or symbol. The record shows 582 warriors, and their camp had 113 huts. This camp was opposite the camp of the fleeing Illinis on the north bank. Not all of the Illinis were cowardly. When the Iroquois massacred the Tamaroa women and children, a party of 100 Kaskaskia warriors followed the Iroquois all the way to the Miami country, assaulting their camp three times and attempting to release the women and children they were carrying off. Father Membré stated that the Iroquois appeared near the Illini village on September 10; another French account said a week later. The pursuit of the fleeing Illinis probably lasted for several weeks, as part of the Iroquois followed the fugitives to the Osage country.

CHAPTER NINE

From the Great Lakes to the Ohio

THE EVENTS recorded in the preceding chapter and, in particular, the shocking story of the Iroquois activities on Illinois River in September, 1680, strikingly illustrate the sad truth that the Woodland tribes of the north-central area had been brought to the verge of ruin by war, disunity, and hatred, and that this was the work of the Indians themselves. In prehistoric times, these tribes had a vision of God, a revelation of a purely Indian spiritual life that led them to strive for a better way of living, to form great religious centers in the Ohio Valley extending westward into Illinois and Wisconsin, and to attempt to live in ordered communities, obtaining their support mainly from the peaceful growing of crops. Their social life and material culture became enriched, and their population grew. But then hate and war came among them and began their work of destruction. The great Mound Builder centers in Ohio lay uninhabited and forlorn; the great temple mounds of Cahokia and those of Kincaid and Angel on the lower Ohio were deserted by their former populations. The fine pottery and artistic work in stone, shell, and copper, material manifestations of a growing Indian culture, were no longer produced. Men's minds were occupied with thoughts of war, slave-catching, and butchery. They had no time or taste for spiritual or aesthetic matters. They had all been brothers once, or had come near to such an ideal—all friends, striving for renown as the leaders in a world of peace and useful labor. Now no man was brother to any other man unless they had come out of the same womb. The Miami betrayed and destroyed the Illini, who was his brother by blood and language. The Chickasaw, yearning for more English guns and kettles, invited his closest blood kindred, the Choctaws, to come on friendly visits to the Chickasaw villages, and then sold the unsuspecting Choctaw families to the English traders to be sent to die in the slave camps of the West Indies.

History, Indian tradition, and archaeology all add their testimony to this sad tale of ruin and desolation. In the Ohio Valley the Mound Builders made their great contribution toward a world of Indian culture. War ended that, but the population remained, and the coming of southern Temple Mound culture began to lift the general level of material life. Then came the collapse, with the flight of the tribes before the Iroquois assault. On the upper Mississippi the story was similar. The old Mound Builder culture began to fade. The Temple Mound folk came to the Cahokia center, and Old Village Cahokian culture began to thrive and spread. The population in Illinois grew; villages were larger, culture was growing. Then came the flowering, in the later Cahokian phase, with new pottery types and fine work in stone, shell, and copper, followed by the collapse in which the Indian population dwindled away. There was no more fine Indian work, no big and thriving settlements. When the French came, they found all the tribes at war and no man trusting any other.

We must here return to archaeology for a time. That is essential; for half of the Indian population from the Ohio Valley and from the region east of the upper Mississippi had fled into the lands beyond the Mississippi before the actual beginning of the historic period. We must make use of archaeology in attempting to trace the movements of these fugitive tribes. The archaeologists have found village ruins, mounds, and burials; but they have given most of these remains an impossible dating—at times as far back as the year 1300—which simply will not fit in with the traditional and historical evidence. It is not reasonable to assume that only ancient Indian remains are here and that all indications of the Indian population of the period 1650–1700 have vanished.

Reviewing briefly the situation in this area, we learn from archae-

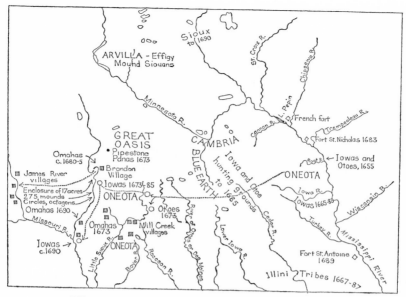

The Protohistoric Period in Northern Iowa

ology that Siouan tribes were in Minnesota and farther south in Iowa at least as far back as Effigy Mound times. These Indians left many groups of effigy mounds and the linear and conical mounds typical of that culture along the west side of the Mississippi, from southern Minnesota into Missouri State. This was before the rise of the southern Indian center at Cahokia Old Village, a higher culture than that of the Siouan tribes. This culture spread among those tribes, bringing crop-growing, the forming of permanent villages, and a higher material culture. As to the identity of the Siouan Indians who were west of the Mississippi at this period, we have no definite information. They may have included the Mandans and the Hidatsa-Crow group, offshoots from the Winnebagoes of Wisconsin. The languages of the Mandans, Hidatsas, and Crows indicate that they had been long separated from the Winnebago group. The other tribes that left the Winnebagoes—the Iowas, Otoes, and Missouris—spoke dialects very close to the Winnebago tongue; and they had in traditions a fairly clear memory of their separation from the Winnebagoes in Wisconsin, probably after the year 1600.

Returning to archaeology, middle Woodland was the period of

Effigy Mound culture among the Siouans of Wisconsin, northern Illinois, and eastern Iowa. At this period Minnesota north of Minnesota River was held mainly by the Sioux, a numerous people who, as the scanty evidence indicates, were wandering about in small camps, hunting and fishing. They do not seem to have had villages, but probably came together at certain favored centers in the spring to hold a rendezvous at which they exchanged news, held councils, and conducted the tribal ceremonies of the Feast of the Dead. The Sioux culture was of a simple and primitive type. They exposed their dead on scaffolds and then cleaned the bones to be taken to the rendezvous, where a communal funeral ceremony was held and the dead were buried in small mounds. With unlimited quantities of wild rice in their marshes and lakes, they had little incentive for growing crops.

The Siouan Indians to the south of Minnesota River were clearly of a different group and probably belonged to the Winnebago stock. They had the Effigy Mound culture, which apparently had not been taken up by the Sioux; but the actual building of large effigy mounds was confined to southern Wisconsin, northwestern Illinois, and northeastern Iowa, with a very few such effigies along the Mississippi in southern Minnesota. The main culture in southern Minnesota at this period was what the archaeologists term Southern Minnesota aspect. It extended from near the upper Des Moines northward to near the big southern bend of Minnesota River, and it was so nearly like the culture of the Sioux that the two are difficult to distinguish from each other. The Southern Minnesota pots had a single cord-mark decoration, a trait that turns up later in village ruins in Dakota. At this early period pottery types and other cultural features from southern Minnesota found their way westward to Split Rock Creek, an eastern tributary of the Big Sioux near the present town of Sioux Falls, and to localities in eastern Dakota.[1]

1 Here we may have clues as to the early location of the Mandans, Hidatsas, and Crows. Split Rock Creek culture is of the Minnesota middle Woodland type. Hiawatha Beach, in Roberts County, South Dakota, and the Devil's Lake culture seem to be a little later; and W. D. Strong noted relationships between these two and the Arvilla culture on upper Red River, close at hand. Waldo R. Wedel remarked that mounds in eastern North Dakota seem to be of recent date, while L. A. Wilford places Arvilla in late Woodland times. The fact that the Arvilla Indians had linear mounds, a holdover from the earlier Effigy Mound culture, points to a connection with the Hidatsa group or with the Mandans because these tribes used linear mounds and boulder outline effigies until quite late. Again, the Arvilla In-

It would be natural to seek here in southern Minnesota for clues concerning the Mandans and the related Hidatsa-Crow group, the earliest known offshoots from the Winnebago group; but there seem to be no such clues until late Woodland times.

The middle Woodland period opened. The southern Indians established the great mound center across the Mississippi to the east of the present St. Louis. Agriculture came into the upper Mississippi lands, with the concomitant forming of permanent villages. In Wisconsin the Cahokian Indians formed the great fortified town of Aztalan and spread their superior culture among the Winnebagoes. This we may date about 1600–40, and farther west on the Mississippi we have the date 1655 from Radisson for the Iowa and Oto villages and their crop-growing. Even the Sioux seem to have formed one village, in the Mille Lacs district, east of the Mississippi and north of the present St. Paul. Radisson, when he was among the Sioux about 1660, did not refer to a village; but Hennepin and Duluth both were in this village in 1680.

In southern Minnesota in these late Woodland times there was a group of Indians whose remains have been termed by archaeology Great Oasis, from a small lake of that name in Murray County. These Indians made a fairly good type of pottery with the globular shape and a decoration that was in some features reminiscent of Cahokia pottery, but the Great Oasis pots have the older Woodland grit tempering. These Indians had two villages in Murray County and one village or campsite farther west, near Lake Benton. Great Oasis would be of little interest if it were not for the fact that the pottery of this

dians had a peculiar custom of burying bodies without heads and sometimes without arms and then placing many skulls and some arm bones together in a separate grave. This practice reminds one of the Mandan custom of placing a small mound in the cemetery near the village with two poles on the mound with bearskins hung on the poles. They said the poles symbolized the sun and moon, and they placed the skulls of their dead in a circle around the mound and probably later gathered the skulls and buried them in a common grave. Again, both the Mandans and Hidatsas had a tradition that their people first dwelt under the ground and later came out into the light of day—a religious myth seemingly of southern origin —and the Hidatsas added that it was at Devil's Lake that their people came out to the surface of the earth. These clues, together with the extension of Effigy Mound cultural traits to the Red River district and on west to the Missouri and north into Manitoba, hint at the route of migration of these Siouan groups, and even at the date of the migration.

group found its way to Indian villages in northwestern Iowa and on west to the Missouri in South Dakota, and then turned up in the Omaha tribe's village in northern Nebraska in the eighteenth century.

The Indians called Cambria by archaeologists had their first center on the south side of Minnesota River, about fifteen miles west of the present town of Mankato. Cambria seems to be a bit later in date than Great Oasis, but Cambria pottery is found in the upper levels of Great Oasis refuse heaps, indicating that the two aspects were partly contemporary. Like Great Oasis, Cambria seems to have had three centers, two villages in Blue Earth County south of Minnesota River and one higher up Minnesota River at Granite Falls. The Cambria folk either lived for a time or visited on the Mississippi in the Lake Pepin district, where some of their pottery is found. Like Great Oasis, the Cambria aspect is interesting because the pottery is found in village ruins in South Dakota. A third aspect, called Silvernale, is known only on Cannon River, just west of the town of Red Wing, Minnesota. Silvernale seems to date to late Cambria times, and the pottery differs from Cambria in that it is shell tempered.

The last and latest of these southern Minnesota archaeological aspects is termed Blue Earth. It is represented by three large village ruins far up Blue Earth River near the town of Blue Earth and close to the present Iowa line. There is also a Blue Earth village ruin on the southern end of Prairie Island in Lake Pepin, the island on which the refugee Tobacco Hurons and Ottawas had a village, starting evidently in 1654. A Blue Earth village ruin is also found east of the Mississippi, on the St. Croix River near the present town of Stillwater. As Blue Earth is obviously more recent, we might assume that the last two villages had been drawn eastward to obtain trade with the French or with the Ottawas and other Indians who had French goods to trade; but no trade articles have been found in Blue Earth village remains. Blue Earth is evidently later than both Cambria and Silvernale. The shell tempering in Silvernale pottery has leached out with age; but the shell temper in Blue Earth pottery is well preserved.

Blue Earth is probably contemporary with Orr Oneota culture, which is found along the Mississippi in northeastern Iowa and across the river in Wisconsin. These two aspects are connected with the very late Cahokia period termed Trappist, while Great Oasis and Cambria have many traits from Cahokia Old Village and from the

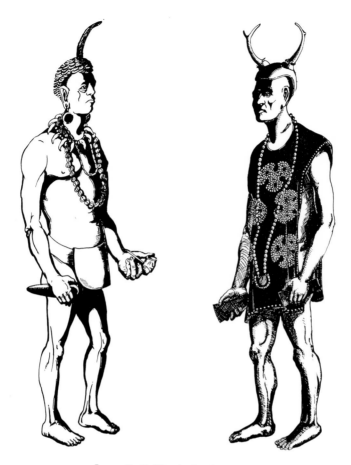

James B. Griffin, Archeology of the Eastern United States;
Courtesy University of Chicago Press

At left is a Hopewell male with dress and accoutrements chosen from finds in the Baehr Mounds of Brown County, Illinois. These finds included the copper earspools, copper plume, the human-portrait clay pipe, bear's teeth, stone celt, and bone beads, and indicated the shape of the headdress and the kind of breechcloth. At right is a Hopewell official in ceremonial dress. He wears a necklace of silver beads with a human-maxillary pendant and carries copper hatchets. The pearls are sewn on his breechcloth in a design which occurred in sheet copper at the Hopewell site in Ohio.

Two views of an unpainted pottery statuette from Jackson County, Illinois. The young girl wears earspools, and a portion of her head is shaved, while the remainder of her hair is pulled over into a roll.

Old Village fortified town of Aztalan in southern Wisconsin. Blue Earth started with pots with loop handles, a type developed by Cahokia Old Village and Aztalan, and went into the flat strap-handle period, which belongs to late Cahokia or Trappist.

Reviewing these late Woodland aspects in southern Minnesota, it may be remarked that none of them was extensive except Oneota. Great Oasis had three villages or occupation centers, none of them very large. Cambria had three, Silvernale one, and Blue Earth about five. None of the villages show indications of long occupation. The culture is simple, probably that of Indians who did little planting at their village but spent most of every year roving in hunting camps. The culture is so similar in all sites that one suspects it was the work of Indians of one stock and perhaps of one tribe. Most conjectures attribute all the remains, or most of them, to the Otoes or to the very closely related Iowas. As for dating, these aspects, starting with the earliest one, Great Oasis, are all connected with Cahokia—first with Old Village and Aztalan, then with the late Cahokian phase. Moreover, these supposedly Siouan groups in southern Minnesota were being affected by the culture in northwestern Illinois which is termed Apple River by archaeology. Apple River seems to be late Cahokian culture with Siouan traits resembling Oneota. This connection with Apple River again suggests that the southern Minnesota aspects are late prehistoric and protohistoric. Here we have another hint of Siouan occupation of northern Illinois, for the Apple River folk may have been Siouans. The archaeological reports concerning these minor aspects are merely confusing to most minds. The probability is that all these aspects—Great Oasis, Blue Earth, Cambria, Apple River, and the rest—are the remains of Siouan camps and villages occupied by groups of the Iowa and Oto tribes, people of the same blood and language whose primitive culture differed in minor respects only.

As was written in an earlier chapter of the present work, the Old Village and Aztalan culture seems to have begun to influence the Winnebago group of Siouans in Wisconsin around 1600, and the Aztalan period ended around the year 1650. By that time the Iowas probably had developed Oneota culture; they certainly had villages and grew crops, as is confirmed by the Radisson reference to the Iowas and Otoes in 1655. The southern Minnesota cultural aspects under discussion here are earlier than Oneota, but some of them appear to have continued in existence until after 1673, being thus contemporary with Oneota.

A shift in Iowa and Oto occupation of lands along the Mississippi came in 1665, when the Iroquois drove the Illinis, Miamis, and some other Algonquians to or beyond the Mississippi. These fugitive Algonquians established themselves along the river and began to hunt on lands that had formerly been the exclusive domain of the Iowas and Otoes. Moreover, the Algonquians, too weak to face the Iroquois, began to raid the native tribes west of the Mississippi, and there can be little doubt that the Iowas and Otoes, the tribes nearest, were among the first to be attacked. Thus when Joliet and Marquette came down the river in 1673, they appear to have heard of the Otoes and Iowas in a new location, in northern Iowa, near the upper Des Moines, and placed these tribes on their maps near the Mahas (Omahas) and the Panas, a Pawnee group. This confirms the Omaha and Ponca tradition that they migrated northward from the Missouri into Iowa, met a village of Iowas near the present city of Des Moines, and accompanied these Iowas to a location near the head of the Des Moines and near the red pipestone quarry in southwestern Minnesota. Some of the traditions state that the Skidi Pawnees or Panimahas accompanied the Omaha group in their migration out of the Ohio Valley and into northern Iowa. The Panas set down on the Marquette and other French maps have been conjectured to have been Pawnees, Arikaras, or even Poncas. It seems more reasonable to identify them as the Skidi Pawnees and to explain the French name for that tribe, Panimaha, as meaning simply that these were the Pawnees who lived with the Mahas or Omahas.[2]

In Cherokee and Buena Vista counties in northwestern Iowa, mainly on branches of Mill Creek, a tributary of the Little Sioux River, modern archaeology has uncovered a striking group of village ruins which have been termed the Mill Creek aspect. These vil-

2 Wedel has given an earlier dating, middle sixteenth century, to the Lower Loup culture in Nebraska, which is supposed to be Skidi Pawnee, and this would seem to make it impossible that the Skidis were with the Omahas, about 1673, in northern Iowa. But Wedel noted that the pottery types of the Lower Loup culture closely resemble pottery in sites of late date in the Iroquois country of western New York. Most of our troubles in dealing with more recent archaeological sites come from confusion in regard to dating. This should be cleared up in time, but all the evidence must be taken into account to reach a reasonable conclusion.

lages are in the district where the French located the Omaha group at the period 1673-85. There are village remains of the Oneota culture, attributed to the Iowas and Otoes, in the same district, and the layout fits the French map locations of all these tribes. Some archaeologists conjecture that the Mill Creek villages date back to about the year 1200, an estimate based on the depth of village refuse, which is supposed, rather arbitrarily, to indicate several hundred years of occupation. This method of fixing dates is, however, little more than guessing; and we may point out that at the village ruins in Saline County, Missouri, which are attributed to the Osages or the Missouri tribe, the depth of village refuse is about the same as at the Mill Creek sites, three to five feet. On the upper Ohio there is at least one village ruin of Fort Ancient culture, belonging to this same time period, and it has the same depth of village refuse. These Indians had the habit of throwing all their refuse on the ground in the village area; they lived in perishable huts that had to be renewed frequently, and the remains of old huts added to the depth of village refuse. It did not take centuries, but only a few years, to add a foot to the refuse heaps. Even the ashes from the fires were enough in themselves to build up the heaps of refuse rapidly.

The Mill Creek culture is of Mississippian pattern. So is the culture of the Quapaws, Kansas, and Osages of the same group with the Omahas and Poncas. Mill Creek culture is said to be of Old Village Cahokian culture, as is also the Oneota or Iowa culture; but the Mill Creek pottery seems to be more diversified in types and more elaborately finished than Oneota pottery.

It is not reasonable to assume that a Siouan group came to the Mill Creek district around the date 1200 and remained in the same location and in the same villages until Old Village Cahokian times (1600 to 1650). It is even less reasonable to assume that, with many ancient village ruins dotting the land in northwestern Iowa, there should be no trace left of the large Siouan population of the period 1670-90. These Mill Creek village ruins fit in with the Omaha and Ponca migration traditions. Moreover, the village ruins farther west, on the Big Sioux and in southern South Dakota, agree with both the migration traditions and the Mill Creek archaeological pattern.

In their surmises concerning the Mill Creek village ruins and those farther to the west, on the Big Sioux and in South Dakota, most of the archaeologists have not displayed much inclination to take a broad view or to consider all the facts in the case. They cling to the notion that the depth of refuse in the village ruins proves a very early date of occupation, although their own reports seem to prove that the refuse heaps have the same traces of high culture from the lowest levels to the upper ones, indicating a short period of occupation. Some archaeologists admit that the Mill Creek villages were those of the Omahas; but, led by their strange belief that Omaha migration tradition is unreliable, they then make a conjecture that Omaha culture was, first of all, that of the Great Oasis and Cambria groups in southern Minnesota, and that Mill Creek developed out of these earlier cultural manifestations. To the historian such a view gives the impression that some archaeologists are grasping at straws in an effort to maintain the opinion that Siouan tradition is not reliable. The verdict of tradition and history is that these Dhegihan tribes came out of the Ohio Valley, probably about the middle of the seventeenth century, the Omaha group going to the Mill Creek district and then on westward to the Big Sioux and to the Missouri in South Dakota. The archaeologists themselves suggest that all these Dhegihan tribes had a late Mississippian culture, and that is a fair description of the culture at Mill Creek. It is late Mississippian culture with a trace of the old Hopewell, Mound Builder, culture. The Omahas continued on special occasions to bury their dead in large mounds, reminiscent of Hopewell, down to 1730.

The policy of Count Frontenac, to extend French control to the upper Great Lakes and the Mississippi Valley, was in effect in 1679. La Salle reached Illinois River and left Henri de Tonty and part of his men there to build a small vessel for an expedition to the mouth of the Mississippi. He sent Accault and another Frenchman, accompanied by Father Hennepin, to explore up the Mississippi; but they fell into the hands of the Sioux. This was in the spring of 1680. The Sioux treated their French captives well. In July, Duluth, Tonty's cousin, who had established a French post on Lake Superior, came among the Sioux with five French soldiers, took possession of the land in the name of the King of France, and obtained the release of Father Hennepin and his companions. Meantime, Tonty was deserted on Illinois River by part of his men, and then in September, 1680, the Iroquois came down on the great Illini village of Kaskaskia and drove the Illinis beyond the Mississippi.

The French were trying hard enough with the small resources at their command; but the Iroquois were creating havoc. They were now coming down the Ohio in fleets of canoes to raid tribes along the Mississippi as far down as the Quapaws, and Father Hennepin stated that in 1679 he saw a Seneca war party near Niagara River that had just raided the Sioux of the Prairie on the west side of the upper Mississippi and was bringing a number of Sioux captives home, probably to be tortured and then cooked and eaten. To add to the French difficulties, the tribes in Wisconsin, Illinois, and Minnesota were raiding each other. The Foxes of Wisconsin hated the French, and they were doing all that they could to break up the French fur trade and force the French out of their country. The Foxes had revived the old Ottawa plan, to drive the Sioux out of their country and take possession, and with the aid of other Wisconsin Algonquians they were warring on the Sioux. The Sioux were also being attacked by the Illinis and were returning the compliment by sending big war parties down the Mississippi to raid the Illini villages. By 1680, the Foxes had blocked the main canoe route to the Mississippi, by way of the Fox and Wisconsin rivers, and there were reports that this tribe was obtaining British goods by some roundabout way, perhaps through the Miamis, who were on good terms with the Iroquois of New York.[3]

In these years of turmoil, at least part of the Miamis had been driven to or beyond the Mississippi by the Iroquois; and like all the other fugitive groups, they had promptly started raiding tribes that still had no French weapons, even going down the Mississippi in canoes to attack the Michigameas. The Kickapoos also moved to the Mississippi River. There was a tributary of the lower Wisconsin River called Kickapoo River, and the same name was later applied to a western tributary of the Mississippi that came in about opposite to the mouth of the Wisconsin River. During their stay on the Mississippi, the Kickapoos evidently opened friendly relations with the Iowa tribe; for in 1680 Father Membré noted that a camp of Ainoves was with the Kickapoos in Wisconsin, probably a camp of Iowas that had come to trade for French knives and hatchets.

La Salle, who had gone to Montreal and Quebec to face his enemies

---

[3] Blair, *Indian Tribes in the Upper Mississippi,* I, 246; Temple, "Indian Villages of the Illinois Country," *Illinois State Museum Scientific Papers,* vol. II, part 2, 32, 34; Thwaites, *Jesuit Relations,* LV, 193; Schlarman, *From Quebec to New Orleans,* 211.

and creditors and to recruit more men, came back to Illinois River late in 1680, only to find the Illini Indians gone and their great village of Kaskaskia burned and full of wolves and buzzards feasting on the dead bodies the Iroquois had left on the ground. Going down the river to Fort Crèvecoeur, he found the fort abandoned, Tonty and his men gone, and the vessel in which the exploration of the Mississippi was to be made lying unfinished on the river side. Thwarted in all his plans, La Salle returned to his little post, Fort Miami, on the St. Joseph River near the southern end of Lake Michigan, where he spent the winter. He now heard from Tonty, who was at Mackinac Island with a few men, and Tonty came to join him. They spent the winter striving to build up an Algonquian alliance against the Iroquois and planning a chain of French forts to block Iroquois and English intrusion into the Great Lakes country. During the winter La Salle and Tonty returned to Montreal. La Salle gained the aid of Count Frontenac in putting off his creditors, obtaining more credit, recruiting men, and purchasing a new stock of needed supplies. He returned in the autumn of 1681 to Fort Miami with a party of twenty-three men. The land was full of groups of refugee Indians, driven from their old homes by the Iroquois. La Salle now met bands of Abnakis and Mohegans and induced them to bring their families and join his forces. With forty-nine followers, including the Indians and their women and children, La Salle reached Illinois River, marching overland. They found the great Indian village of Kaskaskia still deserted. Continuing their march along the frozen river, they came to Fort Crèvecoeur and found it in good condition. Here they made canoes for the Illinois River was not frozen below Lake Peoria. Leaving some men at Fort Crèvecoeur, La Salle embarked the rest of his party in the canoes and in February, 1682, entered the Mississippi and began the descent of the great unknown river.

La Salle found most of the tribes on the Mississippi, from the Arkansas to the mouth, friendly. One tribe tried to attack him. He reached the river mouth on April 7, 1682, and on the ninth he took possession of the land in the name of the King of France, calling it Louisiana in the King's honor. He also took possession of the Ohio Valley, and all this he did with the pretense that the tribes concerned had given their consent, although he had not consulted any of them. Returning up the river, he left Tonty with part of his men to build

Fort St. Louis on Starved Rock, close to the great village of Kaskaskia. La Salle then returned to Montreal and Quebec and sailed for France to obtain support for his next great enterprise, the founding of a French settlement near the mouth of the Mississippi.

This time he obtained the support of the King and the royal government. He was given naval vessels to transport his colonists and the needed supplies; but, when the little fleet reached the gulf coast in 1685, they missed the mouth of the Mississippi. Sailing on westward, La Salle landed part of his colonists and supplies on the Texas coast. He had quarreled with the naval officer, who now sailed away to France, taking part of the colonists and stores with him. La Salle lost the vessel he had retained, and he and his colonists were stranded in a strange land, with no knowledge of where the Mississippi might be. The Indians grew hostile; the colonists quarreled among themselves; and when, in 1687, La Salle set out eastward, to seek the Mississippi, some of the men with him made a plot and assassinated him.

Meanwhile, the faithful Tonty went down the Mississippi to its mouth, seeking for La Salle. Finding no trace of the French, he left a message for La Salle among the Indians near the mouth of the river and returned upstream, leaving a few of his men, to establish a post among the Quapaws on Arkansas River. It was to this little post that La Salle's brother, Father Douay, Henri Joutel, and some others made their way from Texas, going on up the Mississippi and reaching Tonty's Fort St. Louis safely. They concealed from Tonty the news of his leader's death and went on eastward to Montreal and Quebec.

When La Salle left Tonty on Illinois River in 1682 to build Fort St. Louis and gather the Indian tribes near the fort, he probably expected to return and assume command; but on reaching Quebec, he found a situation that hardly could have been worse. His enemies and creditors were preparing to act against him; his patron, Count Frontenac, was being removed from his position as governor of Canada, and La Barre, the new governor, was no friend of La Salle's. La Salle therefore decided to go to France and seek royal support for his plan to colonize the Mississippi.

Tonty, left on Illinois River with only a few men and a slender stock of supplies, built Fort St. Louis at Starved Rock, and then traveled over one hundred leagues through the prairies, seeking the Illinis and inducing them to return to their old village near Starved

Rock, from which the Iroquois had driven them in September, 1680. In 1683, he had about six thousand Illinis and also a big village of Miamis near his new fort. Franquelin's map of 1684 shows four thousand warriors in the new Indian villages around Fort St. Louis. Tonty even had a village of Shawnees from the Ohio Valley, and La Salle's own plan was to induce the Chickasaws to join the confederated tribes on Illinois River and use them against the Iroquois.[4]

But Tonty received no aid, in the form of men and supplies, and it soon became obvious that he would be unable to hold his Indian allies together. The Illinis were undependable. La Salle feared that if he armed these Indians with French guns, they would use the weapons to destroy the Ottawas, and it was the widespread Ottawa trade with the tribes near the upper Mississippi that was the backbone of French influence.

The Indian trade was the source of wealth and power. La Salle had built up wide trade controls, and when he went east in 1682, Tonty or another of his agents established a monopoly of the Wisconsin and Sioux trade. La Salle's men even turned back rival traders, or confiscated their goods; but Governor de la Barre now sent his own man, Nicolas Perrot, to Green Bay as commandant. He sent a dragoon officer, De Baugis, to relieve Tonty and take command in Illinois, and the old La Salle organization seemed to be ended. But La Barre was soon removed, and the new governor, Denonville, restored Tonty to command in Illinois, also sending Tonty's cousin, Duluth, with forty Frenchmen to take over at Green Bay.

La Salle's dream of a great Indian confederacy on the upper Mississippi under French leadership was now doomed. Governor de la

---

4 The Miamis at this period were divided, part of them inclined to be friendly with the French and with the Illinis, the others, living near the southern end of Lake Michigan, inclined to be friendly with the Iroquois. This latter group began to drift southward, occupying the Wabash lands which had been vacant since the Iroquois had forced the old inhabitants to flee. The Miamis who were friendly with the Illinis were frequenting Illinois River. They had been driven to or beyond the Mississippi by the Iroquois before 1670, and in the 1680's were still going to the Mississippi, to hunt and to raid. The Shawnee on Illinois River had two hundred men and their families. They were in part from a Shawnee group that had joined the Miamis about 1680, the rest being people from the Ohio, probably from a village on Cumberland River. Tonty even had Mohegans from New York and Abnakis from New England in the big Indian villages near Fort St. Louis.

Barre had broken the peace with the Iroquois; and that nation, disturbed by French activities in the west, was planning to resume the raids on the tribes along the upper Mississippi and to drive the last of the Shawnees from the Ohio country before the French could arm them. Nicolas Perrot's memoirs and the material from unpublished Perrot manuscripts, used by de la Potherie, give a lively account of events near the upper Mississippi at this period. The dating and some of the details are obscure. Perrot was apparently sent to Green Bay by La Barre in 1683, and he at once pressed on to the Mississippi and built a trading post for the Sioux and other distant tribes that had, up to this time, not had direct trade with the French.[5] The Fox tribe and their allies, the Mascoutens and Kickapoos, were no friends of the French. They were jealous of the Sioux and other tribes beyond the Mississippi, and they did not relish the idea of the French trading arms to those tribes. They had themselves traded French trinkets to the western Indians from time to time; and this may explain why Father Membré reported in 1680 that a camp of Iowas was east of the Mississippi, visiting the Mascoutens and Kickapoos. The Iowas had perhaps gone there, seeking French articles in trade.

Perrot had hardly established his fort, probably on the east bank of the Mississippi, above Wisconsin River and below Lake Pepin in that river, when a camp of Mascoutens came to live near the fort. They pretended friendship. They told Perrot that they would induce a village of their Illini friends to come and live near the fort; but Perrot knew that the Illinis were cannibals, and he was afraid that if they came to his fort, they would attack the Iowas, with whom he wished to trade. From this we may suppose that the Illinis had already made war on the Iowas, during the 1665–80 period, when they had been driven beyond the Mississippi by the Iroquois and

[5] When Perrot came west, he had Le Sueur with him, and the La Harpe historical journal states that Le Sueur first came west in 1683 and that he had seven years' service, at different periods, in the Sioux country. Perrot and his men apparently were on Green Bay in 1683 and went to the Mississippi in 1685, where they built Fort St. Antoine near the lower end of Lake Pepin. Perrot then sent Indians to find the Iowa tribe. The Iowas came to visit him, and he and his men then went among the Sioux during the winter of 1685–86. He was trading among the Sioux when he received orders to come east to join the Denonville expedition against the Iroquois in 1687. (See William Watts Folwell, *History of Minnesota*, I, 37–38.)

had promptly employed the French weapons in their hands against the native tribes, who had only flint weapons.[6]

At this period, around 1680–85, the Algonquian tribes of Wisconsin were keeping up their old effort to drive the Sioux out of their lands and take possession. The Foxes were leaders in this movement. The Sioux had only two tribes allied with them, the Ojibwas of Lake Superior and the Iowas of what is now Iowa State. To add to the Sioux difficulties, the English had established posts on Hudson Bay, and the Crees and Assiniboines (old enemies of the Sioux) had now obtained guns in quantity from the English and were attacking the Sioux from the north, while the Algonquians of Wisconsin assailed them from the east and the Illinis from the south. The Sioux, however, were holding their lands strongly and striking back at all their foes.

Perrot had no sooner established his post on the Mississippi than he sent some friendly Winnebagoes and Potawatomis beyond the river to inform the native tribes that he was prepared to welcome their trade at his establishment. The Potawatomis brought a camp of Iowas to the fort, and all went well for a time. Then the treacherous Mascoutens, having obtained arms in trade from Perrot, went across the Mississippi and attacked and destroyed the main Iowa village, taking many Iowa captives.

At this point, it seems important to clear up the early evidence concerning the Iowas and Otoes. Sioux traditions, gathered about the year 1850, asserted that the Iowas had first dwelled on the banks of the Minnesota River and had been driven from there by the Sioux; but the Sioux seemed confused about these matters, and the small oval mounds they said were ruins of Iowa huts turned out to be burial mounds of some early Indians. Radisson certainly met both the Iowas and Otoes on the Mississippi, above Wisconsin River, in 1655. The Iowas and Otoes were evidently forced to leave the Mississippi and remove westward into Iowa State when the Illinis, Miamis, and other Algonquians were driven west of the Mississippi by the Iroquois, in the 1660's. Marquette, in 1673, put the Iowas and Otoes in northern Iowa on his map, apparently near the upper Des Moines. Father André, in the *Jesuit Relations* for 1676, termed the Iowas the Na-

---

6 This account of Perrot's operations is taken from Blair, *Indian Tribes of the Upper Mississippi*. I shall quote page references only for the more important points.

douesie Mascoutens (Prairie Sioux), and said that their village was very large but that they were poor people, their wealth consisting in ox hides (buffalo skins) and red calumet pipes. He placed their village 200 leagues west of Green Bay, which would have been in the district near the upper Des Moines, and the reference to red calumets seems to show that the tribe had access to the pipestone quarry in southwest Minnesota. Father Membré, in 1679–80, states that the Ainoves (Iowas) were in two villages near the Kickapoos, who were to the west of the Foxes and Mascoutens. This may place the Iowas east of the Mississippi; but much more probably they were on the west of the river. To this he added that the Anthoutantes (Otoes) and Mascoutens Nadouessions were in three great villages on a river 130 leagues or ten days' journey west of La Salle's Fort Crèvecoeur at Peoria Lake on Illinois River.

The references in these French reports to the Mascoutens Nadouessies or Prairie Sioux clearly indicate that at the period 1660–90 the Algonquians of Wisconsin applied this name either to the Otoes or the Iowas or to both groups. After 1690 the name was applied to the Teton Sioux, who by that time had moved into the prairies south of Minnesota River. Father André seems to make the Iowas the Mascoutens Nadouessies, but Father Membré seems to mean that they were the Otoes. The Franquelin map appears to confirm this, as it sets down the Otoutantes or Mascoutens Nadouessies as a single tribe in northern Iowa.

When Nicolas Perrot came to the Mississippi, probably in 1685, he found the Iowas allied with the Sioux. He called the Iowas by that name only and set down that they had two, perhaps more, villages. The two villages were in northeastern Iowa; but the third or Paoutet Iowa group was in northwestern Iowa, with the Omahas. Perrot did not mention the Otoes at all. La Salle had been visited near Peoria, Illinois, in 1679 by Otoes, who said that their village was ten days to the west, and that five days to the west of their village Indians were fighting on horseback. One Oto chief in this party had a horse hoof tied to his belt as a trophy.

The fact that the Iowas are never mentioned as visiting the Illini village on Illinois River, taken with Perrot's statement that the Illinis were man-eaters and enemies of the Iowas, suggests that the Iowas had been driven from their old location on the Mississippi by the Illinis. Here we seem to have a glimpse into conditions before 1680.

The Iowas were allies of the Sioux; the Otoes were not, but seem to have been on good terms with the Illinis, who were enemies of the Sioux. The Iowas frequented the Mississippi near the Wisconsin River, and the Otoes did not.

La Potherie, quoting from Perrot manuscripts, gives an account of events after Perrot reached the Mississippi and built his fort. He gives no date, but it was apparently in the fall of 1685 and the following winter. Perrot, he says, went to the Iowa village and was received with great honor, the tribe performing the calumet ceremonies and promising to hunt beaver for Perrot in the ensuing winter and to bring furs to his fort to trade. Perrot then sent men to inform the Sioux of his establishment, and that tribe was also very much pleased. But in the following spring the Iroquois appeared. They attacked the Miamis on or near Chicago River and then invaded the Illini lands. Part of the Miamis fled to the Mississippi and established themselves at a point sixty miles below Perrot's fort.[7]

We must presume that the Iowas Perrot was dealing with had villages on upper Iowa River in northeastern Iowa, or perhaps a little farther north, in the extreme southeastern corner of Minnesota; for it is here that archaeology has found village ruins and numerous burials of late Oneota culture, attributed to the Iowa tribe, and in these remains there are good quantities of glass beads and metal articles, clearly indicating a trade in European goods. We may here note that the Iowa group shown on the French maps in northwestern Iowa, near the Omahas, was usually termed the Paoutets, which was the name Radisson applied to the Iowas on the Mississippi River in 1655. Perrot and the other Frenchmen, who met the Iowas on the Mississippi after 1680, termed them Iowas and rarely used the name Paoutet. This may indicate that the Paoutets of northwestern Iowa

---

[7] These Miamis were later attacked by the Sioux and driven away from the Mississippi. This was a very important time in Sioux history, but Perrot did not make the sequence of events clear. The Wisconsin Algonquian tribes gathered an army of fifteen hundred men and set out to drive the Sioux from their country. These Indians came to Perrot's fort (spring of 1687?) and said they were going on a friendly visit to the Sioux. They tried to induce Perrot to join them with his men, but he refused. They invaded the Sioux country and were defeated and driven out. In the spring of 1689, these Algonquians apparently attempted to prevent Perrot's going to trade among the Sioux; but the Sioux came with a strong force and conducted Perrot's men to their villages.

belonged to a separate and somewhat different Iowa group, a group that had fled south to the Des Moines River, had met the Omahas there, and had accompanied them to the head of the Des Moines, later moving west to the Big Sioux and finally to the mouth of that stream.

In the winter of 1685–86 Perrot left part of his men at Fort St. Antoine and with the others went among the Sioux to trade. He met a party of Sioux, whose canoes were frozen in the ice. They received him with great pleasure, and he began trade with them. He received a message ordering him to return east to join the Denonville expedition against the Iroquois, which was planned for the season of 1687. It is difficult to make out from the Perrot and La Potherie narratives just what the dating is here. Perhaps Perrot traded among the Sioux in the winter, 1685–86, and again the next winter and was ordered to come east in the winter of 1686–87. At any rate, he left the Sioux in the spring, reached Fort St. Antoine, and was there warned by friendly Indians that the Mascoutens, Foxes, and Kickapoos were coming in pretended friendship, but with the purpose of capturing his fort and using the French arms thus obtained to attack the Sioux. Perrot at the moment had only four men at the fort; but when the Indian army appeared, he marched and countermarched his men, persuading the Indians that he had a force of forty. This so discouraged them that they gave up the plan to attack the fort.

La Barre had now been removed, and Denonville, the new governor of Canada, had reversed the La Barre policy of appeasing the Iroquois. Denonville sent orders to Perrot and Tonty to gather all the French in the west, to collect Indian allies, and to march to join his army for an invasion of the Iroquois lands. The Iroquois, greatly alarmed at the force being brought against them, fled, and the French plundered the Seneca villages and ruthlessly destroyed all the growing crops. This blow greatly disheartened the Iroquois, and for a time they were very careful not to offend the French.[8]

Perrot returned from the Denonville expedition in 1688. He built a new post, Fort St. Nicolas, somewhere near the mouth of Wisconsin River. He now received orders to take possession of the western lands

---

[8] The dating here is clear. In 1687, Perrot was with the Denonville expedition; he was in Montreal early in 1688, returned to the Mississippi and took possession of the country in 1689. In 1690, the English captured Quebec, and that put a sudden stop to Perrot's career in the west.

in a formal ceremony, and this he did "at Fort St. Antoine on the Mississippi, May 8, 1689." He took formal possession of Green Bay, Lake Michigan, Fox River, the Wisconsin and Mississippi, "the St. Croix, St. Peter River (Minnesota River), and places more removed." Boisguillot, commandant at Green Bay, Father Marest, missionary to the Sioux, and "the *voyageur* Le Sueur" signed as witness.[9]

Perrot on the upper Mississippi and Tonty on Illinois River must have been perfectly familiar with the tribes west of the Mississippi; but neither of them recorded any details concerning them. The Otoes are rarely mentioned, the Omahas never; but the French map makers, obtaining information from the men in the field, set these tribes down on their maps. The tribes that made the most trouble were mentioned most often. Duluth came to Green Bay after the Denonville expedition against the Iroquois. He had forty Frenchmen and a big stock of trade goods and was going to the Mississippi to trade with the Sioux. At Green Bay he found that the Foxes and Ojibwas had gone to war. He did what he could to stop that trouble, then found that the hostile Foxes had blocked the main canoe route, up Fox River and down Wisconsin River. In 1689, Tonty visited an Illini village at the mouth of Illinois River and found that these Indians had just made a slave-catching raid on the Osages. The attackers had lost 13 men, but had brought home 130 Osage slaves.[10] These Indian slaves were usually tortured to death, then cooked and eaten; but the white traders were now interested in slaves, and the French were trading for them. In the south the English were making fortunes out of the Indian slave trade. They supplied arms to the Cherokees, Chickasaws, and other tribes and sent them to raid neighboring tribes and bring in slaves to trade to the English. The Carolina traders exported these slaves to the West Indies. The French in the north seem to have bought Indian slaves mainly for the use of French families in Canada, who found Indian servants very useful. The French generally termed the Indian slaves Panis, as many of them were Pawnees from the lands west of the Mississippi; but we know that the slaves were in some instances Osages, Quapaws, and Iowas, and as early as 1682 La Salle obtained a Padouca slave in Illinois, brought from the plains beyond

9 Folwell, *History of Minnesota,* I, 38; Blair, *Indian Tribes of the Upper Mississippi,* 1, 244, footnote.

10 Tonty, in French, *Historical Collections of Louisiana,* I, 71.

the Missouri. Perrot said nothing about Indian slaves; but we know from later French reports that the trade with the Sioux and Iowas, which Perrot started in 1685, soon developed into a brisk slave trade, evidently encouraged by the French traders. The Iowas, attacked by the Mascoutens, withdrew from the Mississippi; but the Sioux traded French goods and arms to the Iowas, and the Iowas went to the Missouri and raided the Panis or Pawnees, trading the slaves they caught to the Sioux for more French goods and firearms. By 1720, the Iowas were allied to the Panis and were obtaining Padouca slaves from them.

The closing years of the seventeenth century were marked by many changes among the tribes near the upper Mississippi. The Miamis were drifting down into the Wabash country. The Potawatomis were leaving Wisconsin and going into northern Illinois and Indiana. The Illinis were steadily losing strength. A French priest among the Illinis reported enthusiastically that he had baptized two thousand members of the tribe; but the Illinis were now very weak and their hold on their lands along Illinois River was precarious. The Foxes, Mascoutens, and Kickapoos were attacking them from the north. The Sioux were coming down the Mississippi in canoes to raid them, and the vindictive Iroquois were still sending war parties against them. In 1691, a party of three hundred Iroquois was lurking near the old Kaskaskia village at Starved Rock. Most of the Illini men were away, raiding the Osages and other badly armed tribes west of the Mississippi, and the Iroquois were calmly waiting for the Illini corn crop to ripen before attacking. They needed the corn to provide them with food on their homeward march.[11]

Perrot was still on the Mississippi in 1689, mainly interested in the Sioux trade; but the constant state of war was ruining trade. He made peace between the Sioux and a band of Miamis who were camped near his fort, which was evidently Fort St. Nicolas. The Ottawas, still engaged in trading French goods to other tribes, now induced the Sioux, Ojibwas, and Iowas to raise a force of twelve hundred warriors and attack the Miamis, Mascoutens, and Foxes. This great war party destroyed the Miami village near Perrot's fort, carrying off many captives. Now the Miamis, Mascoutens, and Foxes began to prepare to invade the Sioux country, when winter covered

---

[11] Temple, "Indian Villages of the Illinois Country," *Illinois State Museum Scientific Papers*, vol. II, part 2, 30.

the innumerable lakes and marshes with ice, making their operations against the Sioux more effective. Perrot was so discouraged by this ceaseless state of war, which made trade almost impossible, that he planned to withdraw all his traders from the Sioux country. He had his main post near the mouth of Wisconsin River and a small one somewhere in the Sioux land, perhaps the one near Lake Pepin. Whether he withdrew his traders or not, we do not know, but he does not seem to be mentioned in the west after 1690.[12]

In any effort to extend our knowledge of the Siouan tribes in northern Iowa and southern South Dakota at this period, we must attempt to fit in the known village ruins and other Indian remains of the region; but, when we attempt to do so, we find that archaeological opinion is fairly united in the view that the village ruins and mounds are all of very early date and therefore cannot be the remains of Iowa, Oto, and Omaha occupation. This has been the view of archaeologists for many years, and their contention has been confirmed to some extent in recent years by the use of the new Carbon-14 laboratory test.[13] To the historian, however, it seems incredible that in an area known to have been occupied by large groups of Siouan Indians from the year 1660 until after the year 1700 there should be no remains of these historic tribes but, on the other hand, numerous remains of an earlier Indian occupation. This situation is not acceptable to either historians or ethnologists.

In the preceding chapter the evidence was given of the flight of the Osage-Omaha and the Quapaw groups from the Ohio Valley because of Iroquois attacks around 1650, and of the migration of the Omahas from the lower Missouri northward through Iowa, where

12 Blair, *Indian Tribes of the Upper Mississippi*, II, 112. This information seems important, as it proves that up to 1690 the Ojibwas were allied to the Sioux. It must have been after this date that the Ojibwas began the war on the Sioux that forced that tribe to retire from their lands near the head of the Mississippi.

13 The Smithsonian Institution recently released the latest Carbon–14 datings, taken from bits of charcoal found in village ruins. The tests gave a date for Cahokia Old Village of A.D. 1200 or earlier. For the Swanson village in South Dakota, which one would suppose to be late seventeenth century, the date was A.D. 858, and for the Thomas Riggs site, also presumably of the seventeenth century, the date was A.D. 1228. To the mind of the present writer, this is really shocking. From the previously announced archaeological findings, one would suppose that the Swanson and Thomas Riggs villages were nearly contemporary and of a much later time than the Carbon–14 test dates.

This Hopewell woman with her child was reconstructed by B. M. Frost from the Hopewellians represented by the Knight statuettes from Calhoun County.

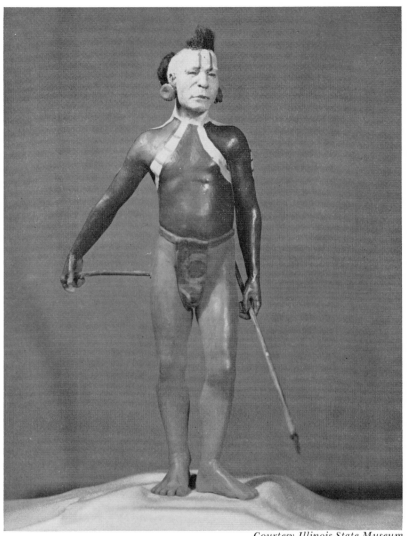

The Ohio Hopewell or Mound Builder culture succeeded Adena culture. The Mound Builders made a deep impression on the minds of the northern Indians with imponderable things of the spirit—sky deities and a future life. This Hopewell warrior was reconstructed by B. M. Frost from the Hopewellians represented by the Knight statuettes from Calhoun County, Illinois.

they picked up a village of Iowas on the lower Des Moines, and the two groups moved into northern Iowa, where the Marquette map places them around 1673. This location of the Omahas, Iowas, Otoes, and Panas is confirmed by the Franquelin maps, made after 1680; and later maps indicate that these Indians had all moved westward and were located on or near the Missouri in southern South Dakota around 1690–1720. The Omaha and Ponca traditions agree that these two tribes moved northward through Iowa and dwelt for a time near the pipestone quarry. This does not necessarily mean in that immediate locality. The quarry is mentioned probably because it was the outstanding feature of the general district. Being attacked here by enemies and having many people slaughtered, the Omahas and Poncas fled west to the Big Sioux, were there attacked again and fled to the Missouri in South Dakota. This story is confirmed to some degree by the historical evidence, which shows that at the period 1680–90 the tribes in northern Iowa were being raided by the tribes along the Mississippi, who were equipped with French weapons, while the tribes in Iowa were still armed only with flint weapons and were at the mercy of Indians bearing French weapons.

It seems a fair assumption that the Omahas and Poncas brought a rather high type of culture from the Ohio Valley and that they had a highly organized social life, that of permanent village Indians of the Ohio country. Being driven west of the Mississippi, they were forced to readjust their whole manner of life to fit the conditions in the Iowa prairies. They were Woodland Indians, and in northern Iowa there were only occasional groves on the prairies and belts of timber along the streams. The buffalo were an all-important source of food.

The Omahas and Poncas were a numerous group. In 1700, Jean François Le Sueur gave the Omahas twelve hundred families as compared with four thousand families for the great Sioux nation; and the Omahas had probably lost almost half of their people to enemy attacks and disease by 1700. The French always introduced smallpox into any tribe they came among, and this dread disease spread to more distant tribes. The Quapaws, close kindred of the Omahas, lost half of their population in a single smallpox epidemic late in the seventeenth century.

In any attempt to locate the Omaha group at this period we must take their large population into account and must consider the fact that they were living in northern Iowa, near the pipestone quarry, and with Iowa and Oto villages not far away. The only village ruins that agree with this description seem to be the Mill Creek sites, on a tributary of the Little Sioux, mainly in Cherokee County, Iowa. Shetrone stated that there were twelve of these village ruins. They were not big towns, but the huts or lodges were of a size that would accommodate two or more families each. It did not require many such huts to make a sizable community. The villages were not near each other, as Indians who lived largely by hunting could not dwell in big and compact communities.

The Mill Creek villages seem to have had up to about twenty huts in each community, and we may surmise that the huts held twenty or more persons each. This is highly conjectural; but it gives a rough idea of the Mill Creek population, perhaps five to seven thousand persons. Some of the villages were on high ground in good defensive positions and had protecting ditches and possibly palisades. All the village sites are notable for the thick layer of refuse left by the Indian population. The refuse has a depth of from three to twelve feet. It forms moundlike areas, and in some villages the huts were set near enough to each other to form a continuous raised area or mound. In the Whittrock and Chan-ya-ta villages, the huts were set farther apart, each with its own mound of refuse. One Chan-ya-ta hut was forty by thirty-two feet in size.

Indian villages with such depth of refuse spread over the ground are not common in the Iowa area, and it is to be surmised that the Omaha-Osage-Quapaw group of tribes may have had habits of daily life that caused such accumulation of rubbish in their villages. The situation at Mill Creek seems quite similar to that at the Pinnacles, in Saline County, Missouri, which is supposed to be an old Osage village. There the huts were placed far apart, each on its own thick area of refuse, as at Whittrock and Chan-ya-ta. The Walls–Pecan Point village ruins, which we have conjectured may have been Quapaw villages of the period 1650, also feature heavy depth of refuse.[14]

14 For descriptions of Mill Creek village ruins see Shetrone, *The Mound Builders,* 336; W. R. Hurt, Jr., *The Thomas Riggs Site, Archeological Studies,* Circular 5, 52–54; Reynold J. Ruppe, paper on Mill Creek Culture, *Yearbook of the American Philosophical Society,* 1955), 335–39. It seems significant that, whenever the archaeologists are struck by an unusual depth of rubbish on a site, that site is one we might attribute to the Dhegiha group—the Quapaws, Osages, Omahas, and per-

This great depth of refuse lying on the Mill Creek sites has led some archaeologists to assume that the villages were occupied over a very long period of time. Estimating so many inches of village rubbish to a century is, however, pure conjecture, and it does not take into account the fact that these Indians were bringing carcasses of buffalo, elk, and other game into their villages and then tossing the bones and other refuse on the ground. Their huts seem to have been of a perishable type, made of poles covered with bark, mats, or skins. These huts did not last long. They often caught fire, and the debris of ruined huts was added to the layer of rubbish in the village. Broken pots, broken flint and bone tools, shells, fish bones, turtle shells and bones, and probably masses of corn cobs were added to the refuse heaps. How can any man estimate whether it took a century or a year to build up a foot of rubbish in such a village?

Many really old village sites gave a clear indication of their age in the fact that the lower levels show an earlier and cruder type of culture while the upper levels exhibit a later and more refined type. In the Mill Creek villages the process is reversed. The lowest level, presenting the situation when the villages were first established, shows a high type of culture very similar to Cahokia Old Village, with well-built rectangular huts, superior pottery of wide variety of types, and corn, bean, and squash seed. The upper levels seem to exhibit a poorer type of pottery and some form of flimsy shelters, compared by archaeologists to wickiups.[15] In effect, there seems to be a degeneration in culture from the lower levels to the top layers, and this situation would coincide with what we might expect happened to the Omaha and Ponca Indians. They came from a settled area in the Ohio Valley bringing a rather high type of culture; and in the Iowa prairies they had to face new conditions, a harder and more nomadic life. They met native groups in northern Iowa, people of their own

haps the Kansas. At the Pinnacles the refuse heaps were rather widely separated, forming mounds three to five feet high, made of village rubbish, with hut ruins on top of the heaps. The village was apparently of about forty huts. Wedel excavated a site in Platte County, Missouri, which he suggested was either a village of the Kansa tribe or of Oneota culture. This village had huts apparently of perishable type, as at Mill Creek and the Pinnacles. The refuse heaps at the Walls–Pecan Point villages had a depth of three to five feet, similar to that at the Pinnacles and at some Mill Creek sites.

[15] Hurt, *The Swanson Site*, 32.

stock, speaking kindred dialects, who had a cruder way of life than that of the Indians of the Ohio Valley; and the Omahas probably learned much from these native groups, and began to adopt some of their ways.

The upper layers of refuse in the Mill Creek village ruins indicate that the pottery was changing in type, becoming cruder, with some traits of the Great Oasis pottery of southwestern Minnesota. Another condition was the raiding of the Iowa tribes by Indians from east of the Mississippi. The Omahas and most of their neighbors were still equipped only with flint weapons, and they could not fight successfully against their attackers. Their one recourse was flight, and the Omaha and Ponca traditions state that, after dwelling for some time near the pipestone quarry their people were slaughtered by enemies, and the survivors fled west to the Big Sioux near the present Sioux Falls and built a fort there. Shetrone stated that there were about two hundred burial mounds near the Mill Creek villages. If we assume, as both history and tradition seem to show, that these Indians were not in the Mill Creek villages for more than about fifty years at most, this is a surprising number of burials, which might be accounted for by the slaughter of the people by enemy groups. But there is too much conjecture here. More excavation in the Mill Creek sites is needed to clear up the situation.

Returning again briefly to the question of the date of the Mill Creek villages, we may note that Reynold J. Ruppe stated that the Mill Creek sites were probably occupied by groups "ancestral to the Omaha" and that these villages were abandoned at about the time the Omahas left Iowa and fled farther west into South Dakota.[16] Ruppe had already given his opinion that the villages were established as far back as the year 1200 and that the date of the Omaha flight from Iowa was about 1685 or 1690. We may leave it to the good judgment of the archaeologists to decide whether the Mill Creek villages, despite their heavy layers of refuse, could possibly have been occupied for nearly five centuries. It would be astonishing for any tribe in the Iowa region to live in one locality for such a length of time, especially if they started, as the Mill Creek folk did, with a high type of culture and then let it degenerate. The signs of degenera-

16 Ruppe, paper on Mill Creek Culture, *Yearbook of the American Philosophical Society* (1955), 335–39.

tion in this same area, in the Blue Earth villages and in the Oneota culture, are shown in pottery changes, as at Mill Creek, and are a matter of very recent date. The cultural deterioration was probably caused by confused conditions and war induced by the obtaining of French weapons. This points to a time after 1650.

The Mill Creek lower-layer pottery has been termed almost identical with Cahokia Old Village pottery, but the Mill Creek pots are grit tempered. The Mill Creek culture has also been termed very similar to Oneota, the culture of the Iowas and Otoes, but the Oneota pots were shell tempered. The tree-ring dating at Kinkaid in southern Illinois showed 1450–1520 for early Kinkaid, which is said to be contemporary with Cahokia Old Village. James B. Griffin stated that Fort Ancient culture in the Ohio Valley was contemporary with early Kinkaid, and Fort Ancient has Oneota traits. Again, Griffin terms Oneota contemporary with middle Kinkaid, which had a tree-ring date of 1523–98. W. R. Hurt, the South Dakota archaeologist, gave his opinion that Mill Creek dated 1300–1400. George F. Will gave a tree-ring dating for the Huff Mandan village ruin of 1485–1543, and this site is said to have some Oneota traits. It has elaborate fortifications, somewhat similar to the Arzberger site on the Missouri in South Dakota, which has Mill Creek traits. Will also remarked that the Mandan archaic villages, somewhat older than the Huff village, have Mill Creek, Mitchell, and Nebraska Culture traits, indicating that these Mandan villages belong to the time of confusion and flight that brought the Omahas and other fugitive tribes into South Dakota. If the reader is still present and conscious, I should like to ask him if he regards archaeological datings as clear and conclusive.

Let us get back to earth. The Marquette map of 1673 set down the Mahas or Omahas apparently in northwestern Iowa, with the Otoes to the east of them, the Panas to the north, between the Omahas and Otoes, and the Iowas to the northwest of the Omahas. Marquette had no accurate knowledge of either the country west of the Mississippi or these tribes. His location of them was only relative and very general. The Joliet map of 1674 put the Mahas apparently between the Des Moines and Missouri rivers, with the Otoes north of them, the Iowas to the west of the Mahas, and the Panas to the southwest. The draft of the Franquelin map of 1684 shows the Des Moines as River of the Otoes, with that tribe near its head and the Mahas north of them. The Franquelin map of 1684 is much more interesting. It shows the Otoes on the head of a tributary of the Mississippi, terming them Ototanta or Mascoutens Nadouesioux. This is repeated on the later Franquelin maps, and it seems to refute the nineteenth-century identification of the tribe called Mascoutens Nadouesioux with the Iowas. The name was evidently applied to both the Iowas and the Otoes. This Franquelin map shows two widely separated Iowa divisions. There is the one termed Paoutet on all the early French maps. This is the native name of the Iowa tribe, and this Paoutet division is shown on the maps to the west of the Otoes and Omahas; but the map of 1684 also shows the Aiounoue tribe or Iowas on Aiounoue River (Upper Iowa River) on the west side of the Mississippi near the mouth of Wisconsin River, and it was undoubtedly this Iowa group that Father Membré said was in Wisconsin in 1680, near or with the Kickapoos and Mascoutens. This group was also the one that Perrot had dealings with in 1685–86. He visited their village, and he reported that the Mascoutens destroyed their village and captured many of the people. This group, always called Iowas, was the one that was allied to the Sioux and was active along the Mississippi in 1680–90.

These French maps, and the information in the French documents, make it clear that, between 1670 and 1683, the group of tribes in northwestern Iowa, near the head of the Des Moines and perhaps west to the Big Sioux, were the Omahas, with the Otoes to the northeast of them and the Paoutet group of Iowas to the northwest; a Pana group to the north. The identity of the Panas is conjectural. La Salle obtained a slave of this tribe on Illinois River in 1679, and the boy said that his tribe lived in two villages on a branch of the Mississippi. Yet the French maps place the Panas near the Omahas in northwestern Iowa, and the Franquelin map of 1684 attempts to show the Missouri River and marks on it two Pana villages and a big group of Panimaha villages, evidently in Nebraska. Along the Missouri is a mass of Panitocka, White Pawnees. The Panimaha we know were the Skidi Pawnees, who brought to the Loup Fork of the Platte in Nebraska a culture closely resembling that of the Iroquoian tribes of New York State. They are said by tradition to have accompanied the Omaha group on their migration out of the Ohio Valley; but there are no archaeological indications that any Pawnee group had villages in northwestern Iowa, in the Mill Creek area. Judging both from the La Salle information and from the French maps, the Panimahas were in Nebraska by 1680 and probably for quite a time prior to that date. The Pana village or villages placed near the Omahas in northwestern Iowa are a mystery.

Obviously, this French information and the French maps do not afford clear enough evidence to locate any of these tribes in north-western Iowa with accuracy. From the French material we cannot adduce anything beyond the fact that these tribes were in northern Iowa, evidently between the upper Des Moines and the Big Sioux; but the archaeological material (leaving out archaeological dating) strongly hints that the Mill Creek villages were those of the Omaha group. We have to locate that group in this particular area, and there are no other village ruins except the Mill Creek ones that fit the situation.

As for the Otoes and Iowas (Paoutet group), who were neighbors of the Omahas at this period, there are Oneota sites in every direction from the Mill Creek villages—near the upper Des Moines, on the upper Little Sioux, to the south of Mill Creek on the Little Sioux, and to the west of Mill Creek on the Big Sioux. Again, we cannot point to any of these Oneota sites and say with certainty that they were the villages of the Iowas or the Otoes; but, in a general way, the French information that the Mill Creek and neighboring districts were the home of the Omahas, Poncas, Iowas, and Otoes at the period 1673–88 is borne out. We might here quote archaeology to confirm this view, but the archaeological dating will not agree. The Omahas, Poncas, Iowas, and Otoes all had forms of Mississippi culture; and W. R. Hurt, head of the museum at the University of South Dakota, observes that Indians with Mississippi culture came from the southeast and east, tarrying in northwestern Iowa near the pipestone quarry, moving on westward to the Big Sioux, to James River, and to the Missouri, between the mouths of the Big Sioux and White River. Hurt dates this movement around 1400–1500, but he appears to believe that it was a second group of Indians, migrating westward from southern Minnesota, that embraced the Omahas, Iowas, and Otoes and that they did not reach South Dakota until about 1690–1700. The theory of two waves of Mississippian culture moving westward into Dakota would be difficult to substantiate; but Mr. Hurt's date of 1690–1700 for the arrival of the Omahas, Iowas, and others on the Missouri in South Dakota is probably correct.

The Omaha and Ponca traditions state that they dwelt in villages near the pipestone quarry for some time. Some of the traditions assert that the Poncas separated from the Omahas at this period and later rejoined them. Enemies, possibly Yankton Sioux, attacked. The Omahas and Poncas fled to the Big Sioux, where they built a fortified village. The Iowas were with or near them, but the Otoes are not mentioned. This seems to be borne out by the French information, for the French mention that the Otoes, or part of them, were with the Missouri tribe on the lower Missouri River about 1687–90. Tonty places them there at the latter date; but Le Sueur, who was in southern Minnesota in 1700, was told by the Sioux that the Blue Earth country south of Minnesota River belonged to the Otoes, Iowas, and Sioux of the Prairie, and that the Otoes and Iowas had recently removed toward the Missouri, to live near the Omahas. The Otoes, however, are never mentioned by the French as being on the Missouri in South Dakota. Instead, they crossed the Missouri and established themselves on the Great Nemaha, in southeastern Nebraska, where they were noted from about 1700 on.[17]

The ruined Indian villages and mounds along the Big Sioux, to the west of the Mill Creek district, are numerous and impressive. It was here that by tradition the Omahas, Poncas, and Iowas lived for a time; and here the Omahas and Poncas were again attacked and slaughtered. They buried their dead in a large mound, which the Omahas stated was still to be seen down to the middle of the nineteenth century.[18] Four of the sites on the Big Sioux are definitely

[17] The culture of the Otoes in the Nemaha district in Nebraska exhibits traits similar to those of an Oneota area on the Mississippi near Burlington, Iowa. This suggests that the Otoes may have gone to the Burlington district, then to join the Missouri tribe, and finally to Nebraska; but such a theory does not account for the presence of a large Oto group in southern Minnesota and northern Iowa down almost to the year 1700. Probably the Otoes, like the Iowas, were in more than one group.

[18] The Omahas called the Big Sioux River "Xe," meaning "Buried" and referring to the burial of their slaughtered people in the mound. The tradition placed this burial mound below Sioux Falls and said that it had a stone wall encircling its base, which seems to be a trait of the Ohio Valley Indians. Some of the traditions state that it was the Sioux who slaughtered the Omahas on the Big Sioux. J. O. Dorsey, "Migrations of the Siouan Indians," *American Naturalist,* Vol. XX, prints a map showing the halts of the migrating Indians. Site No. 15 is the Mill Creek district, south of the pipestone quarry. No. 16 is southwest of the quarry, on an eastern branch of the Big Sioux, and the site is described by tradition as cliffs about one hundred feet high on each bank of the creek, with the village on

of Mill Creek culture and presumably Omaha tribal sites. These are Brandon village, two sites in Plymouth County, Iowa, and the Broken Kettle site near the mouth of the Big Sioux.

Mound building was a characteristic trait of the Omahas, Iowas, and Otoes. They kept this custom in northwestern Iowa, and took it to the Big Sioux River, but when they came to the Big Sioux they evidently began to abandon their old custom of building large burial mounds. This may have been because the attack by enemies had thrown them into confusion, and with their principal preoccupation being one of survival, they had no leisure for building mounds or making superior types of pottery.

The remains along the Big Sioux have been neglected by archaeologists, little real work having been done beyond an excavation at Brandon village ruins and at Split Rock Creek. Cyrus Thomas stated over fifty years ago that there were about 275 mounds along the Big Sioux, south of Sioux Falls in Lyon County, Iowa, and to the north in Minnehaha County, South Dakota; but the mere description of the remains proves little. Thomas stated that the mounds were in groups on high bluffs and terraces, overlooking the river.[19] One notable group of fifty mounds, in the northwestern corner of Lyon County, had stone circles and oblongs made by placing boulders on the ground among the mounds, and these stone outlines outnumbered the mounds by three to one. A theory was advanced that these

its south bank. No. 17 is a fort built by the Indians on the east bank of this same creek near its junction with the Big Sioux. This is the most detailed statement from traditions concerning the location of the Omahas and Poncas when they moved to the Big Sioux. Site No. 18 shows them near Lake Andes, on the Missouri in South Dakota. The French scientist, I. N. Nicollet, and his aides explored and mapped this area in 1836–38, and in his report Nicollet called the Little Sioux "Inyanyanke," Rock River, and stated that the rock for which the stream was named was on or near an upper tributary, Otcheyedan, which meant "The Spot Where They Cry" or "The Place of Mourning." The name, he said, came from a small hillock where the Indians went to mourn their dead relatives. This hillock was in Osceola County, immediately north of the Mill Creek Indian village ruins in Cherokee County, Iowa. The Otcheyedan Creek is a western tributary of the Little Sioux, and the hillock is shown on Nicollet's map a short distance south of Lake Poinsett. The Otcheyedan Creek heads quite near to the Red Stone (Pipestone) branch of the Big Sioux. Nicollet did not state what Indians came to this hillock to mourn their dead; but it seems possible that he is here referring to the spot where the Omahas buried their slaughtered people, about the year 1690.

[19] Thomas, *Report on the Mound Exploration of the Bureau of Ethnology, Twelfth Annual Report*, B.A.E.

boulders were used to hold down the bottom edges of tipi covers. As some of the circles were over thirty feet in diameter, it seems unlikely that these were tipi sites. Perhaps the people were using their old type of large dwellings, circular, or oblong, but were no longer at leisure to build strong structures and made them light with some kind of covering like hides. This might require stones to hold down the edges of the covering.

About half a mile up the river from this group of fifty mounds was another site, apparently a village ruin, with the same type of boulder outlines set among the mounds. These village sites were usually on the terraces. On high points of bluff were small conical mounds containing burials. Another earthwork was on an octagonal enclosure embracing ten acres. It stood immediately south of the group of fifty mounds. This might be the remains of the fort the Omaha and Ponca traditions state their people built when they fled westward to the Big Sioux. In this same locality was the Blood Run site, covering one hundred acres and including an enclosure of fifteen acres. According to Dorsey, the Omahas and the Poncas had a village and fort here on the Big Sioux, but were presently attacked by the Sioux and driven into South Dakota.[20]

Further archaeological work along the Big Sioux should clear up this situation. The excavations at Brandon showed a village of the Mill Creek culture, with evidence that it had been occupied only a short time. Here the Mill Creek hut type was clearly indicated. They were rectangular, and one hut had three fireplaces down the center, indicating three families, or six, as fires were often shared by two families. The hut had no center poles, indicating light construction, and an interior vestibule was inside the hut door. The hut floor was excavated, being about eighteen inches below the level of the ground outside. This village stood on a terrace on the bank of the Big Sioux. It was fortified, being defended by the natural steep slopes on three sides and by a ditch on the fourth. There were apparently thirty-seven huts, and the few articles of stone and bone found suggested a brief occupation.

The Mill Creek Indians were agricultural, and the lack of indications of crop-growing at Brandon was another hint of a short occupation. This village most closely resembled the Mill Creek village north of Alta, Iowa; but it contained pots of mixed types, part of

20 Dorsey, *Omaha Traditions, Sixth Annual Report,* B.A.E.

which were of the old southern Minnesota Cambria culture. Part of the pots had loop handles and part strap handles, the latter suggesting a date around 1650–90. There were no burial mounds near the Brandon village. The pots at Brandon resembled those at the Kimball site, much farther down the Big Sioux, and the Broken Kettle site near the mouth of that stream. These sites are Mill Creek village ruins. Again, the Brandon culture is close in type to that on James River, at the Mitchell and Twelve-Mile Creek sites. All this hints at a situation that one might expect from the Omaha and Ponca traditions. These Indians fled, probably in confusion, made a brief stand on the Big Sioux, and then split up, moving to widely separated localities in South Dakota and near the mouth of the Big Sioux.[21]

The archaeological remains at Brandon and farther down the Big Sioux at Kimball and Broken Kettle, and on James River, seem to fit well the conditions we may assume from the Omaha and Ponca story. Here were tribes—the Omahas, Poncas, Iowas, and Otoes—all with Mississippian type of late culture. The people at Mill Creek must have come into contact with Siouan Indians in southern Minnesota, for they adopted some traits from the pottery of the Great Oasis culture of southwestern Minnesota. Then they fled before enemy attacks to the Big Sioux; and here they picked up pottery traits from Woodland cultural groups of the southern Minnesota district, traits of the Great Oasis culture and Cambria aspects. This seems to mean that the Indians of these aspects were still living in southern Minnesota as late as 1680 and that they were driven westward at the same time that the Indians in northern Iowa were driven out. The refugee groups then mingled on the Big Sioux and fled on into South Dakota, where they arrived in a confused mass. The tribes with the higher Mississippian culture, the Omahas, Poncas, and Iowas, having to live under new and harder conditions, then adopted features of the simpler culture of the Woodland Indians from Minnesota and of the Panis of the Missouri.

We have considerable confirmation of these conjectures from Indian tradition, French information, and French maps. The Omaha

---

[21] For the Indian remains along the Big Sioux, see Thomas, *Report on the Mound Exploration of the Bureau of Ethnology, Twelfth Annual Report,* B.A.E., 38; Hurt, *The Swanson Site, Archeological Studies,* Circular 3; W. H. Over and E. E. Meleen, *A Report on the Brandon Village Site and the Split Rock Creek Mounds, Archeological Studies,* Circular 4.

and Ponca traditions make it perfectly clear that they fled to the Big
Sioux near Sioux Falls and lived there in a village and fort. The
so-called Le Sueur map of 1701 places an Iowa village in this vicinity,
which supports some of the Omaha traditions that they lived on the
Big Sioux near the Iowas. A French trader named La Chesnaye told
Le Sueur that (apparently in 1690) he was married to an Iowa girl
and had been living in an Iowa village near the Missouri and that
these Iowas were constantly raiding the Panis along the Missouri.[22]
French maps from 1701 on show a Trader's Trail starting from the
Mississippi opposite the mouth of the Wisconsin River and going
west through northern Iowa to the Big Sioux near Sioux Falls. In
that locality an Iowa village is shown. The trail then goes down the
east bank of the Big Sioux to another Iowa village. It crosses the Big
Sioux and goes to a third Iowa village, apparently on Vermillion
River. This suggests that the French were trading with the Iowas
from 1690 on. With Perrot trading with the Iowas as late as 1689,
this is a reasonable assumption.

The French maps naturally do not give the exact date at which
these tribes lived in any particular locality. The maps were based
mainly on information obtained from French traders, whose names
often are unknown to us; and some of the map makers continue to
place the tribes in the same locations over a period of many years
when it is pretty obvious that the Indians had left those locations and
moved elsewhere. However, the maps seem to confirm the Indian traditions, that the Omahas and Iowas were living near each other from
about 1670 on and that they moved from near Sioux Falls down the
Big Sioux and then up the north bank of the Missouri to the point
where the French traders, coming up the Missouri, discovered them
in 1717, finding a confused mass of Omahas, Iowas, and assorted
Pani or Pawnee and Arikara groups. From this French material we
cannot date the movements of these tribes; but many years ago a
stone was found on the north side of the Missouri near Lake Andes
with the date 1691 scratched on it and a Christian cross. This hints
the presence of a French trader near Lake Andes, and it was near
that lake that the Omaha tribe assembled after their flight from the
Sioux Falls area.

The apparent flight of the Woodland Indians (Great Oasis and

22 La Chesnaye, in Marc, Baron de Villiers du Terrage, *La Découverte du Missouri,* 32.

Cambria folk) from southwestern Minnesota and their mingling with the Omahas and Iowas in South Dakota may be connected with the movement of the Teton or Prairie Sioux into southern Minnesota, which apparently dates after 1680. The Omaha and Ponca traditions assert that the Yankton Sioux attacked them in northwestern Iowa and drove them to the Big Sioux, then attacked and drove them farther on, into South Dakota.

The Omaha and Ponca tradition that they were attacked in northwestern Iowa and later on the Big Sioux near Sioux Falls by the Yankton Sioux is supported by French evidence that the Yanktons were nearest to the area occupied by the Omahas and that the Yanktons later occupied that area, rather than by direct assertion that these Sioux attacked the Omahas. There was a movement of the Teton Sioux and the Yankton group from their old lands near the head of the Mississippi southward to Minnesota River late in the seventeenth century, the Yanktons evidently going on toward the red pipestone quarry in the southwestern corner of Minnesota. Thus Le Sueur in 1700 called the Yanktons the "Village of the Red Stone Quarry," and in later times the other Sioux admitted the right of the Yanktons to control the pipestone quarry by discovery and occupation. This right was confirmed to the Yanktons by the United States government in the treaty of 1858. The De l'Isle map of 1718 shows the Tetons around a big lake at the head of Minnesota River and a village of the Yanktons on the north bank of the river, about midway between the big bend of the river and the lake at its head. Here the Yanktons perhaps had their center, with their hunting grounds to the south, extending to or beyond the pipestone quarry. In other words, they were probably occupying, after 1700, the lands from which they are said to have driven the Omahas, Poncas, and Iowas at a date around 1690. Again, the French merchant of St. Louis, Auguste Chouteau, wrote a historical memoir in 1816, and in it he asserted that at the beginning of the eighteenth century a tribe of Sioux occupied the Des Moines River in Iowa. In 1700, Iberville was planning to build a post on the lower Des Moines for the trade of these Sioux, and we know from later French reports that the Sioux of the Des Moines in the eighteenth century were the Yanktons, and our government recognized the Yankton claim to lands on the upper Des Moines down to about the year 1820.

Le Sueur stated in 1700 that the country along the Blue Earth

River in southern Minnesota had belonged to the Iowas, Otoes, and the Sioux of the Prairie; but that recently the Iowas and Otoes had left, going to live near the Omahas on the Missouri. Since it is quite clear that at least one village of Iowas had been with or near the Omahas for a number of years, back to the 1670 period, here again we have a suggestion that the Iowas, and probably the Otoes were in more than one group. Indeed, the French reported one Oto group with the Missouri tribe on the lower Missouri in 1687, and Tonty confirmed this report in 1690. In 1700, Iberville reported, evidently from Le Sueur's information, that the Otoes and Iowas were with the Omahas at a point about one hundred leagues west of the Illinois, which meant west of the Mississippi.

Much of this material, from Indian tradition and French sources, would fit in nicely with the archaeological situation in northwestern Iowa, on the Big Sioux, and in South Dakota, if it were not for the insistence of archaeologists that all the village ruins and other remains date back to the year 1200, or at least to 1500. These Indian remains, they insist, are all very old. They have found no clear trace of the tribes that swarmed through northwestern Iowa, on the Big Sioux and in South Dakota near the Missouri in 1670–1700, and some archaeologists seem to think that this casts doubt on the authenticity of Indian traditions and even on the truth of French evidence. It only casts doubt on archaeological dating.

The amazing tangle of archaeological traits found on and near the Missouri in southern South Dakota is in itself strongly suggestive of a late dating for these village ruins and other remains. The conditions are strikingly similar to those found by archaeologists in the Piedmont district in Virginia and Carolina at a very late prehistoric date. There the old native cultures broke down and became greatly confused soon after the whites began to form settlements along the coast. It was about the same in other areas, and James B. Griffin noted the confused archaeological conditions on the Ohio in late prehistoric times and attributed this by inference to Iroquois attacks after that tribe obtained European weapons.

When the French trader Bourgmont met the Omahas on the Missouri in South Dakota in 1717, he described them as a noble nation, peaceful folk, wanderers; and they were wandering because they had been driven to it by the attacks of tribes who had obtained French weapons. Tradition, the vestiges this tribe still had in the nineteenth century of a formerly high social organization, fits in with what we know of the other tribes of the Ohio Valley. Most of these Indians were probably survivors of the old Mound Builder population or their neighbors, people used to a settled and well-organized way of life under conditions of relative peacefulness. They probably did not make ruthless war on their neighbors. Then the Iroquois obtained European arms and cleared all the tribes out of the great valley, driving most of the survivors westward or southward. War and turmoil spread to Michigan, Wisconsin, and Illinois. No man was any longer any other man's brother. He could trust only his closest blood relations. There was no such thing as pity. Tribe after tribe became the victims of neighbors who had obtained French weapons; and when the victims in their turn obtained such arms, instead of using them against their oppressors, they went and massacred neighbor nations still armed only with flint weapons. Slavery on a commercial scale entered the field; and by 1690 there were French and English traders who specialized in buying Indian slaves, and in trading arms to certain tribes and urging them to attack their harmless neighbors and obtain more slaves for barter. By 1690, one village of Iowas, probably former victims of the Illini and Mascouten raiders, were living on the Missouri and raiding the Pawnees, trading the captives they took to the slave-dealers for more French weapons. Under such conditions native culture began to wane. People who had to be on the watch day and night against raiders had little leisure for building handsome villages or making fine pottery and other native products.

Even the Sioux, who had held out so long against the Algonquian plans to take their country, now suffered the fate of weaker tribes. Attacked from the north by the Crees and Assiniboines, armed with guns from Hudson Bay, and with their old allies, the Ojibwas, now armed with French guns and urged on by the vindictive Ottawas, the Sioux began to retire from their land of lakes and marshes near the head of the Mississippi, the Tetons and Yanktons leading the movement southward to the Blue Earth and prairie land near upper Minnesota River. By 1700, the Tetons had started their long migration westward, which was to end within sight of the Rockies, in the plains of Colorado, Wyoming, and Montana.

CHAPTER TEN

From Woodland
to Prairie

TOWARD THE CLOSE of the seventeenth century the tribes of the north-central Woodlands were in a bad way. Contact with Europeans was causing their native culture to wither away, and their old belief in themselves and in the power of their gods was steadily weakening. The only ambition they had left was to seek glory in petty warfare and to gain small advantages by attacking neighbor tribes. The dawn of the eighteenth century witnessed the growing domination of the whites in most areas and the end of the Indian world as it had been visioned by the ancestors of the contemporary tribes.

This last phase had already destroyed many tribes near the Atlantic coast and along the lower Mississippi. These tribes had welcomed the coming of the whites, who were so friendly and helpful at first, but the European settlements hardly had been formed before the whites began to push the Indians out of their way and to establish white control. As an Iroquois chief said with deep bitterness, the white man took the Indian by the hand in pretended friendship and then threw him behind him. That was true. The Indian was to be the follower from now on, and haughty tribes, like the Iroquois, found the new situation intolerable.

In the view of most of the tribes, the French were less obnoxious than the English or the Spaniards of Florida. Most of the French colonists accepted the Indian as an equal and even adopted many Indian ways. The Indian was their brother. But the English and Spaniards regarded themselves as far above any Indian, and their attitude was usually that the Indian must give up his heathen ways if he wished to survive. The Indian's retort was to attack the white intruders, and most of the early wars were near the coast, where the English and Spaniards had formed settlements. The French had little trouble, except with the two haughty nations, the Iroquois in the northeast and the Natchez on the lower Mississippi.

There is little left to record concerning the Woodland Indians of the north-central areas. The drift into white control went steadily on after the French had established themselves on the upper Mississippi and formed a colony near the mouth of the river. There are interesting episodes to be set down, and we may attempt to reconcile modern archaeology with the known movements of actual tribes between the dates 1680 and 1725. In particular we may try to follow the fate of some of the tribes the Iroquois had driven out of the Ohio Valley, the Omahas and Poncas and their Siouan neighbors, the Iowas and Otoes; and we may also attempt to give some account of the great block of White Panis or Pawnees that held both banks of the Missouri River before the coming of the Siouan tribes.

Archaeology tells us that these Pawnees occupied the east bank of the Missouri from the Little Platte River, near the present Kansas City, up to a point near the present Sioux City. On the west bank their villages extended northward from northeastern Kansas, at a point near the present St. Joseph, into northeastern Nebraska. On the east bank the cultural remains of these Pawnees are termed in archaeology the Glenwood aspect. On the Nebraska bank the same culture has been given the name Nebraska Culture or aspect.

The French divided the Pawnee tribes into Black Pawnees and White Pawnees, the first group in the south, the second in the north; and early French maps set down a great mass of Panis Blancs or White Pawnees along the Missouri. These maps are so inaccurate and distorted that it is impossible to judge just where these Pawnees were, but it seems to be a safe conjecture that the French map makers were attempting to locate the villages that modern archaeology has found in ruins and accurately described.

These Pawnees lived in earth lodges with subsurface floors, a type

of dwelling that has been found in village ruins of the related Caddoan Indians in western Arkansas and eastern Oklahoma. Unlike
the Woodland tribes of the region east of the Mississippi, the primitive Pawnees did not gather in compact villages, often fortified, but
each one built his earth lodges at a considerable distance from the
nearest neighbors. Often the lodges stood in a long row along the
bank of a stream, forming what the Pawnees and the kindred Arikaras called a long village extending along the stream for several
miles. The Indians measured the length of their village in bowshots,
and the group with the longest village was proud of that fact. These
Pawnees cultivated crops, hunted, and caught fish. The wide-open
condition of their villages suggests a time of peace, or that war was
a matter of small raids that did not threaten the destruction of entire villages. But in the middle of the seventeenth century the Indians in the Plains to the west—Plains Apaches or Padoucas—obtained horses and Spanish weapons and began to make destructive
mounted attacks on the Pawnees. These raids fell mainly on the
Pawnee villages out in the Plains, in the upper Republican River
district in southwestern Nebraska. The Pawnees along the Missouri
were evidently first affected by Mississippian culture of the Cahokian
type, probably brought to them by Siouan tribes living in Iowa and
Missouri, and this was evidently a peaceful intrusion of culture. But,
by 1680, the Pawnees were being raided by the Indians along and
near the Mississippi, the tribes that had obtained French arms evidently leading in these raids. They carried off numbers of Pawnee
captives, so many that Pani became the French term for an Indian
slave of any origin. The Siouan tribes in Iowa and Missouri, themselves recent victims of savage raids, began making slave-catching
raids on the Pawnees of the Missouri River; and by about the date
1710 the great group of White Pawnee villages along the Iowa and
Nebraska banks of the river had been destroyed and the inhabitants
killed, carried away as slaves, or forced to flee. By the time the French
began to find their way up the Missouri (1710–20), the Pawnee villages along the river banks had vanished; but the French found a
new Pawnee tribe called Arikaras, perhaps first contacting them in
eastern Nebraska and later visiting them on the Missouri in South
Dakota. To this tribe they gave the old name of White Pawnee. This
fact and some additional evidence seems to show that the Arikaras

of Dakota were, in part at least, the survivors of the old White Pawnee nation who had fled up the Missouri into Dakota.

The French might have held the upper Mississippi lands strongly if it had not been for the vacillating policy of the officials at Paris and Quebec. After the Denonville expedition into the Iroquois country in 1687, peace was made with the Iroquois and an order was sent out for all Frenchmen to leave the lands near the upper Mississippi. This meant the temporary ruin of trade and an end to the hold the French had on tribes like the Sioux. Nicolas Perrot seems to have held out, as he was reported at his fort as late as 1690. He then left, and his lieutenant, Le Sueur, was appointed French commandant in the West, with headquarters at Chequamegon on Lake Superior. Le Sueur continued to send traders among the Sioux and to visit that tribe in person. In 1695, he took a Sioux chief, Tioscate, to Montreal where the chief died.[1]

The Algonquians, headed by the Ottawas, had tried for half a century to drive the Sioux from their lands near the head of the Mississippi, which the Algonquians coveted for themselves; but the Sioux fought off all attackers. After 1670, the Ojibwas were the most important tribe on Lake Superior, and they had made an alliance with the Sioux, the latter tribe permitting the Ojibwas to hunt and trap on their lands. When Le Sueur was sent to Chequamegon in 1693, one of his instructions was to continue the alliance of the Ojibwas and Sioux; but presently the vindictive Ottawas, still smarting from the old defeats at the hand of the Sioux, used their influence to set the Ojibwas against the Sioux. War followed, and the Sioux hold was loosened on their land of lakes and marshes at the headwaters of the Mississippi. When Le Sueur came up the Mississippi from its mouth in 1700, he found part of the Sioux of the East living along the Mississippi from the mouth of Minnesota River southward. The lands south of Minnesota River were now held by the Sioux of the West or Tetons, and they apparently extended their hunts as far westward as the pipestone quarry in southwestern Minnesota, for Le Sueur called the Yankton Sioux the Village of the Red Rock. Here we have something to employ in checking the Omaha and Ponca

---

[1] *Minnesota Historical Society Collections,* I, 272. This chief was evidently of the Mantanton Sioux division. That band told Le Sueur in 1700 that the chief was their relative.

traditions. Those traditions state that the Yanktons attacked them in northwestern Iowa and drove them west to the Big Sioux near Sioux Falls; then attacked again and forced them to flee farther west, into Dakota. We have no evidence when the Yanktons came into southwestern Minnesota. They were evidently on the head of the Mississippi when Hennepin was among the Sioux in 1680; they were in southwestern Minnesota before 1700. Their attacks on the Omaha group probably date somewhere between 1685 and 1695, and this seems to fit in with other French information, which places the Omaha group in northwestern Iowa from about 1670 to about 1685.[2]

The Sioux were still very strong, and did not need to fear any of the Algonquians, except those in the north, the Ojibwas and Crees, who were fully equipped with firearms. Twice the Sioux struck savage blows against the Miamis, the group that had a village on the Mississippi, south of the mouth of Wisconsin River; and the Sioux attacked the Foxes, the tribe the French feared. The Foxes and their allies, the Sacs, Mascoutens, and Kickapoos, often blocked the main canoe route from Green Bay up Fox River and across a portage to Wisconsin River and down that to the Mississippi. By doing this, they stopped French trade on the Mississippi for a season and made endless trouble for the traders. At times the Foxes won the Sioux over to their side, and at other times the Sioux were at war with them. The Sioux were always at war with the Illinis, going down the great river in fleets of dugout canoes to attack Illini villages.

The Illinis were about finished as a great nation. In some manner they had won the intense hatred of their own Algonquian kinsmen; and a generation of enemy attacks, plus the attentions of the French, had ruined them. The French now had a mission among them on Illinois River and the Jesuits, counting baptisms as upward progress, were very optimistic; but the Illinis knew that their hold on their old lands along the Illinois River was weakening, and they seemed to realize that when they were driven from that river valley their fate was sealed. That time was rapidly approaching. In 1693, the Kas-

2 Folwell, *History of Minnesota*, I, 81. Dorsey, "Migrations of the Siouan Indians," *American Naturalist*, Vol. XX, states that the enemies who slaughtered the Omaha people were called *Jan-a-ta ni-ka-cin-ga,* Forest People, in the Omaha tradition, and that the Yanktons then lived near the Mississippi in forested country. The tradition states that the Omahas were living on the Big Sioux near Sioux Falls when the Yanktons attacked and "killed one thousand warriors."

kaskia and Peoria chiefs, whose tribes had formerly raided the Osages and Missouris as a pastime, went to visit those tribes, seeking an alliance with them against their enemies. This alliance evidently failed, and the movement away from Illinois River began. In 1697, the Tamaroa villages were on the east bank of the Mississippi, at Prairie du Rocher, far below the mouth of Illinois River, and the Michigameas were living nearby on the west bank of the Mississippi. Tonty, La Salle's faithful lieutenant, was still in Illinois in 1698, warning the French authorities that if they did not act the English would soon be in control of the Illinois country. In 1699, Iberville established a French colony near the mouth of the Mississippi, at Mobile Bay, and the principal chief of the Illinis now decided to take all his people in canoes and go to live under the shelter of the French at Mobile. The Jesuits and French traders were aghast at this decision to abandon Illinois River, and they did what they could to thwart the chief. In the end the plan was given up, but a large part of the Illinis abandoned their country and went down to Arkansas River to seek the protection of the Quapaws. While they were there, the Quapaws got smallpox and lost most of their people. The Illinis also must have suffered heavy loss; and presently they drifted back to their old lands in Illinois, but not to Illinois River. The remnants of their nation now settled at Cahokia and Kaskaskia, on the east bank of the Mississippi, below Illinois River, and here the French came and settled among the Indians. A mission was formed, and then a French fort was established; but it was too late to save the Illinis. As an important tribe, their day was past.[3]

The Illinis abandoned Illinois River and northern Illinois, and the Algonquian tribes of Wisconsin moved down and occupied these lands. They also moved into the abandoned lands of the Ohio Valley, mainly to the Wabash country, where the Miamis, Mascoutens, Weas, and Piankashaws established themselves. The Iroquois were now permitting the Delawares and part of the Shawnees to return to the Ohio as tribes dependent on the Iroquois, and the Scioto country on the upper Ohio was soon recognized as the land of the Delawares and

---

[3] Schlarman, *From Quebec to New Orleans,* 111–59; Temple, "Indian Villages of the Illinois Country," *Illinois State Museum Scientific Papers,* Vol. II, part 2, 35–36. The Shawnees, old friends of the Illinis, came with the Chickasaws in the autumn of 1698 and attacked the Illinis with English guns, killing ten persons and carrying off one hundred slaves. (Schlarman, *From Quebec to New Orleans,* 138.)

Shawnees. Using the Iroquois as a lever, the English traders pushed westward and came to the Mississippi, finding their way as far as the Quapaws on Arkansas River. But now the French officials, both in Canada and on the lower Mississippi, recognized the importance of the Illinois country as the key to French control of the upper Mississippi, the Ohio, and the Missouri. They built Fort de Chartres near Kaskaskia and sent Frenchmen to establish themselves among the Indians on the Wabash. By 1720, there was no escape for any tribes within reach of the whites. Both French and English were working to establish control over the Indians, and to use the tribes in the white interest.

The tribes west of the Mississippi were not affected by French policy; but they were being harassed by Indians armed with French weapons, who came across the Mississippi and carried their slave-catching operations as far west as the Missouri. The Siouan tribes of northwestern Iowa—the Iowas, Omahas, Poncas, and perhaps part of the Otoes—were victims of these attacks; but the worst blows seem to have been struck against the White Panis or Panitokas along the Missouri, who were almost destroyed.

The Panitokas were set down on the French maps, particularly the Franquelin maps, after 1680 in a large area along the Missouri. The French heard of the Panitokas from tribes along the Mississippi and obtained Pawnee slaves; but by the time the French actually went up the Missouri, after the year 1700, the Panitokas had disappeared. Since modern archaeology shows that there was a great block of Pawnee or Caddoan Indians dwelling in earth lodge villages along the Missouri in what seems to be late prehistoric times, one is strongly inclined to assume that the village ruins found by archaeologists along the Missouri in western Iowa and eastern Nebraska are the remains of the Panitoka nation. There is no other possible explanation of these village ruins, unless we accept them as the Panitoka villages of the French maps.

Since the same French maps that placed the White Pawnees along the Missouri also placed the Siouan tribes—Iowas, Otoes, and Omahas—in northwestern Iowa, these White Pawnees were obviously close neighbors of this Siouan group. This would explain the adoption of some Mississippian cultural traits, particularly in pottery, by the Pawnees along the Missouri, and also by those farther west, on the Loup Fork of the Platte. And this was not a matter of a very

246

early date, as some archaeologists have supposed; it was of the period 1650–1700.[4]

At this period the tribes near the upper Mississippi had obtained French weapons and were making slave-catching raids on the Pawnees along the Missouri. At the same period the Padoucas or Apaches in the western plains had obtained horses and some Spanish weapons and were attacking the Pawnees in southwestern Nebraska. Indeed the mounted attacks were being made on Caddoan tribes along the eastern borders of the plains, all the way from Texas up into Dakota. Thus the Indians of the Pawnee groups were under pressure by tribes equipped to some extent with European weapons, both in the east and in the west. The result was that the primitive Pawnees of southwestern Nebraska removed farther to the northeast, some of them settling on the Loup Fork of the Platte, others drifting on northward to the Missouri in South Dakota. And the White Pawnees along the Missouri also had to abandon their villages, which were deserted and forgotten by the time the French came up the Missouri, soon after 1700.

We do not know enough about the White Pawnees, the early Arikaras, and the Pawnees of Loup Fork in Nebraska to give a clear-cut account of them.[5] Our information comes from a few early French

[4] The dating seems obvious. The Siouan tribes apparently picked up Cahokia culture after 1600, and they passed some traits on to the Pawnees along the Missouri, probably in the period 1650–80, and then the Otoes came and settled in southeastern Nebraska and exchanged cultural traits with the Pawnees on Loup Fork. This must have been close to 1700, as the Otoes were with or near the Missouri tribe in Missouri State during the period 1684–94, and they seem to have come into Nebraska after leaving the Missouris. Again, the Osage-Omaha group of Siouans was in the Ohio Valley up to about 1650, and they could not have made contact with the White Pawnees on the Missouri until after that date. The French information shows that the White Pawnee villages were still occupied up to about 1690.

[5] When I wrote my history of the Pawnees and, later, "The Mystery of the Arikaras," I had no knowledge of the linguistic and cultural relationship between the Skidi Pawnees and the Iroquoian tribes of the western New York and Pennsylvania country. This led me into making assertions which I now regret. It does seem, from present knowledge, at least possible that the Skidi Pawnees were in the Iroquoian area up to about the middle of the seventeenth century and that the Dhegiha Siouan tradition that states the Skidis accompanied their tribes on their migration out of the Ohio Valley may be correct. The Loup Fork protohistoric pottery, Skidi, is strikingly like the eastern Iroquoian pottery of a late

references to these Pawnee groups, from entries on French maps, and from archaeology; and we have the additional difficulty that archaeologists prefer to give an impossibly early date to some of the Pawnee village remains. However, from Indian tradition and some early French material, we may suppose that the Arikaras were in eastern Nebraska up almost to the year 1700, that their tribal name, meaning Elkhorn or Horned Elk, was given to the Elkhorn River in eastern Nebraska, and that, before 1700, they moved up into South Dakota. This would seem to make the Arikaras a part of the Nebraska Culture folk, and since the Glenwood Culture, on the Iowa side of the Missouri, is identical with Nebraska Culture, we may assume that the Glenwood folk were also Pawnees, and probably the White Pawnees of the French maps. When their villages were no longer safe, the surviving White Pawnees, or part of them, evidently went northward into South Dakota; and even as late as 1795 the French gave the name of White Pawnee at times to the Arikara tribe along the Missouri in Dakota.[6]

Indeed, we here have fragmentary evidence of a great disaster that overtook the Pawnees of Nebraska and western Iowa toward the end of the seventeenth century, and this disaster also involved the Siouan tribes of northern Iowa. These Indians were all without any European articles, as far as we know, and they were still armed only with flint weapons. Attacked by enemies coming from the Mississippi, equipped with French arms, these Siouan and Pawnee groups were slaughtered, and the survivors fled to the Missouri in southern South Dakota.

Here we may bring in the Panas. This group was never considered important. Most authors were content to term the Panas a group of Pawnees, or a group of Arikaras. J. O. Dorsey, who could see only Siouan Indians, identified them as Poncas, evidently on the surmise that Pana was a poor rendering of the name Ponca. There are two things that make the Pana worth more consideration than they have had in the past. Presumably they are the Skidi Pawnees, said by tradition to have accompanied the Omaha group on its migration

---

period. There is really nothing to show that the Skidis were on Loup Fork in Nebraska until well toward the year 1700.

6 See Nasatir, *Before Lewis and Clark*, Pani Hoca (Panitoka, White Pawnee), in index; Hyde, "The Mystery of the Arikaras," *North Dakota History*, XVIII, 192–94, 202.

out of the Ohio Valley, and they are therefore presumably the group that brought typical Iroquoian pottery to the Missouri and to the Loup Fork of the Platte. Marquette, on his map, 1673, put the Panas north of the Omahas, Iowas, and Otoes, apparently in northwestern Iowa. La Salle in 1680 referred to the Panas as living in two villages on or near the Missouri and trading for horses with two tribes, the Gatakas and Manrhoat. La Salle's brief notice of the tribe seems to be the only French statement concerning them, but the French map makers took the Panas up and attempted to put them on their maps where Marquette and La Salle had located them. The Franquelin maps followed La Salle, putting the Panas on the Missouri with the Gatakas and Manrhoats near them; but the Franquelin maps had the Missouri terribly distorted and apparently put in as two rivers. It is therefore impossible to state just where the Pana tribe was supposed to be. The Minet map of 1685, made from La Salle's talks with Minet, puts the Panas evidently west of the Missouri, with the Apaches to the west of them. This is the first use of the name Apache in any French document or map. On this map the Omaha group is to the northeast of the Panas, and a Pentoca (Panitoka or White Pawnee) group in three villages is on a stream with two branches, between the Omahas and the Panas. This stream is evidently the one shown on the Franquelin maps and on French and English maps, down to 1763. It looks like the Vermillion River, a northern tributary of the Missouri in South Dakota. At first Panitoka villages are marked on it; but later maps place Arikara villages there. There seem to be no village ruins of any type on the upper Vermillion, and the map makers must have intended some other stream.[7]

Of the Panas, archaeologists do not say a word; but they have found the peculiar Iroquoian type of pottery, which we might assume the Panas brought from the Ohio, at the great Arzberger fortress on the Missouri, above the Great Bend, and also in the late Pawnee villages of the Loup Fork. The Arzberger fortress was a mighty work. It enclosed within its wall and ditch from sixty to seventy acres and was ten to twenty times the size of any other fortified village on the Missouri. The wall of the fort had looped bastions, the type used in the great Angel fortified village on the north side of the Ohio, near

[7] The Franquelin and Minet maps are in Griffin, *Fort Ancient*. Other French and English maps are in Winsor. *The Mississippi Basin*, and Winsor, *Cartier to Frontenac*.

Evansville, Indiana. The builders of the Arzberger fortress must have been a very strong group, playing an important role in the history of their day. Our present knowledge is not sufficient for forming an opinion; but we might conjecture that the Panas came west with the Omahas, left them before 1680 and moved farther west to be with their kinsmen of the Pawnee stock. La Salle's two villages may have been two widely separated Pana centers, one on the Missouri near the Great Bend, one on Loup Fork in Nebraska.

The period of the attacks on the Pawnees and on the Omaha group appears to have been about 1670 to 1695. The Panas were perhaps the first to leave northern Iowa and go to the Missouri. Then, after 1680, the tribes on and east of the Mississippi attacked the Omahas, Iowas, and Otoes. Perrot speaks of an Iowa village being destroyed; but perhaps this Iowa group survived and was the village that lived near the Omahas when they moved to the Big Sioux. An Iowa group remained on the Mississippi, allied to the Sioux and trading with the French. The Otoes, or part of them, fled to the Missouri tribe on the lower Missouri River, evidently about 1680 or 1683. This Oto group later left the Missouris and moved to the Great Nemaha River in southwestern Nebraska.

We have no direct historical evidence concerning the Omaha and Ponca flight from northwestern Iowa to the Big Sioux and on to the Missouri; but one suspects that the flight to the Big Sioux was in the 1680's and that to the Missouri in the late 1680's or early 1690's. Nicolas Perrot stated that the Iowas were in alliance with the Sioux in 1685–1690; then the Iowas withdrew toward the Missouri, and the Yankton Sioux were apparently on the headwaters of the Des Moines River from about 1700 on. The Sioux are stated by the French documents to have been trading French goods and arms to the Iowas, who were too far to the west to have any direct trade with the French. By 1723, the Iowas had stopped slave-raiding the Pawnees of the Missouri and were trading French goods, which they obtained from the Sioux and sometimes from the Sacs and Foxes, for Padouca slaves, which they obtained from the Otoes, Pawnees of Nebraska, and the Kansa tribe of Kansas. Villiers refers to this Sioux trade with Iowas during the period 1700–1724, and the Sioux concerned were evidently the Yanktons.

The Omaha and Ponca traditions depict the movement of these tribes from northwestern Iowa to the Missouri as a sudden movement, with all the people together. The French maps seem to deny this, and if we again assume that the Mill Creek village ruins in northwestern Iowa are the old Omaha and Ponca villages, archaeology also contradicts the Indian tradition. The maps first show the Omahas in northwestern Iowa, with the Iowas, Otoes, and Panas near them. Then the Panas vanish, and the Omahas are on the Big Sioux near Sioux Falls, with an Iowa village north of them. Next the Omahas are near the mouth of the Big Sioux, and again an Iowa village is near them. The De l'Isle map of 1722 puts the Omahas on the north bank of the Missouri, in the Lake Andes district near Chouteau Creek. It was here that, in the nineteenth century, a stone was found near the town of Wagner, with the date 1691 and a Christian cross scratched on it. In this same area, the town of Vermillion at the mouth of Vermillion River is said to have been built over the ruins of an Indian village, and archaeologists think the village remains were Oneota, meaning Iowa tribal remains. This may have been the place where La Chesnaye lived in an Iowa village about the year 1690.

Assuming that Mill Creek culture was that of the Omahas and Poncas, archaeology adds interesting details to the meager Omaha and Ponca traditions. It shows that part of the Mill Creek people moved to the Big Sioux near Sioux Falls and built the Brandon village and probably others; and near them was a big Oneota (Iowa Indian) center. The Mill Creek people then extended down the Big Sioux, on its eastern bank, building burial mounds at two points near the lower Big Sioux, in western Plymouth County, Iowa. Meanwhile, an Indian group with a culture very close to Mill Creek in type established a group of villages on James River, near the present town of Mitchell. Here on James River the Mill Creek type of pottery is mixed with the Cambria type from southern Minnesota, which suggests that Indians fleeing from Minnesota joined the Mill Creek people on James River. From this James River location it is only about forty miles to the Lake Andes district near the Missouri; and it was near Lake Andes that the Omahas and Poncas acquired their sacred pole. This pole was a symbol of tribal unity. The pole is supposed to have been found by a kind of miracle; but one is inclined to suspect that the Omahas and Poncas had become separated and that both groups had probably split into smaller sections. When the tribal leaders saw the vital need to draw the people together for mutual defense, they probably invented the sacred pole, made it and then found it by a miracle, thus impressing the common people with the idea that the spiritual powers were watching over them and warning them to reunite and stand together. The Poncas, according to some of the traditions, were never really united with the Omahas. They are said to have left the Omahas in northern Iowa. They rejoined them when the sacred pole was discovered near Lake Andes but left them soon after, crossed the Missouri, and went up the west bank with the Arikaras. At about this period (1690) a big group of Poncas was living with the Quapaw tribe, hundreds of miles away toward the southeast, on Arkansas River.

By this time, 1690–1700, there was a mass of fugitive groups gathered along the Missouri, from the Big Sioux north to the Great Bend. They were, as far as we know, all Siouan and Pawnee groups, and they were nearly all still without European arms, the easy victims of raiders coming from the Mississippi. The French were now starting to trade up the Missouri; but the trade at first seems to have been in the hands of adventurous peddlers, who came up the great river in canoes with a few French knives, hatchets, and trinkets. Bourgmont was trading on the Missouri in 1714, and he claimed that in 1717 he went up as far as the mouth of White River in South Dakota. He placed the Iowas on the left bank and the Omahas above them, on the east bank near the mouth of White River. He termed the Omahas a noble nation. Le Sueur had reported in 1700 that the Omahas had twelve hundred families, or at least six thousand people. They had probably lost half of their population, between the time of their flight from the Ohio Valley and their arrival on the Missouri in South Dakota, and the Panis or Pawnees they found there had suffered similar loss. Most of the Indians concentrated on the Missouri above the Big Sioux were still armed only with flint weapons; but some of them were beginning to obtain horses from Indians out in the plains, and once they learned to fight on horseback they could hold their own, even against enemies armed with guns and coming against them on foot.

In 1717, Bourgmont put an Iowa village on the left or east bank of the Missouri, and the Omahas on the east bank near the mouth of White River. He stated that the Omahas were wanderers—that is, that they had no permanent village—but that the mouth of White River was their rendezvous, where the tribe, separated in groups when hunting, met seasonally. He put three villages of Arikaras on the left or northeast side of the Missouri above the Omahas, and above these Arikaras, on both banks of the Missouri, forty villages of Caricaras. As we know from later information that the Arikara tribe was made up of one or two villages of Arikaras Proper and many villages of Panis, it is obvious that Bourgmont's Caricaras were the Pani group. In 1723, Renaudière added to the Bourgmont account the information that the Omahas were allied to the Nations of the Ricaras, whose villages were on the Missouri, ten leagues or about twenty-five miles above the Omahas.[8]

Thus, from French reports, we find that in 1717–23 there was a mass of Indians along the Missouri, between the Big Sioux and the Great Bend. Here were the Omahas, with about six thousand people, an Iowa village, and a mass of Panis and Arikaras. Later information was that, before the smallpox epidemics between 1765 and 1790, the Arikaras (and Panis) had four thousand warriors, or a population of at least twenty thousand. But this mass of Siouans and Pawnees on the Missouri were without proper arms, and Indians from the Mississippi were hunting them like birds. Before 1700 the French were buying quantities of slaves, brought home by the raiders; but now the French began to trade up the Missouri, and they could not very well continue to trade for Pani slaves while they were trading on friendly terms with the Panis. However, tribes from the Mississippi continued to make slave raids. The Osages were raiding the Panis in the south, but the greatest number of slaves were now probably Padoucas from the plains. The Iowas, like the Osages, were evidently engaged in the business of catching Pani slaves up to 1700; but after 1720 the Panis had French knives and hatchets, and many of them were mounted and too dangerous for the Iowas to attack. The Iowas therefore went into the trading business, bringing European goods to the Missouri and trading with the Otoes and Omahas for slaves, horses, and furs. French maps after the year 1700 show a *chemin des voyageurs,* or traders' trail, running from a point on the Mississippi near the mouth of Wisconsin River to an Iowa village on the upper Big Sioux near Sioux Falls, then down the east bank of the Big Sioux to an Iowa village on the Missouri, then up the northern bank of the Missouri to another Iowa village. On later maps this trail went to an Iowa village at or near the mouth of the Little

[8] Villiers, *La Découverte du Missouri,* 62; Renaudiere in Margry, *Découvertes et établissements des Français,* VI, 394.

Sioux, then across the Missouri to the Omaha village in northeastern Nebraska, and then the Pawnee villages on the Platte.[9]

Indian traditions are not very detailed, and if the narrators attempt to put in details they usually only confuse the story and con-

[9] It is difficult to follow the Iowa tribe's movement from the French maps as these maps were often added to for years after their supposed date, and it is hard to judge how many Iowa villages there were at any given date, or where they were at any period. The map of migrations made by an Iowa chief in the nineteenth century and printed in Schoolcraft is not helpful. This chief either did not know the facts of his tribe's movements, or he was confused. The tribe clearly had at least two villages from 1680 on, and they were usually in different locations at the same date.

Nicolas Perrot reported that the main Iowa village was destroyed by Algonquian raiders in the 1680's, but this is probably an exaggeration. The French maps from 1673 to the late 1680's put the Paoutet Iowa village in northwestern Iowa, near the Omahas, and this group of Iowas must have gone on to the Big Sioux, first near Sioux Falls, then on the east bank of the Big Sioux near its mouth. Thus the Big Sioux may be the "Fish Creek" of the Iowa chief's migration map. The Iowas are supposed to have had a village at the mouth of Vermillion River. Later they removed to the Little Sioux. The Jeffreys map of 1762 shows the Iowa village on the Little Sioux, with the traders' trail from the Mississippi going to their village, across the Missouri to the Omaha village, then to the Pawnees on the Platte or Loup Fork.

The Bowen and Gibson map, dated 1763, shows the Paoutez or Iowa village of the tribe on Iowa River, the Little Sioux. Perhaps another group of Iowas were in the south, for the so-called Le Sueur map, supposed to date around 1701 but clearly added to as late as 1730 at least, shows three Iowa villages on the east side of the Missouri, near the southern boundary of Iowa State. About 1740, an Iowa village was on the east bank of the Missouri, in the northern edge of the present city of Council Bluffs, with an Oto village opposite on the west bank in the northeastern edge of the present Omaha. After this date, the Iowas evidently all went to the Des Moines, below the present city of Des Moines, and they remained in that location on into the nineteenth century.

If the Iowas were ever a great tribe and great warriors, it was before the French met them, around 1655. Perrot stated that they were allied to the Sioux in the 1680's, but the Sioux probably obtained little advantage from the alliance beyond some trade in French goods the Iowas may have brought to their villages. From 1690 on at least one village of Iowas was engaged in slave-raiding the Panis. After that they traded French goods to the tribes on and west of the Missouri. They seem to have been in partnership with the Sacs and Foxes, obtaining European goods from those tribes. Like the Sacs and Foxes, the Iowas were hostile toward the French, but not in the brave and open manner of those tribes. The Iowas were friendly toward any strong party of French, but often murdered French traders when they caught one or two of them alone and off their guard. In all their later history, the Iowas did not perform one noble act, unless it has failed to be recorded.

tradict each other. French information concerning the tribes on and near the Missouri is scanty up to 1717, and the maps do not agree on some points. One would suppose that modern archaeology should be a great aid in clearing up obscure points concerning these Indians in South Dakota between 1680 and 1750. Intensive archaeological work has been carried on in this area for many years under federal subsidy, and many reports have been published; but when one examines these reports, he becomes only more confused about what the situation among the tribes in South Dakota really was at the period 1680–1750. These archaeological reports add many important facts to our previous knowledge, and then make it impossible for us to use these facts by insisting that all the village ruins and other Indian remains are of a time prior to 1600 and that most of them date before 1500. However, the archaeological dating is mainly conjectural, and even when tree-ring analysis is employed the dating is still far from satisfactory. This being admitted, the historian is justified in setting aside the archaeological dating, at least for the purpose of attempting to fit archaeology in with the other materials and attempting to reach a reasonable solution to a very vexing problem.

We may observe that all the Indians who were assembled in South Dakota after the year 1690, with the exception of one village of Iowas, were fugitive groups, tribes that had been savagely raided by enemies armed with European weapons, had lost most of their people, and had probably had their old tribal organization and ordered way of life violently disrupted. The situation was similar to that among the tribes of the Piedmont in Virginia and Carolina in late prehistoric times, and also similar to conditions on the Ohio at an equally late date. The same breakdown of native culture and confusion of cultural traits is present in the Piedmont and on the Missouri in South Dakota. The archaeological attempt to explain the flight of tribes into South Dakota has mainly to do with a supposed great drought in the high plains to the westward; but, even if that theory is acceptable as an explanation of the flight of the Pawnees from southwestern Nebraska to Dakota, it cannot explain the flight of the Siouan tribes westward from the woodlands of the Ohio, of Wisconsin, and of Minnesota.

As far as the Siouans are concerned—the Iowas, Otoes, Omahas, and Poncas—we know from French information that they did not go to the Missouri in South Dakota until after 1680. The White Pawnees, along both banks of the Missouri, in Iowa and Nebraska, were in that location in the 1680's, but had disappeared before the French came up the Missouri, after the year 1700. Broken White Pawnee groups were then noted on or near the Missouri, and even after 1795 the French sometimes termed all the Arikaras of the Missouri White Pawnees.[10] These facts throw considerable light on the movement of the various Indian groups to the Missouri in Dakota and give an idea as to the date of these movements.

Archaeology, as we might expect, adds new facts to the scanty Omaha and Ponca migration traditions. The traditions hint that the Poncas left the Omahas in northwestern Iowa, near the Pipestone quarry, rejoined them later near the Missouri. Then, as we know, the Poncas left the Omahas again and set themselves up as a separate tribe. Archaeology shows that there was such a split in the Mill Creek Indians, whom the present author believes were the Omahas and Poncas. The Omaha tradition states that the tribe was attacked in the pipestone district, retired westward to the Big Sioux near Sioux Falls, and built a fort and village there near the Iowas. The tribe was attacked there and massacred, and those who survived fled toward the Missouri. Archaeology tells a somewhat different story. It shows that the Mill Creek Indians probably did not move to the Big Sioux in one group or perhaps at one time, and it shows that part of them went west of the Big Sioux and established villages on James River, near the present town of Mitchell. It shows further that part of the Mill Creek Indians moved down the Big Sioux, along the east bank of the river, living at a site called Kimball and then establishing a village at Broken Kettle farther down the river. The Broken Kettle village might be the Omaha village on the eastern bank of the Big Sioux near its mouth shown on French maps around the date 1700.

Leaving out archaeological dating, this situation disclosed by the archaeologists might fit the Omaha and Ponca movements after they left the Mill Creek villages in northwestern Iowa, probably in the

---

10 Nasatir, *Before Lewis and Clark,* 331–34, 389, records the story of two Frenchmen who came to the Mandan villages in the employ of a British trading company of Canada. These men ran off and went down the Missouri, finding the Pani Hoca tribe in two big groups. Pani Hoca is clearly a corrupt form of Panitoka, White Pawnee, and the location of the two groups shows that they were the Arikaras.

1680.'s. These tribes, when attacked by the Iroquois in the Ohio Valley, had split up during their flight, the Quapaws going down the Mississippi accompanied by part of the Poncas—the Osage, Kansa, Omaha, and Ponca group going up the Mississippi and then up the Missouri. It is logical to assume that when the Omahas and Poncas were driven out of the Mill Creek district, they also split up into groups and moved to separate locations; but the French maps seem to show that the main Omaha group kept to the Big Sioux, first establishing a village or villages near Sioux Falls, then at Broken Kettle, about twelve miles above the mouth of the Big Sioux, then going to a location on the Missouri near Chouteau Creek or a little farther up, near Lake Andes.

The Brandon village ruin, on the Big Sioux near Sioux Falls, is of Mill Creek type; but it is a small village that would not have held a fraction of the Omaha population. It seems to have been occupied only a short time, and for this reason there was not an extensive group of pottery types and other remains found by the excavators. The hut type was rectangular, with small wall posts along only two sides (the long sides) of the hut. Each hut had fireplaces for two or more families. This type of hut is also found at the Swanson site, on the east bank of the Missouri, just below Crow Creek. The hut type is similar to that described by Zimmerman from Ponca tradition. The Poncas stated that two lines of small posts or poles were set in the ground; the upper ends of the poles were then bent from each side of the hut toward the center, the ends of the poles then being fastened toegther, forming a long arbor with curved roof. This pole framework was then covered with bark. The Ponca medicine lodge was constructed in the same form, but was much larger than the common huts.[11]

The Brandon village ruins show a culture that is Mill Creek in

[11] Charles Leroy Zimmerman, *White Eagle, Chief of the Poncas*, 84, 140. The Poncas said these bark huts had two fireplaces and two smoke holes in the roof. Griffin, *Archeology of the Eastern United States*, Fig. 64, shows Osage lodges very similar in form to the Mill Creek and Brandon huts, and we know that historic Osage huts were long, rectangular structures of poles bent together at the tops in an arch and covered with bark. The Quapaw huts in the late seventeenth century were "long houses" of bark, larger than the Caddoan grass lodges of East Texas, which accommodated about twenty persons to each dwelling. See the Douay and Tonty account of the Quapaws. Mildred Mott, in her book on Iowa archaeology, stated that the old-time hut of the Iowa tribe was a dwelling of poles covered with bark.

type but with some new traits. Brandon closely resembles the Mill Creek village ruin at Alta, Iowa, and also the Mitchell village ruins on James River in South Dakota. W. H. Over and E. E. Meleen, after some excavation at Brandon village and at the Mitchell and Twelve-Mile Creek sites on James River[12] established the Over focus in archaeology. This focus was supposed to form an archaeological entity, with a close relationship to the Mill Creek village ruins, so close that only minor variations distinguished the Over focus from Mill Creek. From the historical point of view, these differences amount to little, and the Indians who made the Mill Creek and Over focus villages are still most probably the Omaha group.

The Broken Kettle and Kimball sites on the east side of the Big Sioux certainly represent a large community of Mill Creek folk, who must have dwelt there for quite a long time because the refuse deposit at Broken Kettle has a depth of eleven feet. This is comparable to the depth of refuse at some of the Mill Creek villages, and it suggests that even while the main body of the Omahas was living at Mill Creek a group had gone to the lower Big Sioux, to the Broken Kettle site. We might conjecture that the group were Poncas.

The James River villages and other remains are in four sites, termed by archaeology the Mitchell, Twelve-Mile Creek, Ethan, and Bloom sites. These sites indicate that a much larger group of Mill Creek folk were settled on the James than at Brandon, and the villages on the James seem to have been occupied for a longer time than the Brandon village was. The James River sites are Mill Creek in culture, with certain added features. Here on the James the fine and varied pottery types of Mill Creek turn up again and perhaps reach their final flowering. The pottery shows certain traits from the Cambria aspect in southern Minnesota, indicating contacts between the Cambria folk and those on James River. At Mill Creek there was a similar indication of Minnesota influence, but it consisted only in certain pottery traits from the Great Oasis aspect in southwestern Minnesota. At both Brandon and on the James there are some collared pots and pots with cord-marked surfaces, indicating contacts with the Pawnees of the Missouri.

12 Over and Meleen. *A Report on the Brandon Village Site and the Split Rock Creek Mounds, Archeological Studies*, Circular 4; Hurt, *The Swanson Site, Archeological Studies*, Circular 3.

The Bloom site on the James is a village on a terrace that juts out into the river valley. It is a good defensive location and is strengthened by an entrenchment running across the unprotected side, in rear of the village. There are indications of twenty-five huts, and nearby are some fifty burial mounds, some of them 150 to 200 feet in diameter. The Mitchell village was also fortified, with a double ditch, such as that of at least one of the old Mandan villages on the Missouri in North Dakota.

The Swanson village ruin, on the east side of the Missouri just below Crow Creek, also belongs to the Mill Creek cultural group, although it was placed by the archaeologists in the Over focus, along with Brandon and the James River villages. The Swanson site is unlike most Missouri River Indian villages, for it is on the bottomlands, while most villages are on higher locations. It is a small village of less than twenty lodges, and it is very close to the big Arikara fortified village which Prince Maximilian saw in ruins in 1833. The lodges at Swanson are like those at Brandon on the Big Sioux. The culture at Swanson is clearly connected with that at Brandon and the sites on James River, but the Swanson pottery has few traits in common with Mill Creek pottery, or the Cambria pottery that is found on James River. The Swanson pottery is much affected by Pawnee influence, and the rim decoration of some pots is Great Oasis in type. This is what we might expect, for Swanson is far west of the other villages of the Mill Creek culture. It is in a Pawnee district, and it naturally shows Pawnee influence.

One of the most interesting discoveries at the Swanson site was a cache of four red catlinite stone pipes; another was a catlinite bannerstone. The pipes and bannerstone must have been tribal ceremonial objects, carefully guarded by the Indians, and such finds in South Dakota sites are rare. W. R. Hurt, Jr., in his monograph on the Swanson site, suggested that the pipes did not belong to the lodge ruins but were intrusive and of a later date. The pipes were found some feet above the floor of the ruined lodge; but, this type of ceremonial pipe was kept in a leather sacred bundle and usually hung high on a post in a lodge. Thus, when a lodge fell in ruins, the post the pipe sack was hung on might have kept it above the floor until after the settling of debris.

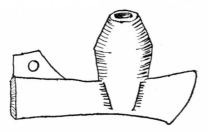 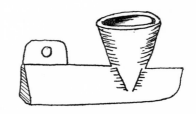

These fine Swanson-site pipes are obviously important; too important to be brushed aside as late period material, buried in the earth long after the Swanson village ceased to be occupied. These Swanson pipes are not late-date ones. They are winged pipes, sacred pipes with wings or fins atop the stem, back of the bowl. They are the same type of pipes that are in the Omaha tribe's sacred war bundle, and this fact, taken with the type of culture in the Swanson village, may connect the pipes with the early history of the Omahas or Poncas.

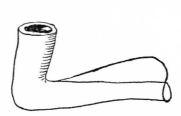 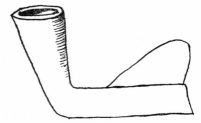

Such winged pipes seem to have been unknown among the tribes east of the Mississippi; the known specimens are all western pipes, and all the early ones are of catlinite. They are in the Omaha tribe's sacred bundle, and they were found in the Swanson village and by Waldo R. Wedel in village remains in Kansas, evidently remains of the early Kansa, who belonged originally to the same group with the Omahas. Wedel also reported winged catlinite pipes in the Tobias site, on the Little Arkansas River, and this may be an early Pawnee site. In the Kaskaskia district in western Illinois, winged catlinite pipes were found in graves of the Illini Indians; but as such pipes were unknown elsewhere in Illinois, it is assumed that they were obtained in trade by the Illinis after the year 1700 from Indians in Iowa or Dakota. Winged catlinite pipes were also noted among the Nebraska Pawnees and continued to be used by the Pawnees as sacred pipes on into the nineteenth century. Whether the sacred pipes of the Poncas were of the winged type or not, does not seem to be recorded.[13]

The finding of these winged catlinite pipes in sites in South Dakota and eastern Kansas may in time prove to be a most important clue to the movements of the Dhegiha group of Siouans, and may even assist in dating their migrations. The pipes in the Omaha sacred war bundle do not have a hole bored through the wing on top of the stem; the Swanson site pipes do have such a hole, and some pipes of this type in use among the Sioux in the nineteenth century also have a hole bored through the wing. The purpose of the hole was, perhaps, to pass a cord through to bind the stone pipe firmly to its long wooden stem. We might conjecture that the pipes with holes in the wings are a later development and that the pipes in the Omaha sacred bundle are of a somewhat earlier date. Some of the winged pipes Wedel found in Kansas had holes in the wings.

Clay or pottery pipes are common in the Mill Creek village ruins. As far as reported, catlinite is not found in the northwestern Iowa

[13] The contents of the Omaha tribe's sacred bundles show that all the sacred pipes in these bundles are of red catlinite and usually the platform type, similar to those found at the Swanson village ruin. The winged pipes are in the war bundle. The pipe in the sacred pole bundle is a red catlinite platform pipe without a wing on the stem, and what looks like a serpent nose in front of the bowl and serpent eyes incised on the side of the stone stem.

Howard D. Winters, curator of the Museum at Southern Illinois University, Carbondale, Illinois, informs me that red catlinite pipes with wings on the stem have been found in Indian graves at the historic Kaskaskia Indian village that dates from 1700 on. Because such pipes are unknown elsewhere in Illinois, Mr. Winters suggests that, as Kaskaskia was a French trading center, the pipes were brought in trade or perhaps by visiting Indians from the west. The winged pipes found among the Santee Sioux in the nineteenth century are of black serpentine stone. The wings on the stems are not of the eighteenth-century shape, but are rectangular, with one to four holes in the wing, and the pipes are all decorated with lead inlays.

In Griffin's great work, *Archeology of the Eastern United States*, there are no winged pipes comparable to those of the Omahas or the Swanson site pipes, but one pipe of Ohio Intrusive Mound culture, which preceded Fort Ancient, may be termed a winged pipe. Waldo R. Wedel in his new work, "An Introduction to Kansas Archeology," *Bulletin 174*, B.A.E., reports winged pipes of catlinite in three Kansas sites, including a Kansa tribal site. These sacred pipes were, at the apparent time of their origin, peculiar to the Dhegiha tribes—Omahas, Poncas, Kansas—and to their allies, the Skidi Pawnees.

Mill Creek villages, and as far as is known the Dhegiha group of Siouans had only pottery pipes when they emerged from the Ohio Valley.

The whole question of the use of catlinite by early Indians needs to be reassessed. The story of the red pipestone quarry in southwestern Minnesota is largely romantic nonsense. Archaeology shows that catlinite from this quarry was seldom used by the early Indians. The first cultural group that used this stone to any large degree was the Blue Earth aspect, in all probability an Oto tribal group, with villages on Blue Earth River. But, we have to take into account the French reports that large red stone calumet pipes were in use by the tribes of the upper Mississippi as far back as 1650. Radisson mentions them in his rambling narrative, and around the year 1680 the French reported that the Iowas (perhaps they were in error and it was the Otoes) had many great red stone calumets. This seems to contradict the archaeological dictum that the Oneota (Iowa and Oto) stone pipes were usually small disc pipes; but we must bear in mind that the big calumets of peace and war were sacred tribal pipes, carefully kept and guarded, and they did not turn up in village ruins or in graves except on rare occasions. The small stone pipes and the pottery pipes belonged to individuals and were often lost or buried with the owner. In the nineteenth century, tribal controls were much relaxed, and any man who could afford one had the right to own a big red catlinite pipe for his personal use.

The Swanson village ruin is the farthest west of the Mill Creek type of culture. It might be termed the fading out of that culture, the last attempt to keep to the old way of life the Omahas and Poncas had brought out of the Ohio Valley. These two tribes had been driven from their villages in northwestern Iowa, and all that their traditions tell us is that they went to the Big Sioux near Sioux Falls and then to the Missouri near Lake Andes. The new archaeological material adds details that make the story more interesting. It shows that these Indians split up. Some groups established new villages and attempted to hold to the old way of life, making fine pottery and implements of stone and bone. Other groups took to wandering in hunting camps; and by the time Bourgmont described the Omahas in 1717 they were all wanderers. If they still had any permanent villages, these were so small and inconspicuous that Bourgmont did not refer to them.

Most of the archaeological work along the Missouri, in eastern

Nebraska, western Iowa, and southern South Dakota, has been done in village ruins of the Caddoan or Pawnee groups. Here, as in the case of the Siouan tribes, archaeological dating stands in the way of any attempt to connect these village ruins with known tribes; yet, as with the Siouan tribes, archaeology seems to confirm the general outline given by Indian tradition and French reports. These Indians along the Missouri in Nebraska and Iowa were the kinsmen of the primitive Pawnees of the upper Republican region in southwestern Nebraska, and at a date we may conjecture was around the year 1650 or a bit later both the upper Republican Pawnees and those along the Missouri were displaced, evidently by enemy raids. One would suppose that the upper Republicans were driven from their old location by the mounded Padoucas of the plains, and that the White Pawnees along the Missouri were raided by Indians on the Mississippi, who now had French arms. The result of these attacks was that the upper Republican Pawnees moved northeast to the Loup Fork of the Platte, and part of them went on northward to the Missouri in South Dakota, while the White Pawnees along the Missouri moved up the river, their surviving groups also coming into South Dakota.

The French had some knowledge of these Pawnees of the Missouri; but the French map makers did not know the course of the river and its main tributaries, and it is impossible from the crude maps to state exactly where the Pawnee groups were at any given period. One curious feature is the placing of Pawnee villages on what seems to be a northeastern tributary of the Missouri, perhaps the Vermillion River of South Dakota. Franquelin placed four White Pawnee villages near the head of this stream in 1684–99. Maps made after 1700 changed the name of the Indians of this location to Arikaras and usually showed two villages. There are no Caddoan or Pawnee village ruins either on the upper Vermillion or on James River; and since the French placed the Arikaras and Pawnees on the main Missouri and nowhere else in 1717 and 1723, and as these Pawnee or Arikara villages are really important, we are justified in suggesting that the first few French traders to reach these Pawnee villages followed a trail west from near Sioux Falls to the Pawnee villages near the Great Bend of the Missouri and that, like Bourgmont in 1717, they regarded White River as the main Missouri and informed the French map makers that the Pawnee villages were on a northern branch of the Missouri. If this is correct, it may mean that the Pawnees or Arikaras near the Great Bend had small quantities of French trade articles before 1700, but not earlier than 1680 or 1690.

This movement of the Pawnee groups to the Missouri in South Dakota is not, from the historical point of view, an event of the period 1400–1500, as some archaeologists believe, but of a date after 1650. By 1717 the movement was apparently completed, and the Pawnees and Arikaras were established in their new locations in South Dakota, along both banks of the Missouri, and mainly in the Great Bend district. Here they had fortified their main villages and obtained some horses from tribes in the plains. According to Bourgmont, the Arikara villages farthest down the Missouri were trading furs, presumably for French articles, but probably not directly to Frenchmen but to some tribe that traded with the French, probably the Iowas.

Here we have the curious situation that the Omahas and Poncas, when forced to flee to the Missouri, gave up settled village life and took to wandering; but the Pawnees and Arikaras clung to village life and began to fortify their principal villages for the first time in their history. Thus, when the Indians on and near the Mississippi continued their raids on the tribes on the Missouri (the French reported large raids in 1726 or 1727), the Omaha group had to retreat west of the Missouri, but the Arikaras and Pawnees held their villages and remained where they were.

The Arikaras, who became the dominant group in the nation in later times, said that this nation was made up of three main tribes, Arikaras, Panis, and Sinin. The Sinin were said to have come from the east, and we have to take into account the Siouan tradition that the Skidi Pawnees came with them from the Ohio Valley and were evidently still with the Omaha group in northwestern Iowa in the 1670's. Presumably, these Skidis brought with them the peculiar collared pottery of the Iroquoian tribes of New York, Pennsylvania, and the upper Ohio valley, and these collared pots have been found by archaeologists both in the Arikara area near the Great Bend of the Missouri and in the Skidi Pawnee district on the Loup Fork in Nebraska.[14] On the Loup the Skidi village remains are termed proto-

14 When I wrote "The Mystery of the Arikaras" in 1950, I had only faint clues suggesting that the Pawnees of Nebraska were related in language to the Iroquoian tribes of the east, and I knew nothing of the story of the Skidi Pawnee migration from the upper Ohio Valley. I therefore made use of the alternative view, that

historic by archaeologists, but by the French these Skidi villages are dated 1700–50.

The most interesting of the Pawnee or Arikara fortified villages is the one called Arzberger by archaeologists. It is on the east bank of the Missouri above the Great Bend, and it consists of about forty lodges, defended by a log stockade with a ditch outside the stockade and looped bastions. The site seems very important because the looped bastions are a feature of Mississippian sites, such as the great Angel village on the north bank of the Ohio, near Evansville, Indiana. Angel is just east of the Wabash and in the very district that the Osages, and in all likelihood the Omahas, occupied before they were driven from the Ohio Valley by the Iroquois. Moreover, part of the pots at Arzberger are of the peculiar collared type, which very closely resemble the pottery of the Iroquoian tribes in western New York and Pennsylvania, and the Skidi Pawnees, if the Omaha tradition is correct, may have brought this type of pottery to the Missouri in South Dakota and to the Loup in Nebraska. In the latter location this pottery type is proved to be Skidi because of the location of the Skidi villages on the Loup from the year 1700 onward.

The Arzberger culture is basically primitive Pawnee from the upper Republican River in southwestern Nebraska. So is the culture at the three St. Helena village ruins, on the south bank of the Missouri, opposite the mouth of James River; and at both Arzberger and St. Helena the old Pawnee culture is affected, mainly in pottery traits, by the culture of the Mill Creek villages near the present Mitchell on James River. Moreover, in 1867, F. V. Hayden found broken pottery in a Skidi Pawnee village ruin on Loup Fork that was not Pawnee, and Waldo R. Wedel has recently identified this pottery as Mitchell or Mill Creek.

There is here too much evidence to be brushed aside, because archaeology prefers to term all these village ruins of the period 1400–1500. We first have the story that the Skidi Pawnees accompanied the Omaha group when it fled from the Ohio about the date 1650. The Panas, presumably a Pawnee and therefore an Iroquoian group, were north of the Omahas in northwestern Iowa about 1673, when Marquette put them on his map. The looped earthworks at Pipestone re-

the Skidis were the old upper Republican group of Pawnees. This I now have reason to doubt.

semble in a way the looped bastions of the Arzberger fortress. The Panas, by La Salle information, were in two villages on or near the Missouri in contact with tribes that traded with the Spaniards in 1680. The Arzberger and St. Helena groups were contemporary with the Mill Creek group on James River and were exchanging cultural traits with them. The French found the Omahas on the Missouri near the mouth of White River in 1717–23, with the Panis and Arikaras up near the Great Bend in over fifty villages. We may well wonder why archaeology has found no trace of these Indian groups of the period 1673–1723, but numerous village ruins of Indians of the same stocks, all supposed to date back to the year 1500.[15]

Paul L. Cooper presented a study of the pottery along the Missouri in South Dakota, in *American Antiquity*, April, 1949. He divided the pottery into Categories A, B, C, and Minaric II. Minaric II was probably the pottery of the Ponca tribe after they left the Omahas near the mouth of White River, crossed west of the Missouri, and joined Pani and Arikara groups, going with them as far up as the mouth of Cheyenne River. The Poncas then turned back down the Missouri and went to their historic location on Ponca Creek in northwestern Nebraska. Cooper's Category A pottery is pretty clearly that of the Arikaras Proper, a late type, not found below a point on the river near the city of Pierre. His Category C is the pottery of a group who built villages, several of them fortified, along both banks of the Missouri, below the Great Bend. As the Category C pots have some collars, they seem to be related to the Arzberger pottery. This Category C ware continued to be in use until the Arikaras and Panis had migrated up the river to the villages below Cheyenne River, which were occupied in 1795. The Category B pottery is in village sites below the Great Bend, and like the Category C it persisted in use until 1795 or later. The Category B pots are thinner and in some ways better made than most wares found along the Missouri. These pots seem to have some Siouan traits, and the rim decoration is said to resemble that of the Great Oasis pottery, which has surprisingly turned up in Omaha village ruins in northeastern Nebraska. In time archaeology may, by a study of these pottery types, add much infor-

15 The archaeological sources used here are mainly Cooper, "Recent Investigations in Fort Randall and Oahe Reservoirs," *American Antiquity*, Vol. XIV, No 4; Hurt, *The Swanson Site, Archeological Studies*, Circular 3; Hurt, *Thomas Riggs Site, Archeological Studies*, Circular 5.

mation concerning the early history and relations of the Pani, Arikara, and Siouan tribes along the Missouri in South Dakota from 1650 to 1750.

The French information shows that the confusion among the tribes in western Iowa and along the Missouri, due mainly to slave-catching raids from tribes along the Mississippi, dated about 1660 to 1695. By the latter date, the fugitive tribes had regained some equilibrium, had drawn together and fortified some of their villages. They now had obtained some horses from the plains and were learning to fight on horseback.[16] They could no longer be hunted like birds, and, led by an Iowa village that went to live near the mouth of the Big Sioux, the Indians on the Mississippi began to trade French articles to their former victims along the Missouri, obtaining in return Padouca slaves from the plains and also furs and horses. The Sacs and Foxes, enemies of the French, soon joined the Iowas in this trade with the tribes on the Missouri; and by 1724 we find Boisbriant, French commandant in Illinois, and Bourgmont on the Missouri warning the French authorities that, if something were not done quickly to strengthen the French position on the Missouri the Sacs, Foxes, and Iowas would win the trade and turn the Missouri River tribes against the French.[17]

The fortification of Indian villages along the Missouri probably did more than anything else to stop the raids on the Missouri Valley tribes. Some theorists have assumed that these fortified villages could be easily stormed; but we have evidence that even the bold Teton Sioux had neither the courage nor the skill to storm a fortified village. When David Thompson was among the Mandans in 1797, he was told by the chiefs that the fortified villages were safe

[16] We may say that apparently the Omahas and Poncas, because of dire need, abandoned their villages and became wandering hunters for a time. This hardened the people and made it much more difficult for raiders from the east to strike telling blows. At a later period, about 1760, the Cheyennes abandoned their village life and crop growing because, as wandering hunters, they would be able to defend themselves against the Teton Sioux, who were turning the Cheyenne villages into death traps for their inhabitants.

[17] Hyde, *Indians of the High Plains*, 81. On October 5, 1724, Boisbriant, commandant in Illinois, reported that an Otoe chief had told him that the Otoes were trading Padouca slaves to the Foxes, from whom they obtained a much higher price than the French traders gave them. (Villiers, *La découverte du Missouri et l'histoire du Fort d'Orléans*, 3.)

from the Sioux, although that tribe now had firearms. The worst the Sioux could accomplish, the chiefs stated, was to set fire to a short length of the log palisades on a dark and stormy night. It was when the Mandans left their villages to go on their semiannual buffalo hunts that the Sioux assaulted and defeated them, forcing them to give up their hunting and return to their villages. In 1797, the Mandan chiefs were considering the giving up of dangerous tribal hunts, staying at home, growing more crops, and obtaining meat, skins, and horses from the wandering hunting tribes, such as the Cheyennes, Arapahoes, and Kiowas, who were eager to trade for the corn, dried pumpkin, beans, tobacco, and other products of the Mandans. Thus, at the end of our narrative, we find that tribes who were striving to maintain a higher culture facing the same old threat of destruction by the hands of hardier wandering tribes, and that they had the same hard choice: either to coop themselves up in fortified towns and try to defend their culture or else to abandon culture and resume the life of wandering hunters.

Epilogue

B Y T H E C L O S E of the seventeenth century all of the tribes of the north-central Woodlands were facing destruction, mainly because they could not forget their petty feuds and present a united front to oppose the intrusion of Europeans into their lands. Their old dream of an Indian world was almost forgotten. Their native culture was dying because they preferred the trinkets, metal pots, and weapons brought by white traders. Tribes that had developed fine and varied types of pottery lost the art within a generation or two. The arts of flint chipping, stone polishing, and work in shell and bone disappeared.

The once mighty Iroquois were being bridled by the English, and they soon found that they were no longer free to continue their career of conquest. In the lands near the upper Mississippi, the only tribes that were keeping their strength were the Sioux and Ojibwas, who were farthest from the French and dwelled in lands that were difficult to penetrate. The Foxes of Wisconsin were making a great reputation by opposing the French; but they were a small tribe, and their efforts to form a solid confederacy to block French intrusion were not successful.

The Sioux, apparently after the year 1689, began to retire from their lands near the head of the Mississippi. The Teton or Prairie

Sioux seem to have moved first, occupying lands at the head of Minnesota River. The generally accepted view that the Ojibwas forced the Sioux southward appears to be incorrect. The contemporary French reports suggest that it was the Crees and Assiniboines who had obtained large quantities of firearms from the English trading houses on Hudson Bay, who attacked the Sioux from the north and forced them to remove south to Minnesota River. The Crees and Assiniboines had adopted the practice of using big war parties in their attacks on the Sioux. At times they put as many as five hundred warriors into a single war party. It was after 1700 that the Pillager group of Ojibwas drove the Sioux from the upper value of the River St. Croix and then advanced westward to occupy the old Sioux district around Sandy Lake. The Ojibwas were better equipped with guns than the Sioux. They were better canoemen and woodsmen than their opponents; for the Sioux spent much of their time in open country and marshes, and their boats were rather clumsy wooden dugouts, not to be compared in efficiency with the light but strong bark canoes of the Ojibwas. After the year 1800, the Sioux were reported to be trading with the Chippewas for bark canoes, which the Sioux had not the skill to make properly.

The old group of Hurons and Upper Algonquians had held all the lands from east of Lake Huron west to Lake Michigan before the Iroquois had attacked and almost exterminated the Hurons. The survivors had fled to Wisconsin, some even taking refuge in the prairies of eastern Iowa. They had then attempted to destroy or drive out the Sioux and take their fine country; but they had failed and had found themselves involved in endless petty warfare, steadily losing strength. Because of feuds the Hurons and Algonquians could not adopt the reasonable solution for their troubles by forming a strong confederacy; and after the year 1680 they began to drift back eastward into the vacant lands of the southern Michigan peninsula. Some of these tribes moved down into the Ohio country, left empty since the Iroquois wolf packs had destroyed or driven out the native inhabitants. In moving toward the Ohio, these tribes had to have some kind of friendly arrangement with the Iroquois and with the English; and this was not at all to the liking of the French officials in Canada, who presently ordered the building of a fort at Detroit, ostensibly for military operations against the Iroquois, but apparently with the object of keeping out British trade.

The English at Albany were trading better goods at lower prices than the French could meet, and this English trade was already reaching out to take the tribes along the lakes and in Wisconsin away from the French. The Foxes in Wisconsin were obtaining English goods and guns, which they used effectively in their bitter warfare against the French and their Indian allies.

After 1685, affairs in Canada were not prospering. War was rife; trade was precarious; the Indian missions were dying. An angry Jesuit, writing from Michilimackinac, accused the Canadian officials of destroying the missions by favoring traders, who were demoralizing the Indians by trading liquor to them in unlimited quantities. Instead of converting the Indians to Christianity, this priest asserted, the authorities had permitted a host of young Frenchmen to run wild in the woods, debauching the Indian women and turning themselves into worse savages than any Indians could be.[1]

It took the Iroquois invasion of Montreal Island, the home of most of the French merchants and traders, to awaken the French authorities. In August, 1689, an army of 1,400 Iroquois, accompanied by a few Englishmen, invaded the island, took the French by surprise, and drove their attack to the very gates of Montreal. They killed from 150 to 200 persons, plundered and burned, and then withdrew, taking a great number of captives with them.[2]

Frontenac was now returned to Canada as governor. He attempted to revive the French trade in the west and to form an Indian alliance against the Iroquois. Le Sueur built a fort at Chequamegon on Lake Superior and then one on the Mississippi in the Sioux country. In 1696, he took an Ojibwa and a Sioux chief to Montreal, where the Sioux died. Le Sueur then went to France to seek a ten-year monopoly of trade on Lake Superior and the upper Mississippi and mining rights. He was given only the mining rights. The French government had decided to form a colony at the mouth of the Mississippi, and this was done in 1699. Le Sueur also went by ship to the mouth of the Mississippi and then started up the river in a shallop with his men and equipment to begin mining for copper in Minnesota.[3]

Frontenac's efforts to form an alliance among the western tribes,

1 Thwaites, *Jesuit Relations*, LXV, 189.

2 Schlarman, *From Quebec to New Orleans*, 46.

3 *Minnesota Historical Society Collections*, Vol. X, part 2, 261; Schlarman, *From Quebec to New Orleans*, 268.

to deal with the Iroquois and to keep English trade away from the upper lakes and the Mississippi, was a failure. The French court altered its policy, ordering all the traders and woodrunners to leave the Indian country and return to Montreal. The fort among the Sioux was abandoned. The Fox tribe blocked the canoe route to the Mississippi and made French trade almost impossible. The Foxes had won over at least part of the Sioux, turning them against the French.

In 1701, the French built a fort at Detroit because the plan made in Paris to withdraw all traders from the Indian country and persuade the Indians to bring their furs to Montreal had failed. There were reports that the Foxes and other tribes were now trading for English goods, some of them even going to Albany to trade directly with the English. The fort at Detroit, it was hoped, would draw the Foxes there, win their trade back to the French, and induce them to leave the canoe route to the Mississippi open. But it did not. The Foxes remained implacably hostile. The Ottawas, Hurons, Potawatomis, and Miamis of the Lakes at first thought the Detroit post was to be the base for active war on the Iroquois, and they were pleased; but when they learned that the fort was to be only a trading place and that the French in truth were attempting to placate the Iroquois and make peace with them, the Hurons and Upper Algonquians were furious.

The withdrawal of the French from the upper Mississippi was bringing ruin to the Illinis, who were the only Indians in the region consistently friendly toward the French. The Illinis, raided by the Foxes and their allies, by the Sioux from the north, and by the Chickasaws and other English-armed tribes from the south, had to withdraw from Illinois River. Then they learned of the new French colony, established near the mouth of the Mississippi, and the Illini chiefs decided to remove their people to the lower Mississippi and live under the protection of the French. The chiefs were persuaded by French missionaries and others not to leave Illinois; but La Salle's dream of using the Illinis as the central core of a great Indian confederacy allied to the French was now dead. The Illinis were facing extermination.[4]

One of the results of the French withdrawal from the upper Mis-

---

[4] Thwaites, *Jesuit Relations*, LXV, 102–103; Schlarman, *From Quebec to New Orleans*, 117, 252; French, *Historical Collections of Louisiana*, I, 79, 82.

sissippi, about the year 1696, was that the Sioux were placed in a very precarious position. They could no longer obtain French arms and goods, while their principal enemies, the Crees and Assiniboines, continued to obtain arms from the Hudson Bay traders. The Foxes of Wisconsin were getting English weapons and goods from Albany and were alternately trading with and raiding the Sioux. It would seem that the Foxes were inclined to be friendly with the Sioux of the East but were raiding the Sioux of the West or Prairie Sioux. In 1700, Le Sueur reported that the district along the Mississippi near Lake Pepin was unsafe for French traders as it was the war ground between the Foxes and Sioux. War parties frequently passed, and if they encountered French traders, they robbed them. By 1700 the Sioux had lost the fine reputation the French had given them in earlier times. The truth probably was that the Sioux at first had regarded the French as spirits, beings with more power than any human creatures; but now they knew the French were only men like themselves, and they robbed and abused Frenchmen when they thought it safe to do so, although there was still no record of the Sioux having killed a white man. In 1700, Le Sueur reported that the Sioux still did no planting. They had wild rice but no corn.[5] At this time the French were greatly alarmed because the Foxes were trading English goods to the Sioux for fine furs. This seems to mean that the Foxes were not always at war with the Sioux; but perhaps they were at war with the Prairie Sioux and at peace with the eastern Sioux of the Mississippi. The Sioux in turn were said to be trading European articles to the Iowas.

Le Sueur's mining venture into southern Minnesota was a failure. His party reached the Blue Earth River late in 1700 and built a small fort. The Sioux of the East visited the fort and complained that it was in the lands of the Sioux of the West. They wanted Le Sueur to come into their lands and trade with them, but he had come to mine blue earth on Blue Earth River. He believed that this blue earth was pure copper, and in 1701 he had his men dig enough of it to load his shallop. Two large canoes were loaded with furs, traded by the Sioux. Le Sueur now left part of his men to continue trade

[5] *Minnesota Historical Society Collections,* Vol. X, part 2, 562; French, *Historical Collections of Louisiana,* III, 23; Margry, *Découvertes et établissements des Français,* 79.

at the fort and with the rest of his party set out for the mouth of the Mississippi with his load of blue earth and furs. He took ship for France, and there he was stunned to learn that his blue earth was just that. It had not a trace of copper in it. And that ended another French effort to imitate the Spaniards of Mexico and South America and obtain great fortunes by mining. Le Sueur's men stayed at his fort until 1702; then, as no supplies or reinforcements arrived, they abandoned the fort. They reported that the Foxes had killed three of their companions near the fort.[6]

Le Sueur had evidently traded with the Iowas and Otoes in southern Minnesota in 1693–96, and when he returned in 1700, he expected to find them there and to induce them to settle near his fort as they were the only local tribes that grew crops and he wanted corn and vegetables for his men; but he was told that the Iowas and Otoes had moved toward the Missouri. By 1700 the lands in southern Minnesota and northern Iowa were held by the Sioux of the West, with the Yankton group at or near the pipestone quarry and probably extending down into northwestern Iowa. The Yanktons were raiding the Omahas and Panis on the Missouri.

The Foxes, for such a small tribe, were making a great deal of trouble for the French. Their location in Wisconsin enabled them to block the French canoe route to the Mississippi, and their trade with the English apparently made them independent of French trade. When the French established the post at Detroit, they attempted to use it to wean the Foxes away from the English by urging them to trade at Detroit, or even to settle there. Part of the Foxes went to Detroit. In 1712 they led in an Indian plot to take the French post by surprise, but the plot failed and the Foxes withdrew from the vicinity of Detroit. The French organized an expedition and caught the Foxes in their fortified village on Wisconsin River, punishing them severely.[7] That only made the Foxes more determined than ever to fight on; and when the French encouraged their Indian allies to burn any Foxes that fell into their hands, the result was only an increased determination on the part of the Foxes never to give in to the French. In 1721, Father Charlevoix reported that the Illini tribe had captured thirty-seven Foxes and had burned all or most

6 Folwell, *History of Minnesota*, I, 42.

7 Temple, "Indian Villages of the Illinois Country," *Illinois State Museum Scientific Papers*, Vol. II, part 2, 88.

of them. This probably meant that they were tortured at the stake and their bodies cooked and eaten.[8]

In 1726 the French sent an expedition into Wisconsin, led by De Lignery. He was urged to exterminate the Foxes; but he was afraid that if attacked the Foxes would escape, flee to the Sioux, and cause more trouble than ever. In June, he made a peace with the Foxes and their allies, but neither the Indians nor the French observed the peace conditions, and the Fox war went on.

The French settlement at the mouth of the Mississippi, weak from its birth, did not prosper. At first the settlement was at Biloxi, then at Mobile. Bienville was in command. He and his brother, Iberville, were Canadians, both men of strong character and vigorous in action; but they had very few resources in men and supplies. The boundless ambition of Louis XIV had involved France in the War of the Spanish Succession, with England and the principal Continental powers in alliance against him. The great Marlborough in a long and bitter war tore the French military power to pieces, and when Louis died, he left France in an exhausted condition. The new king was little more than a pleasure-seeker and wastrel. John Law, an adventurer from Scotland, now persuaded the French government to turn over to him the French colonies, not including Canada, and he was given a twenty-five year lease. His companies sold stock, and, rich and poor, the people of France went mad and gambled every sou they could find in Law's company shares. The mania for speculation in land in distant parts of the earth spread to other countries.

Law not only gained control of the lands along the lower Mississippi, now called Louisiana, but even some control in Illinois. His company sent colonists to the lower Mississippi, including a colony of Germans. He had another colony on Arkansas River, but his company had no solid basis. John Law's whole program was based on inducing the public to gamble in stocks and bonds, paying gold and silver for worthless securities. On his advice, the French government was issuing limitless quantities of paper money which had nothing back of it to maintain its supposed value. When the inevitable crash came, the colonists in Louisiana were left destitute, with no hope of help from the French government. Even the troops in Louisiana were destitute, without pay and facing starvation. The end came when

[8] Schlarman, *From Quebec to New Orleans*, 212–13. This expedition was in 1716. Louis la Porte commanded the French force.

the French and Swiss soldiers marched off to surrender to the English in Carolina where at least they might hope to be fed.[9]

The English were not attempting to occupy lands in the west; but their Indian traders were constantly striving to extend their control to new tribes. They already had the Cherokees and Chickasaws in their hands and were reaching out to extend their trade among the tribes on the lower Mississippi and even in Illinois. The Foxes in Wisconsin were obtaining English arms and goods fairly regularly. The French had to fight two little wars to maintain control of the tribes near the lower Mississippi. Their gains were small, for they had almost to exterminate the Natchez nation and they failed to strike any telling blow against the Chickasaws. In Illinois their loyal allies of the Illini confederacy were facing destruction by enemy tribes. The surviving Illinis were now living in little communities along the east bank of the Mississippi, near the mouth of the Missouri. A considerable number of French had settled among them, and there was a mission, a French trading center at Cahokia, and a French farming settlement at Kaskaskia. The Illinis still had two hundred warriors in their Kaskaskia village, but the tribe was being attacked by many enemies, and in a single year the Foxes had killed seventy-seven Illinis. The Illinis were big, lusty, and handsome men. In their own villages they were proud and fierce; but a French officer stated in 1723 that, out of sight of their villages, they were the greatest cowards in all the Indian lands.[10]

The movement among the Indians to reoccupy the vacant Ohio country, which was well under way at the beginning of the eighteenth century, seems to have had no special significance. The Indians concerned apparently wished to move into new country, and they drifted down from Wisconsin and Michigan into the Wabash lands and farther east to the Great Miami. They belonged mainly to the Illini and Miami groups—Weas, Piankashaws, part of the Miamis, part of the Mascoutens—and later they were joined by the rest of the Kickapoos and Mascoutens from Wisconsin. The Iroquois claimed the Ohio country by conquest but had not occupied any of the lands. It was now the Iroquois policy to permit the Delawares and Shawnees to occupy the lands near the Scioto, the Iroquois claiming a kind of sovereignty over these tribes whom they said they had conquered in

9 Schlarman, *From Quebec to New Orleans*, 173–79.
10 *Ibid.*, 196.

earlier times. The surviving Hurons, now called Wyandots, were also moving down into northern Ohio. They were making large claims to being important, insisting that by ancient custom it was their right to light the council fire and take the lead in councils.

If these tribes in the Ohio country imagined that they were getting away from their troubles and the interference of whites by moving to their new locations, they were soon disillusioned. The French, fearful of losing control over these tribes, sent Vincennes to establish a French trading center on the Wabash and to strive to keep the Indians loyal to the French interest. The English were trying to extend their trade through the Ohio country and were attempting to make use of the Iroquois to draw the tribes away from the French. It was soon apparent that, if trouble came, the Ohio country would be a battleground in which the French and English would clash.

From the time the French ships had first entered the mouth of the St. Lawrence, they had imagined that China was not far off and that by going up the river they would find a sea route to the Orient. Coming to the Great Lakes, they heard rumors that made them believe Tartar tribes were in Wisconsin, near the Winnebagoes and Sioux, and that Chinese mandarins were visiting that region. By 1700 they realized that China was a long way toward the west, and their quest now was for a route to the Western Sea and across it to China. Father Charlevoix was traveling through Canada in 1720, and in 1721 he came west into Illinois. He was a good observer, and he was collecting all the information he could from both the French and the Indians. When he returned to France, he put forward a plan for reaching the Western Sea through the Sioux country, and he proposed that a French establishment, including a fort and a mission, should be placed on the Mississippi in the Sioux lands as a base from which explorations toward the west might be carried out. This plan met approval at the French court; and in 1727 an expedition left the St. Lawrence, passed along the Great Lakes, crossed Wisconsin and the Mississippi, and established Fort Beauharnois on Sioux lands in southeastern Minnesota.

Charlevoix had misjudged the situation on the upper Mississippi. From the moment the new French post was built on the west bank, there was trouble. The Foxes now had wide trade arrangements, mainly in English goods, with the Sioux and other tribes, as far west as Nebraska, and they were using part of the Sioux and Iowas as middlemen in this trade. The intrusion of the French in 1727 produced immediate and violent reaction, the Foxes renewing their hostilities and part of the Sioux evidently siding with them. But the opportunity for the Sioux to obtain arms and trade goods direct from the French at a post in their own country drew part of the Sioux to Fort Beauharnois, and their trading with the French probably enraged the Foxes and their allies.

The reports concerning events at Fort Beauharnois are fragmentary and confused, but there was clearly trouble from the day the post was built. Father Guignas, a missionary for the Sioux who was with the French, reported in September, 1727, the building of the fort "in the middle of the north shore" of Lake Pepin. This priest evidently had no success in his missionary efforts; for in the following year he started down the Mississippi to go to the more friendly Kaskaskias, and on his way he was captured by the Mascoutens and Kickapoos, allies of the Foxes. In 1727 the Foxes and Sioux of the Prairie gathered a big war party and went to the Missouri to raid the Omahas. In 1728 the French acted against the Foxes and also aroused the Iroquois, who burned a Fox village. The Foxes then attacked their old allies, the Kickapoos. All the Algonquian tribes now turned against the Foxes, and one Fox village set out to march eastward to seek the protection of the Iroquois. The French at once urged the Potawatomis, Mascoutens, and Kickapoos to block the trails near the southern end of Lake Michigan. The marching Fox village had 350 men and a total of about 1,000 persons. The Foxes crossed upper Illinois River, starting on toward the southeast; then, finding their way blocked, they halted and fortified a position. The French and their Indian allies moved in from three directions and beset the Fox fort. The Foxes managed to steal out of the fort and get away, but they had gone only twenty-five miles when they were overtaken and surrounded. In the ensuing massacre, 200 to 300 Fox warriors were killed or taken and some 600 women and children butchered. The French were not satisfied. Only the extermination of the Foxes would content them. In the winter of 1730–31, the French aroused the Iroquois again, with the result that another Fox village was captured and some 300 Foxes killed.[11]

The surviving Foxes fought on. They were of the same blood as

11 Temple, "Indian Villages of the Illinois Country," *Illinois State Museum Scientific Papers,* Vol. II, part 2, 89–91.

the Cheyennes, who in the plains of the distant West a century and a half later defied the power of the United States and fought to the death. What the Sioux were doing is not clearly evident. Le Sueur, when he had stated in 1700 that the district near Lake Pepin was a war ground and not a suitable place to establish a trading fort, had put it rather mildly. In 1729, the Sioux, probably armed with French weapons obtained at Fort Beauharnois, again set out in force to raid the Omahas on the Missouri. The French then abandoned their fort; but they came back (1732?) and reoccupied it, only to abandon it again soon after. The missionaries and the traders were convinced that the place was unsafe, and they agreed that it was better to go and to lose all their property rather than to stay and lose their lives.

Here we may end the story. The old dream of an Indian world in which the Indians could build a civilization along lines of their own choice was dead; and, in a welter of petty warfare, one tribe after another was losing its strength and facing extinction. There was no end of this futile fighting until the coming of the French and Indian War with its operations on a greater scale, ending in the English conquest of Canada.

Bibliography

American Antiquity, Vol. V, No. 4 (April, 1940), 341. "Notes and News" column.

American Antiquity, Vol. XXI, No. 2 (October, 1955), 192. "Reviews" section.

Beach, W. W. *The Indian Miscellany.* Albany, 1877.

Blair, Emma H. *The Indian Tribes of the Upper Mississippi Valley and Region of the Great Lakes* . . . . 2 vols. Cleveland, 1911.

Bossu, Jean-Bernard. *Jean Bernard Bossu's Travels in the Interior of North America, 1751–1762.* Translated and edited by Seymour Feiler. Norman, 1962.

Champlain, Samuel de. *Voyages of Samuel de Champlain, 1604–1618.* 3 vols. Boston, 1878–82.

Colden, Cadwallader. *The History of the Five Indian Nations of Canada, Which Are Dependent on the Province of New York in America, and Are a Barrier between the English and the French in That Part of the World.* 2 vols. New York, 1902.

Collection of the State Historical Society of Wisconsin, Vol. XI.

Cooper, Paul. "Recent Investigations in Fort Randall and Oahe Reservoirs, South Dakota," *American Antiquity,* Vol. XIV, No. 4 (April, 1949), 300–10.

Chouteau, Auguste. Historical Notes on the Indians of North America. Manuscript dated St. Louis, February 21, 1816; National Archives, Indian Bureau Papers, Ancient and Miscellaneous Surveys, Vol. IV (RG 75).

Dixon, Roland B. *Some Aspects of North American Archeology*. Pamphlet; reprint from *American Anthropologist*, Vol. XV, No. 4 (1913), 549–77.

Dorsey, J. Owen. "Migrations of the Siouan Indians," *American Naturalist*, Vol. XX, No. 3 (March, 1886), 211–22.

———. *Omaha Sociology*. *Third Annual Report*, Bureau of American Ethnology, 1884.

———. *Omaha Traditions, Sixth Annual Report*, Bureau of American Ethnology, 1888.

———. *Osage Traditions. Sixth Annual Report*, Bureau of American Ethnology, 1888.

———. *Siouan Sociology. Fifteenth Annual Report*, Bureau of American Ethnology, 1897.

Fenton, W. N. *Problems Arising from the Historic Northeastern Position of the Iroquois. Smithsonian Miscellaneous Collections*. Vol. C (1940).

Fletcher, Alice, and Francis LaFlesche. *The Omaha. Twenty-seventh Annual Report*, Bureau of American Ethnology, 1911.

French, Benjamin Franklin. *Historical Collections of Louisiana*. 5 vols. New York, 1846–58.

Folwell, William Watts. *A History of Minnesota*. 4 vols. St. Paul, 1956.

Griffin, James B. *Archeology of the Eastern United States*. Chicago, 1952.

———. *Fort Ancient*. Ann Arbor, 1943.

———. *Late Prehistoric Cultures of the Ohio Valley*. Reprint from *Ohio Archaeological and Historical Quarterly*, Vol. LXI, No. 2 (1952).

Harrison, William Henry. *A Discourse on the Aborigines of the Ohio Valley*. First printed in pamphlet form; Cincinnati, 1838. Reprinted in *North American Review,* Vol. LI, No. CVIII (July, 1840), 46–68.

Heckewelder, John. *The Indian Nations Who Once Inhabited Pennsylvania and the Neighboring States*. Philadelphia, 1876.

Hewitt, J. N. B. *Iroquoian Cosmology. Twenty-first Annual Report,*

Bureau of American Ethnology, 1903, and *Forty-third Annual Report,* Bureau of American Ethnology, 1928.

Hodge, F. W., ed. *Handbook of Indians North of Mexico, Bulletin 30,* Bureau of American Ethnology, 2 vols. Washington, 1907.

Hurt, W. R., Jr. *The Swanson Site. Archeological Studies,* Circular 3, Pierre, 1951.

———. *The Thomas Riggs Site. Archeological Studies,* Circular 5, Pierre, 1953.

Hyde, George E. *Indians of the High Plains.* Norman, 1959.

———. *The Early Blackfeet and Their Neighbors.* Denver, 1933.

———. "The Mystery of the Arikaras," *North Dakota History,* Vol. XVIII, No. 4 (October, 1951), and Vol. XIX, No. 1 (January, 1952).

Iowa Archaeological Society Journal, Vol. V, 13–16.

James, Edwin. Vol. XV of Thwaites' *Early Western Travels* (*q.v.*).

Lapham, Increase Allen. *Antiquities of Wisconsin. Smithsonian Contributions to Knowledge,* Vol. VII, Washington, 1865.

Lorant, Stefan. *The New World.* New York, 1946.

Margry, Pierre. *Découvertes et établissements des Français dans l'ouest et dans le sud de l'Amérique Septentrionale, 1614–1754.* 6 vols. Paris, 1876–86.

Martin, Paul S., George I. Quimby, and Donald Collier. *Indians Before Columbus.* Chicago, 1947.

McGee, W. J. *The Siouan Indians: A Preliminary Sketch. Fifteenth Annual Report,* Bureau of American Ethnology, Washington, 1897.

Minnesota Historical Society Collections, volumes I and X.

Mooney, James. "The Siouan Tribes of the East," *Bulletin 22,* Bureau of American Ethnology, 1895.

Mott, Mildred. "The Relation of Historic Indian Tribes to Archaeological Manifestations in Iowa," *Iowa Journal of History and Politics,* Vol. XXVI, No. 3 (July, 1938), 227–314.

Nasatir, A. P., ed. *Before Lewis and Clark.* 2 vols. St. Louis, 1952.

Over, W. H., and E. E. Meleen. *A Report on the Brandon Village Site and the Split Rock Creek Mounds. Archeological Studies,* Circular 4, University of South Dakota, Vermillion, 1941.

Parkman, Francis. *The Jesuits in North America in the Seventeenth Century.* Boston, 1880. Many editions.

————. *La Salle and the Discovery of the Great West.* Boston, 1880. Many editions.

————. *Pioneers of France in the New World.* Boston, 1907. Many editions.

Quimby, George I. *Indian Life in the Upper Great Lakes.* Chicago, 1960.

Radisson, Pierre E. *Voyages of Peter Esprit Radisson, Being an Account of His Travels and Experiences among the North American Indians, from 1652 to 1684.* With historical illustrations and an introduction by Gideon D. Scull. Boston, Prince Society, 1855.

Ritchie, William A. "A Perspective of Northeastern Archaeology," *American Antiquity,* Vol. IV, No. 2 (October, 1938), 94–112.

————. "Cultural Influences from Ohio in New York Archaeology," *American Antiquity,* Vol. II, No. 3 (January, 1937), 182–83.

Rowe, C. W. *The Effigy Mound Culture of Wisconsin. Milwaukee Public Museum Publications in Anthropology,* No. 3, Milwaukee, 1956.

Ruppe, Reynold J. "The Earliest Indians of Iowa," *Journal of the Iowa Archeological Society,* Vol. V (1955–56).

————. Paper on Mill Creek Culture, *Yearbook of the American Philosophical Society* (1955), 335–39.

Schlarman, J. H. *From Quebec to New Orleans.* Belleville, Illinois, 1930.

Schoolcraft, Henry R. *Historical and Statistical Information Respecting the History, Condition and Prospects of the Indian Tribes of the United States.* 6 vols. Philadelphia, 1851–57.

Shea, John Dawson Gilmary. *Early Voyages Up and Down the Mississippi.* Albany, 1902.

Shetrone, H. C. *The Mound Builders.* New York, 1930.

Short, J. T. *North Americans of Antiquity.* New York, 1880.

Spaulding, A. C., in *Fifth Plains Conference Notebook,* I, 106–107.

Squier, E. G., and E. H. Davis. *Ancient Monuments of the Mississippi Valley. Smithsonian Contributions to Knowledge,* Vol. I, Washington, 1848.

Strong, W. D. *An Introduction to Nebraska Archaeology.* 1935.

Swanton, John R. "Early History of the Creek Indians and Their Neighbors," *Bulletin 73,* Bureau of American Ethnology, 1922.

————. "The Indian Tribes of North America," *Bulletin 145,* Bureau of American Ethnology, Washington, 1953.

Temple, W. C. "Indian Villages of the Illinois Country," *Illinois State Museum Scientific Papers*, Vol. II, part 2, Springfield, 1958.

Thomas, Cyrus. "Catalogue of Prehistoric Works East of the Rocky Mountains," *Bulletin 12*, Bureau of American Ethnology, 1891.

———. *Report on the Mound Exploration of the Bureau of Ethnology. Twelfth Annual Report,* Bureau of American Ethnology, 1894.

———. "The Circular, Square and Octagonal Earthworks of Ohio," *Bulletin 10*, Bureau of American Ethnology, 1880.

Thwaites, Reuben Gold, ed. *Early Western Travels, 1748–1846.* . . . 32 vols. Cleveland, 1904–1907.

———, ed. *The Jesuit Relations and Allied Documents.* 73 vols. Cleveland, 1896–1901.

Upham, Warren, "Groseilliers and Radisson, the First White men in Minnesota, 1655–56, and 1659–60, and their Discovery of the Upper Mississippi River," *Minnesota Historical Society Collections*, Vol. X, part 2, 449–594.

Villiers du Terrage, Marc, baron de. *La découverte du Missouri et l'histoire du Fort d'Orléans (1673–1729).* Paris, 1925.

———. *Documents concernant l'histoire des Indiens de la région orientale de la Louisiane.* Paris, 1922.

Webb, William Snyder, and William Delbert Funkhouser, *Ancient Life in Kentucky, The Kentucky Geological Survey,* 1928.

Wedel, Waldo R. "An Introduction to Pawnee Archeology," *Bulletin 112*, Bureau of American Ethnology, 1936.

———. "Culture Chronology in the Central Great Plains," *American Antiquity*, Vol. XII, No. 3 (1947), 148–56.

———. "An Introduction to Kansas Archeology," *Bulletin 174*, Bureau of American Ethnology, 1959.

Whitman, William. *The Oto. Columbia University Contributions to Anthropology,* New York, 1937.

Wilford, L. A. "Revised Classification of the Prehistoric Cultures of Minnesota," *American Antiquity*, Vol. XXI, No. 2, (October, 1955), 130–42.

Will, George F. "Archaeology of the Missouri Valley," *Anthropological Papers of the American Museum of Natural History,* Vol. XXII, part 4 (1924), 285–344.

———. "Tree Ring Studies in North Dakota," *Bulletin 338*, North Dakota Agricultural College, 1940.

————, and T. C. Hecker. "Upper Missouri Valley Culture in North Dakota," North Dakota History, Vol. XI, Nos. 1 and 2 (Bismarck, 1944).

Winsor, Justin. Cartier to Frontenac. Boston and New York, 1894.

————. Narrative and Critical History of America. 8 vols. Boston and New York, 1884–89.

————. The Mississippi Basin. Boston and New York, 1895.

Witthoft, John, and W. A. Hunter, "Seventeenth-century Origins of the Shawnee," Ethnohistory, Vol. II, No. 1 (1955).

Zimmerman, Charles Leroy. White Eagle, Chief of the Poncas. Harrisburg, 1941.

Index

Abnakis: 216n.

Accault, Michael: 195, 212

Adders: 58

Adena culture: 9ff., 19ff., 24–28, 67, 71

Adena folk: x, 17–24, 27, 41, 60, 67, 145, 150

Adirondacks: 58, 59, 86

Aganatchi: 190

Ainoves: 192, 213, 219

Aiounoue: 230

Akansea: 61, 62, 63, 64, 65, 66, 156, 157, 159, 160, 167, 170, 171, 173, 175n., 188, 190, 191n.

Akowini: 55

Algonquians: x, xi, 7, 28, 40, 46, 56, 57, 58, 67, 71, 76, 77, 81n., 84, 85, 86, 87, 88, 89, 90, 91, 92, 93, 94, 95, 96, 97n., 98, 102, 104, 105, 107, 108, 109, 110, 112, 114, 115, 116, 117, 121, 124, 125, 127, 128, 131, 135, 136, 142, 143, 144, 145, 146, 148, 151, 152, 153, 154, 174, 178, 179, 180, 182, 183, 184, 185, 186, 187, 188, 192, 196, 210, 214, 218, 219, 220n., 239, 244–45; origin of, 3; in early Woodland times, 3–6, 16; culture of, 3ff., 67, 107–10; in archaic times, 51–53; traditions of, 5–53, 55–58; in Mound Builder times, 52–53; in Ohio Valley, 60; at war with Winnebagoes, 100–103, 142; in Michigan, 115; listed by La Salle, 162–63; attacked by Iroquois, 177–81; in Wisconsin, 178; raided by Sioux, 182ff.; migrations of, 55, 164–66, 178, 245, 270; unite against Foxes, 278–79

Allouez, Father: 138, 184, 193, 198

Amikwa (Beaver) tribe: 96

Anahotaha: 132

Andastes: 84, 90, 165

Anderson focus: 149, 150

André, Father: 219

Angel Colony: 78, 82, 160, 163, 203, 265

Anthouantes (Otoes): 219

Antlered King: 31

Apaches: 249

Apple River culture: 209

Arapahoes: 268

Arikaras: 236, 242–43, 247n., 248–49, 252, 253, 256, 259, 263ff.

Arzberger fortress: 229, 249–50, 265, 266

Assiniboines: 239, 270, 273

Atlatl: 8

of which *Indians of the Woodlands: From Prehistoric Times to 1725* is the sixty-fourth volume, was inaugurated in 1932 by the University of Oklahoma Press, and has as its purpose the reconstruction of American Indian civilization by presenting aboriginal, historical, and contemporary Indian life. The following list is complete as of the date of publication of this volume:

1. Alfred Barnaby Thomas. *Forgotten Frontiers*: A study of the Spanish Indian Policy of Don Juan Bautista de Anza, Governor of New Mexico, 1777–1787. Out of print.
2. Grant Foreman. *Indian Removal*: The Emigration of the Five Civilized Tribes of Indians.
3. John Joseph Mathews. *Wah'Kon-Tah*: The Osage and the White Man's Road. Out of print.
4. Grant Foreman. *Advancing the Frontier, 1830–1860.* Out of print.
5. John Homer Seger. *Early Days Among the Cheyenne and Arapahoe Indians.* Edited by Stanley Vestal. New edition (1956).
6. Angie Debo. *The Rise and Fall of the Choctaw Republic.* Out of print.
7. Stanley Vestal (ed.). *New Sources of Indian History, 1850–1891.* Out of print.
8. Grant Foreman. *The Five Civilized Tribes.* Out of print.
9. Alfred Barnaby Thomas. *After Coronado*: Spanish Exploration Northeast of New Mexico, 1696–1727. Out of print.
10. Frank G. Speck. *Naskapi*: The Savage Hunters of the Labrador Peninsula. Out of print.
11. Elaine Goodale Eastman. *Pratt*: The Red Man's Moses. Out of print.
12. Althea Bass. *Cherokee Messenger*: A Life of Samuel Austin Worcester. Out of print.
13. Thomas Wildcat Alford. *Civilization*. As told to Florence Drake. Out of print.
14. Grant Foreman. *Indians and Pioneers*: The Story of the American Southwest before 1830. Out of print.
15. George E. Hyde. *Red Cloud's Folk*: A History of the Oglala Sioux Indians.
16. Grant Foreman. *Sequoyah.*
17. Morris L. Wardell. *A Political History of the Cherokee Nation, 1838–1907.* Out of print.
18. John Walton Caughey. *McGillivray of the Creeks.*
19. Edward Everett Dale and Gaston Litton. *Cherokee Cavaliers*:

Forty Years of Cherokee History as Told in the Correspondence of the Ridge-Watie-Boudinot Family. Out of print.

20. Ralph Henry Gabriel. *Elias Boudinot, Cherokee, and His America.*

21. Karl N. Llewellyn and E. Adamson Hoebel. *The Cheyenne Way*: Conflict and Case Law in Primitive Jurisprudence.

22. Angie Debo. *The Road to Disappearance.* Out of print.

23. Oliver La Farge and others. *The Changing Indian.* Out of print.

24. Carolyn Thomas Foreman. *Indians Abroad.* Out of print.

25. John Adair. *The Navajo and Pueblo Silversmiths.*

26. Alice Marriott. *The Ten Grandmothers.*

27. Alice Marriott. *María*: The Potter of San Ildefonso.

28. Edward Everett Dale. *The Indians of the Southwest*: A Century of Development Under the United States. Out of print.

29. Adrián Recinos. *Popol Vuh*: The Sacred Book of the Ancient Quiché Maya. English version by Delia Goetz and Sylvanus G. Morley from the translation of Adrián Recinos.

30. Walter Collins O'Kane. *Sun in the Sky.*

31. Stanley A. Stubbs. *Bird's-Eye View of the Pueblos.*

32. Katharine C. Turner. *Red Men Calling on the Great White Father.*

33. Muriel H. Wright. *A Guide to the Indian Tribes of Oklahoma.*

34. Ernest Wallace and E. Adamson Hoebel. *The Comanches*: Lords of the South Plains.

35. Walter Collins O'Kane. *The Hopis*: Portrait of a Desert People. Out of print.

36. Joseph Epes Brown. *The Sacred Pipe*: Black Elk's Account of the Seven Rites of the Oglala Sioux.

37. Adrián Recinos and Delia Goetz. *The Annals of the Cakchiquels.* Translated from the Cakchiquel Maya, with *Title of the Lords of Totonicapán,* translated from the Quiché text into Spanish by Dionisio José Chonay, English version by Delia Goetz.

38. R. S. Cotterill. *The Southern Indians*: The Story of the Civilized Tribes Before Removal.

39. J. Eric S. Thompson. *The Rise and Fall of Maya Civilization.*

40. Robert Emmitt. *The Last War Trail*: The Utes and the Settlement of Colorado.

41. Frank Gilbert Roe. *The Indian and the Horse.*

42. Francis Haines. *The Nez Percés*: Tribesmen of the Columbia Plateau. Out of print.

43. Ruth M. Underhill. *The Navajos.*

44. George Bird Grinnell. *The Fighting Cheyennes.*

INDIANS OF THE WOODLANDS

has been set in ten-point Baskerville, a Linotype face adapted from John Baskerville's eighteenth-century design. While modern designers are attracted to the refined simplicity of this type, it had admirers during Baskerville's time, despite his controversial innovations of paper and design. Succeeding years have proved its legibility, so that today Baskerville's original design is one of the most popular book faces.

UNIVERSITY OF OKLAHOMA PRESS : NORMAN